GDPR

by Suzanne Dibble

GDPR For Dummies®

Published by: **John Wiley & Sons, Inc.,** 111 River Street, Hoboken, NJ 07030-5774, www.wiley.com

Copyright © 2020 by John Wiley & Sons, Inc., Hoboken, New Jersey

Published simultaneously in Canada

For general information on our other products and services, please contact our Customer Care Department within the U.S. at 877-762-2974, outside the U.S. at 317-572-3993, or fax 317-572-4002. For technical support, please visit https://hub.wiley.com/community/support/dummies.

Wiley publishes in a variety of print and electronic formats and by print-on-demand. Some material included with standard print versions of this book may not be included in e-books or in print-on-demand. If this book refers to media such as a CD or DVD that is not included in the version you purchased, you may download this material at http://booksupport.wiley.com. For more information about Wiley products, visit www.wiley.com.

Library of Congress Control Number: 2019954068

ISBN: 978-1-119-54609-2; 978-1-119-54614-6 (ebk); 978-1-119-54617-7 (ebk)

Manufactured in the United States of America

V10015633_111419

DEC 2 4 2019

Contents at a Glance

Table of Contents

Introduction

The General Data Protection Regulation — the GDPR — seeks to unify data protection legislation across Europe. It is the successor to the EU Data Protection Directive [of] 1995 and came into effect on May 25, 2018.

A complex regulation composed of 11 chapters, 99 articles (which dictate the compliance requirements), 173 recitals (which provide context to the articles), and 88 pages, the GDPR might not be something you care to read.

I was inspired to write this book — designed to help anyone who needs to quickly and easily come to grips with the GDPR and related data-protection legislation — following the success of my Facebook group, GDPR for Online Entrepreneurs. (I tell you more about that topic later in this introduction.) In this group, the largest social media group on the topic of the GDPR, I have been able to help tens of thousands of small-business owners via my numerous video guides, online training sessions, and live Q&As.

Although the Facebook group has helped many thousands of small-business owners around the world understand the GDPR and how to implement compliance in their own organization, I know that many more still need help. Some aren't on Facebook, some will never find my group, and some prefer a comprehensive book over watching videos.

It is my hope that, in writing this book, I can help many more tens of thousands (and maybe someday, hundreds of thousands) when dealing with the complex set of issues associated with the GDPR.

About This Book

The book explains the complexities of the GDPR in language that anyone can understand. It is practical, it is relevant, and it is comprehensive. If you're processing personal data — whether you're part of a company, a charity, or an association — this is the book for you.

Due to its ease of reading and the comprehensive nature of the book, the book may be not only a useful guide for small-business owners, charities, and associations but also a useful resource for Data Protection Officers (or anyone responsible for data processing) of larger companies.

WARNING

Although reading this book might save you the headache of reading the entire text of the GDPR, you might still need to obtain legal advice concerning certain activities related to achieving and maintaining GDPR compliance.

Foolish Assumptions

If you're reading this book, I assume the following about you (issues that relate to the material scope of the GDPR, which is a topic I discuss further in Chapter 2):

- ➤➤ You either run your own business (or an association or a charity) or work for one and are to some extent the responsible party when it comes to data protection.

- ➤➤ You process personal data in an automated way or as part of a manual filing system.

Note: If you process personal data purely as part of a personal or household activity, you need not read this book, because the GDPR doesn't apply to you.

The following list shows what I'll ask you *not* to assume, to help you begin to understand how the GDPR works and when it applies to you:

- ➤➤ **Territorial scope of the GDPR:** Don't assume that just because you're established *outside* of the EU that the GDPR doesn't apply to you. If either of the following bullet items applies to you, the GDPR applies to you:

  - • *You offer goods or services (whether payment is required or not) to data subjects within the EU.*

  - • *You monitor the behavior of data subjects in the EU — for example, by using tracking cookies.*

- ➤➤ **Size threshold for the GDPR:** Don't assume, because your company, charity, or association is very small, that the GDPR doesn't apply to you. No threshold of size dictates whether the GDPR applies. There are derogations (exemptions) for certain GDPR obligations for organizations that employ more than 250 employees, but many people confuse this with an absolute exemption from the application of the GDPR. That is not the case.

- ➤➤ **Compliance:** If the GDPR does apply to you, don't assume that you can play fast-and-loose with the rules and never be fined or that you can ignore the rules because your competitors aren't compliant. Supervisory authorities respond to complaints; if they investigate you and find non-compliance, they have a wide range of sanctions at their disposal. (See Chapter 21 for more on this topic.)

Equally, don't assume the worst because a complaint has been made. If you cooperate with the supervisory authority and show that you have been trying to become compliant, you will in all likelihood be spared a fine. If you bury your head in the sand and ignore the GDPR, however, the supervisory authorities won't hesitate to use the full sanctions at their disposal.

>> **Investment to become compliant:** You may not be overjoyed about having to find the time to learn about the GDPR and then implement compliance, but it's important, and it's necessary. Yet you don't have to spend a fortune on expensive lawyers and you don't need to become an expert on the GDPR.

If you put aside just a few days to read this book, buy my GDPR Compliance Pack (find out more about this later in the Introduction), and put in place the necessary documents, you will be in good shape to fend off complaints, cope with regulatory investigations, avoid fines, and develop customer loyalty by respecting their data.

>> **People don't care about compliance:** At a talk I gave at the Digital Marketer's Internet marketing conference in San Diego about the GDPR and the new ePrivacy Regulations (see Appendix A for more on the ePD), I shared research from a report by Axciom, which surveyed over 10,000 people in ten different countries. The report shows that the vast majority of people are very concerned about the issue of online privacy.

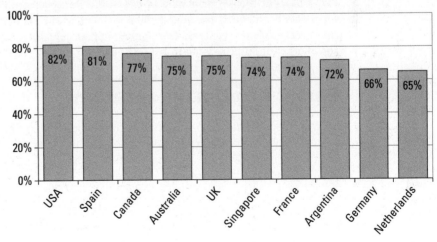

On a scale from 1 to 10 where 1 is 'not at all concerned' and 10 is 'very concerned', how do you rate your levels of concern about the issue of online privacy these days? |% who answer 7-10

So, don't assume that your prospects and your customers don't care about your compliance with the GDPR. As public awareness increases about GDPR compliance, it's in your best interest to comply; not doing so means that your prospects and customers' concerns about how you use their personal data won't be alleviated. By showing that you're complying with the GDPR, you'll likely be rewarded by your customers with their loyalty, and your prospects will be more likely to become customers.

How This Book Is Organized

I've organized this book into several chapters divided into seven parts. In this section I briefly describe each part to give you a high-level look into what information is covered and where. You can find a more granular breakdown of the topics in the table of contents at the front of this book. And, if you're searching for information on a specific issue, you can check the index to find where in the book it's located.

Part 1: Getting Started with GDPR

Part 1 walks you through the fundamentals of data protection law and the changes introduced by the GDPR.

Part 2: The Key Principles of GDPR

Part 2 is about the key principles of the GDPR. Here's where I look at what personal data is and what processing data is — and at the six data protection principles. This part also contains one chapter on data controllers and data processors and another on international transfers of data.

Part 3: Key Documentation

Part 3 is about the key documentation needed in order to become GDPR compliant. I explain what needs to be contained in the Data Inventory, the Privacy Notice, the Cookie Policy, Data Processing Agreements, Data Sharing Agreements, Opt-in wording, and Legitimate Interest Assessments.

I also touch briefly on Data Protection Impact Assessment forms, Data Subject Access Requests, Data Breach Records, and Data Protection Policies.

Part 4: Data Subject Rights, Protection, and Security

In this part, I look at each of the data subject rights, paying particular attention to Data Subject Access Requests and the right to be forgotten. I take a more in-depth look at Data Protection Impact Assessments, Privacy Impact Assessments, and Data Protection Officers. This part also contains a chapter each on data security and data breaches (including the reporting requirements in the case of a breach).

Part 5: The Workplace, Marketing, and Beyond

This part looks at the lawful grounds of processing for employees, the vital ingredients of an employee Privacy Notice, the handling of Data Subject Access Requests from employees, employee monitoring, employee data breaches, and staff training. I also delve into the lawful grounds of processing for marketing, the GDPR's interrelationship with the ePrivacy Directive, and the impact of the GDPR on various types of offline and online marketing. This part covers how the GDPR affects children, charities, and associations and ends with a chapter on supervisory authorities and remedies, liabilities, and penalties.

Part 6: The Part of Tens

The Part of Tens is a traditional part of the *For Dummies* series, and I use it to provide three helpful lists:

- >> The ten best GDPR resources
- >> The ten must-have skills for a Data Protection Officer (DPO)
- >> The ten best ways to train employees to be good stewards of data

Part 7: Appendixes

I've included three appendixes (and a glossary of terms), each providing useful information that doesn't fit elsewhere in the book:

- >> Appendix A gives an overview of impending changes inspired by the GDPR, including proposed amendments to the ePrivacy Directive, US data protection laws, and data protection legislation around the world.

>> Appendix B provides a list of all the supervisory authorities in each EU member state and their contact details.

>> Appendix C contains a handy checklist of all the activities you must complete to maintain GDPR compliance.

>> Appendix D is a glossary of terms, related to the GDPR and data protection, that I use throughout the book. Although I define the terms when I introduce them, the glossary is a handy reference.

Icons Used in This Book

Throughout this book, I use various icons to draw your attention to specific information — here's a description of what they mean:

TIP

This icon highlights pointers to an easier way of doing something or a suggestion that can save you time. This icon may also point out where I give advice to help keep you out of trouble.

REMEMBER

When you see this icon, you know that it highlights information to keep in mind — or a topic I've discussed elsewhere, and I'm reminding you of it.

WARNING

I use this icon to point out pitfalls to avoid or actions (or a lack of actions) that can land you in legal trouble.

TECHNICAL STUFF

Sometimes I provide particularly sticky details about an issue, which can get technical and not exactly interesting. You can ignore any text marked with this icon and not miss it a whit.

What You're Not to Read

Many small business owners are familiar with concepts such as consent and legitimate interests and the requirements to have a Privacy Notice and a Cookie Policy and to keep data secure. What many of them ignore, however, are matters such as using data processors and subprocessors, international transfers and data protection by design and by default.

If you're familiar with basic concepts but haven't ventured beyond that, I recommend that you skip Part 1 and most of Part 2 to start at Chapter 6 and then read on from there.

I see many business owners who took action when the GDPR came into effect by putting new documentation into place but haven't revisited it since then. The supervisory authorities are clear that treating the GDPR lightly, as a one-off exercise or a tick-the-box exercise, is not sufficient. Compliance has to be ongoing, and privacy must be at the heart of the organization. If this is you and you need to revisit your ongoing compliance, I recommend skipping Parts 1–3 (for now) and paying particular attention to Chapter 14 onward.

If you're an expert on the GDPR and are using this book as a reference point only, just dip in and out as you see fit.

Where to Go from Here

Unless you are an expert in the GDPR (and are using this book as a reference point), I suggest that you start at Chapter 1 and read the entire book from start to finish.

You can read chapters out of order if you need to focus on certain areas before others. I provide cross-references to relevant chapters on topics you might need to know more about.

If you are new to GDPR compliance or you haven't kept on top of ongoing compliance, start with the GDPR checklist in Appendix C, which will highlight your areas of noncompliance.

If you receive a data subject right request, such as a Data Subject Access Request or a right to be forgotten, you can refer quickly to the relevant section in Chapter 14.

GDPR Facebook group

After having worked with multinational companies for many years as a City of London lawyer at one of the world's largest law firms, I have dedicated the past ten years to working exclusively with small businesses. I have always felt strongly about the injustice of traditional legal services being inaccessible to small business owners, often leaving them without protection for their businesses.

Though I had been running my Small Business Legal Academy for many years and helping thousands of small businesses with not just data protection law but also wider business law matters (www.smallbusinesslegalacademy.co.uk/sbla), I set up my GDPR Facebook group (GDPR for Online Entrepreneurs) after realizing that the majority of small-business owners:

>> Know absolutely nothing about data protection laws

>> Rely on incorrect advice from the loudest voice at their networking meetings

Because of this, I posted, for 90 days, one video guide per day on the GDPR, helping tens of thousands of small businesses in the process. I regularly post updates of cases, updated guidance from the European Data Protection Board or supervisory authorities, and updates on new related legislation. I also answer questions about the general application of the GDPR.

TIP

Ensure that you answer the questions that you are asked when you apply to join my Facebook group — or you won't be let in.

GDPR Compliance Pack

In my Facebook group, many small-business owners were panicking about the introduction of the GDPR and the huge fines they might face for non-compliance. Some were considering closing their small businesses because they lacked the resources to consult a lawyer in the traditional way. Part of my role in the Facebook group was to calm that panic and explain the reality: Small business owners wouldn't be fined 20 million euros the day after the GDPR went into effect because of a small breach of the GDPR.

As I continued to educate group members on the ins and outs of the GDPR, they started asking how to implement their newfound knowledge. They realized that they needed a Privacy Notice, agreements with their data processors, and other documents, but they didn't know where to get them from.

In response to this demand, I put together my GDPR Compliance Pack and sold it as affordably as possible. It has all the documents (over 20) a small business needs in order to become GDPR-compliant. After selling many thousands of copies of this Compliance Pack to organizations around the world, I have received huge accolades from happy customers — even asking whether they can nominate me for an award for the help I have provided. (That MBE is on its way, I am sure!)

If my Compliance Pack would help you, find out more about it here: www. suzannedibble.com/gdprpack.

Other ways to stay in the know

You can sign up for my GDPR updates by email by going to www.suzannedibble. com/gdprupdates.

TIP

If you don't receive any updates, check the spam folder in your email program and then whitelist the email address.

I also provide free training sessions on all areas of the GDPR that offer practical guidance on how to comply. The dates and registration links for those webinars are in my update emails.

If any areas of this book need to be updated, I will post the information at www.suzannedibble.com/gdprfordummies.

In addition to what you're reading right now, this book comes with a free access-anywhere Cheat Sheet that offers a number of GDPR-related tips, techniques, and resources. To get this Cheat Sheet, visit www.dummies.com and type **GDPR For Dummies cheat sheet** in the Search box.

One-on-one legal advice

Although this book, the Facebook group, and my Compliance Pack can help you enormously with the GDPR, they don't comprise a complete substitute for one-on-one legal advice. If you have a particularly complex business or are processing data in a complex way, I recommend that you obtain legal advice. For one-to-one advice, email me via my website and I'll either provide you with a quote or refer you to a trusted data protection colleague.

www.suzannedibble.com

1
Getting Started with GDPR

Chapter **1**

Grasping the Fundamentals of GDPR and Data Protection

The General Data Protection Regulation (GDPR), which came into effect on May 25, 2018, is the successor to the European Union's Data Protection Directive [of] 1995 (Directive 95/46/EC).

One aim of the GDPR was to harmonize data protection laws across Europe — so its legal form is a *regulation* (an order that must be executed) as opposed to a *directive* (a result to achieve, though the means to achieve aren't dictated). Unlike a directive, when the European Union (EU) enacts a regulation, it becomes national legislation in each EU member state, with member states having no opportunity to change it via national legislation.

However, EU member states are permitted to make certain *derogations* (a fancy term for *exemptions*) from the GDPR (such as in the case of the need to uphold a country's security), so data protection laws across Europe aren't quite as harmonized as may have been desired by some of the legislators.

Although EU member states cannot change the GDPR, each member state requires national legislation to accompany the GDPR, for two reasons:

>> The GDPR needs to fit into the member state's legal framework.

>> National legislation is needed to choose from the exemptions permitted by the GDPR.

At the time this book was written, all but three member states had passed national legislation to sit alongside the GDPR. So, you need to familiarize yourself with not only the GDPR but also the legislation that was implemented in the EU member state(s) in which your organization is established.

Understanding Data Protection Laws

Data protection laws exist to balance the rights of individuals to privacy and the ability of organizations to use data for the purposes of their business. Data protection laws provide important rights for data subjects and for the enforcement of such rights.

This list describes a handful of additional points about these laws to keep in mind. Data protection laws:

>> **Protect data subjects:** A *data subject* is an individual whose personal data is collected, held, and/or processed.

>> **Apply to organizations that control the processing of personal data (known as *data controllers*) and also organizations that process personal data under the instructions of data controllers (known as *data processors*):** These include companies (both private and public), charities (not-for-profit, political, and so on), and associations (such as churches, sports clubs, and professional leagues, to name only a few).

>> **Apply throughout the world.** The concept of privacy originated in the United States in the 1890s. Although the EU has been a front-runner in establishing the laws protecting data and sees itself as setting the gold standard of data protections laws, the vast majority of countries around the world have some form of data protection laws.

>> **Do not prevent organizations from using personal data:** Organizations can legitimately use personal data to their benefit as long as they comply with applicable data protection laws. Every organization is likely to process some personal data — of its clients, employees, suppliers, prospects, and so on.

» **Prevent common misuses of personal data:** Organizations often fail to (i) put in place appropriate measures to keep personal data secure, (ii) inform the data subject at the point of data collection about what it is intending to do with the personal data and where necessary to obtain consent, and (iii) transfer personal data to third parties without the knowledge of the data subject. Data protection laws generally prevent these common misuses.

Countries hold to varying degrees of regulation and enforcement and some countries don't have any data protection laws. Table 1-1 rates the strength of various countries' efforts to protect data.

TABLE 1-1 **Regulation/Enforcement Strength of Data Protection Laws Worldwide**

Type of Regulation/ Enforcement	Countries
Tough	Australia, Canada, Hong Kong, South Korea
Strong	Argentina, China, Estonia, Finland, Iceland, Japan, Latvia, Malaysia, Monaco, Morocco, New Zealand
Light	Angola, Belarus, Costa Rica, Egypt, Ghana, Lithuania, Mexico, Nigeria, Russia, Saudi Arabia/UAE, South Africa, Turkey, Ukraine
Limited	Honduras, India, Indonesia, Pakistan, Panama, Thailand, Uruguay

The Ten Most Important Obligations of the GDPR

The *obligations* I refer to in this section's heading are the ten most important actions you need to take to comply with the GDPR; I've only summarized these obligations in the following list because I discuss them further throughout this book:

» **Prepare a data inventory to map your data flows** so that you can understand exactly what personal data you're processing and what you're doing with it. (See Chapter 7 for more on this topic.)

» **Work out the lawful grounds for processing each type of personal data** for each purpose for which you're processing it. (Chapter 3 has more on this topic.)

>> **Ensure that your data security strategy is robust** and that you have implemented appropriate technical and organizational measures to ensure a level of security appropriate to the risk of a data breach or other security incident. (See Chapter 16 for more about data security.)

>> **Ensure that an appropriate safeguard is in place** whenever you transfer personal data outside of the European Economic Area (EEA). (See Chapter 6 for more about transferring personal data.)

>> **Update your Privacy Notice** to ensure that you're being transparent about the means and purposes of your data-processing. (See Chapter 8 for more on Privacy Notices.)

>> **Update your Cookie Policy** to ensure that you aren't relying on implied consent, that browsers of your website are taking affirmative action to consent to non-essential cookies being used, and that the cookies are fired only after consent is obtained. (For more on the concept of implied consent as well as details about cookie policies, see Chapter 9.)

>> **Ensure that your staff are appropriately trained** in relevant areas of the GDPR. (Chapter 18 has more on this topic and Chapter 24 has tips for training employees to help you maintain GDPR compliance.)

>> **Ensure that you have reviewed the grounds on which you process employee data,** and issue a revised employee Privacy Notice where necessary. (See Chapter 18 for more on this topic.)

>> **Determine whether you need to appoint a Data Protection Officer (DPO).** If you do, take the necessary steps to hire a suitable candidate. (See Chapter 15 for more on DPOs.)

>> **Review all of your processor and subprocessor arrangements** and ensure that appropriate contracts are in place. Ensure that the data processors (and subprocessors) are compliant with the GDPR and that they have adequate security in place to protect the personal data. (See Chapter 5 for more on this topic. Chapter 10 covers data processor and subprocessor contracts.)

Facing the Consequences

Think of this section as a description of not only the consequences you face if you aren't compliant but also the reasons you should care about being compliant.

Increased fines and sanctions

The GDPR has introduced significant increases in the maximum fines for breaches of its requirements.

Under the GDPR, the fine for certain breaches of the GDPR have been increased to €20 million or 4 percent of global turnover for the past financial year, whichever is higher. For "lesser" breaches, the maximum fines have increased to €10 million or 2 percent of global turnover for the past financial year, whichever is higher.

This significant increase in fines indicates the increasing importance of data protection within the EU as the value of personal data increases and the processing becomes even more sophisticated.

This is not to say that you will be fined these amounts for any infringements of the GDPR — you would have to do something that significantly impacts on the rights and freedoms of a large number of data subjects to incur a maximum fine. (See Chapter 21 for examples of fines issued and the considerations that will be taken into account when supervisory authorities are deciding on the appropriate sanction. I also discuss throughout this book, fines and sanctions as pertinent to the topics at hand.)

REMEMBER

Supervisory authorities are the regulatory authorities (often known as *data protection authorities*) within individual EU member states that are responsible for the enforcement of the GDPR. There is a list of supervisory authorities in Appendix B.

Civil claims

Data subjects can now bring civil claims against data controllers for infringements of their data subject rights. So, if, for example, you don't respond appropriately to a data subject right request (namely where the data subject can request details of the personal data you process for that data subject — see Chapter 14 for more detail on this) or if you experience a data breach that affects the data subject's personal data (see Chapter 17 for more on this), you could find yourself on the receiving end of a civil claim.

As you may have noticed in recent high-profile data breaches, such as the British Airways data breach in 2019, data protection lawyers are placing advertisements encouraging victims of data breaches to join group actions against the data controller.

A civil claim against you would not only damage your reputation further but would also cost a significant amount of time and money to defend the claim.

Data subject complaints

The general public is much savvier about their data protection rights than they used to be — for these reasons:

>> The introduction of the GDPR garnered a lot of publicity due to the increased sanctions.

>> Supervisory authorities ran various awareness campaigns to ensure that data subjects were aware of their rights.

>> Certain high profile cases, such as the Facebook and Cambridge Analytica cases (where personal data was misused for political profiling) and the British Airways data breach case, have received broad coverage in the media.

This savviness has led to an increase in the number of complaints from data subjects whose personal data hasn't been processed in accordance with the GDPR. Data subjects are lodging complaints both directly to the data controller and to supervisory authorities. The two situations require two different responses:

>> **If the data subject complains directly to you (the data controller):** Although a complaint signals that an element of reputational damage has occurred, you have an opportunity to repair the relationship — which is particularly important if the data subject is a customer or a potential customer.

>> **If the data subject complains to the supervisory authority:** Because the supervisory authority is bound to investigate that complaint, you might face more serious consequences. The supervisory authority will review all your data processing activities, policies, and procedures in relation to that complaint. If it finds that the complaint is valid, the supervisory authority will use its corrective powers in relation to such complaints.

These corrective powers include the ability to issue fines, to impose a temporary or definitive ban on the processing of personal data, or to force you to respond to the data subject's requests to exercise their rights. Chapter 21 contains more information about the powers of supervisory authorities.

Brand damage

When a data subject brings a claim against you, you risk not only sanctions from the relevant supervisory but also brand damage. A report by Axciom (a consulting firm providing marketers with data and technology assistance) entitled "Global data privacy: What the consumer really thinks" showed that individuals from around the world are, in the vast majority, quite concerned about how their personal data is used and protected. If you aren't compliant with the GDPR, you're showing your prospects, customers, and employees that you aren't concerned about the protection of their personal data.

You can see the Axciom report at: `https://dma.org.uk/uploads/misc/5b0522b113a23-global-data-privacy-report---final-2_5b0522b11396e.pdf`.

Loss of trust

If you don't comply with the GDPR and, for example, you experience a data breach or don't respond appropriately to data subject requests, you are likely to lose trust from your customers and prospects. When they don't trust you, they don't want to buy from you or otherwise do business with you. Similarly, when your employees don't trust you, they no longer want to work for you.

In unfortunate timing, British Airways sent an email to all of its customers to assure them that they could trust British Airways with their personal data. Just a couple of months later, British Airways suffered a large data breach that compromised the financial details of 185,000 customers, details that were sold on the dark web. As a result of this data breach, the share price of IAG (British Airways' parent company) decreased by 5.8 percent (equivalent to a loss of £350m).

In 2018, CompariTech carried out a report finding that, in the long term, organizations that have suffered data breaches financially underperformed.

You can find that report at `www.comparitech.com/blog/information-security/data-breach-share-price-2018/`.

Being a Market Leader

By embracing the GDPR and showing your customers, prospects, and employees that you care about the protection of their personal data, you gain a competitive advantage.

Elizabeth Denham, the UK information commissioner, summed up this idea nicely:

"Accountability encourages an upfront investment in privacy fundamentals, but it offers a payoff down the line, not just in better legal compliance, but a competitive edge. We believe there is a real opportunity for organisations to present themselves on the basis of how they respect the privacy of individuals and over time this can play more of a role in consumer choice."

Chapter **2**

Key Changes Introduced by GDPR

Though it's true that the GDPR introduces some key changes in European data protection law, the changes aren't as numerous as many organizations' leaders may think. If you aren't familiar with existing data protection laws, however, and the threat of increased sanctions has aroused your interest in being compliant with them, it may all be quite new to you. And, of course, if you're established outside the EU and this is the first time that European data protection laws are relevant to you, it's all new to you.

In this chapter, I walk you through the key changes to data protection that the General Data Protection Regulation (GDPR) introduces. Many of the changes relate to topics I explore in more depth throughout this book, so, where applicable, I point you to chapters containing more information.

Increased Territorial Scope

Arguably, the biggest change the General Data Protection Regulation (GDPR) introduces is that of the increased territorial scope. Indeed, if you're established mainly outside of the EU, the data protection laid out in the GDPR may all be new to you.

Pre-GDPR, if your main establishment was outside of the EU but you had establishments within the EU, you would have to have complied with the local law of the country within the EU in which you had establishments. Although EU Member States have implemented their national law on data protection on the basis of the Data Protection Directive [of] 1995 (the EU legislation governing data protection that was succeeded by the GDPR), there still existed certain differences in the implementation of that directive into local law.

For example, EU member states differed on their views, amongst many other things, as to:

>> Whether encoded or pseudonymous data should be regarded as personal data

>> Whether personal data should also extend to legal persons such as companies

>> The definition of "filing system"

>> The definition of "controller" and "processor"

>> The applicability to deceased persons

>> Whether implied consent is permissible

REMEMBER

A *Directive* is a legislative act of the EU Parliament and the Council of the European Union that sets out a goal that all EU member states must achieve within a certain period of time. However, individual member states have flexibility on how to implement laws to achieve those goals. A *Regulation*, however (such as the General Data Protection Regulations), is a binding legislative act that is applied in its entirety across all member states and is immediately applicable and enforceable.

One aim of the GDPR was to harmonize data protection laws across Europe — hence it's being a *regulation* (an order that must be executed) as opposed to a *directive* (a result to achieve though the means to achieve aren't dictated) and being directly applicable across all EU member states. This brings good and bad news for these two situations:

>> **If you have many establishments within the EU,** this is good news because you now have to comply only with one data protection law. This one comes with certain exemptions, and so forth, on a country-by-country basis, but that's still better than having to comply with many different data protection laws.

>> **If you don't have an establishment within the EU** but the GDPR applies to you (because you offer goods or services to or monitor the behavior of individuals within the EU), this is bad news. You have to get up to speed with (and become compliant with) a long, complex, and far-reaching regulation.

You might feel somewhat indignant that a country that isn't your own can subject you to these complex regulations. This was the initial response of many business owners from outside the EU when they first came into my Facebook group (GDPR for Online Entrepreneurs), where I provide GDPR updates and answer related questions. "How dare the EU impose rules on us," some of them lambasted.

TIP

If you share that sentiment, let me invite you to reconsider your thinking on this. If you're established outside of the EU, the law applies *only to the extent that you process the personal data of people within the EU.* The EU is looking after its people. If you were exporting physical goods into the EU, you would expect to comply with the laws of the country you're exporting to. Just because personal data is intangible doesn't mean that it isn't worthy of protection.

Indeed, arguably, personal data should be subject to even greater protection because of the advances in processing and the potential consequences of its being abused, such as personal data being used covertly to influence democratic elections.

In any event, just remember that whether the GDPR applies to you — and the extent to which it applies to you — depends on whether you're an EU-established controller:

>> **If you're established within the EU,** the GDPR applies to the entirety of your processing, including the processing of personal data of data subjects who are outside of the EU.

>> **If you aren't established within the EU,** and if the GDPR applies to you, it applies only to the processing of personal data of data subjects who are within the EU.

I separately discuss EU-established controllers and non-EU-established controllers to take a closer look at these scenarios. In this context, controllers are *data controllers*, in the simplest terms, the entities — whether a person, organization, or public authority, for example — who control the data that's processed. I discuss controllers and processors in Chapter 5.

EU established data controllers

Article 3(1) of the GDPR provides that the GDPR applies "to the processing of personal data in the context of the activities of an establishment of a controller or processor in the [European] Union, regardless of whether the processing takes place in the [European] Union or not."

TIP

The European Data Protection Board (EDPB), an independent European body, provides guidance regarding how to apply data protection rules throughout the European Union (EU). You can read more about this entity at https://edpb. europa.eu/edpb_en.

The EDPB recommends a threefold approach to the question of whether the processing of personal data falls within the scope of the GDPR due to Article 3(1) — namely, considerations of whether

>> You have an establishment within the EU.

>> Your processing is in the context of the activities of the establishment.

>> You're a controller or a processor.

I explain these concepts further throughout the rest of this section.

Establishment

There's no definition of establishment within the GDPR, but Recital 22 suggests that it implies the "effective and real exercise of activity through stable arrangements. The legal form of such arrangements, whether through a branch or a subsidiary with a legal personality, is not the determining factor in that respect."

This would mean that if an entity is merely incorporated in a territory or has, for example, a single server in that territory, it would not necessarily be established in such a territory. See the nearby sidebar, "Weltimmo v. NAIH," regarding a court case that provides some guidance on the meaning of establishment.

REMEMBER

If you have any presence in an EU member state, whether it's a single representative such as an employee or agent, you need to carefully consider whether you have an establishment in that EU member state. If you do, you need to comply with the GDPR in the entirety of your processing, including in relation to data subjects who are outside of the EU.

WELTIMMO V. NAIH

A 2015 case *(Weltimmo v NAIH)* provides some guidance on the meaning of establishment. Weltimmo was incorporated in Slovakia, and its business was advertising properties on its website. The target market, however, was Hungary, with Hungarian properties being featured and the text of the adverts on the website being written in Hungarian. Complaints were made to the Hungarian Data Protection Authority because properties weren't being removed when requested. Weltimmo argued that the Hungarian Data Protection Authority [Nemzeti Adatvédelmiés Információszabadság Hivatal (NAIH)] did not have jurisdiction to take action against it because it was incorporated in Slovakia.

The Court of Justice of the European Union (CJEU) confirmed that the place of incorporation wasn't a deciding factor and that the presence of a single representative may be sufficient to have an establishment within a certain territory if that representative acts with a sufficient degree of stability. The Court also considered these circumstances:

- The website was solely targeted to Hungarians.
- Weltimmo had a representative in Hungary who represented Weltimmo in administrative and legal proceedings.
- Weltimmo had a bank account in Hungary for recovery of debts.
- Weltimmo used a letterbox in Hungary for management of day-to-day business matters.

The court commented that the nationality of the data subjects was irrelevant.

However, if you're a non-EU entity, the mere fact that your website is accessible by people within the EU doesn't mean that you have an establishment within the EU. Nor does having a Representative in accordance with Article 27 of the GDPR (see Chapter 6 for more details on Representatives), nor using a data processor established in the EU.

In the context of its activities

Where you're processing personal data "in the context of the activities" of the establishment, then GDPR will apply to you whether the processing takes place within the EU or not.

Therefore, if you're mainly based outside of the EU and this is where the processing takes place, but you have an establishment within the EU and the processing carried out is in the context of the activities of the entity based outside of the EU, then the GDPR will apply regardless of the fact that the processing is being carried out outside of the EU.

REMEMBER

Having an establishment within the EU could just be the presence of one sales agent, one employee, or other such representative in an EU country.

For the processing to be in the context of the activities of the establishment, there needs to be an inextricable link between the activities of the establishment based outside the EU (the one carrying out the processing) and the establishment based in the EU. *Inextricable* means that the two establishments are indeed connected and cannot be separated.

The independent European Working Party (known as the Article 29 Working Party) was a guiding entity regarding data protection issues. The Party ceased to formally exist when the GDPR came into effect, but its advice can still be helpful. The Working Party stated that this *inextricable link* should not be stretched too far. Just because two entities are part of the same group of companies doesn't mean that there's an inextricable link.

REMEMBER

If processing by a non-EU entity is inextricably linked to the activities of an establishment in the EU, then the GDPR applies to all processing (even of data subjects outside of the EU), even though the EU establishment isn't carrying out (or taking any part in) the data processing itself.

Data controller or data processor

Because Article 3(1) of the GDPR refers to data controllers as well as data processors, EU-based data processors who are dealing with non-EU data controllers need to comply with the relevant GDPR obligations on processors, including entering into a Data Processing Agreement (DPA). (See Chapter 5 for more about data controllers and data processors.)

A DPA is a legally binding document to be entered into between the data controller and the data processor in writing or in electronic form. It regulates the particularities of data processing — such as its scope and purpose — as well as the relationship between the data controller and the data processor.

A DPA is important because it forces data controllers to take measures to ensure the protection of the personal data they handle. If data controllers decide, for example, to outsource certain data processing activities, they must be able to demonstrate that their suppliers and sub-processors also provide enough guarantees to protect the data and act in a GDPR compliant manner.

This arguably puts these data processors at a disadvantage to data processors based outside of the EU in terms of compliance documentation. However, it could be argued that these data processors being subject to a higher level of data protection regulations than their non-EU counterparts is a good thing, in terms of protection of the data, therefore providing such data processors with a competitive advantage.

Chapter 5 covers the relationship between (and obligations of) data controllers and data processors. Chapter 10 covers Data Processing Agreements.

Non-EU established controllers

Article 3(2) of the GDPR states that the GDPR applies to "the processing of personal data of data subjects who are in the [European] Union by a controller or processor not established in the [European] Union, where the processing activities are related to" either of the following or both:

>> You offer goods and services to data subjects who are in the European Union. Whether the data subject is required to pay for those goods or services isn't relevant.

>> You monitor the behavior of data subjects, as far as that behavior takes place within the European Union.

I explain these concepts further throughout the rest of this section.

Data subjects who are in the EU

The data processing must relate to data subjects located in the EU at the moment when the relevant *trigger activity* takes place — that is, when the goods or services are offered or when the behavior is monitored. The citizenship, place of residence, or other legal status of the data subject has no relevance.

Offering of goods or services

It's irrelevant whether payment has been made for goods or services — the mere offering will suffice.

Recital 23 of the GDPR provides that when considering whether you're offering goods or services to data subjects within the EU, you need to look at whether it was actually an active part of your business plan to offer goods or services to data subjects within the EU. If you have a few one-off sales in the EU or sign-ups to your newsletter from data subjects in the EU, for example, you may not be within the scope of the GDPR. Just because your website is accessible by data subjects within EU countries doesn't mean that the GDPR applies to you.

The following factors are considered in determining whether the GDPR applies to you:

>> Your text is in an EU language.

>> You're displaying prices in an EU currency.

>> You've enabled the ability for people to place orders in EU languages.

>> You make references to the country of EU users or customers.

>> You have advertisements directed to people within EU member states.

>> You display telephone numbers with international codes.

>> You're using a domain of the European member state (for example, . de or . eu).

>> You mention clients or customers in European member states.

This isn't an exhaustive list — all circumstances need to be considered.

Monitoring of behavior

If you monitor or profile EU individuals' behavior, where that behavior is occurring within the EU, then the GDPR applies to you.

Monitoring here includes the tracking of individuals online to create profiles, particularly where this is in order to make decisions concerning that individual or for analyzing or predicting the individual's preferences, behaviors, and attitudes.

If you're using cookies to track an individual's activity on the Internet, for example, and that individual is within the EU, the GDPR applies to you.

Understanding the Representative's Role and When to Appoint One

A *Representative* is a person or organization that you, as a data controller or data processor, may be obliged to appoint in writing to act as a liaison between your organization and supervisory authorities.

If you, as a data controller or a data processor, do not have an establishment within the EU and the GDPR applies to you (see Chapter 1 for more on this), you're required to appoint a Representative in writing.

You don't have to appoint a Representative if your processing of personal data meets all three of these criteria:

>> It's occasional.

>> It doesn't include processing of special categories of data or criminal convictions data on a large scale, AND

>> It's unlikely to result in a risk to the rights and freedoms of natural persons, taking into account the nature, context, scope, and purposes of the processing.

Responsibilities of the Representative

The Representative represents the data controller or data processor with respect to their obligations under the GDPR and has primarily a passive role, with the following two main responsibilities:

>> The Representative is mandated by you, as the data controller or data processor, to receive correspondence from the supervisory authorities and data subjects on all issues related to the processing of personal data. The Representative can receive correspondence in addition to or instead of you.

>> The Representative must also make available to the supervisory authority, at their request, the Article 30 processing records of the data controller or data processor. One of the main changes to data protection law that the GDPR has brought about is the fact that data controllers and data processors are required to keep internal systems and records; see Chapter 7 for more about these items.

The Representative may be fined if they fail to fulfil their obligations under the GDPR. Recital 81 of the GDPR states that "the designated Representative should be subject to enforcement proceedings in the event of noncompliance by the data controller or data processor." This statement seems to suggest that the Representative can be liable for the noncompliance of the data controller or data processor. Guidance from the European Data Protection board (EDPB) suggests that this is the case.

Qualifications of the Representative

A Representative may be an individual or a business but must be established in the EU. Guidance from the EDPB suggests that Representatives can include law firms, consultants, and other private companies, as long as they're established within an EU member state where the relevant data subjects are. For example, if you're established in the United States and have no data subjects in Ireland, you cannot appoint a representative in Ireland.

The following points can be helpful as you consider whom to appoint as your Representative:

>> Choose a Representative in a member state in which a significant proportion of data subjects whose personal data are processed are located.

>> The Representative must be able to communicate in the languages of all the relevant data subjects and supervisory authorities (which may be done by way of an external team, if necessary).

>> One Representative may act for lots of different non-EU data controllers or data processors.

>> The Representative should not be an external Data Protection Officer (the DPO, which I discuss in Chapter 15), because the roles are incompatible and may result in a conflict of interest.

>> Appoint your Representative in writing, clarifying the terms of the relationship and the Representative's obligations.

>> If the role is being undertaken by a company or another such organization, a single person should be the lead contact.

THE UK LEAVES EUROPE

When the UK leaves the EU, it will become a third country. If you're established within the UK and don't have a branch, an office, or another establishment within the EU, you may need to appoint a Representative if you are doing either or both of the following:

- Offering goods or services to data subjects in the EEA
- Monitoring the behavior of data subjects located in the EEA

Although it may be tempting to appoint a Representative in Ireland, for language reasons, this is possible only if you have data subjects located in Ireland.

Similarly, if you're established in the EU, without a UK branch or office or another establishment and you are offering goods or services to data subjects in the UK or monitoring the behavior of data subjects located in the UK, you will need to appoint a Representative in the UK.

Consent and Withdrawal of Consent

Although consent isn't a new ground for lawful processing, the GDPR establishes a higher standard of consent. Pre-GDPR, consent could be implied consent with the use of default options, pre-ticked boxes, and opt-outs. Post-GDPR, consent needs to include an *affirmative action*, a concept covered in Chapter 11. To read more about the new standard of consent (and the other lawful grounds of processing), see Chapter 3.

REMEMBER

Withdrawing consent must be as easy as giving consent. For example if you have obtained consent via a tick box on a website, the data subject must be able to withdraw consent online rather than, say, write a letter to withdraw consent.

Data subjects have the right to withdraw consent at any time. So, arguably, merely having an Unsubscribe option at the bottom of emails would not suffice, as an email is not available to a data subject at all times — they may have received one and deleted it and therefore have no link to unsubscribe when they want to do so.

As a result of these changes, you should

>> **Review all your consents and consider whether they meet the GDPR standard of consent.** For example, if you obtained consent using pre-ticked boxes or other default options, this is no longer valid under the GDPR. If your

consents are not of a GDPR standard, you need to refresh those consents. Keep in mind as well that you cannot email individuals to request consent for email or text marketing, due to the provisions of the ePrivacy Directive, as implemented into EU member state law.

>> **Ensure that you have appropriate mechanisms for data subjects to withdraw consent.** Withdrawing consent must be as easy as providing consent, so make sure data subjects can easily find a way to do it — a preference management tool, for example, in which data subjects can unsubscribe from certain types of emails. The place to inform data subjects of their right to withdraw consent is in the Privacy Notice, which I discuss in Chapter 8.

>> **Ensure that you have robust systems for recording evidence of consent.** If data subjects lodge a complaint against you, that could result in an investigation down the line. In that case, you need to produce this evidence. (See Chapter 3 for more about documenting consent.)

Additional Data Subject Rights

Data subjects did enjoy certain rights under previous data protection laws, but the GDPR has extended those rights and added the new right of data portability. (See Chapter 14 for more about data subject rights.)

The enhanced data subject rights are backed up with the ability for data subjects to bring civil claims, which is also a new addition.

As a result of the changes to data subject rights, you need to

>> **Update your Privacy Notice.** See Chapter 8 for more on this topic.

>> **Review your existing lawful grounds for processing in light of the enhanced data subject rights.** For example, if your lawful grounds for processing is consent or performing a contract, the data subject may require the data to be ported over to a new data controller. If your lawful grounds are a different one, this right doesn't apply.

>> **Review subject access request procedures and update them as necessary.** A *data subject access request (DSAR)* is a written request made by the data subject for information that he or she is entitled to ask for under the GDPR. (See Chapter 14 for more on this topic.)

Liability of Processors

The GDPR introduces direct obligations on — and liability for — data processors. A *data processor* is an entity, such as a cloud-based storage provider, that processes data for the data controller upon the instruction of the data controller. (See Chapter 5 for more about data processors.)

Under the GDPR, data processors are required to comply with a number of obligations, including

>> Maintaining adequate documentation of processing of personal data (Article 30); see Chapter 7

>> Implementing appropriate security standards (Article 32); see Chapter 16

>> Carrying out routine Data Protection Impact Assessments (Article 32); see Chapter 15

>> Appointing a Data Protection Officer (Article 37); see Chapter 15

>> Complying with rules on international data transfers (Articles 44-50); see Chapter 6

>> Cooperating with national supervisory authorities (Article 31); see Chapter 21

Data processors are liable for fines and other sanctions (Article 83) if they don't comply with these obligations. In addition, data processors may be subject to civil claims from data subjects (Article 79).

As a result of these changes, you should

>> Decide whether you're a data controller, a data processor, or a joint controller in each case of processing personal data. (See Chapter 5.)

>> Review and renegotiate contracting arrangements with your data processors to ensure compliance. (See Chapter 5.)

>> Review supply chains and ensure compliance by subcontractors that are processing personal data (who are known as "subprocessors").

>> Carry out data privacy impact assessments where necessary. (See Chapter 15.)

>> If you're the data processor, decide whether your customer agreements need to be renegotiated on pricing to reflect the increased risk profile.

Specific Protection for Children's Data

The GDPR is the first data protection law to explicitly state that children's personal data merits specific protection, in the following areas:

>> **Regarding consent:** It introduces new requirements for the online processing of a child's personal data. If you offer online services to a child and you rely on consent as your lawful grounds for processing, only children over a certain age are able to give their own consent. For processing the personal data of children under this age, you will require parental consent and this needs to be verified. In the UK the age of consent is 13, and in other countries the age ranges from 13 to 16. (For more on this topic, see Chapter 20.)

>> **Marketing:** The GDPR also provides that specific protection is necessary where children's personal data is used for marketing purposes or creating personality or user profiles. So, if you do this kind of marketing, you need to consider this carefully and take advice where necessary. For more on marketing, see Chapter 19.

>> **Automated processing:** You should not subject children to decisions based solely on automated processing (including profiling) if these have a legal or similarly significant effect on them. There are certain exceptions to this prohibition, but they apply only if suitable measures are in place to protect the rights, freedoms, and legitimate interests of the child.

WARNING

Recital 71 makes it clear that the exceptions of the prohibition on automated decision-making for children should not be the norm. If you make these types of decisions about children, you need to carefully consider the processing and take advice where necessary.

>> **Transparency:** In terms of the transparency principle (see Chapter 4 for more on this), the GDPR requires you to provide age-appropriate Privacy Notices for children that make it very easy for them to understand how their personal data is being processed — for example, by using videos.

>> **Right to erasure:** The GDPR says that the right to have personal data erased is particularly important when the processing is based on the consent of a child.

REMEMBER

As a result of these changes, if you process children's personal data, you should

>> **Ensure that your consent procedures are compliant.** Where you're offering online services to children and relying on consent as your lawful grounds for processing, make sure you have suitable methods for verifying parental consent.

>> **Review how you use children's personal data for marketing purposes or creating personality or user profiles.** You'll want to consider this advice carefully and take it where necessary.

>> **Review whether you're subjecting children to decisions based solely on automated processing.** Do those decisions have a legal or similarly significant effect on the children? If so, consider this advice very carefully and take it where necessary.

>> **Review your Privacy Notices.** Do you need to simplify the language in your Privacy Notices so that children can understand them?

Data Breach Notification

The GDPR has introduced the requirement to notify supervisory authorities and affected individuals when data breaches occur. Pre-GDPR, in the majority of EU Member States there was either no obligation to notify or, if there was, there were minimal sanctions for failing to do so. (See Chapter 17 for more on the obligations on data controllers and data processors in relation to data breach notifications.)

Data Protection Officers

The GDPR introduces the European-wide obligation for certain data controllers and data processors to appoint a Data Protection Officer (DPO). Under previous data protection legislation, certain EU member states — Germany, for example — required the appointment of a DPO, but for the majority of member states, it's a new requirement. (See Chapter 15 for more about the obligation to appoint a DPO.)

Accountability and Governance

The GDPR introduces a new concept of accountability. It's no longer enough just to do the right thing. You need to keep records of your thought processes and reasons for why you reached a certain conclusion. (One clear example here is justifying the use of legitimate interests as a grounds of processing — see Chapter 12 for more on this topic.)

The GDPR introduces additional governance obligations, including

>> Keeping detailed records of processing activities. (See Chapter 7.)

>> Carrying out Data Protection Impact Assessments (DPIAs) for high-risk processing. (See Chapter 15.)

- >> Appointing a Data Protection Officer. (See Chapter 15.)

- >> Implementing data protection by design and by default. (See Chapter 15.)

- >> Maintaining a record of data breaches. (See Chapter 17.)

- >> Notifying certain data breaches to the supervisory authority and the data subject. (See Chapter 17.)

Increased Fines and Sanctions

The main change that has given the GDPR so much coverage in the press — and that has really made organizations take note of the changes — is the introduction of significant increases in the maximum fines for breaches of its requirements. Pre-GDPR, the maximum fines were £500,000 in the UK and a similar amount in other EU member states, but under GDPR, the fines look like this:

- >> For certain breaches, maximum fines have increased to €20 million or 4 percent of global turnover for the past financial year, whichever is higher.

- >> For "lesser" breaches, the maximum fines have increased to €10 million or 2 percent of global turnover for the past financial year, whichever is higher.

Chapter 21 has more detail on fines and penalties, but throughout this book, I include information regarding fines and sanctions on that chapter's topic, as applicable.

Ability to Bring a Civil Claim

GDPR makes it considerably easier for data subjects to bring civil claims against data controllers and against data processors. The data subject doesn't have to have suffered financial loss or even any *material damage*, such as loss of or destruction of goods or property, and can claim for *nonmaterial damage*, such as distress and hurt feelings.

In addition, data subjects have the right to require a consumer protection body to exercise rights and bring claims on their behalf. This isn't quite the same as the ability to bring class actions, but it increases the risk of group claims.

Data subjects can also lodge a complaint with the supervisory authority, which I discuss in Chapter 21.

The Key
Principles
of GDPR

Chapter **3**

Digging In to Data: What's Personal, What's Sensitive, and How It's Processed

I t's a simple fact that pretty much every organization (no matter what the size) is collecting and using individuals' personal data and of course processing that data to gain benefit from it (such as emailing potential customers or storing personal data of employees).

The GDPR regulates how organizations process personal data. How *processing of data* is defined is exceptionally broad and I cover this in-depth later on in this chapter.

Before I do that, however, I want to describe what is meant by *personal data*, a term that also has a far-reaching definition in the GDPR. *Personal data* is defined in the GDPR as "any information relating to a natural person who is identified or identifiable, directly or indirectly, with particular reference to an identifier, such as name, ID number, location data, or one or more factors relating to the physical, physiological, genetic, mental, economic, cultural, or social identity of that natural person."

REMEMBER

A *natural person is* a living individual. The law often distinguishes between a natural person and a legal person; a legal person being a legal entity, which can be something like a company or limited partnership.

Special-category data concerns certain, specific categories of personal data that require additional protection because they are clearly sensitive in nature (such as medical health data) or are at particularly high risk of being used to negatively target or discriminate against data subjects (data regarding race, religion, or sexual orientation, for example).

Related to the idea of personal data is the concept of a *data subject:* an individual whose personal data is collected, held, or processed. This concept is important to understand as you read about personal and special-category data and how it's processed.

REMEMBER

For the purposes of the GDPR, personal data relates to *all* personal data processed by organizations established within the European Union (EU). Regarding organizations that are not established in the EU, it relates only to the personal data of people within the EU. (See Chapter 2 for more about the territorial scope of the GDPR.)

Dissecting the Definition of Personal Data

The GDPR's far-reaching definition of personal data is far broader than most other jurisdictions' definition of personal data. One notable exception to this is the California Consumer Privacy Act that comes into force on 1 January, 2020, which is generally considered to be as wide as the GDPR definition of personal data.

The GDPR's definition of personal data once again is "any information relating to a natural person who is identified or identifiable, directly or indirectly, with particular reference to an identifier, such as name, ID number, location data, or one or more factors relating to the physical, physiological, genetic, mental, economic, cultural, or social identity of that natural person."

TIP

If you have difficulty determining whether data is personal data, erring on the side of caution is always best.

To help you understand what is and is not personal data, I take each part of the GDPR's definition and explain it in turn.

Information

The definition of personal data refers to "any information," which is obviously very broad. When looking at whether the information in question falls within the scope of personal data, you need to look at the nature, content, and format of that information.

Nature

Personal data may be either objective or subjective in nature. *Objective* information is information that is factual in nature whereas *subjective* information includes someone's opinions and assessments about the data subject. An example of objective information is "the basketball player is six foot five and has scored 53 goals over the last season." An example of subjective information is that his coach thinks the basketball player is ready for promotion to the A team.

The information (whether factual or opinion) does not need to be true to be personal data.

Content

Personal data can be directly about the individual, such as their employee record, their medical history or a criminal record, or it may relate to an individual's activities, such as bank statements showing what the individual has purchased or itemized telephone bills showing which numbers the individual has called.

REMEMBER

The content doesn't need to be about the individual's private life. It can be about any activity relating to the individual, including information that's in the public domain or that relates to the individual's professional activities. An individual's name and work email address containing the individual's name are personal data in the same way that the individual's personal email address is also personal data.

In relation to content, the GDPR provides a non-exhaustive list of what might be considered personal data. It lists name, ID number, location data, and online identifiers, which I explain a bit later in this chapter, in the section "Identifiers."

Format

In relation to the format of the information, the information may be in any form — alphabetical, numerical, graphical, photographical or acoustic. The GDPR expressly refers to information processed by automated means, but information held in a paper-based filing system can also fall within the scope of the GDPR. However, if the information is held in unstructured paper records (such as business cards at the bottom of your drawer or handwritten notes in a notebook), the GDPR doesn't apply.

Certain EU member states, however, may provide for additional protection for certain information. The UK's Data Protection Act of 2018 stipulates that the manual unstructured processing of personal data by public authorities can constitute personal data.

If the processing is carried out in the course of a purely personal or household activity (such as a personal address book on your iPhone), GDPR doesn't apply.

Relating to

It's time to look at the "relating to" part of the definition of personal data. *Relating to* means that the information must be about an individual. This means more than simply identifying the individual — the information must concern the person in some way.

Information can contain references to an individual or in some way be linked to the individual but not relate to them. An example is a scenario in which the relevant information isn't about that individual, but is about something else entirely. In that case, depending on the circumstances, the information may or may not be personal data.

The example that the UK's Information Commissioner's Office (ICO) uses to demonstrate this point is when a lawyer sends an email to opposing counsel about a client's case. The lawyer's name and email address are personal data about the lawyer, but the content of the email is about the client and the client's case. So, although the lawyer is identified in the email, the content of the email isn't the lawyer's personal data where it's relating to legal advice about the client. If, however, a complaint was made about the lawyer's advice to such a client and the emails were used as part of an investigation of the lawyer's actions, the content of the email would become personal data of the lawyer.

For information to relate to an individual, one of the elements described in the next three sections must be present: the content element, the purpose element, or the result element. Their characteristics are described below:

Content

The *content element* is present when the information clearly relates to the individual — the results of a test that the individual has taken, for example.

Purpose

The *purpose element* is present when the information is processed to evaluate, consider, or analyze the individual — information about a job or about a house when linked to an individual may be personal data, for example. If an organization measures aggregated productivity levels across departments, this information is not in and of itself personal data, but when productivity is linked to an individual in order to work out a pay raise for that individual, it becomes personal data because the purpose relates to the individual.

Even if the information is about objects (such as cars and houses) that aren't currently used to provide information about an individual but *could* be used to provide such information, it's likely to be personal data.

TIP

What you need to look at is whether the processing has or *could* have a resulting impact on the individual, even if there's currently no intention to use the information to determine or influence the way an individual is treated. This is obviously a broad definition of *purpose* because you must consider *possibilities* of impact rather than definite impact.

If the purpose of the processing of data is to identify somebody — by using CCTV cameras, for example — that data is personal data even though the vast majority of information isn't used to identify an individual (because, for example, CCTV is viewed only in specific time frames when looking for an individual).

Result

In relation to the *result element*, this is present when the processing of information has an impact on an individual's rights and interests. The independent working party opinion on personal data provides the following example:

> "A system of satellite location is set up by a taxi company which makes it possible to determine the position of available taxis in real time. The purpose of the processing is to provide better service and save fuel, by assigning to each client ordering a cab the car that is closest to the client's address. Strictly speaking the data needed for that system is data relating to cars, not about the drivers. The purpose of the processing is not to evaluate the performance of taxi drivers, for instance through the optimization of their itineraries. Yet, the system does allow monitoring the performance of taxi drivers and checking whether they respect speed limits, seek appropriate itineraries, are at the steering wheel or are resting outside, etc. It can therefore have a considerable impact on these individuals, and as such the data may be considered to also relate to natural persons. The processing should be subject to data protection rules."

Natural person

As stated in the GDPR, information must relate to a "natural person" for it to be considered personal data, which means that the information must be about a living, breathing person who is living. It doesn't include data in relation to "*legal persons*" (that is, corporations or other organizations with a separate legal status) or data in relation to public authorities.

Some countries protect data after death. For example, Denmark protects information for ten years after the death of an individual. In Hungary, close relatives of the deceased or a person appointed by the data subject during his or her lifetime have the right to exercise data subject rights on behalf of the deceased. Similarly, in Italy, an agent of the deceased data subject can exercise data subjects on behalf of the deceased data subject. In Spain, heirs or executors of the deceased data subject are entitled to exercise certain data subject rights (namely the right of access, the right of erasure and the right of rectification — see Chapter 14 for more on these). French law allows for data subjects to provide instructions for the management of their personal data after their death.

Data relating to sole traders (that is, people who run a business but not through a separate legal entity), employees, partners, and directors (where the information relates to them as individuals) may be personal data. For example, an employee's name within a corporate email address (such as paulsmith@xyz.com) will still be personal data, but the content of work emails will not necessarily be their personal data unless it "relates" to them or has an impact upon them.

Identified or identifiable

Another part of the definition of personal data is "identified or identifiable." This means that it must be possible to identify and distinguish an individual from others using that information. A hypothetical possibility of identification isn't enough — there must be a reasonable likelihood. Obviously data that directly identifies a data subject by name will be personal data, but data may also be used to identify someone indirectly — for example, by reference to an online identifier — and you need to consider the likelihood of this possibility.

When you're assessing the possibility of identification, you must consider these factors:

>> The cost and the amount of time required for identification

>> The technology that's available at the time of the processing

>> The likely technological developments

The rise of big data increases the chance that individuals can be identified. *Big data* refers to extremely large data sets that are analyzed by computers to show patterns, trends, and associations relating to human behavior. Other issues to consider include

>> Whether the information is in the public domain

>> All the means that any person is reasonably likely to use to identify the individual

>> The lengths that a determined person would go to in order to identify an individual — a spurned ex-partner, for example, or a stalker, a journalist, or an industrial spy

>> The perceived value of the information — information relating to a high-profile individual such as a politician or well-known businessperson or celebrity

TIP

You have a duty to consider whether the likelihood of identification has changed over time. To help you with this task, as you assess the possibility of identification, document what you assess, and how, and keep it under review.

WARNING

Considering the possibility of potential identification, it is important that you don't inadvertently disclose information that could be linked with other information to identify somebody, thereby causing a data breach.

Directly or indirectly

The GDPR also talks about an individual being identified or identifiable "indirectly or directly." An example of where an individual can be identified *directly* is by a unique identifier, such as a passport number or a name and address. Being identified *indirectly* is when you combine the data that you hold with other data to identify an individual (postal code and date of birth, for example). Another example is a vehicle registration: By itself, it may be insufficient to identify an individual, but if you link it to other data — the data held by a country's motor vehicle registration agency, for example — it can become possible to identify the owner.

REMEMBER

Even if you never find out who the individual is in real life, if the purpose behind the processing of the information is to single out somebody (for advertising, for instance), it constitutes personal data.

Identifier

Another part of the GDPR's definition of personal data is "with particular reference to an identifier, such as name, ID number, [or] location data." In this section, I explore various identifiers, though keep in mind that this isn't an exhaustive list.

Names

A name by itself may not be enough to identify an individual, as explained in this list using someone named Michael Jones as an example:

>> If it's a common name, such as Michael Jones, and you hold only this information by itself, it's unlikely to be sufficient information to identify an individual; therefore, the name by itself isn't personal data.

>> If you have the information that reveals that Michael Jones lives in a small village called "Littleville" and only one Michael Jones lives in Littleville, this is likely to be sufficient information to identify him.

>> If the location in which Michael Jones lives is a big city where more than one Michael Jones lives, you may need more identifiers for the information to constitute personal data, such as physical characteristics: Michael Jones, who lives in Big City and has gray hair, walks with a limp on his left leg, and is taller than six feet.

You don't need to know a name to identify an individual. A combination of other identifiers may be sufficient. For example, you might be able to identify an individual from a description of gender and salary and the name of the organization they work for. An example is "women earning over $200,000 at XYZ Corporation": If only one woman is earning over that amount at the company, this is sufficient to identify an individual and is therefore likely to be personal data. If, however, dozens of women earn more than that amount at that organization, this isn't personal data without additional identifiers.

ID numbers

An example of an ID number is a passport number, Social Security number, driver's license number, or any other number that directly identifies an individual.

Location data

Location data isn't specifically defined in the GDPR, nor does it provide any specific guidance on how to deal with it. Obviously, an individual's home address constitutes personal data. However, location data also includes information that's processed electronically, indicating the geographical position of terminal equipment of the individual, such as a laptop or mobile phone.

Remember the following in relation to location data:

>> **If that location data relates to an identifiable individual,** it qualifies as personal data.

>> **If the information is anonymized so that it can't be linked to any individual,** it isn't personal data and the GDPR doesn't apply.

APPS THAT TRACK LOCATION DATA

Apps increasingly track location data and the organization that owns the app sells this data to third parties. European data protection regulators are increasingly concerned about the use of location data with no transparency to individuals about what this location data is being used for. A number of cases have arisen in which regulators have required organizations (such as Fidzup and Teemo) to come into compliance with GDPR within a specified period in relation to the use of such location data. If the organizations fail to become compliant, sanctions are levied. There was no discussion of potential liability on the part of the app publishers.

>> **If the location data is processed with other information relating to an individual, the device, or the individual's behavior, or is used in a way to single out one individual from others,** it's personal data even if identifiers such as name and address are not known.

In certain circumstances, location data could reveal special-category data; for example, if the individual has visited hospitals or places of worship or has been present at political demonstrations. (I discuss special-category data in the later section "Defining Special-Category Data.")

Location data should also be considered in the context of employee data and any GPS tracking that an organization carries out (such as tracking on vans, company cars, and other company vehicles).

Online identifiers

When it comes to online identifiers, I'm talking about IP addresses (which I discuss further below) and the other items in this list:

>> **Cookie:** This is a small text file that a web server delivers to a web browser to create web pages tailored to the user — usually to serve the user advertisements or to save site login information or shopping basket contents. Cookies can be used to track users' behavior on a single site or across different sites.

>> **Radio frequency identification (RFID) tag:** This tag is attached to an object for the purpose of using radio waves to read and capture information stored on the tag.

>> **Advertising ID:** A user-resettable ID is assigned by a device or operating system. When sent to advertisers and other third parties, this ID helps advertising services because it can be used to track how the person uses applications.

- » **MAC address:** A MAC address — short for media access control address — is a unique identifier linked to your mobile device. Again, even if you don't know the name of the individual, if you use this data to single out individuals and treat them differently, this constitutes personal data.

- » **Pixel tag:** These are small image files (also called *clear GIFs* or *web beacons*) loaded through a web page that can cause websites to place and read cookies. They can trigger the collection of information, such as a person's IP address, the time the person viewed the pixel, and what browser the person is using.

- » **Device fingerprint:** Information about the specific characteristics of a device (the operating system used, the screen resolution, the fonts installed, and so on) that can be used for tracking the device. This is also known as a *machine fingerprint* or *browser fingerprint*.

- » **Account handle:** This term refers to one of your social media usernames. A social media handle is still sufficient to identify an individual by itself without reference to a real name. It's still personal data if it distinguishes one individual from another, even if it's not possible to link the online identity with the real-world identity.

IP addresses

An *IP address* is a unique address identifying a device connected to the Internet or a local network. A series of digits separated by periods — such as 123.45.67.89 — can be either static or dynamic:

- » **Static:** A static IP address, manually configured, doesn't change. Static IP addresses are clearly personal data when it comes to the user using the device to which the IP address has been assigned.

- » **Dynamic:** A dynamic IP address is automatically configured and assigned every time a computing device is connected to a network (such as the Internet). As such, it is temporary and changes. Dynamic IP addresses may be personal data under certain circumstances.

    If the dynamic IP address can be combined with other data by the data controller or other interested parties — data held by the Internet service provider for example, such as the time of the connection and the pages that were visited — the address could be regarded as personal data, following the case of *Breyer v. Bundesrepublik Deutschland, case C-582/14,* May 12, 2016.

REMEMBER

If there is a risk, even a small one, that individuals can be identified from IP addresses — whether static or dynamic — treat those IP addresses as personal data.

Photographs

Whether photographs are personal data depends on the purpose of the photograph:

Consider a photo of a sporting event in a newspaper that includes a crowd shot. Individuals within that crowd can be identified, but it isn't personal data where the purpose was not to learn anything about those individuals but instead to celebrate the sporting event in the local newspaper.

Now consider that somebody sees in that picture an individual who told his boss that he was ill and couldn't work that day. If the person who saw the photograph sends the photo to that individual's manager, who then adds the photograph to the personnel file for disciplinary proceedings, this would be personal data.

TIP

If it isn't likely that a photograph would ever be processed for the purpose of learning anything about individuals, it generally isn't considered personal data. If it's likely that there would be a case for using the data to learn about individuals, it would be personal data.

Anonymization

With regard to anonymization, if information that relates to an individual and that can identify a natural person is truly anonymized, it's no longer personal data, and GDPR doesn't apply to that data.

Anonymization is where the data subject is no longer identifiable and where it is not possible at any point in the future to reidentify the individual. If at any point you can reidentify the individual, that data isn't anonymized; it still remains personal data, and the GDPR applies to it. If you continue to process the underlying information, that will still be personal data. For example, if you carry out an employee survey and create a report that only contains statistics such as 53% of employees were in favor of shorter working days, this in and of itself would not be personal data. However, if you continue to store (or process in any other way) the underlying data that contains the names of the employees or other identifiers of the employees, you will still be processing personal data.

REMEMBER

It's often difficult within an organization to fully anonymize the data, so care must be taken with this. You can view guidance notes from the ICO here: https://ico. org.uk/media/for-organisations/documents/1061/anonymisation-code.pdf.

Note that these notes refer to the legislation that was pre-GDPR but the concepts remain the same. The ICO are working on updating the guidance.

Aggregation of data for statistical purposes generally isn't considered to be personal data, but be careful: If the sample size is too small, this may enable identification, in which case it's personal data and the GDPR applies.

REMEMBER

While you're anonymizing the data, you're still processing personal data, which means the GDPR applies to that processing.

Pseudonymization

The GDPR describes pseudonymization as

> "...the processing of personal data in such a manner that the personal data can no longer be attributed to a specific data subject without the use of additional information, provided that such additional information is kept separately and is subject to technical and organisational measures to ensure that the personal data are not attributed to an identified or identifiable natural person."

So in other words, *pseudonymization* is where you (i) remove names or other identifiers from a data set (by using techniques such as hashing or data masking or even something as simple as substituting numbers for names and other identifiers) so that the data can no longer be attributed to any individual, (ii) keep the removed data separate from the pseudonymized data, and (iii) ensure the removed data and the pseudonymized data is subject to technical and organizational measures (such as restricting access to the removed data to employees who have a need to know to perform their functions) to ensure that the pseudonymized data isn't attributed to that individual.

REMEMBER

Pseudonymization is an important safeguard for data minimization, but data that has been pseudonymized is still personal data and subject to GDPR.

Defining Special-Category Data

The GDPR refers to what was called "sensitive data" under old data protection laws as *special-category data*.

Special-category data is data that requires additional protection because it refers to data that is clearly sensitive in nature or which has a particularly high risk of being used to negatively target or discriminate data subjects if the information is not protected properly. As such, the GDPR provides for even greater protection for special-category data — which I discuss in this chapter.

But first, take a look at what special-category data actually is. Special-category data includes information that relates to

>> Racial or ethnic origin

>> Political opinions

>> Religious or philosophical beliefs

>> Trade union membership

>> The processing of genetic data

>> Biometric data for the purpose of uniquely identifying a natural person

>> Data concerning health

>> Data concerning a natural person's sex life or sexual orientation

Personal data concerning health is defined by the GDPR as "personal data related to the physical or mental health of a natural person, including the provision of health care services, which reveal information about his or her health status."

Health data includes all data relating to the health status of an individual that reveals information relating to the past, current, or future physical or mental health status of that individual. *Health* is defined in the dictionary as a person's "mental or physical condition."

In many cases, you must consider the purpose for which the data is being used to work out whether it's special-category data. Consider these two examples:

>> A photograph of somebody with one arm in a cast isn't special-category data when it's posted on social media for friends to see. If the same photograph is in a personnel file, however, it's special-category data.

>> If a supermarket is tracking kosher preferences to improve procedures for stocking shelves, it isn't special-category data. If, however, the data is tracking an individual's purchasing habits of kosher food or the data is linked to an individual to target ads for Jewish people, it's special-category data.

The definition of special-category data under the GDPR does not include criminal records data (which is dealt with separately under the GDPR) or financial data or social security numbers. However, other laws will often apply special protections to these data. In Tables 3-1 and 3-2, I further highlight examples of what is and is not special-category data, respectively, and provide the reasoning for why.

TABLE 3-1   **What's Special-Category Data and Why**

Scenario	Type of Data
Pregnancy	Health, generally (for example, a person's physical condition)
Medical data being passed to mountaineering instructors	Health
Students completing a health questionnaire when signing up for exercise class	Health
A health questionnaire for children's activity classes outside of school	Health
An astrologer collecting details of past traumas in order to treat an illness	Health
A therapist being told about physical or mental conditions	Health
Leadership and management coaches and trainers implementing psychometric or behavioral assessments	Health
Medical secretaries processing patients' case notes	Health
Equal opportunities forms	Ethnic origin
Job application forms revealing health issues	Health
An x-ray of a broken leg	Health (assuming that you can link this to the patient)
A fingerprint used to access a secure area of a building	Biometric

TABLE 3-2   **What's Not Special-Category Data and Why**

Scenario	Rationale
A passport	Neither the photograph nor the information on the passport confirms the ethnic origin of the person. Guesses aren't definitive. If the passport is a biometric passport, this would be special-category data.
A photograph of somebody wearing an "I am gay" T-shirt	The message on the shirt doesn't confirm the person's sexual orientation. The person may have a number of other reasons for wearing it, so unless the photograph is being processed to single out the individual in some way, this isn't special-category data.
A photograph of a couple marrying in a Hindu ceremony	This doesn't confirm that the two people getting married are Hindu and, again, unless the photograph is being processed to single out the individuals in some way, this isn't special-category data.

Scenario	Rationale
Body measurements for making patterns and clothing	Although this is data relating to a person's physical condition, if somebody is a particularly extreme size, you may be able to take educated guesses about their health. If you're processing only for the purpose of making clothes, this isn't special-category data.
Health data about animals	Data about animals isn't covered by the GDPR, but if special-category data relating to an individual is linked to it — a hearing dog for the blind and the individual is blind, for example — then that data would be special-category data.
Photographs that don't automatically comprise special-category data	Photographs are only biometric data (and therefore special-category data) where processed through specific technical means and used for the purposes of uniquely identifying somebody — at airport security barriers, for example.
Someone smoking a cigarette	This in and of itself isn't health data and therefore isn't special-category data. However, if this data is being used to single out someone and treat them differently (by an insurance company, for example), it would be special-category data.

Understanding the Processing of Data

As with the other definitions under GDPR, explored earlier in this chapter, the definition of *processing* is exceptionally wide. It covers any operation (whether automated or not) performed on personal data, including

>> Collecting

>> Recording

>> Organizing

>> Structuring

>> Storing

>> Adapting or altering

>> Retrieving

>> Consulting

>> Using

>> Disclosing by transmission

>> Disseminating or otherwise making available

>> Aligning or combining

>> Restricting

>> Erasing or destroying

If you just have the *potential* to access data on someone else's systems but don't *actually* access it, you are not processing that data until you do access it. A website hosting company clearly processes data because it stores data. A mail delivery service doesn't process information within an envelope or a parcel just because it delivers it. To process personal data, you need to have a degree of access to the data or the ability to control or use the data itself. That being said, the delivery service will, of course, be a data controller in its own right in relation to any information it holds to make the deliveries, such as the name and address of the sender and the recipient.

REMEMBER

If the processing isn't by automated means but forms part of a paper filing system, the GDPR applies to that processing. If the processing is in the form of unstructured paper records, such as business cards lying in the bottom of your drawer, GDPR doesn't apply.

Processing Personal Data Lawfully

To process personal data, you need to have lawful grounds for processing, as provided for in the GDPR. If you don't, you're processing that data illegally — unless you can establish an exemption, such as for journalism or research, or on free-speech grounds. See Chapter 1 for more about the exemptions to the GDPR.

TIP

Many people think that GDPR is all about consent, but that isn't true — consent is just one of six potential lawful grounds for processing personal data.

The lawful grounds for processing, other than consent, are:

>> Contractual necessity

>> Legal obligation necessity

>> Vital interests necessity

>> Public interest necessity

>> Legitimate interests

I describe the six lawful grounds in the next few sections, after first explaining what is meant by the *compatibility of purposes* and the concept of *necessity*. Understanding both concepts is crucial to your understanding of the six lawful grounds for processing personal data.

You must choose which ground you're relying on to process the data before you start the processing. Swapping lawful grounds after you have chosen one is difficult to justify, so be certain about your lawful ground before processing the data. If the circumstances relating to the processing have genuinely changed, you may be able to rely on a new ground for processing, but you must first inform the data subject.

Compatibility of purposes

In accordance with the principles of fairness, lawfulness, and transparency (see Chapter 4 for more on these principles), you may process the personal data only for the purpose for which you collected it. Where the lawful grounds for processing isn't based on consent or on a legal obligation under EU or member state law, then processing for further purposes may be lawful if that further purpose is *compatible* with the original purpose.

To ascertain whether a further purpose is compatible, you must consider these factors:

>> Any link between the original purpose and the further purpose

>> The context in which the data has been collected, especially the reasonable expectations of the data subject with regard to the further processing based on the relationship between the data controller and the data subject

>> The nature of the personal data

(Obviously, if the data is sensitive, it's harder to justify the compatibility of a further purpose.)

>> The consequences of the further processing for the data subject

>> The existence of appropriate safeguards in the original processing and the further purpose processing (such as encryption or pseudonymization)

Here's a concrete example: Picture an insurance broker that uses its client's personal data at the end of the insurance year to determine whether that client could benefit from additional types of insurance. This is a compatible purpose. If, however the insurance broker shares its clients' personal data with loan providers for their own marketing purposes, this processing isn't permitted without the consent of the clients — the purpose isn't compatible with the original purpose for which the data was collected.

If the lawful grounds for processing is consent, you always need to gain fresh consent for processing for further purposes.

Necessity

Five of the lawful grounds for processing (namely, contractual necessity, legal obligation necessity, vital interests necessity, public interest necessity, and legitimate interests) are focused on certain things being *necessary* in order for that ground to apply. If you can achieve the same purpose but without the processing, then you won't have lawful grounds for processing the personal data.

In this context, necessary does *not* mean that the processing is absolutely essential. If you decide on the processing merely because it's convenient for you, in your interests to do so, or simply the way you've always done things, this would not be *necessary* for the purposes of these grounds of processing. The ICO's guidance is that "it must be more than just useful and more than standard practice."

The processing must be a "targeted and proportionate" way of achieving your specified purpose. If you could process the data in a less intrusive way or you could minimize the amount of data that is processed, the lawful ground doesn't apply. This is an objective test, so you need to look outside of your business to determine the answer to this question. Just saying, "Well, that's the way we've always done it" won't satisfy the necessary criteria.

Consent

Consent is likely to be the appropriate ground where you want to offer a real choice to people — for example, whether they want to receive your marketing emails. But I caution you to carefully consider consent as a lawful grounds for processing:

>> Consent can always be withdrawn, so if you need the data for the stated purposes, it's always wise to rely on another lawful grounds for processing where possible.

   Or in other words, if the data subject withdraws their consent and you would try to continue processing the data under a different lawful ground, consent isn't the appropriate grounds for processing.

>> If the relationship has a power imbalance (such as during employment or during processing by a public authority), proving that consent is freely given (one of the elements of a valid consent) is difficult.

>> Consent provides data subjects with stronger rights in relation to their data than other grounds for processing — the right to erasure and the right to data portability, for example. (See Chapter 14 for more on data subject rights.)

A valid consent has various elements. Consent must be

>> Freely given

>> Specific

>> Informed

>> An unambiguous indication of wishes

I explore each of these elements in turn throughout this chapter, in addition to other issues regarding consent — including the need to obtain fresh consent, consent required under the ePrivacy Directive and the consent concerns specific to documentation, children, and third parties.

Freely given

Freely given means that the data subject is free to choose whether to give consent, without any detriment, and has genuine choice and control over what personal data they provide.

Incentivizing consent is possible. If you offer money-off/discount vouchers for subscribing to an email marketing list, for example, this would still be valid consent. If, however, the data subject suffers a detriment or is unfairly penalized as a result of not providing consent, the consents that were obtained aren't valid. An example of a detriment is charging higher prices for a service if the data subject refuses to consent to their data being shared with third parties.

If consents are bundled so that a data subject can only consent to all of the processing, this consent isn't valid because the consent hasn't been freely given — perhaps the data subject wanted to sign up for one type of processing but was forced to sign up for another as well, because the consents were bundled. The consent needs to be granular, as shown in Figure 3-1. You need to offer separate consents for one of these:

>> **Different types of processing:** For example, to be contacted by email, phone, or postal mail

>> **Different purposes:** For example, sending email marketing and sharing details with third parties

Note that the preferences form in Figure 3-1 requires opt-in consent for SMS (text) updates but opt-out consent for communications by postal mail or telephone. This is because the ePrivacy Directive (as implemented in the UK as the Privacy and Electronic Communications Regulations, known as PECR) requires consent for text marketing (amongst other electronic marketing) but not for postal or telephone marketing. Hence, this organization is relying on consent (which must be the opt-in type to be valid under the GDPR) for text marketing and on the legitimate Interests grounds for processing to send postal and telephone marketing; this is compliant with the GDPR. If you rely on the legitimate interests grounds for processing, you must provide the ability for data subjects to opt out at any time — and that's what this web page is doing.

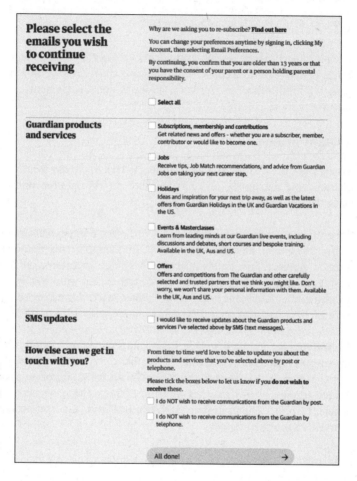

FIGURE 3-1:
An example of granular consent for different types of processing and purposes, from the Guardian UK website.

REMEMBER

the ePrivacy Directive (as implemented into EU member states through their national legislation) requires consent for certain electronic direct marketing communications. If the relevant national legislation (such as the PECR in the UK) requires consent, then the GDPR will also require consent for such processing.

If consent to a processing of personal data is a condition of service and the service provider will not provide the service without the consent to the processing being given, then the consent isn't freely given. However, if the data is required in order to fulfil the service (for example, passing a customer's name and address to a delivery company), then the appropriate lawful grounds for processing would be contractual necessity, and consent wouldn't be required.

REMEMBER

It's difficult for employers to show that consent by employees has been freely given, because of the imbalance of power in the working relationship. As such, employers should look at other grounds of lawful processing for key employee data and rely on consent only for processing of such personal data as responses to surveys, competitions, or similar matters. In addition, consent can always be withdrawn, so if you need to retain certain key employee data, relying on consent as a lawful grounds for processing is unwise. See Chapter 18 for more on this.

Specific

The consent must be given for a specific purpose, such as for sending marketing emails. In accordance with the transparency principle (discussed in Chapter 4), you must clarify what the personal data is being used for, and you must be as specific as possible. If you're processing personal data for multiple purposes, you must obtain consent for each purpose.

Specificity is often problematic because you may not know what you want to use the data for at a later date after you have collected it. The GDPR provides for processing for compatible purposes. If your lawful grounds for processing is consent, however, then even if the new purpose is compatible, in order to comply with the principles of fairness and lawfulness, you need to obtain fresh consent for the new purpose.

One exception to this rule relates to processing for scientific research purposes. The GDPR states that, where it is not possible to fully identify the purpose of data processing for scientific research purposes, data subjects can legally give their consent to certain areas of scientific research consistent with recognized ethical standards for scientific research.

The specified purpose must be set out in your Privacy Notice (see Chapter 8) as well as in any processing records you may be obliged to keep under Article 30 of the GDPR. (See Chapter 7.)

REMEMBER

You should regularly review your processing in consideration of your stated purpose and, if you notice any "purpose creep," obtain fresh consent if the new purposes are not compatible with the original purposes. Note that the consent needs to be obtained before the commencement of the processing for the new purpose.

Informed

You must provide the data subject with all necessary information about the processing at the point that the person provides consent. The place for this information is in your Privacy Notice, which I discuss in Chapter 8. This must be in a form and in a language that's easy to understand. Language that's likely to confuse (such as double negatives and inconsistent terminology) will invalidate consents.

Recital 32 of the GDPR makes clear that if a consent is to be given by electronic means, such as ticking a box on an online form, the request for consent must be clear, concise, and not unnecessarily disruptive to the user experience. Suppose that a lengthy and confusing Privacy Notice pops up and blocks content until the user of the website clicks to make it disappear. Having to click the notice is disruptive to the user experience and falls afoul of this provision.

TIP

A better strategy here is to use a layered Privacy Notice like the one shown in Figure 3-2. Where possible, you should combine this type of notice with a *just-in-time notice* — a note on a web page that appears at the point where the data subject inputs personal data, as shown in Figure 3-3. (Note how a just-in-time notice provides a brief message about how the submitted information will be used and a link to the longer Privacy Policy.) Some level of disruption may be necessary to obtain the consent, but you can minimize it as much as possible.

Full Privacy Policy

Show all | Hide all

⌄ Controller of Personal Information

⌃ What do we mean by personal information?

Personal information means details which identify you or could be used to identify you, such as your name and contact details, your travel arrangements and purchase history. It may also include information about how you use our websites and mobile applications.

⌄ When does this policy apply?

⌄ How can you keep your personal information secure?

⌄ When do we collect personal information about you?

⌄ What types of personal information do we collect and retain?

⌄ What do we use your personal information for?

⌄ When will we send you marketing?

⌄ How can you change what marketing communications you receive, how you receive them and unsubscribe?

FIGURE 3-2: Here's how British Airways presents its Privacy Notice.

For the data subject to be informed, the person must know at least the identity of the data controller and the purposes of the processing. If you're sharing the data with any third parties who are relying on that consent, the identities of those third parties must also be named.

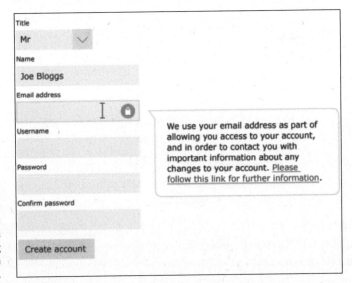

FIGURE 3-3:
An example of a
just-in-time notice
from the UK's
Direct Marketing
Association
(DMA).

REMEMBER

You don't need to name all third parties to whom you disclose the data, because many are relying on other lawful grounds for processing to process the data (contractual necessity, for example). If you're sharing data with a third party for the purposes of it marketing to the data subject, consent is the likely grounds for processing. In this case, the third party should be named in the consent from the original data controller, as it should be in any other cases where the third party will be relying on that consent in order to process the data.

You should ensure that the consent is separate from other terms and conditions so that it isn't buried in lots of legalese.

THE IMPORTANCE OF OBTAINING SPECIFIC THIRD-PARTY CONSENT

The enforcement action in September 2018 by the UK's supervisory authority, the ICO, against the marketing agency Everything DM underscores the importance of obtaining specific consent to share data with named third parties and shows that generic third-party consent is insufficient.

The ICO stated that "firms providing marketing services to other organizations need to double-check whether they have valid consent from people to send marketing emails to them. Generic third-party consent is not enough, and companies will be fined if they break the law."

Unambiguous indication of wishes

In order for consent to be valid, there must be no doubt about the data subject's wishes. If there is any uncertainty about whether the data subject has consented, the presumption is that they have *not* consented.

Recital 32 to the GDPR states that a clear, affirmative act may include a written statement, including by electronic means or an oral statement. This might include having the user tick a box when visiting a website, choosing technical settings for online services, or by acting in a way that clearly indicates acceptance of the processing (for example, asking individuals to drop their business cards in a bowl if they want to receive your newsletter).

In this context, a *clear, affirmative act* means that someone has taken deliberate and specific action to consent to the processing. Hence, pre-ticked boxes and opt-out actions aren't ways of obtaining valid consent, because the data subject hasn't had to take affirmative action. Therefore, this isn't an unambiguous indication of the person's wishes. They simply may not have seen the check box or the opportunity to opt out.

Similarly, silence doesn't constitute an effective consent. For example, if you ask someone by phone to say something specific in order to opt out of the processing of their data, the data subject's silence isn't a valid consent, because the person may not even be listening. To actively confirm consent over the telephone or in person, the data subject must speak certain words, such as "Yes, I consent." Keeping records of this oral consent is vital.

An element of *implied consent* can come with a positive act that makes it clear the data subject is consenting to the processing. For example, if you ask attendees of an event to drop their business cards into a bowl for a chance at winning a prize, that would imply consent for them to be entered into that prize drawing. However, the data can't be used for marketing to those individuals without their further consent.

Consent obtained by way of duress or coercion doesn't constitute valid consent.

Obtaining fresh consent

The GDPR has introduced a higher standard of consent than what existed under the previous regulations. If your existing consents don't meet the new GDPR standard (you previously relied on pre-ticked boxes to indicate consent or you don't have satisfactory records of your consents, for example), you must update those consents to meet the higher standard to be valid.

SHRINKING YOUR EMAIL LIST: GOOD OR BAD?

Many small businesses saw their email lists cut by up to 80 percent on the introduction of GDPR as a result of them needing their email subscribers to opt in again for marketing communications because their existing consents weren't to a GDPR standard of consent. Many people did not opt in again due to "opt in fatigue"; just before the GDPR coming into force, they each received hundreds of emails from different organizations asking them to re-opt in. Other people were simply not engaged in the emails they received from organizations and chose not to re-opt in, whilst other emails requesting the re-opt in were simply not delivered to inboxes and were hidden by spam filters or directed into marketing folders that are not obvious to the individual.

In my experience, after the initial shock, many of these businesses consider the cut beneficial because the remaining email subscribers are the ones who are engaged in their content and are loyal to the brand — and who are customers or potential purchasers. It has improved deliverability of their marketing emails so that those who truly want to see their content actually get to see it.

WARNING

Be wary of attempting to obtain fresh consent to marketing communications by emailing data subjects on your mailing list — to do so would be processing the data without a valid lawful grounds for processing. Also, consent is generally required for email and text marketing communications under the ePrivacy Directive. See the next section (and Chapter 19 and Appendix A) for more about the ePrivacy Directive.

TIP

You can have on your website a sign-up box to obtain fresh consent for email marketing communications (and use various advertising methods to direct people to it), but, obviously, it takes some time to obtain consents in this way, and people who have consented previously may invariably be "lost." See the nearby sidebar, "Shrinking your email list: Good or bad?" to see what I mean.

Regarding the ePrivacy Directive and consent

Consent is required for communications covered by the ePrivacy Directive, such as for email and text marketing to individuals. Currently, the ePrivacy Directive (as implemented in EU member states national legislation) applies only to organizations that provide electronic communications services within that member state, but this is soon to be extended to have a similar global reach as the GDPR. Be mindful of these regulations when deciding your lawful grounds for processing. If you need to obtain consent under the ePrivacy Directive, this needs to be to the same standard of consent as the GDPR. See Chapter 19 and Appendix A for more on the ePrivacy Directive.

Withdrawing consent

If you rely on consent as your lawful grounds for processing, you need to inform data subjects of their right to withdraw consent. The place to do this is in your Privacy Notice (which I discuss in Chapter 8).

You also need to offer data subjects easy and free ways to withdraw consent. You may want to consider using a preference management tool to do so, as shown in Figure 3-4. You might also include an online form to withdraw consent at the bottom of each page of your website.

Welcome to the British Airways Permissions Centre

This is where you can view, manage and change how we use the personal information you have given us, including exercising your right to be forgotten.

If you're not sure where to start, we recommend you view the information we hold on you before taking any other action.

We are committed to respecting your privacy and protecting your personal information and will always treat it with the upmost care. You can find out how we handle your data and all the ways we use it to provide you with a better service in our Privacy Policy.

What would you like to do?

○ Unsubscribe from emails and other marketing
This will remove an email address from all marketing communications. If you only want to unsubscribe from one channel (say email or text messages) you can do this in your Executive Club or ba.com account area.

○ Opt out of email surveys
This will ensure we no longer use an email address for feedback following a flight or at any other time.

⦿ View and manage my personal information
See a report of all the information we hold on you and manage how that information is used, including exercising your **right to be forgotten.**

To find your personal information in our systems, we need at least your first name, last name, email address and date of birth. We will only use this information to process your request.

If you have used multiple email addresses with us or your email address has been used for someone travelling with you, you may need to make more than one request.

First name *as used in a booking or your ba.com account*

FIGURE 3-4: A preference management tool from British Airways provides a way for data subjects to unsubscribe or opt out.

TIP

The GDPR states that data subjects must be able to withdraw consent at any time. Arguably, merely having an Unsubscribe option at the bottom of emails would not suffice as an email is not available to a data subject at all times — they may have received one and deleted it and therefore have no link to unsubscribe when they want to do so.

Keep the following points in mind as you consider how to enable data subjects to withdraw consent:

>> **Withdrawing consent must be as easy as providing it.** If a data subject provided consent by ticking a box on an online form, specifying in your Privacy Notice that they have to call a telephone number or even write to an email address to withdraw consent isn't compliant. If, however, consent was

obtained over the telephone, it is compliant to provide a telephone number for the data subject to call to withdraw their consent.

>> **A data subject must not suffer any detriment by withdrawing their consent.** If the data subject suffers, the consent is invalid.

>> **When consent is withdrawn, you must stop processing the data immediately.** Where this isn't possible, it must be stopped as soon as possible.

>> **If a data subject withdraws consent, you don't necessarily need to delete all their data.** For example, if a data subject opts out of email marketing (effectively withdrawing consent to you for processing their data to send email marketing), you can properly keep this data on a suppression list (so that you have a record of the data subject's opting out).

   Similarly, if you need to retain data for legal or auditing purposes, you can do so, but at the point of obtaining the consent you must be upfront with the data subject about your intentions to continue to process the data for certain purposes. The place to do this is, of course, in your Privacy Notice.

>> **A third party can withdraw consent on behalf of a data subject.** You must, however, satisfy yourself that the third party has the authority to do so. This may cause difficulties where data subjects use automated software tools for unsubscribing.

>> **No set time limit dictates how long consents are valid.** However, you need to monitor consents and refresh them where necessary depending on the context, including data subjects' expectations and how often you email them. For example, if you haven't emailed people for a long time, you may need to obtain fresh consents. If in doubt, the UK's supervisory authority, the ICO, recommends refreshing consents every two years. You should also consider contacting data subjects regularly (every six months, for example), to remind them of their right to withdraw consent.

Documenting consent

You must be able to prove that consent has been provided and you must keep records of consents. If complaints are lodged or investigations begin down the line, you'll need to produce this evidence. You should keep records of the following consent-related information:

>> Who consented, such as name or another online identifier (username, for example)

>> The date on which the consent was given

>> Details that were provided at the time about the processing and the purposes

REMEMBER

>> How someone consented (for example, in writing or by submitting data into an online sign-up form for newsletter subscription)

>> Whether the person has withdrawn consent and, if so, on what date

You can accomplish documenting the details of the processing and the purposes that were provided at the time of the processing by referring to your Privacy Notice that was in force at the time. Keep notes of how Privacy Notices are amended over time so that you know which version was shown to each data subject. This can be as low tech as keeping a hard copy file of Privacy Notices and writing the dates on the top from when and to they were effective.

Children's consent for online services

If a child is signing up to use online services (other than preventive or counseling services), such as online games or education platforms, and the lawful grounds you rely on to process their data is consent, then consent must be obtained from a parent or guardian if the child is under a certain age. This list includes matters that you need to consider when obtaining consent for children's use of online services:

>> **The relevant age of consent for children differs from country to country.** In the UK, it's 13. The map shown in Figure 3-5 shows the relevant age for other countries.

FIGURE 3-5:
Ages of consent for children in individual EU member states.

- >> **You might need to take age verification measures.** For example, if you choose to rely on the child's consent because they state that they're older than the relevant age, you need to verify their age.

  For example, if you choose to rely on the child's consent because they state that they are older than the age required for parental consent, you may need to take additional measures to verify their age — don't just take their word for it.

- >> **You might need to confirm a parent's responsibility.** If a parent's consent is provided, you need to make reasonable efforts to verify the parent's responsibility for the child.

- >> **Parental consent doesn't automatically expire when the child reaches the age of consent.** You may need to refresh this consent more regularly.

Third-party consent

A third party may be able to provide consent on behalf of another person, but you need to ensure that they're duly authorized to do so. If a third party is providing consent, the data subject still needs to be fully informed about the processing and the purposes by way of a Privacy Notice.

In practice, a third party providing consent for the processing of personal data of adults is likely only in circumstances where the third party has power of attorney for the data subject and can act on their behalf.

You can assume that adults have the capacity to consent, unless you have any reason to believe otherwise.

Contractual necessity

Article 6(1)(b) of the GDPR states that "processing shall be lawful if the processing is necessary for the performance of a contract to which the data subject is party or in order to take steps at the request of the data subject prior to entering into a contract." This list provides some examples of when the first part of this ground applies:

- >> **When you enter into a contract with a customer:** If you require certain data from the customer so that you can provide services to the customer, such as their name, address, email address, and financial details, you should rely on this ground for processing such personal data.

- >> **When you need to fulfil an order:** If you require certain data to be processed so that you can fulfil the order for your services or products, such as body measurements to make tailored suits, you should rely on this grounds for processing.

>> **When you need to deliver an order:** Similarly, if you need a name and address to send goods to a data subject, your lawful grounds for processing is contractual necessity because you require this information in order to perform the contract.

>> **When you are paying your employees:** In order to comply with your obligations in your employment contracts to pay your employees, you will need to process certain personal data relating to those employees, such as their name, address, and payment details.

REMEMBER

The lawful processing ground of contractual necessity relates only to contracts you enter into with the data subject. Other parties to the contract may exist in addition to you and the data subject, but if you aren't, or the data subject isn't, a party to the contract, this ground cannot apply.

TIP

Contracts can be in oral form, so you don't necessarily need a written agreement for this ground to apply.

The second part of this grounds for processing is when you need to "take steps at the request of the data subject prior to entering into a contract." An obvious example is when a data subject has asked for a quote but the contract hasn't yet been entered into.

Legal obligation necessity

Article 6(1)(c) of the GDPR states that processing shall be lawful if processing is necessary for compliance with a legal obligation to which the data controller is subject.

Recital 45 of the GDPR states that the processing should have a basis in EU or member state law — that is, that the legal obligation emanates from a law passed at the level of either the EU or an individual country. Laws passed in countries outside the EU don't apply.

This ground applies to statutory or common-law obligations, but not to contractual obligations. (*Common law* is law that derives from court judgments.) Regulatory requirements also satisfy this grounds for processing as long as the regulatory requirements are required by law.

REMEMBER

The legal necessity ground doesn't require a legal obligation to process — rather, the overall purpose is to comply with a legal obligation you're subject to.

Here are a few examples of the processing allowed under the legal necessity ground:

>> Sharing employee data with the tax authorities

>> Processing data under money laundering regulations

>> Disclosing data as a result of a court order

If you process data in order to be in compliance with an EU or member state legal obligation, the data subject cannot generally exercise its right to erasure, right to data portability, or right to object to processing (see Chapter 14 for more on data subject rights).

Vital interests necessity

Article 6(1)(d) of the GDPR provides a lawful basis for processing where "processing is necessary in order to protect the vital interests of the data subject or of another natural person."

Recital 46 defines "vital interests" as being "an interest which is essential for the life of the data subject or that of another natural person." This clarifies that this grounds for processing is available only in life-or-death situations and when the processing is necessary for the data subject's survival. This is likely to be the case only in emergency situations, such as when the data subject is so ill that they cannot consent to processing.

Recital 46 goes on to state that processing under this ground should take place only where the processing cannot be based on another legal basis — so it's a grounds of last resort.

Recital 46 further anticipates that this ground can be used not just for saving the life of an individual but also on a larger scale, referring to processing being necessary for "humanitarian purposes, including for monitoring epidemics and their spread," referring also to natural and manmade disasters.

It seems clear that data processing for scheduled medical procedures should not use this grounds for processing and should instead look to another ground, such as consent.

The reference to "or of another natural person" makes clear that the personal data doesn't need to be about the person who is in the life-or-death situation. An example here is when you need to process data about a parent to save the life of a child. *Natural person* isn't defined in the GDPR, but it is unlikely that a fetus would be deemed to be a natural person. Hence, if the processing of data is in relation to a mother to save an unborn child, arguably this grounds for processing doesn't apply.

If the personal data being processed is data relating to health, which it often is in emergency situations, a further condition needs to be satisfied for processing special-category data. The related condition for processing special-category data is when the processing "is necessary to protect the vital interests of the data subject or of another natural person where the data subject is physically or legally incapable of giving consent." If the parent, for example, is able to give consent, this condition for processing special-category data wouldn't apply and an alternative condition for processing special-category data would need to be relied on.

Public interests necessity

Article 6(1)(e) of the GDPR provides a lawful basis for processing when "processing is necessary for the performance of a task carried out in the public interest or in the exercise of official authority vested in the controller." Unless you're able to exercise official authority, this grounds for processing isn't relevant to you. You don't need a specific statutory power for this ground to apply, but the task must have a clear basis in law.

Member states may implement their own legislation to specify what constitutes public interest. The UK has done so in Part 2, Chapter 2 of the Data Protection Act of 2018. Public interest matters include the ones in this list:

>> The administration of justice

>> The exercise of a function of either House of Parliament

>> The exercise of a function conferred on a person by an enactment or rule of law

>> The exercise of a function of the Crown, a Minister of the Crown, or a government department, or

>> An activity that supports or promotes democratic engagement

Legitimate interests

Article 6(1)(f) of the GDPR gives you a lawful basis for processing when "processing is necessary for the purposes of the legitimate interests pursued by the controller or by a third party except where such interests are overridden by the interests or fundamental rights and freedoms of the data subject which require protection of personal data, in particular where the data subject is a child."

Relying on the legitimate interests ground is likely to be appropriate when you, as the data controller, have an existing relationship with the data subject (with an employee or a customer, for example) and when there's little impact on the data subject.

Although this grounds for processing is a relatively flexible one, it is not an easy answer, because you must balance your interests in processing the data with the rights and freedoms of your data subjects and you have to navigate many gray areas in your decision-making. Sometimes it's better to put the matter beyond doubt and obtain consent, where this is practicable.

Processing under legitimate interests

The GDPR provides some guidance on what personal data might be processed under the grounds of legitimate interests, though this list isn't an exhaustive one.

Recital 47 states that the processing of personal data for direct marketing purposes may be regarded as carried out for a legitimate interest. However, you must consider the ePrivacy Directive and the obligation, in certain circumstances, to obtain prior consent for sending marketing emails and texts. (See Chapter 19 for more on the ePrivacy Directive.)

Recital 48 states that data controllers who are part of the same group of companies may rely on the legitimate interests ground for internal administrative purposes, including the processing of clients' or employees' data. This doesn't, however, affect the principles of international transfers of data within those group companies. (See Chapter 6 for more on international transfers.)

Recitals 47 to 49 of the GDPR state that a legitimate interest can be to:

>> Ensure network and information security, which could include processing to

- *Prevent unauthorized access to networks*

- *Prevent malicious code distribution*

- *Stop denial-of-service (DoS) attacks and damage to computer and electronic communication systems*

>> Prevent fraud

>> Disclose information about criminal acts or security threats to the authorities

TIP

Certain countries, such as Italy, are more prescriptive about what constitutes legitimate interests, so check each relevant jurisdiction.

Relying on legitimate interests

To rely on the legitimate interests grounds for processing, you must conduct the 3-step Legitimate Interests Assessment test — document the text, keep it on file, and regularly review it:

1. **Identify a legitimate interest.**

You must identify a legitimate interest of yours and be comfortable explaining why it's a legitimate interest. A *legitimate interest* simply means that the processing is done for the purpose of an interest that isn't unlawful or unethical. Sending spam emails isn't a legitimate interest because it's unlawful and unethical.

A wide range of interests may be legitimate interests. The interests can be yours or a third party's, and they can relate to your business interests or to benefits for society as a whole or part. The interests don't need to meet a certain standard, but if they aren't compelling, the rights and freedoms of the data subject will more easily override these interests when you carry out the Balancing test (in Step 3 of the Legitimate Interests Assessment).

REMEMBER

Your Privacy Notice must clearly and transparently inform the data subject not only that you're processing their personal data based on legitimate interests but also *why* the legitimate interest you've identified is in fact legitimate. Here's an example: "We process your name and email address to send you direct marketing because it is a legitimate interest of ours to seek to gain new customers and grow our business."

2. **Carry out the Necessity test.**

To perform a *Necessity test* is to work out whether the processing of the personal data is necessary for the pursuit of your commercial or business objectives. That doesn't necessarily mean indispensable, but it's more than ordinary, useful, reasonable, and desirable.

TIP

Probably the easiest question to ask yourself is this: "Is there another way to achieve the identified interest?"

To answer this question, you're looking at the processing here and asking yourself whether a less intrusive way of processing the information would achieve your goal. If the processing isn't necessary, you can't rely on legitimate interest as a lawful basis.

3. **Carry out the Balancing test.**

A *Balancing test* ensures that the rights and freedoms of the data subject have been evaluated and that their interests don't override your legitimate interest. This evaluation should always be conducted fairly and in an unbiased way, which is fairly hard to do when you're focused on your own interests. But you always have to give due regard and weighting to the rights and freedoms of the data subjects.

You should document the Balancing test, including your thought process on it, in case you're ever challenged over your use of legitimate interests as a lawful ground of processing. Consider, and then document, the nature of your legitimate interest, the impact of the processing, and any safeguards you can put in place.

In carrying out the Balancing test, consider these factors:

- *The reasonable expectations of the individual:* Would or should they expect the processing to take place? If they would, the impact of the processing is likely to have already been considered and accepted. If they have no expectation, the impact is greater and is given more weight in the Balancing test.

- *When the data was collected:* If you collected the data long ago and the data subject hasn't heard from you since, receiving marketing literature out of the blue for example may not be expected.

- *The potential nuisance factor of the processing:* Also consider the effect that your chosen method of processing and frequency of any communication might have on more vulnerable individuals — ads targeted at people who are struggling financially, for example, or gamblers or alcoholics.

- *The type of data:* If it's special-category data, you need to give more weight to protecting the rights and freedoms of the data subject (as well as satisfying an Article 9 condition in order to process the special-category data).

- *The nature of your interest as a data controller:* Does the processing add value, or is it only for your convenience? Is it also in the interest of the data subject?

- *The impact of the processing on the data subject:* Consider both positive and negative impacts. Will there be any harm to the data subject as a result of the processing? What is the likelihood of the impact on the data subject and its severity?

- *The status of the data subject:* Is the data subject a customer, a child, an employee, or someone else?

- *Your status in comparison to the data subject:* Are you in a dominant position?

- *The ways in which the data is processed:* Does it involve profiling or data mining, publication, or disclosure to a large number of people? Is the processing on a large scale?

You must then decide whether you have satisfied the Balancing test for each category of data subjects and for each processing and for each purpose.

Each instance of relying on the legitimate interests grounds of processing requires its own evaluation, and, unfortunately, there's no definitive method for checking whether you're correct in your considerations. If you have any doubt about whether you can rely on legitimate interests, choosing an alternative grounds for processing is the wiser path.

Right to object

Data subjects have the right to object to processing under the grounds of legitimate interests.

If somebody objects to your processing on the grounds of legitimate interests, you must stop that processing unless you can either:

>> Demonstrate compelling, legitimate grounds for the processing that override the interests, rights, and freedoms of the data subject

>> Show that the processing is for the establishment, exercise, or defense of legal claims

If you receive an objection to processing personal data for direct marketing purposes from a data subject, you must stop processing that personal data as soon as you receive an objection. You have no exemptions or grounds to refuse that right.

Processing special-category data

Processing special categories of data is prohibited under the GDPR unless an exemption to such prohibition applies, as set out in Article 9 of the GDPR. I describe these exemptions in this section.

The lawful grounds for processing (such as consent or legitimate interests) that you rely on to process the special-category data does not necessarily need to be linked to the exemption to the prohibition for processing special-category data, although it often will be. Consider these examples:

>> **If you're relying on legitimate interests to process the data:** You will need to rely on an exemption such as that the processing is necessary to establish, exercise, or defend legal claims or that the data has manifestly been made public by the data subject.

>> **If, however, you're relying on the grounds for processing data, where the processing is necessary to protect the vital interests of the data subject:** Chances are good that the exemption you will rely on for processing special-category data is also that the processing is necessary to protect the vital interests of the data subject.

Set out below are the exemptions to the prohibition against processing special-category data (only one exemption need apply):

>> **Explicit consent:** The data subject has given *explicit consent* to the processing for one or more specified purposes.

>> **Employment:** The processing is necessary for the purposes of carrying out the obligations and exercising specific rights of the data controller or of the data subject in the field of employment and Social Security and social protection law insofar as it's authorized by EU or member state law (or a collective agreement pursuant to member state law) providing for appropriate safeguards of fundamental rights in the interests of the data subject.

>> **Vital interests:** The processing is necessary to protect the vital interests of the data subject or of another natural person where the data subject is physically or legally incapable of giving consent.

>> **Not-for-profits:** The processing is carried out in the course of its legitimate activities with appropriate safeguards by a foundation, association, or any other not-for-profit body with a political, philosophical, religious, or trade union aim and on the condition that the processing relates solely to the members or former members of the body (or to persons who have regular contact with it in connection with its purposes) and that the personal data isn't disclosed outside that body without the consent of the data subjects.

>> **Made public:** The processing relates to personal data that is manifestly made public by the data subject.

>> **Legal claims:** The processing is necessary for the establishment, exercise, or defense of legal claims or whenever courts are acting in their judicial capacity.

>> **Public Interest:** The processing is necessary for reasons of substantial public interest on the basis of EU or member state law which shall be proportionate to the aim pursued, respect the essence of the right to data protection, and provide for suitable and specific measures to safeguard the fundamental rights and the interests of the data subject.

>> **Health:** The processing is necessary for the purposes of preventive or occupational medicine, for the assessment of the working capacity of the employee, medical diagnosis, the provision of health or social care systems or services (or the management of health or social care systems and services) on the basis of EU or member state law or pursuant to a contract with a health professional and subject to certain conditions and safeguards (as discussed below this list of bullet points).

>> **Public health:** The processing is necessary for reasons of public interest in the area of public health, such as protecting against serious cross-border threats to health or ensuring high standards of quality and safety of health

care and of medicinal products or medical devices, on the basis of EU or member state law which provides for suitable and specific measures to safeguard the rights and freedoms of the data subject, in particular professional secrecy.

>> **Archiving:** The processing is necessary for archiving purposes either in the public interest or for scientific purposes, historical research purposes, or statistical purposes which are based on EU or member state law. The only caveat is that such processing must:

- *Be proportionate to the aim pursued;*
- *Respect the essence of the right to data protection; and*
- *Provide for suitable and specific measures to safeguard the fundamental rights and the interest of the data subject.*

Special-category data may be processed for the health purposes referred to in the eighth bullet point in the preceding list when that data is processed by, or under the responsibility of, a professional who's subject to an obligation of professional secrecy or by another person who's also subject to an obligation of secrecy under EU or member state law or rules established by national competent bodies.

Member states may introduce further conditions, including limitations with regard to the processing of genetic data, biometric data, or data concerning health.

REMEMBER

If you're processing special-category data of people within the UK, consider also Part 2 of schedule 2 of the Data Protection Act of 2018, which sets out further conditions for processing under the employment, health, research conditions, and substantial public interest conditions.

Exploring the explicit consent exemption for processing special-category data

Explicit consent isn't defined in the GDPR, but the word *explicit* suggests an even higher standard of consent than the usual standard of consent for GDPR purposes.

Consent can at times be implicit — dropping a business card in a bowl to enter a prize drawing, for example. Explicit consent, however, seems to require a clear statement of consent, though this doesn't necessarily need to be in writing or even online, because it can, in theory, be obtained orally (though you would have to keep careful notes, in this case).

An online form needs to make a statement similar to this one: "By entering my medical details below, I explicitly consent to my medical questionnaire (including any data in it about my physical and mental health) being processed by Fit Limited for the purpose of ensuring my safety when using its premises."

As is demonstrated above, the purpose of the processing must be included in the statement of explicit consent. In addition, you should include

» The identity of the person(s) who will process the special-category data

» The nature of the special-category data (medical details, for example)

» The details of any automated decision-making with legal or significant effects

» The details of any data to be transferred and the risks of the transfer

If explicit consent is withdrawn, you need to find a different exemption to rely on to continue to process the special-category data. You must inform the data subject of this different exemption and ensure that it's fair.

Health processing

The Data Protection Act of 2018 sets out the definition of both a *health professional* and a *social work professional*. The latter is defined as "a person registered as a social worker." A health professional may be one of the following:

» Registered medical practitioner

» Registered nurse or midwife

» Registered dentist

» Registered dispensing optician or registered optometrist

» Registered osteopath

» Registered chiropractor

» Registered pharmacist or registered pharmacy technician

» Child psychotherapist

» Scientist employed by a health service body as the head of a department

» Art therapist, chiropodist, clinical scientist, dietitian, medical laboratory technician, occupational therapist, orthoptist, paramedic, physiotherapist, prosthetist, orthotist, radiographer, or speech and language therapist

TIP

These definitions may vary from country to country, so if this is likely to affect your business because you process the health data of individuals within the EU, be sure to check the legislation of each relevant jurisdiction.

If you're a life coach, a therapist, an executive coach, a behavioral expert, or anyone else who may process health data but you don't fall under the definition of health professional in the relevant jurisdiction's law, you must look to another processing condition to process the special-category data.

Other considerations when processing special-category data

When processing special-category data, you should protect that data to higher security standards, since the consequences of a data breach will be much more harmful to data subjects. If you are collecting special-category data from data subjects online, then consider encryption or other security methods to protect that data during its transmission to you.

Also, carefully consider your retention policy and how long to keep special-category data. See Chapter 13 for more on retention policies.

The Consequences of Getting Processing Wrong

If you process personal data unlawfully because you lack a valid grounds for lawful processing or have chosen the wrong grounds (or your processing of special-category data does not fall within a specified exemption), this can not only cause harm to your reputation and lead to diminished trust in you and your brand, but also cause you to face significant fines or other sanctions.

Under Article 83(5)(a) of the GDPR, you could be fined up to €20 million, or 4 percent of your total worldwide annual turnover in the previous financial year, whichever is higher, if you process personal data without a lawful ground (or your processing of special-category data does not fall within a specified exemption).

Before you start to panic, fines are always proportionate — if you are a small business who has unintentionally processed data unlawfully but you have taken steps to comply with GDPR and are cooperating with the supervisory authority, then this should be taken into account and your fines (if any) are likely to be minimal. (See Chapter 21 for more on how supervisory authorities set fines.)

Chapter **4**

The Six Data Protection Principles

At the heart of data protection compliance (and aside from the overarching accountability principle) lie these six specific data protection principles:

» Lawfulness, fairness, and transparency

» Purpose limitation

» Data minimization

» Accuracy

» Storage limitation

» Integrity and confidentiality

The GDPR doesn't introduce many changes to the principles that existed under the previous European data protection legislation. However, in my experience, I find that most small-business owners weren't familiar with the principles that were in place before the GDPR came into force, so a lot of this is new to them, even if it isn't new to data protection legislation.

The GDPR and its increased sanctions have focused attention on data protection, making it more important than ever for you to truly understand the GDPR and the six principles — and to reflect this understanding in every element of your business.

Accountability

In addition to the six specific principles, which I describe in this chapter, an accountability principle runs across all GDPR compliance. This accountability principle places the onus on you — as the data controller — to comply with the GDPR and to document that fact as well.

Accountability is not merely a tick-the-box exercise — you need to consider how to demonstrate your accountability dependent on your particular circumstances. However, the following examples show you what you may need to do to in order to demonstrate your compliance:

>> Adopt and implement certain policies, put certain documents in place, and sign certain contracts. (See Part 3 for more on this.)

>> Ensure that data protection is embedded in your organization by design and by default. (See Chapter 15 for more in this.)

>> Maintain records of your data processing. (See Chapter 7 for more on this.)

>> Carry out Data Protecton Impact Assessments (DPIAs) where necessary. (See Chapter 15 for more on this.)

>> Record and report personal data breaches. (See Chapter 15 for more on this.)

>> Appoint a Data Protection Officer (DPO) where necessary. (See Chapter 15 for more on this.)

>> Put appropriate security measures in place. (See Chapter 16 for more on this.)

>> Ensure appropriate staff training, monitoring, and auditing. (See Chapters 18 and 24 for more on this.)

>> Adhere to certain codes of conduct and certification schemes. (Note that there are none in place at the time of publishing this book.)

>> Put certain reporting structures into place.

>> Adopt assessment and evaluation procedures.

>> Keep records of communications relating to the exercise of data subject rights.

>> Review measures at regular intervals to ensure they are still fit for purpose.

It is important to note that compliance is ongoing. The data protection authorities will not look favorably on organizations that put the requisite policies and documents into place when the GDPR came into force but have not kept up to date with changes in the law or in guidance from the regulators.

Lawfulness, Fairness, and Transparency

Article 5(1)(a) of the GDPR states that personal data shall be "processed lawfully, fairly, and in a transparent manner in relation to the data subject."

Lawfulness

Lawfulness means you must process personal data in accordance with the law. This means satisfying one of the six lawful grounds for processing personal data under the GDPR and also satisfying a condition for processing special category data or criminal offence data when processing such data. (See Chapter 3 for more about what comprises special category data and criminal offence data.) If there are no lawful grounds for processing the personal data or a condition for processing special category data or criminal offence data is not met, then the processing will be unlawful and in breach of this principle.

In addition, the processing must also be lawful in the more general sense — that is, complying with any other laws that are relevant to the processing, such as those regarding employment, taxes, health, copyright, marketing, contract, and any further specific data protection introduced by individual countries.

Chapter 3 details what is and what is not personal data and what the six lawful grounds for processing personal data are.

If you process personal data unlawfully, the affected data subjects may exercise the right of erasure and the right to restrict processing. (See Chapter 14 for more on this.)

Fairness

Fairness means you do not deceive or mislead data subjects when you collect their personal data.

Fairness also means that you should only use personal data in ways that data subjects would reasonably expect. This is particularly important when you are relying on the lawful ground of legitimate interests to process the data. See Chapter 3 for more on this.

Fairness also requires you to consider how the data subject will be impacted by your use of their personal data for your specified purpose. If a negative impact isn't justified, the processing will be unfair. This is particularly important in cases of profiling or automatic decision-making (both discussed in Chapter 14).

In certain limited circumstances, the processing of personal data is deemed fair even though the data subject isn't aware of how it will be used, such as when tax authorities obtain personal data about employees from an employer.

Note that if you are collecting personal data about a group of people and have collected and used the personal data unfairly in relation to just one data subject out of that group, this would still be a breach of this principle.

Finally, the fairness principle requires you to treat data subjects fairly when they exercise their data subject rights. (See Chapter 14 for more about data subject rights.)

Transparency

The principle of transparency is closely linked to the principle of fairness.

Transparency means that you must be open and clear to data subjects in relation to the processing of their personal data, so that data subjects can make informed decisions about whether to provide their personal data or not and whether to exercise their data subject rights or not.

The GDPR prescribes the minimum amount of information you must provide to data subjects about the processing of their personal data. The place to provide this information is in the Privacy Notice. (See Chapter 13 for more on this.)

Article 12(1) of the GDPR states that the information provided to data subjects must be "concise, transparent, intelligible and in an easily accessible form, using clear and plain language." This means that the information must be easy to read and understand and free of jargon. "Accessible" means in practice that Privacy Notices must be clearly and prominently displayed (and not hidden) on your website.

Note however that the information does not have to be provided in writing or indeed on your website and may be provided orally when requested by data subjects (provided that their identity is proven by other means), which may be appropriate where you are collecting personal data on telephone calls.

The UK's Information Commissioner's Office (ICO) recommends just-in-time notices (see glossary), videos, icons and symbols, and a privacy dashboard to ensure that Privacy Notices are also easy to read and to understand. The ICO states that it would be wrong to assume that everyone has the same level of understanding about Privacy Notices.

Transparency is particularly important where you do not have an existing relationship with the data subject and are obtaining the personal data from a third party.

REMEMBER

If you have children as data subjects, ensure that the language you use in the Privacy Notice is simple enough for a child to understand. Using animations or other visualizations is recommended for helping children to understand the information.

Purpose Limitation

The Purpose Limitation principle lets you collect data for only a specific and legitimate purpose that the data subject has been made aware of.

The first step, therefore, when collecting data is to identify the specific purpose for which the data is being processed — collecting customer email addresses to send an electronic invoice on completion of the order or collecting prospect email addresses to send them marketing materials about your services, for example.

If you want to use this data for another purpose that you did not previously inform the data subject about, such as sharing their data with third parties so that the third party can market to them, this is a new purpose — and is outside the scope of your original purpose.

You may process personal data for an additional purpose only if one of the following statements applies:

>> The additional purpose is compatible with the original purpose.

>> You obtain consent to process the personal data for the new purpose.

>> The further processing is required for a task carried out in the public interest.

>> The further processing is for archiving purposes in the public interest, scientific or historical research purposes, or statistical purposes.

>> The processing is based on EU law or the law of any EU member state.

See Chapter 3 for more about compatibility of purpose and other considerations you must think about when deciding whether an additional purpose is a compatible purpose.

REMEMBER

Being able to process for a compatible purpose wouldn't usually be possible where the original processing was based on consent. In this case, if you want to use the data for a purpose other than the one the data subject previously consented to, you need to obtain fresh consent for the purposes of fairness and transparency.

Data Minimization

Data minimization dictates that you identify the minimum amount of personal data necessary to achieve the purposes you communicated to the data subject and not process any further data than is necessary for those purposes. You may process only personal data that is adequate, relevant, and limited to what is necessary to accomplish the purposes for which it is processed.

You therefore first need to understand why you need that data — that is, you need to know the specific purpose of the processing. You cannot collect data that isn't necessary now just in case you might need it in the future or because it might become useful to you.

You may be able to justify processing information for a foreseeable circumstance, even if that circumstance never comes to pass. For example, if you run a dental practice and a patient wants to see you for a free consultation, you do not need the data subject's home address or financial details. You may, however, require an email address or a phone number to send an appointment reminder or to follow up if the patient doesn't show for the appointment.

As part of the data minimization principle, ask yourself whether you could still achieve your purpose if any of the data were to be *anonymized* (lacking information that distinguishes individuals).

TIP

To demonstrate compliance with the accountability principle, keep records of your data minimization considerations and actions. This could be done, for example, by conducting a documented Data Protecton Impact Assessment (DPIA). See Chapter 15 for more about DPIAs.

Accuracy

You must take reasonable measures to ensure that the personal data is accurate and, where necessary, kept up-to-date.

Accuracy isn't defined in the GDPR, but the UK's Data Protection Act of 2018 tells us that it means the personal data isn't incorrect or factually misleading.

Obviously, if a data subject exercises the right to *rectification* — requiring that inaccurate or out-of-date personal data is corrected or updated, in other words) — the data must be rectified as soon as possible to comply with this principle. See Chapter 14 for more on the right to rectification and other data subject rights.

You may keep records of the inaccuracies, if necessary, but the inaccurate data must be recorded as such.

Regarding opinions

An opinion isn't inaccurate just because the data subject doesn't agree with it. If the opinion was based on facts that were incorrect, the opinion might also be incorrect and should be revised based on the accurate facts.

TIP

If an opinion is drawn from personal data, make note of the fact that the opinion is just that — an opinion. If appropriate, make a note of the identity of the person who has the opinion as well. If the opinion turns out to be incorrect, keep notes on that, too.

Taking reasonable measures

You should take every reasonable step to ensure that the personal data is accurate and, where necessary, kept up-to-date. In this context, *measures* means that you should develop processes in your business to ensure that the data is accurate — not just during the collection process but for all of the processing.

What is *reasonable* will depend on all the circumstances, including the nature of the data:

>> **Adverse impact:** If inaccurate data would have an adverse impact on the data subject, you need to take more care to ensure that it is accurate than if it would have no adverse impact.

>> **Sensitive data:** As covered in Chapter 3, you need to put more effort into ensuring that special category data is accurate than you do for non-sensitive data.

>> **Other sources:** If you collect the personal data from a source other than the data subject, you must take further steps to verify the accuracy of the data than you would if you had received the data directly from the data subject.

Updating personal data

Whether you need to keep the personal data up-to-date depends on the purposes of the processing. If, for example, you processed data for a one-off transaction with a one-time customer, you would not be obliged to ensure that the details of their address are up-to-date on an ongoing basis.

If, however, you have an ongoing customer whom you regularly send products to, you can reasonably request at the start of the relationship that they keep you updated if they move. Asking whether their details are still accurate every six months, for example, would be also reasonable and sensible.

Storage Limitation

The Storage Limitation principle stipulates that personal data must not be kept for longer than necessary for the purposes for which the personal data is processed. In other words, you can't keep personal data for longer than you need it. After data is no longer necessary, you must delete it or anonymize it.

Data that has been anonymized can be retained indefinitely — anonymous data is no longer "personal" and so the GDPR's Storage Limitation principle does not apply to it.

As to whether you need to delete backups of the personal data, the UK's ICO's guidance on this is that you need to put the personal data beyond use. They state that "if it is appropriate to delete personal data from a live system, you should also delete it from any backup of the information on that system."

Taking personal data offline is, of course, not the same as deletion and, although it may reduce the risk of security breaches, by holding the personal data you are still processing it and data subject rights and all the other principles will still apply to that personal data.

The GDPR states that you should set time limits for periodic reviews of data to assess whether it is still required. Include the time period in your data retention policy. (See Chapter 13.) For certain types of processing, you may determine the retention period yourself, but check federal, state, and local statutes for any statutory retention periods that might have been established (for legal or accounting purposes, for example). If a statutory retention period exists, you must retain the data for the period mandated by the statute.

The GDPR also states that you can keep personal data for longer periods if it will be processed solely for public interest archiving, scientific or historical research, or statistical purposes and provided you have appropriate safeguards in place. The UK's ICO states that you can hold this personal data "indefinitely."

TIP

When deciding whether the data is still necessary, you may decide you need to delete some data but still retain other data about an individual. For example, if a data subject was a customer five years ago, you may decide that you no longer need to keep all of that data subject's details, but you might decide that you need to keep a record of the transaction in case of a legal claim or for tax records.

Data subjects have a right to erasure if you do not need the personal data any more. See Chapter 14 for more on this.

If you share personal data with third parties, you need to agree between you what happens to the data when it is no longer needed. One solution may be for the parties to transfer it back to the original holder of the data.

Integrity and Confidentiality

Article 5(1)(f) of the GDPR states that personal data must be processed "in a manner that ensures appropriate security of the personal data, including protection against unauthorized or unlawful processing and against accidental loss, destruction, or damage, using appropriate technical or organizational measures."

This principle is also known as the security principle. For more on the security of data, see Chapter 16.

Consequences of Noncompliance with the Six Principles

The six data protection principles are the cornerstones of the GDPR, and hence any noncompliance with any of the principles will potentially result in the highest sanction under the GDPR: namely, a fine of up to 20M euros ($22.7 million) or 4 percent of global worldwide turnover for the preceding financial year (whichever is higher).

The scale of the fine will depend on the seriousness of the infringement, and not every infringement will necessarily result in a fine. Data protection authorities have a range of enforcement options in addition to fines, such as serving an enforcement notice requesting the cessation of processing of personal data.

Data subjects can file civil claims, and class action lawsuits (or collective actions) are now being initiated, particularly in relation to noncompliance regarding the integrity and confidentiality principle with security breaches. A collective action is currently being brought in relation to the British Airways data breach that occurred in September 2018.

Aside from the regulatory consequences and the possibility of civil claims, if you don't comply with these six principles, chances are good that you will lose your customers' trust and, ultimately, their business. Your suppliers may also no longer want to work with you, and you are likely to see a negative impact on your profits.

I look at the consequences of noncompliance in more detail in Chapter 21.

Chapter **5**

Data Controllers and Data Processors

To fully understand the GDPR, you need to grasp the meaning behind the concepts of the data controller, data processor, joint controller, and subprocessor. This chapter defines what each of these terms means and explains their obligations and the relationships between them.

You must know which role you're assuming in relation to each of your processing activities, because obligations under the GDPR differ and sometimes overlap, according to whether you're a data controller, a joint controller, or a processor.

REMEMBER

You can be a data controller and a data processor at the same time for different processing activities, although you cannot be a controller and a processor in relation to the same processing activities. For example, if your business is a cloud hosting provider, you would be a data controller in relation to the contact data (personal data) about each of your clients, and you would be a data processor in relation to the personal data contained within the content that you are hosting for your clients.

If you're a data controller *and* a data processor, you must ensure that you have a separation of systems so that the data you're processing as a controller is processed separately from the data you're processing as a processor.

Recognizing Who's a Data Controller

You are a *data controller* if you are a "natural or legal person, public authority, agency, or other body that, alone or jointly with others, determines the purposes and means of the processing of personal data."

In other words, a data controller is an entity that decides how and why personal data is used.

An individual processing personal data for a purely personal or household activity isn't subject to the GDPR.

As the data controller, you decide which data to collect, how to collect it, and what to do with it. Here are a couple of examples:

>> Your website has a form for people to enter email addresses if they want to have free resources emailed to them. You're the data controller of the personal data (the email addresses) you've collected.

>> You're an employer and you collect personal data from your employees in order to issue security passes. You're a data controller in relation to that personal data.

Because data controllers make decisions about the personal data, they are subject to more obligations under the GDPR than data processors.

Exploring joint controllers

Joint controllers are two or more controllers who together determine the purposes and means of processing — and therefore share the responsibilities of the data controller.

If two or more separate organizations collect and use data for a common purpose, they are joint controllers. Note that they don't need to be processing the data at the same time or in equal parts.

Here are two possible scenarios — one where the entities are joint controllers and another where they are not:

>> A luxury shopping brand, a luxury car manufacturer, and a bank together create an event that people sign up to attend. Using the data collected, they communicate event details (and other event-related matters) to the people who have signed up. The data isn't used for any other purpose. The brand, car manufacturer, and the bank are joint controllers of the data.

>> After the event, each organization uses (within their own organizations) the personal data of those data subjects who opted in to receive more information from that organization. They are not joint controllers in relation to that data, because it isn't being processed for a common purpose.

Joint controllers of Facebook Fan Pages

A real-world example of the complexities involved in determining who is — and who is not — a joint controller is the case of the *Court of Justice of the European Union (CJEU) v. Wirtschaftsakademie Schleswig-Holstein* (a German education company). In June 2018, the CJEU ruled that Facebook Fan Page administrators are joint controllers with Facebook regarding personal data on their Facebook Fan Pages.

The ruling was based on the assertion that Fan Page administrators partly determine the purposes and means of the processing of visitors' personal data by giving Facebook the opportunity to place cookies through the Fan Page on the visitors' devices, regardless of whether the visitor has a Facebook account.

These cookies are used to provide statistical reporting to the administrator — Facebook calls this "Insights Data" — using parameters defined by the administrator to specify the types of statistics it wants. The court noted that "in particular, the administrator of the Fan Page can ask for — and thereby request the processing of — demographic data relating to its target audience, including trends in terms of age, sex, relationship and occupation, information on the lifestyles and centres of interest of the target audience and information on the purchases and online purchasing habits of visitors to its page, the categories of goods and services that appeal the most, and geographical data which tell the Fan Page administrator where to make special offers and where to organise events, and more generally enable it to target best the information it offers."

The judgment states that, because they're joint controllers, the responsibilities aren't necessarily shared equally, and that all circumstances should be considered when assessing the level of responsibility of each of them.

Following this judgment, Facebook issued a Page Insights Controller addendum stating that where you are established in the EU and wherever Insights Data containing personal data is processed under your influence and control (or any other third parties for whom you're creating or administering the page), you (the administrator) acknowledge certain things in relation to such processing. These include (amongst others):

>> You and Facebook are joint controllers for the processing of the Insights Data.

>> Facebook takes primary responsibility for complying with the GDPR.

>> You have a legal basis for the processing of Insights Data under the GDPR.

>> You identify the data controller for the page (i.e. the name of your organization).

>> You comply with any other applicable legal obligations.

>> If you're contacted by data subjects or a supervisory authority under the GDPR with regard to the processing of Insights Data and the obligations assumed by Facebook, you're required to forward all relevant information to Facebook within a maximum of seven calendar days.

REMEMBER

If you're a Facebook Fan Page administrator, you should be transparent about the type of processing taking place. If you use Facebook's cookies on your website, implement a Cookie Policy explaining which cookies are used and for what purpose. You must also ensure you have valid lawful grounds for using the cookies as well as for processing any personal data obtained.

TIP

You should include your Privacy Notice on the Fan Page itself as well as on your website. See Chapter 8 for more on Privacy Notices, and see Chapter 9 for more on Cookie Policies.

Understanding Who's a Data Processor

A *data processor* is an entity who processes data for the data controller upon the instruction of the data controller. A data processor can use its expertise to decide the suitable technical measures necessary to conduct the processing (such as how to store the data, which IT systems to use to collect personal data, and which security systems to use). If the processor decides more than that (for example, what to use the data for — perhaps using it for the purposes of other clients), then the processor may become a data controller in its own right, which can have serious consequences in terms of obligations and liability.

When you think about data processors, think about cloud-based storage providers, data analysts, and email service providers — any entity that deals only with the data that's handed to them and that has no say in which data is collected and what it's used for.

REMEMBER

An employee who processes data in the context of their employment with an organization that acts as a data controller is not a data processor. However, if employees use such personal data outside of the scope of their employment, they will become a data controller in their own right and subject to full compliance and sanctions of the GDPR. The employer would retain responsibility if the new processing by the employee was enabled through inadequate security measures.

Although a one-man freelancer or a contractor processing personal data on behalf of an organization isn't part of the same legal entity of the organization, it would be fairly safe to assume that they can be treated the same as employees, being subject to the same policies and staff training, especially where they are using the same systems as employees. If the contractor is a separate organization as opposed to a one-man freelancer, you would need to look at whether they are a data processor or a joint controller.

A mail delivery company is neither a controller nor a processor when they pick up letters and deliver them to the recipient, since they have no access to the content of the letters they deliver and therefore do not process the personal data within such letters. However, if that mail delivery company keeps electronic records of names and/or addresses or other personal data relating to such deliveries (to confirm that letters have been signed for, for example), then it would be a data controller in relation to that personal data and should comply with all relevant data controller regulations (providing a Privacy Notice, for example).

TIP

If an organization processing personal data on your behalf is subject to certain legal requirements requiring them in certain circumstances to disclose such personal data to regulatory authorities (for example, lawyers and accountants under money laundering regulations), such organizations will not be data processors but will instead be joint controllers.

Determining whether an entity is a controller or a processor is often difficult. The Article 29 Working Party, predecessor to the European Data Protection Board (EDPB), provides the following guidance to help you determine whether the entity is a controller or a processor:

>> **Consider the level of prior instruction given by the data controller.**
This points to the degree of independent judgment that the data processor can exercise.

>> **Consider the monitoring by the data controller of the execution of the service.** The closer the monitoring by the data controller, the more likely that the entity processing the data is a data processor and not a data controller.

>> **Consider the visibility/image portrayed by the data controller to the data subject and the expectations of the data subject on the basis of it.**
If a data processor sent an email on behalf of the data controller but it appeared as though the email was originating from the data processor (because, for example, the processor's name was in the "from box" of the email), the "data processor" would be more likely to actually be a data controller. (See the case of Everything DM, later in this chapter, where an email service provider was held to be a joint controller of personal data.) However, an outsourced call center operator that clearly presents itself as its client will be a data processor.

>> **Consider the expertise of parties.** If the expertise of the entity processing the data plays a predominant role, such as a barrister, the more likely it is that the entity will be a data controller.

Differentiating who are subprocessors

If a data processor subcontracts part of the processing to a third-party entity, that third party is a subprocessor. Just because a separate division within an organization may carry out certain of the processing tasks doesn't mean that the division is a subprocessor. If, however a separate group company (another company under common ownership but set up as a separate legal entity, in other words) is processing the personal data on behalf of another group company that is the data processor, that separate group company is a subprocessor. Sole traders, partnerships, government authorities, and other organizations can also be subprocessors, in the same way that they can be controllers or processors.

An example of a subprocessor arrangement is when a soft drinks manufacturer (SD Limited, in this example) hires a marketing company (M Limited) to carry out its marketing activities on its behalf. M Limited performs certain processing of personal data as a processor (such as sending out marketing emails under the instructions of the controller, SD Limited) and also arranges the hosting of marketing materials and video files on a cloud-based server (C Limited). C Limited is a subprocessor in this arrangement.

Exploring Obligations under the GDPR

Controllers, joint controllers, and processors all have responsibilities under the GDPR. Each has certain obligations that cannot be ignored without facing potential penalties. In this section, I list the most relevant obligations for each role and provide, as applicable, a cross reference to the chapter where I discuss that obligation.

Obligations on controllers

As a data controller, you're subject to the following obligations in the GDPR:

>> Comply with the six data protection principles and the overarching accountability principle (Chapter 4).

>> Process personal data only if you have lawful grounds for processing (Chapter 3).

- Be transparent by providing individuals with the required information regarding your processing activities (Chapter 8).

- Use only a data processor that is compliant with the GDPR (see below).

- Conduct due diligence and enter into a data processor agreement with every processor you use (Chapter 10).

- Use data protection *by design and default* when processing personal data (in other words, take into account data protection issues at the outset of the design of any system, service, product, or process and to only process personal data that is necessary to achieve your specific purpose; Chapter 15).

- Implement appropriate security measures to the data you process in order to keep it secure (Chapter 16).

- Keep appropriate records of processing activities (Chapter 7).

- Where required, notify the relevant supervisory authority and individuals of personal data breaches (Chapter 17).

- Carry out Data Protection Impact Assessments (DPIAs) where necessary (Chapter 15).

- Appoint a Data Protection Officer where necessary (Chapter 15).

- Appoint a representative where necessary (Chapter 15).

- Transfer data internationally only where lawful (Chapter 6).

- Comply with enforcement notices issued by data protection authorities (Chapter 21).

- Comply with data protection rights requests, though note how joint controllers must respond to the exercise of data protection rights, as set out below (Chapter 14).

- Pay data protection fees, if applicable in your jurisdiction (see below).

Certain data protection authorities such as the UK levy a data protection fee on data controllers. The majority of EU member states (including Bulgaria, Austria, and Romania) do not charge such fees.

In the UK, the Data Protection (Charges and Information) Regulations [of] 2018 provide that a data protection fee must be paid by all data controllers (not data processors) unless the data controller is exempted. This replaces the preexisting requirement to "notify" (or register) with the ICO.

The cost of the data protection fee ranges from £40 to £2900 ($44 to $3,228) depending on the size and turnover of the data controller. Charities only pay £40 regardless of their size and turnover.

The tiers are:

>> **Tier 1 — micro organizations:** You have a maximum turnover of £632,000 ($703,574) for your financial year or no more than 10 members of staff. The fee for tier 1 is £40.

>> **Tier 2 – small and medium organizations:** You have a maximum turnover of £36 million ($40,077,036) for your financial year or no more than 250 members of staff. The fee for tier 2 is £60 ($66).

>> **Tier 3 – large organizations:** If you do not meet the criteria for tier 1 or tier 2, you have to pay the tier 3 fee of £2,900.

If you use CCTV for domestic purposes, such as for monitoring your property, even if the CCTV captures images beyond the boundaries of your property, you are exempt from paying the data protection fee.

If you own a number of practices (such as dentist practices) and all the practices are part of the same legal entity, then only one fee is payable that would cover all of the practices. If, however, there are a number of separate legal entities, each legal entity would each need to pay the data protection fee.

You may be exempt from paying the fee if your organization does not fall within a list of specified industries and you only process personal data for:

>> Staff administration (including payroll)

>> Accounts or records (invoices and payments, for example) in connection with your own business activity

>> Advertising, marketing, and public relations in connection with your own business activity

The UK's ICO has a free online tool that you can use to work out whether you need to pay the fee or not. You can see it at: https://ico.org.uk/for-organisations/data-protection-fee/self-assessment/.

REMEMBER

The UK data protection fee is only payable by organizations that are processing personal data within the UK (for example, via a subsidiary, a branch, or an office). If you are processing personal data related to individuals within the UK but you are processing that data from outside of the UK, you do not have to pay the fee.

Obligations on joint controllers

As joint controllers, you share the obligations placed on data controllers under the GDPR in respect of the data set that you jointly control. You need to decide which of the joint controllers is responsible for complying with each of the data controller's obligations, especially with regard to data protection rights. Make this clear in your Privacy Notice. (See Chapter 8 for more.) The GDPR requires that an "arrangement" is in place (which would normally take the form of a written agreement) between the joint controllers in order to reflect their respective duties. The essence of such an arrangement needs to be communicated to the data subjects.

In the Privacy Notice, you should state details of each of the joint controllers and specify which of the joint controllers is responsible for responding to certain data subject rights. If, however, the data subject decides to send a notice of exercise of data protection rights to the joint controller who isn't responsible, that joint controller must still reply.

Joint controllers are wholly liable for the actions of the other joint controllers, unless they can show that they were not responsible. For example, a data subject may file a claim against one joint controller and that joint controller would be wholly liable, unless that joint controller was not responsible for the circumstances giving rise to the claim. The joint controller against whom a data subject makes a claim may be able to bring a claim against the other joint controller(s) for a contribution to that liability if they were also responsible for the matters giving rise to the claim. Equally, according to ICO guidance, joint controllers are all fully accountable to supervisory authorities. Following the case of *Independent Data Protection Centre for the Land of Schleswig-Holstein v. Wirtschaftsakademie Schleswig-Holstein GmbH*, Case No. C-210/, it seems that it is not the case that there is equal responsibility for joint controllers and that the supervisory authorities may look at which of the joint controllers was responsible for the noncompliance.

Obligations on processors

As a processor, you're subject to the following obligations in the GDPR: You must

>> Provide sufficient guarantees that technical and organizational measures have been taken to ensure compliance with GDPR [Article 28(1)] and ensure the protection of the rights of the individuals. This includes taking into account issues such as pseudonymization, encryption, confidentiality, integrity, restorability, and regular testing.

>> Only process personal data on instructions from the data controller (except where required to do so by law) [Article 29].

>> Ensure that a contract is in place between the data controller and the data processor that specifies duration, subject matter of processing, type and categories of data, as well as other mandatory terms required by the GDPR [Article 28(3)]. (See Chapter 10 for more.) This can either be a stand-alone contract or be incorporated into a party's terms and conditions.

- >> Notify the controller of any breaches — without undue delay [Article 33(2)].

- >> Transfer data only to a third country where appropriate safeguards are in place [Article 44]. (See Chapter 6.)

- >> If necessary, appoint a Data Protection Officer [Article 37(1)]. (See Chapter 15.)

- >> Maintain in writing a record of all categories of processing activities carried out on behalf of the controller and the details thereof [Article 30(2)]. (See Chapter 13.)

- >> Obtain consent from the data controller before engaging a subprocessor [Article 28(2)].

- >> Where appointing a subprocessor, ensure that the same contract as between the processor and controller is entered into by the processor and the subprocessor [Article 28(4)].

Before allowing a subprocessor to process data on behalf of the data controller, the data processor must notify the controller of this arrangement and obtain either:

- >> **Prior specific written consent:** The subprocessor is named.

- >> **General written consent:** The categories of subprocessor are named.

If relying on a general consent, then the data processor must inform the data controller before appointing or replacing any subprocessors in order to give the data controller the opportunity to raise objections. If consent is provided, the data processor must put in place a contract with the subprocessor that reflects the terms of the agreement between the data processor and the data controller. (See Chapter 10 for more on such agreements.)

Obligations on the data controller to use GDPR-compliant data processors

One of the obligations in the GDPR [Article 28(1)] on the data controller is to use only data processors providing "sufficient guarantees to implement appropriate technical and organizational measures in such a manner that processing will meet the requirements of the GDPR and ensure the protection of the rights of the data subject."

In practice, this means that a data controller must carry out thorough due diligence on the data processor before letting it process personal data. Merely relying on the assurances found in a contract won't suffice. The GDPR doesn't specify what due diligence is necessary, and each case varies, depending on the nature of the processing, the sensitivity of the data, and the risks to the data subjects.

The recitals to the GDPR provide some assistance by stating that we should pay particular attention to these areas:

>> Expert knowledge

>> Reliability

>> Resources

>> Adherence to an approved code of conduct

>> Approved certification

The UK's Information Commissioner's Office (ICO) adds that data controllers should also review relevant documentation such as the data processor's record management policy and information security policy.

At the date of publishing this book, there is no approved code of conduct or certification scheme.

After the data controller has determined that the data processor is providing sufficient guarantees and wants it to commence the processing of the personal data, the data controller and the data processor must enter into a written agreement, which I discuss further in Chapter 10.

That isn't the end of the matter. The data controller must continuously review the actions (and omissions, if relevant) of the data processor to ensure that the data processor is meeting the guarantees and complying with the contract. (In Chapter 10, I talk about how the contract between the data controller and the data processor provides audit provisions so that the data controller — or its appointed third party — can carry out ongoing checks on the data processor.)

Exploring Liabilities under the GDPR

Just as certain obligations are required of you as a data controller or data processor, certain liabilities come with those roles, too. I outline those liabilities in this section.

Liability for data controller for using a noncompliant data processor

A data controller is responsible not just for its own compliance, but also for that of its data processors (and subprocessors).

Even if the data processor breaches its contract with you as a data controller and even where the data processor has agreed to indemnify you under that contract, data subjects and supervisory authorities may still hold you fully responsible for the actions or omissions of your data processor and do one of the following:

>> File a complaint against you with a supervisory authority (in the case of data subjects).

>> Claim against you (in the case of data subjects).

>> Enforce against you or fine you (in the case of a supervisory authority).

You're the data controller, so the onus would be on you to recover any costs from the data processor for liability suffered by you as a result of the data processor's actions or omissions through settlement or a court of law.

You, as a data controller, aren't liable for damage resulting from a breach of the GDPR if you can prove you weren't in any way responsible for the event that caused the damage. However, if the damage has been caused by your data processor (or subprocessor), you can still be responsible for that damage as you chose to allow the data processor to carry out the processing. You may, however, claim against the data processor to the extent that they're responsible for the damage giving rise to the claim or for breach of contract. The maximum fine for using a noncompliant data processor is 10 million euros or 2 percent of the total worldwide annual turnover of the preceding financial year, whichever is higher. (See Chapter 21 for more on fines; Chapter 2 discusses how fines have increased under the GDPR.)

Liability of data processors

Data subjects can also choose to claim directly against the data processor, and similarly, supervisory authorities can proceed directly against the data processor (or subprocessor). A data processor is liable to the extent that it did not comply with the GDPR obligations on data processors and to the extent that it did not follow the instructions of the data controller. The data processor isn't liable if it can prove that it isn't responsible for the event giving rise to the damage.

The maximum fines that can be levied against data processors are 20 million euros ($22,265,000) or 4% of the total worldwide annual turnover of the preceding financial year, whichever is higher. See Chapter 21 for more on fines; Chapter 2 discusses how fines have increased under the GDPR.

A subprocessor may also be liable for a breach of GDPR or for a breach of the contract with the data processor. See Chapter 6 for more information.

Chapter **6**

Transfers of Data Outside of the EEA

With the GDPR in place, the European Union (EU) now considers that it has the gold standard of data protection and that transfers of personal data outside of the EU need to have special protection. This chapter describes those protections and tells you how to comply with the GDPR when you transfer personal data outside of the EU.

At the end of the chapter, I describe the role of your organization's *Representative* — a necessary appointee when you don't have an establishment within the EU but the GDPR applies to you — and when you may need one.

Principles of Data Transfer Outside of the EEA

An *international transfer* of personal data occurs whenever personal data that is being processed (or will be processed) is sent to a third country or an international organization.

TECHNICAL STUFF

A *third country* is any country outside the European Economic Area (EEA), which includes the EU member states and Iceland, Norway, and Liechtenstein. (The last-named three countries have adopted a national law that implements the GDPR.)

In this chapter, I refer to the EU for familiarity, but actually all references to the EU in this chapter are to the EEA.

Chapter 5 of the GDPR sets out the rules on making international transfers. Article 44 of the GDPR, states that international transfers may take place only if "the conditions laid down in this Chapter are complied with by the controller and processor, including for onward transfers of personal data from the third country or an international organisation to another third country or to another international organisation."

TECHNICAL STUFF

An *onward transfer* is an indirect transfer, which I discuss in the section "Working with Data in Transit and Onward Transfers," later in this chapter.

The receiver of the personal data outside of the EU can be either an organization or an individual. The receiver can also be an affiliate or a subsidiary of the transferring entity, because these are separate legal entities from the transferring entity.

The transfer may happen by

>> **Sending personal data outside of the EU:** For example, when a data controller within the EU send names and email addresses to a digital marketing agency outside of the EU

>> **Making personal data accessible outside of the EU:** For example, when a data controller within the EU uses a hosting company outside of the EU that has access to the personal data

However, if personal data is *in transit* (that is, electronically routed between EU countries via a country outside of the EU) rather than being transferred outside of the EU, the restrictions on international transfer don't apply. See the later section "Working with Data in Transit and Onward Transfers."

Countries with an Adequacy Finding

Article 45 of the GDPR states that the international data transfer may take place as long as the receiver — whether it's a third country, an international organization, or a territory within the third country — provides an "adequate level of protection." If there is adequate protection, no specific authorization of the transfer or any further acts are required.

The European Commission decides whether individual countries have sufficient data protection laws so that the transfer of personal data doesn't need additional protection. This is called an *adequacy finding*.

At the time this book was published, the European Commission had approved the following countries as having adequate protection for data transfers — having an "adequacy finding," in other words:

>> Andorra

>> Argentina

>> Canada (commercial organizations only)

>> Faroe Islands

>> Guernsey

>> Isle of Man

>> Israel

>> Japan

>> Jersey

>> New Zealand

>> Switzerland

>> Uruguay

>> United States of America (limited to the privacy shield framework, which I discuss in the next section)

At the time of publishing this book, the European Commission is in adequacy talks with South Korea to grant an adequacy finding in relation to transfers of personal data to South Korea.

Adequacy findings are kept under review, and the European Commission can revoke satisfactory adequacy findings if it sees fit.

REMEMBER

Following Brexit, the UK will be a third country, and the provisions on international transfers will apply to transfers from countries within the EU to the UK. This list spells out two possible scenarios:

>> **If the UK leaves the EU with transitional arrangements in place:** Transfers from the EU to the UK won't be restricted (and the UK will effectively have an adequacy finding).

>> **If the UK leaves without transitional arrangements in place (known as a *no-deal Brexit*):** It will need to apply for an adequacy finding, a process that could take up to three years. In the meantime, transfers to the EU to the UK would be restricted transfers and additional safeguards will need to be put into place. See the next section for more about the position on transfers between the UK and the EU after Brexit.

Becoming Part of the US Privacy Shield

The EU–US Privacy Shield Framework was designed by the US Department of Commerce in conjunction with the European Commission and the Swiss government to support transatlantic commerce. The framework provides a means for companies (on both sides of the Atlantic) to comply with data protection requirements when transferring personal data from the EU and Switzerland to the United States.

TIP

Organizations in the United States can self-certify under the Privacy Shield Framework so that transfers of personal data from the EU to such organizations can be made without restriction. They need to recertify annually.

If a US organization wants to be part of the Privacy Shield Framework, certain procedures must be followed. You can read about the requirements at www.privacyshield.gov/article?id=How-to-Join-Privacy-Shield-part-1.

In essence, you need to:

>> Create a Privacy Notice that complies with Privacy Shield standards.

>> Identify an independent recourse mechanism for data subjects.

>> Self-certify by way of this website: www.privacyshield.gov.

If your organization in the EU wants to determine whether a US organization is part of the Privacy Shield, you can check the searchable database at `www.privacyshield.gov/list`.

REMEMBER

The Privacy Shield was being challenged at the time this book was published, via two cases to be heard by the Court of Justice of the European Union (CJEU). Max Schrems, the privacy activist who brought down the Safe Harbour (the transfer framework preceding the Privacy Shield) is behind the two cases.

However, a big complaint of the European Commission has been removed by President Trump appointing Keith Krach as a permanent Ombudsperson. In addition, the European Data Protection Board released its own report in early 2019 which, although still referring to the ongoing CJEU challenges, was much less threatening about a referral of the Privacy Shield to the CJEU than it had been in its previous report.

When the UK leaves the EU, transfers of personal data from the UK to the US will proceed as they did before Brexit. This means that if the transfer is to an organization that has Privacy Shield certification, the transfer can proceed with no further restrictions. However, the US organization must update its Privacy Notice as spelled out here:

> [INSERT your organization name] complies with the EU–US Privacy Shield Framework and the Swiss–US Privacy Shield Frameworks (Privacy Shield) as set forth by the US Department of Commerce regarding the collection, use, and retention of personal information transferred from the [INSERT European Union and the United Kingdom and/or Switzerland, as applicable] to the United States in reliance on Privacy Shield. [INSERT your organization name] has certified to the Department of Commerce that it adheres to the Privacy Shield Principles with respect to such information. If there is any conflict between the terms in this Privacy Policy and the Privacy Shield Principles, the Privacy Shield Principles shall govern. To learn more about the Privacy Shield program, and to view our certification, please visit `www.privacyshield.gov`.

Working with Data in Transit and Onward Transfers

A *direct transfer* of personal data is where the receiving organization is based outside of the EEA. An *indirect transfer* (also known as an *onward transfer*) is where the receiving organization is based inside the EEA but the data is processed by processors or subprocessors outside of the EEA. This includes affiliates, subsidiaries, and other group companies that are processors or subprocessors.

The GDPR recognizes that personal data will flow between, to, and from countries outside the EU — if that were not the case, international trade and cooperation as it's currently formulated could not exist. Because that flow of data is increasing, so too has concern for — and the challenges of — protecting that data. Recital 101 states, "When personal data are transferred from the Union to controllers, processors or other recipients in third countries or to international organisations, the level of protection of natural persons ensured in the Union by this Regulation should not be undermined."

Recital 101 emphasizes that data controllers still have the responsibility to protect personal data and data subject rights. This includes cases of "onward transfers of personal data from the third country or international organisation to controllers, processors in the same or another third country or international organisation[s]."

What we can see from that recital is that restrictions on transferring personal data outside of the EU also extend to onward transfers of personal data from a third country to another third country. Take the following scenario, for example:

1. A French data controller transfers personal data relating to its customers to its Indian IT service provider that acts as data processor.

2. The Indian subsidiary then transfers the data to a Brazilian specialist IT company that acts as a subprocessor.

The transfer from the Indian company to the Brazilian company (or indeed a transfer from the Indian company to another organization within India) is an onward transfer.

That means it's subject to the GDPR.

REMEMBER

Personal data is *in transit* when it's merely electronically routed between two organizations in the EU via a non-EU organization, such as a server in Venezuela. In this case, if there's no intention to access or manipulate the data during transit, the "transfer" of the data to Venezuela is not a restricted transfer.

Understanding Standard Contractual Clauses

If the recipient organization is in a country that doesn't have an adequacy finding, the transferring party may put in place contractual protections in order for the transfer to proceed. (See the list in the section "Countries with an Adequacy Finding," earlier in this chapter.)

These *standard contractual clauses* (sometimes referred to as SCCs) are contracts that govern the transfer of the personal data in the form approved by the European Commission.

You cannot amend the form of the standard contractual clauses. The wording must match what's been approved by the European Commission.

With the GDPR coming into force, data controllers are no longer required to complete an authorization process when using standard contractual clauses, as had previously been the case in certain EU member states.

Determining the type of standard contractual clause to use

Because there are two different types of standard contractual clauses, you must determine whether the transfer is controller-to-controller or controller-to-processor (see Chapter 5 for more on this distinction):

>> **Controller-to-controller:** If the transfer is an EU controller to a non-EU controller transfer, you need to put in place the standard contractual clauses for a controller-to-controller transfer.

>> **Controller-to-processor:** If the transfer is an EU controller to non-EU processor transfer, you need to put in place the standard contractual clauses for a controller-to-processor transfer. You have more to consider in this scenario, as I discuss next.

You can see both variations of the standard contractual clauses at `https://ec.europa.eu/info/law/law-topic/data-protection/international-dimension-data-protection/standard-contractual-clauses-scc_en`.

Regarding the controller-to-processor transfer

When it comes to the controller-to-processor transfer, the standard contractual clauses only anticipate transfers from EU data controllers. They do not contemplate regulated transfers by data controllers that are subject to the GDPR that are established outside of the EU.

For example, a US-based controller that has data subjects in the EU and is subject to the GDPR who transfers personal data to an Indian data processor will find that the standard contractual clauses don't apply to this transfer. Because the standard contractual clauses don't permit amendments, the standard contractual clauses cannot be used; the US controller would need a *derogation* (an exemption) to apply before making the transfer. (See the later section "Derogations for International Transfers," for more about this topic.)

After Brexit, if no transitional arrangements are in place (in the event of a no-deal Brexit, in other words), the following will apply in relation to the use of standard contractual clauses relating to data transfers between EU and UK organizations:

REMEMBER

>> **Where personal data is transferred from an EU controller to a UK controller or UK processor,** the UK will be a third country and the existing standard contractual clauses can be used.

A *third country* is any country that isn't an EU member state or one of the additional EEA countries (Iceland, Norway, or Liechtenstein).

>> **Where personal data is transferred from an EU processor to a UK controller or UK subprocessor,** standard contractual clauses cannot be used. A solution would be to reroute the data to the UK or another non-EU jurisdiction so that the GDPR doesn't apply, but this is unlikely to be an easy process. Data controllers may decide to take a risk-based approach to this situation and continue as before until the European Data Protection Board comes up with a solution.

>> **Where personal data is transferred from the UK to the EU,** the EU country will be recognized as "adequate," and standard contractual clauses won't need to be put into place — nor will any further action need to be taken.

TECHNICAL STUFF

A *no-deal Brexit* refers to the circumstances where the UK leaves the EU with no formal arrangements in place dictating how data transfers will be handled.

Establishing Binding Corporate Rules

If your organization has a number of group companies throughout the world and it needs to transfer personal data freely between such group companies, the most effective way to enable those transfers is to put binding corporate rules into place.

Binding corporate rules (BCRs) are data protection policies that each group company adheres to. This helps to ensure the requisite protection for the personal data, regardless of the country's data protection legislation in which the group company is established.

The following list highlights important points to know regarding BCRs:

>> BCRs must include all general data protection principles and also enforceable rights for data subjects. They must be legally binding and apply to each group company.

>> BCRs must be approved by your lead authority. (See Chapter 21 for more about who your lead authority is.) Keep in mind that it can take 12 months to two years to arrange for the necessary approvals.

Your supervisory authority may need to involve other supervisory authorities and the European Data Protection Board if you have group companies in more than one EU member state.

>> If you put BCRs in place, you will have an ongoing obligation to monitor compliance with the BCRs, including regular audits and staff training.

>> BCRs that were approved before the GDPR went into effect will remain valid until amended, repealed, or replaced.

>> The GDPR provides for BCRs for data processors, such as outsourced services and cloud computing services.

>> The BCRs must be attached to the service agreement with the data controller and must be binding toward the data controller.

In the event of a no-deal Brexit, the UK's ICO will no longer be able to have any authority in relation to BCRs. Organizations will need to identify a new supervisory authority, whether they already have approved BCRs, are in the middle of the application process, or want to apply for BCRs.

Derogations for International Transfers

In simple terms, a *derogation* is an exemption from a rule or law. You must look at the acceptable derogations for international transfer if the following statements are true:

>> The organization to which you're transferring personal data is not established in a country that has an adequacy finding.

>> You do not have BCRs in place.

>> You do not have standard contractual clauses in place.

In this case, if a derogation doesn't apply, any international transfer of personal data would be unlawful.

Rely on a derogation only as a last resort. Derogations do not provide the data subject with adequate protection or appropriate safeguards for their personal data being transferred out of the EU.

Article 49 of the GDPR lists acceptable derogations, which I explain throughout the rest of this section. Notice that some derogations align with the lawful grounds for processing that I discuss in Chapter 3.

Throughout the following derogation discussion, I refer to the European Data Protection Board (EDPB), an EU body charged with the application of the GDPR since it took effect May 25, 2018. Among other activities, the EDPB works to ensure that the GDPR is applied consistently across the EU and provides guidelines on interpreting core concepts (guidelines I rely on here). Learn more at `https://edpb.europa.eu`.

Explicit consent

If "the data subject has explicitly consented to the proposed transfer, after having been informed of the possible risks of such transfers for the data subject due to the absence of an adequacy decision and appropriate safeguards," you will be able to transfer the personal data outside of the EU (as per Article 49(1)(a)).

However, the data subject needs to specifically give consent for the particular data transfer or set of transfers. Obtaining the data subject's prior consent for a future transfer at the time of the collection of the data is likely not possible. The reason for this is that you're unlikely to know all the specific circumstances of an international transfer at the time you collect personal data from a data subject and request their consent.

For example, consider an EU organization that collects personal data for the delivery of goods. At that time of collection, no one anticipated needing to transfer this data to a non-EU organization. If, years later, that EU organization is acquired by a non-EU organization and it's necessary to transfer the personal data outside of the EU, the data subject would need to provide explicit consent for this specific transfer at the time when the transfer is envisaged.

The consent provided at the time you collected the data isn't sufficient to rely on the consent derogation for the transfer of the personal data outside of the EU.

You must specify the following in your consent request:

>> All data recipients or categories of recipients

>> All non-EU countries to which the personal data will be transferred

>> A statement that the non-EU country to which the data will be transferred doesn't provide for an adequate level of data protection based on a European Commission decision

Contractual necessity

Where "the transfer is necessary for the performance of a contract between (i) the data subject and the controller or the implementation of pre-contractual measures taken at the data subject's request" or (ii) "in the interest of the data subject between the controller and another natural or legal person," you may transfer the personal data to a non-EU organization (as per Article 49(1)(b)).

Recital 111 of the GDPR states, "Provisions should be made for the possibility for transfers in certain circumstances . . ., where the transfer is occasional and necessary in relation to a contract." What this means is that you may rely on this derogation only when the transfer is *occasional* and *necessary*.

The necessity test requires a "close and substantial connection between the data transfer and the purposes of the contract" — in other words, without the data transfer, the contract could not be carried out. A couple of examples from the EDPB help to clarify this point:

>> **When the derogation cannot be used:** "This derogation cannot be used, for example, when a corporate group has, for business purposes, centralized its payment and human resources management functions for all its staff in a third country, as there is no direct and objective link between the performance of the employment contract and such transfer. Other grounds for transfer such as standard contractual clauses or Binding Corporate Rules may, however, be suitable for the particular transfer."

>> **When the derogation could be used:** "On the other hand, the transfer by travel agents of personal data concerning their individual clients to hotels or to other commercial partners that would be called upon in the organization of these clients' stay abroad can be deemed necessary for the purposes of the contract entered into by the travel agent and the client, since, in this case, there is a sufficient close and substantial connection between the data transfer and the purposes of the contract (organization of clients' travel)."

The EDPB provides the following examples of when a transfer may be occasional or not:

>> **When the derogation cannot be used:** "Transfers would not qualify as 'occasional' in a case where a multinational company organizes trainings in a training center in a third country and systematically transfers the personal data of those employees who attend a training course (data such as name and job title but potentially also dietary requirements or mobility restrictions). Data transfers regularly occurring within a stable relationship would be deemed as systematic and repeated, hence exceeding an 'occasional' character."

>> **When the derogation can be used:** "A transfer here may be deemed occasional, for example, if personal data of a sales manager, who in the context of an employment contract travels to different clients in third countries, are to be sent to those clients in order to arrange the meetings. A transfer can also be considered as occasional if a bank in the EU transfers personal data to a bank in a third country in order to execute a client's request for making a payment, as long as this transfer doesn't occur in the framework of a stable cooperation relationship between the two banks."

In relation to the contract being "in the interest of the data subject," this derogation won't provide a basis for data transfers where "an organization has, for business purposes, outsourced activities such as payroll management to service providers outside the EU, since no close and substantial link between the transfer and a contract concluded in the data subject's interest can be established even if the end purpose of the transfer is the management of the pay of the employee."

Public interest

If the data transfer is necessary for important reasons of public interest, you may transfer the data internationally (as set out in Article 49(1)(c)). Private organizations are unlikely to be able to use this derogation.

This derogation isn't limited to data transfers that are occasional. (Read the earlier section "Contractual necessity" to see what this means.) This doesn't mean, however, that data transfers can take place under this derogation on a large scale and in a systematic manner.

Legal claim necessity

Where the transfer is necessary for the establishment, exercise, or defense of legal claims, the personal data can be transferred internationally (as set out in Article 49(1)(d)).

Recital 111 states that an international transfer can be made where it's "occasional and necessary in relation to a contract or a legal claim, regardless of whether in a judicial procedure or whether in an administrative or any out-of-court procedure, including procedures before regulatory bodies." The EDPB guidance is that data transfers for the following purposes may fall under this derogation:

>> Formal pre-trial discovery procedures in civil litigation

>> Actions by the data exporter to institute procedures in a third country — for example, commencing litigation or seeking approval for a merger

WARNING

The EDPB further advises that you cannot rely on this derogation to justify transferring personal data because you think it's possible that legal proceedings or formal procedures may be brought at a later date.

You must keep in mind that an international transfer may take place under this derogation only when it's necessary and occasional. The EDPB provides the following guidance on these terms:

>> **Necessary:** This Necessity test requires a "close and substantial connection between the data in question and the specific establishment, exercise, or defense of the legal position."

"The mere interest of third country authorities or possible 'good will' to be obtained from the third country authority as such would not be sufficient."

>> **Occasional:** See the earlier section "Contractual necessity" for more about what *occasional* means in this context.

Vital interests

Where the transfer is "necessary in order to protect the vital interests of the data subject or of other persons, where the data subject is physically or legally incapable of giving consent," personal data may be transferred internationally, as set out in Article 49(1)(e).

This derogation applies when data is transferred in the event of a medical emergency and where it's considered that such transfer is directly necessary in order to give the medical care required.

WARNING

If the data subject has the ability to provide consent, this derogation cannot be relied on. The ability to make a valid decision can be based on physical, mental, or legal incapability.

Open register

The final derogation set out in Article 49(1)(f) of the GDPR is a transfer made from a register that, according to EU or member state law, provides information to the public — to the general public, that is, or to any person who can demonstrate a legitimate interest.

These can include registers of companies, registers of associations, registers of criminal convictions, land title registers, or public vehicle registers.

The EU or member state will specify certain conditions that an individual must meet in order to make transfers from these registers. Only when the conditions are fulfilled may the transfer take place.

Compelling legitimate interests

Article 49(2) of the GDPR states that where no other provisions for transfer outside of the EU apply, a transfer to a third country or an international organization may still take place if the following conditions apply:

>> **The transfer is not repetitive.**

>> **The transfer concerns only a limited number of data subjects.** No threshold has been set as to what a limited number is, and it depends on all of the circumstances. Here's the EDPB guidance on this:

> "If a data controller needs to transfer personal data to detect a unique and serious security incident in order to protect its organization, the question here would be how many employees' data the data controller would have to transfer in order to achieve this compelling legitimate interest. As such, in order for the derogation to apply, this transfer should not apply to *all the employees* of the data controller but rather to a *certain confined few.*"

>> **The transfer is necessary for the purposes of compelling legitimate interests pursued by the data controller and are not overridden by the interests or rights and freedoms of the data subject.** The EDPB provides as an example of "compelling" legitimate interests where a data controller is compelled to transfer the personal data in order to protect its organization or systems from serious immediate harm or from a severe penalty that would seriously affect its business. Although the EDPB does not then go on to provide a practical example of this, one such scenario might be transferring personal data from one server within the EU to a server outside of the EU, where the server within the EU is being subject to a malicious attack.

>> **The data controller has assessed all the circumstances surrounding the data transfer and has on the basis of that assessment provided suitable safeguards with regard to the protection of personal data.** You need to consider (i) the interests, rights, and freedoms of the data subject — including any possible physical, material, and nonmaterial damage (such as loss of reputation), (ii) the risks to such interests, rights, and freedoms, (iii) the appropriate safeguards to put into place, and (iv) these additional factors:

- The nature of the data

- The purpose and duration of the processing

- The situation in the country of origin

- The third country acting as the conduit

- The country of final destination of the transfer

WARNING

You must inform your supervisory authority of the transfer, and you must inform the data subject of the transfer and the compelling legitimate interest pursued. Use this derogation only as a last resort.

The duty to inform the supervisory authority doesn't extend to having to obtain the consent of the supervisory authority before the transfer is made.

REMEMBER

The reference to "compelling" legitimate interests means that the bar here is higher than for the legitimate interests as a lawful ground for processing. See Chapter 3 for more on legitimate interests as a grounds for processing.

3
Key Documentation

Completing a data inventory to help you write other pieces of your key documentation

Using a Privacy Notice to detail how you gather and use personal data

Crafting a Cookie Policy — and understanding why you need it

Writing down agreements between you, joint controllers, and data processors

Communicating to data subjects how you process personal data — and giving them an out

Determining the specific circumstances (and associated risks) of your data processing

Maintaining other GDPR-related documents, such as data breach records and data retention policies

Chapter **7**

Building Your Data Inventory

The very first step of your GDPR compliance journey (after reading this book!) is to map the data flow in and out of your organization in order to fully understand the uses of the data. This key step is one that you cannot skip.

In this chapter, I first explain how to complete your data inventory and then show you how it informs a number of your other compliance documents — particularly, your Privacy Notice.

The data inventory will also help you, as a data controller, with your obligations under these two articles of the GDPR:

» **Article 30:** Mandates you to keep records of your data processing. (More on that topic later in this chapter.)

» **Article 15:** Mandates you to comply with data subject access requests (DSARs), where data subjects have the right to know exactly which of their personal data you are storing. (I talk more about DSARs in Chapter 14.)

Understanding the Rationale for Data Inventory

A key part of the process of becoming GDPR-compliant is understanding the data flow into and out of your organization — and being fully aware of how the data is being used, by you as well as by any third parties you transfer the data to.

Because the data flow and use of data vary from one organization to another, you won't benefit from using non-personalized template documents (or copying other people's documents) in an effort to be compliant. You need to carry out this exercise yourself, in detail, so that you can personalize a template to fit your business.

REMEMBER

Supervisory authorities have clearly specified that organizations cannot merely pay lip service to GDPR compliance and treat it as a tick-the-box exercise. Organizations must put privacy and data protection at the heart of their operations. Carrying out the data inventory is a key part of this process.

The good news is, if your organization is relatively small, completing the data inventory should be fairly simple. To make the process as pain-free as possible, you can use this chapter as a guide. (For more help, check out the data inventory tool, which is part of the Cheat Sheet associated with this book.)

Completing a Data Inventory

To complete your data inventory, you need to understand these concepts:

>> What personal data is (see Chapter 3)

>> What special category data is (see Chapter 3)

>> What processing is (see Chapter 3)

>> What third countries are (see Chapter 6)

>> The kinds of personal data you collect and process

>> The purpose for which you're collecting and using the personal data

>> The lawful ground for each processing (see Chapter 3)

>> Where the personal data is stored (including whether it's on third-party systems, such as servers)

>> Where the data flows from the point of collection throughout your organization to third parties (and where those third parties are geographically located)

>> How long you're retaining the data

>> What security measures you apply to the data

In simple terms, *data mapping* is the process by which you find out what data you have, where, why, and who you share it with, in order to understand the data environment within your organization and to comply with GDPR accountability. The GDPR doesn't specify the form your data mapping is to take — it doesn't even specify that data mapping needs to take place. To comply with the GDPR, though, you'll certainly need to conduct this exercise.

TIP

If you have previously registered with a supervisory authority in relation to the personal data you are processing (with the Information Commissioners Office in the UK, for example), you should be able to use a lot of the information from that registration to prepare your data inventory.

REMEMBER

If your organization is a relatively small one with simple data flows, you should be able to carry out the data inventory yourself, using this chapter and the free Data Inventory template found on this book's Cheat Sheet.

Preparatory steps for data inventory

If you're part of a larger organization or it has a more complex data flow, you may choose to outsource the task to a data privacy professional. You may also want to consider investing in one of the many online tools that can facilitate the data mapping exercise — I list recommended tools in the "Exploring Systems for Managing Data" section, later in this chapter. Whatever you do, be sure to determine which requirements are in place with regard to keeping records of your data processing.

When preparing the data inventory, keep in mind the data protection principles. (See Chapter 4.) Ask yourself:

>> Do I really need this data to achieve this purpose?

>> Is the security appropriate for this type of personal data?

>> Am I legally able to transfer this data to that third party?

Regardless of the size of your organization, I advise involving all relevant individuals within the organization in the process of data mapping, to ensure that you don't miss anything and that you obtain a comprehensive view of all your organization's data processing activities. Equally important is that you ensure that senior management takes a hands-on role in the process.

If your organization is a larger one and you're not outsourcing the data mapping process to data protection professionals, preparing a questionnaire to send to all heads of appropriate functions, such as IT, HR, Finance, Marketing, and Sales can help you collect the information you need. Keep the questions simple, such as these examples:

>> Whom do you hold information about?

>> If you are processing this data to provide a service to another organization, what is the service provided and which organizations?

>> What is the information you hold about them?

>> Why do you hold that information and what do you use it for?

>> How long do you hold that information?

>> With whom do you share that information — both internally and externally — and where are those people geographically located?

>> In what form is the information stored? (Is it electronic file or paper file, for example?)

>> Where is the information stored? (For example, is it in a HR filing cabinet, a sales file directory, or an email marketing tool like Mailchimp or Aweber?)

>> How do you keep the information secure?

It is also a good idea to provide examples of personal data within the questionnaire so that staff don't make incorrect assumptions about what personal data includes or does not include.

You should follow up the questionnaire with face-to-face meetings with the heads of the appropriate functions. You should also decide who within the organization is ultimately responsible for the data mapping exercise and then set appropriate timescales.

The Data Inventory template

In this section, I describe what information goes into each column on a typical Data Inventory template.

Data collected from

In this column, you list the sources that the data is collected from, such as

>> **A form on your website:** To inquire about your goods or services.

>> **A form on your website:** To sign up to your newsletter.

>> **Employee new starter forms:** To provide requisite information when hired by an organization.

>> **Direct from the customer:** When purchasing products or services from you, for example.

>> **Direct from event attendees:** When they add their business cards to enter a prize drawing, for example.

>> **Direct from suppliers:** When pitching for work, for example.

>> **Direct from individuals:** When signing up for a free app or free online service, for example.

>> **A recruitment agency:** When they send you applicant details, for example.

>> **Event organizers:** Who had permission to share with you the personal data of the attendees?

>> **Publicly available sources:** Credit rating agencies and public authorities, for example.

>> **Group companies:** When you share HR or IT functions, for example. (Note that group companies are still third parties as they're separate legal entities.)

>> **Other third parties:** Benefits providers, training course providers, call center providers, or medical providers who may, for example, pass on to you personal data (and possibly special category data) about employees.

>> **Cookies and pixels (see glossary) placed on your website:** If cookies or pixels include personal data, this needs to be included on the data inventory. (See Chapter 3 for more.)

>> **Data brokers:** When buying personal data such as email lists from data brokers. Exercise care here — see Chapter 19.

These examples are intended to prompt you to think about the wide variety of sources from which you might obtain data.

Category of data subject

Putting it simply, the data subject is the individual about whom you hold personal data. (For a more elaborate description, see Chapter 14.)

Here's a list of examples of the kinds of data subjects you'll deal with:

>> Customers

>> Employees

>> Job applicants

>> Prospects

>> Website visitors

>> Representatives of suppliers

>> Affiliates

>> Emergency contacts

>> Beneficiaries

>> Professional advisors

>> Complainants

>> Members and shareholders

>> Individuals recorded on closed circuit TV (CCTV)

Personal data being processed

Personal data is any information relating to a natural person that is identified or identifiable, directly or indirectly. To read more about what constitutes personal data, see Chapter 3.

In the Personal Data column of the data inventory, you describe the types of personal data you're collecting and using. The following list gives you an idea of the range of data involved:

>> Financial

>> Medical

>> Tax

>> Pension

>> Contact

>> Ethnicity

>> Employment history

>> Purchase history

- >> Human resources
- >> Lifestyle
- >> Location
- >> IP address

Purpose

In the Purpose column of the data inventory, you describe the purpose of the specific processing. This list gives you several examples:

- >> Processing financial transactions for customers
- >> Fulfilling contractual obligations
- >> Meeting an insurance requirement
- >> Complying with a legal requirement
- >> Meeting a tax requirement
- >> Sending an order to a customer
- >> Fulfilling marketing needs
- >> Meeting payroll needs
- >> Ensuring equal opportunities
- >> Meeting security needs
- >> Performing market research
- >> Determining customer preferences
- >> Defending (or establishing) legal claims
- >> Sending a newsletter to prospects
- >> Sending (and keeping records of) customer communications
- >> Replying to inquiries
- >> Personalizing the customer experience
- >> Monitoring the use of your website and online services
- >> Keeping records of orders placed
- >> Administering and protecting your business and website

- >> Delivering relevant website content and advertisements
- >> Carrying out credit checks
- >> Obtaining professional advice

REMEMBER

Under the data minimization principle, you must collect only the data you need in order to carry out your specified purpose. See Chapter 4 for more on this topic.

In addition, you must ensure that you have a lawful ground for processing for each purpose and understand whether any ancillary legislation applies. For example, for sending a newsletter to prospects, you are likely to need consent of the data subject (see Chapter 19 for more).

Lawful grounds for processing

Under this column, you state your lawful grounds for processing. You can choose from six lawful grounds; the main four used in a commercial context are consent, contract, legal requirement, and legitimate interests. To read more on this subject, see Chapter 3.

This column is not strictly required in your Article 30 record of processing (see below), but as you need to include your lawful grounds for processing in your Privacy Notice, it is a good idea to include this in any event.

Certain jurisdictions, such as the UK, require records to be kept of the lawful ground of processing for special category data and criminal conviction data.

These examples show typical lawful grounds of processing for data processing activities carried out by most organizations:

- >> Processing tax data for employees would be a legal requirement grounds for processing.
- >> Processing ethnicity for equal opportunities purposes would be based on consent. (Note that, because this is special category data, you would also need an additional explicit consent condition, which I cover in Chapter 3.)
- >> Processing prospect data for marketing purposes would be for legitimate interests. (Note that the ePrivacy Directive as adopted by EU member state law may apply, which means consent may be required; see Chapter 19 for more on this topic.)
- >> Processing financial details for employees would be for contractual reasons (because you have to pay them).

>> General business and website administration would be for legitimate interests.

>> Carrying out credit checks would be for legitimate interests.

>> Keeping records for a statutory retention period would be a legal requirement grounds for processing.

Special category data

It's helpful to flag, in the data inventory, whether the personal data being processed is special category data and, if so, the Article 9 condition for being able to process the special category data. For example, when employees take sick leave and you require them to send you medical reports to ensure that they receive medical benefits, that data is special category data and you would need to meet an Article 9 condition in order to process that data. The additional condition for processing special category data in such cases would be that the processing is, as Article 9 states, "necessary for the purposes of carrying out the obligations and exercising the specific rights of the controller or of the data subject in the field of employment law." See Chapter 3 for more on this.

Note that, although the GDPR does not specify that this is required in the Article 30 record of processing, certain jurisdictions such as the UK have passed their own legislation requiring that the Article 9 condition be documented.

Sometimes, there may be overlapping options for the lawful grounds for processing and for the special category data conditions. You just need to choose one.

REMEMBER

In the employment context, I don't recommend that consent be used as a lawful ground for processing, because of the imbalance in the relationship (meaning that consent is not freely given and therefore cannot be considered valid consent) and the fact that the consent can always be withdrawn. See Chapter 18 for more on this topic.

Volume of data

It isn't critical to include this column in the data inventory, but it may be helpful for you to have an overview of the volume of personal data you're processing. It doesn't have to be a precise number, though it should give you an idea of the scale of the data you're dealing with.

For example, you may have only tens of records for employment histories because you have only 14 employees, but you may have hundreds of thousands of email subscribers.

Retention period

Under the principle of storage limitation, personal data should be retained only for such period as is necessary for the purposes for which the data is processed.

As such, one of the policy documents you should have in place is a document retention policy. This policy sets out how long certain data is to be kept and when it is to be deleted. (See Chapter 13 for more on this topic.)

Certain data may need to be kept according to statutory limits, such as tax and financial information, but for the majority of data, you can choose retention periods based on the usage of such data within your organization, considering all the circumstances, such as the length of buying cycles.

Third party to whom data is transferred and country located in

Any third party that you, as a data controller, transfer data to should be listed here, including those who are data processors for you. (I discuss data processors in Chapter 5.) You should also specify in which country a particular third party is located, because this will prompt you to consider the appropriate safeguard for that international transfer of data (see Chapter 6 for more on this topic).

Here are some examples of third parties to whom you may transfer data:

>> Other group companies

>> Third-party suppliers

>> Fraud prevention organizations

>> Tax authorities

>> Other regulatory authorities

>> Insurance companies

>> Supervising entities

>> Market research agencies

>> Potential purchasers of the business and assets

>> Past employers

>> Claims investigators

- Professional advisors
- Examining bodies
- Healthcare professionals
- Recruitment agencies
- Credit brokers
- Family members

REMEMBER

You only need to include in your Article 30 record of processing the third parties you are actually disclosing personal data to. You do not need to list hypothetical third parties or even third parties that you are likely to share personal data with in the future.

Appropriate safeguard for transfer of data

If you transfer personal data outside the European Economic Area (EEA), ensure that you have legally permitted grounds to do so. (This is covered in more detail in Chapter 6.) Such grounds could include these examples:

- The transferee is located in an "adequate" country.
- You have entered into EU standard contractual clauses with the non-EU partner.
- The data transfer is subject to derogation.

Additional columns

You may also want to add in the following columns to your data inventory, depending on the size of your organization:

- The business function that owns the data
- The physical location of the data
- The name and contact details of any joint controller, if any, as described in Chapter 5
- A description of security measures (for example, encryption)
- Confirmation of whether a DPIA is required (as described in Chapter 15)

Exploring Systems for Managing Data

You'll find many tools on the market for managing data in compliance with the GDPR. When assessing the right tool for your organization, consider these types of tools:

>> Security

>> Compliance assessment

>> Data governance

>> Data management

>> User consent

>> Compliance

The following systems may help you, though you should note that I'm not necessarily endorsing any of these products.

>> GDPR Mentor

>> Trust Arc

>> One Trust

See Chapter 22 for more detail about these solutions.

Article 30: The Obligation to Keep Records of Data Processing

One of the main changes to data protection law that the GDPR has brought about concerns the principle of accountability. Rather than register with a supervisory authority and publicly list the data you process, now the obligation is for you to keep internal systems and records.

Every organization, regardless of size, will likely have to carry out some formal record keeping under Article 30 of the GDPR.

By completing the data inventory discussed earlier, you will have created the records required under Article 30 of the GDPR.

Article 30 provides that organizations with 250 employees or more must keep certain records of *all* of its processing activities, as set out in detail earlier.

Organizations with fewer than 250 employees must also keep records of processing, if the processing

>> Is likely to result in a risk to the rights and freedoms of data subjects

>> Is not occasional, or

>> Includes special category data or criminal conviction data. (See Chapter 3 for more on these types of data.)

If you run an organization of fewer than 250 employees and the particular processing meets all the following requirements, you don't need to record it (otherwise, you do):

>> It isn't likely to impact on the rights and freedoms of data subjects.

>> It's a one-off.

>> It doesn't involve special category data or criminal conviction data.

For example, if you conduct a customer survey as a one-off (or even occasionally, such as every year), you don't generally need to keep records of this particular processing. If, however, this survey involves profiling or special category data (such as health data or ethnicity) or criminal convictions data, then even though the processing is occasional, you must still keep records. This is because profiling can result in risks to the rights and freedoms of data subjects and special category data and criminal convictions data must always be recorded without exception.

Keep this list handy as you prepare records of your data processing:

>> **Even if you don't legally need to record all your processing, recording everything is a good practice.** Doing so helps you to comply with other obligations under the GDPR, such as data subject access requests. (See Chapter 14 to read more about data subject access requests.)

>> **The record of your processing activities is a dynamic record that will change regularly.** It isn't a record that you can complete once and then stash in a drawer. For this reason, assigning the ongoing responsibility for this task to someone within your organization is essential.

>> **Your data inventory is the starting point for your record of processing activities.** However, where the GDPR doesn't prescribe what type of information needs to be detailed in your data inventory or how you carry out your data mapping exercise, the GDPR does prescribe what records you must keep, and this varies, depending on whether you're acting as a data controller or a data processor.

You can act as a data processor and a data controller in relation to different processing activities, so be sure to keep your records duly separated. See Chapter 5 for more on whether you're acting as a data processor or a data controller.

>> **The records must be in writing, and can be in electronic format.** Whether you're acting as a data controller or a data processor, you shall (or your representative shall) make the records available to your supervisory authority, if requested.

Controller's obligations

If you're acting as a data controller for certain personal data processing, you need to keep the following records, all of which are described in detail in the data inventory section above:

>> Your organization's name and contact details (and, where applicable, any joint controller — see Chapter 5 for more on what a joint controller is)

>> The purpose of the processing (marketing or customer management or to comply with legal requirements, for example)

>> A description of the categories of data subjects (employees, customers, and suppliers, for example)

>> A description of the categories of personal data (contact details, transaction history, employment history, for example)

>> The categories of recipients of the data (service providers, insurers, and regulatory authorities, for example)

>> Transfers of personal data to third countries as well as documentation of suitable safeguards

>> Envisaged retention period for different categories of data

>> A general description of the security measures

>> Details of your Data Protection Officer and/or your representative, if you have one (as described in detail in Chapter 15)

Processor's obligations

If you're acting as a data processor, you need to keep the following records of your processing again, all of which are described in detail in the data inventory section above:

>> Your organization's name and contact details

>> The name and contact details of each data controller on behalf of whom you're acting

>> The categories of processing carried out on behalf of each controller (marketing, IT services, or payroll, for example)

>> Transfers of personal data to third countries as well as documentation of suitable safeguards

>> A general description of the security measures

>> Details of your and each data controller's Data Protection Officer or your Representative, to the extent that you/they have one (as described in detail in Chapter 15)

Chapter **8**

Penning a Privacy Notice

I n this chapter, I look at one of the most important documents for GDPR compliance: the *Privacy Notice,* a document — sometimes lengthy and often complicated — that details how you, as the data controller, gather and use personal data. Every business, no matter how small, needs to have a Privacy Notice in place, and it's vital to get it right.

REMEMBER

You do not need to provide a Privacy Notice relating to personal data you are acting as a data processor in relation to, but as a data processor, you will also be a data controller in relation to certain personal data (such as names and emails addresses of your customers) and you will need a Privacy Notice for this personal data.

This chapter will help you understand what you need to include in your Privacy Notice, what to do with the notice, and where you can obtain a template to make this task easy for you.

TIP

A quick word on terminology: Historically, Privacy Notices have been referred to as *Privacy Policies.* The terms are often used interchangeably. However, the purists might make the following distinctions:

>> **Privacy Notice:** This is a document that explains to individuals how their personal data will be used and protected. This is the term I use throughout this chapter.

>> **Privacy Policy:** This is a document that sets out the rules about how an organization will handle the personal data under its control.

Learning the Rationale for a Privacy Notice

One of the principles of GDPR is transparency. What this means is that if you're collecting and using people's data, you have to be open and upfront with people about what you're going to do with their personal data. You inform people of this intent in a document called a *Privacy Notice.*

How you collect personal data — directly or indirectly — from data subjects determines which article (Article 13 or Article 14) of the GDPR specifies what you need to include in the Privacy Notice and when you need to provide the Privacy Notice to the data subject:

>> **Directly:** If you collect personal data directly from data subjects — they input their name and email address into your newsletter sign-up form on your website, for example — look to Article 13 for guidance.

>> **Indirectly:** If you collect personal data indirectly from data subjects — you obtain the data from third parties such as data brokers or from publicly accessible sources such as a telephone book, for example — look to Article 14.

The next two sections look at Article 13 and Article 14 in greater detail.

Privacy Notices where you collect data directly from individuals

Article 13 of the GDPR states that where personal data is collected directly from the data subject, you, as the data controller, shall (at the time the personal data is obtained) provide the data subject with the following information:

>> Your identity and contact details and, where you have one, the identity and contact details of your Representative. (See Chapter 15 for more on whether you need to have a representative.)

>> The contact details of your Data Protection Officer (DPO), if you have one. (See Chapter 15 for more on whether you need to have a DPO.)

>> The purposes of the processing and the legal basis for the processing of the personal data. (See Chapter 3 for more on this topic.)

>> If relying on the legitimate interests ground of processing, a description of the specific legitimate interests that either you have or a third party has. (See Chapter 3 for more on the legitimate-interests ground.)

- The recipients or categories of recipients of the personal data, if any. (See Chapter 7 on data inventories for more on this topic.)

- If you plan on transferring personal data outside of the European Economic Area, provide information about those transfers and the measures you will put in place to ensure your transfers are lawful. (See Chapter 6 for more on international transfers.)

- How long you will keep the data for or, if this isn't possible, the criteria you use to decide that period.

- The rights that individuals have to request access to, correction, deletion, or restriction of their personal data, or to object to processing. (See Chapter 14 for more on data subject rights.)

- Where the processing is based on consent, the existence of the right to withdraw consent at any time without affecting the lawfulness of processing based on consent before its withdrawal.

- The right to lodge a complaint with a supervisory authority.

- Whether the data subject is obliged to provide the data as a result of a statutory or contractual requirement and of the possible consequences of failure to provide such data.

- Whether automated decision-making, including profiling, is being used. If so, meaningful information about the logic involved, as well as the significance and the envisaged consequences of such processing for the data subject, must be provided. (See Chapter 14 for more on automated decision-making.)

If you, as the data controller, intend to further process the personal data for a purpose other than that for which the personal data was collected, you have to provide the data subject with information about that other purpose *before* the further processing takes place. See Chapter 3 for more on processing for other purposes.

REMEMBER

You don't have to provide this information to the data subjects if they already have the information. For example, if a prospect was provided with your Privacy Notice when he signed up for your newsletter, you don't need to send him the Privacy Notice again when he provides more personal data while becoming a customer.

Privacy Notices where you collect data from a third party or publicly available source

Where you haven't collected personal data directly from the data subject but instead have obtained it from a third party or a publicly available source (such as an online directory, a corporate website or a social media page), you must provide the relevant information by the earlier of:

>> One month of collection

>> The date on which you use the personal data to contact the data subject for the first time

>> The date on which you disclose the personal data to a third-party recipient

The relevant information to be provided in the Privacy Notice includes all of what is required under Article 13, together with these two items:

>> The categories of personal data

>> Information about where you obtained the personal data from, including — if applicable — whether you obtained it from publicly accessible sources

TIP

Where it is impossible to name the specific sources of the personal data (because different pieces of data relating to the data subject cannot be attributed to a particular source, for example), you should provide general information to the data subject about the nature of the sources (publicly/privately held sources, in other words) and the types of organization/industry/sector they are in.

You, as the data controller, don't have to provide this information if any of these conditions is true:

>> **The data subject already has the information.**

REMEMBER

The data subject already has the information from *you* about how *you* will process the data. If a third party passed data to you, for instance, this is not the information it may have provided to the data subject about how it would process the data and you will need to provide your own Privacy Notice to the data subject.

>> **The provision of the information proves impossible or would involve a disproportionate effort.**

This might be the case where processing is carried out for archiving purposes in the public interest or for scientific, historical research, or statistical research purposes. You must still take appropriate safeguards to protect the data.

>> **Where the personal data must remain confidential, subject to an obligation of professional secrecy regulated by law.**

WARNING

In reality, relying on any of these exemptions, other than where the data subject already has the information from you, is difficult. You should expect to have to provide this information.

Creating Your Privacy Notice

Your Privacy Notice must be as user friendly and as understandable to the data subject as possible — often a difficult task when including detailed information and references to complex legislation.

Supervisory authorities encourage you to use the following elements — perhaps with icons to draw attention — to communicate your Privacy Notice to data subjects:

>> **Layered Privacy Notice:** This layout makes the text easier to read and understand by "chunking" the text under text underneath collapsible headings that can be expanded to reveal more information, as shown in Figure 8-1. The text of a section is hidden until you expand it by clicking the plus sign (+). This makes the Privacy Notice easier to navigate and to read because the user doesn't encounter a lengthy, plain text document.

1. Introduction	+
2. What is The John Lewis Partnership?	+
3. Explaining the legal bases we rely on	+
4. When do we collect your personal data?	+
5. What sort of personal data do we collect?	+
6. How and why do we use your personal data?	+
7. Combining your data for personalised direct marketing	×

We want to bring you offers and promotions that are most relevant to your interests at particular times. To help us form a better, overall understanding of you as a customer, we combine your personal data gathered across the Partnership as described above, for example your shopping history at both John Lewis & Partners and Waitrose & Partners. For this purpose we also combine the data that we collect directly from you with data that we obtain from third parties to whom you have given your consent to pass that data onto us – such as the Land Registry mentioned above.

8. How we protect your personal data	+
9. How long will we keep your personal data?	+
10. Who do we share your personal data with?	+
11. Where your personal data may be processed	+

FIGURE 8-1:
Users can more easily navigate a layered Privacy Notice.

>> **Privacy dashboard:** A dashboard gives data subjects control over certain privacy settings and can be used to allow them to provide (and withdraw) consent, as shown in Figure 8-2. You should provide links to the Privacy Notice from each of the various preferences to explain how the data would be processed.

Browsing history

If browsing history in Cortana is turned on, your Microsoft Edge browsing history is sent to Microsoft so that Microsoft features and services may use this data to provide you with timely and intelligent answers and proactive personalised suggestions, or to complete tasks for you.

In addition to the browsing history saved here, Microsoft Edge also saves your browsing history on your device. To clear that data, on your device, go to **Microsoft Edge > More ⋯ > Settings**.

When you use InPrivate tabs or windows, your browsing data (like your history, temporary Internet files and cookies) isn't saved on your device once you've finished. Learn more about InPrivate Browsing

VIEW AND CLEAR BROWSING HISTORY >

Search history

Like other search engines, Bing uses your search history to give you better results, including personalisation and autosuggest. Cortana also uses that data to give you timely, intelligent answers and personalised suggestions, and complete other tasks for you.

View and change your search settings

Learn more about InPrivate Browsing

VIEW AND CLEAR SEARCH HISTORY >

☐ Feedback

FIGURE 8-2: Microsoft's privacy dashboard is accessible after logging in.

>> **Video:** A short video clip can be an effective and appropriate way to communicate your Privacy Notice to data subjects. You can view a great example of a video Privacy Notice, prepared by *The Guardian* (a daily newspaper in the UK), at `https://youtu.be/_nUVk1dFsmo`.

>> **Just-in-time notice:** This box on your website pops up at the point where a data subject provides personal data. The notice, as shown in Figure 8-3, gives brief details of how the data is used and provides a link to the full Privacy Notice.

REMEMBER

Often, the technology required for the items in this list — the time and cost of producing videos, for instance — acts as a barrier to small businesses producing Privacy Notices along these lines. That means small businesses get by with having a web page with a Privacy Notice in normal text, without any layering, dashboard, or video — and that's fine. The fact that you don't have all the bells and whistles doesn't mean you won't be compliant.

FIGURE 8-3:
A just-in-time notice.

When it comes to just-in-time notices, however, suppose that you're collecting personal data via your website (for example, through a customer support enquiry) and you decide to obtain consent by virtue of a tick box because you are also going to use their data to send them a newsletter. In this case, you need a technical solution to obtain that tick and keep a record of that consent. Fortunately, affordable solutions do exist, such as Lead Pages, Optimizepress, Click Funnels, Mailchimp, and Aweber, to name but a few.

TIP

Some organizations may think it appropriate to add this wording below the sign-up box: "We will never share your information with third parties." It's likely that this isn't an accurate reflection, because the vast majority of businesses, no matter their size, *will* share certain data with third party data processors, such as cloud service providers or email service providers. What they likely mean, however, is that they won't share your data with third parties so that those third parties can spam you. You might use this wording instead: "We will never sell your data to third parties."

WARNING

You might be tempted to copy another business's Privacy Notice to save time and money. However, I advise against doing this, for these three reasons:

>> **No two businesses' use of personal data will be the same.** If you copy the Privacy Notice of another business, you won't reflect the true data flows and true position about the way you protect personal data within your business. You need to carry out your own data inventory (see Chapter 7) and ensure that all that information is properly reflected in your Privacy Notice.

>> **Copying another business's notice may infringe on its intellectual property rights (or those of the lawyer/attorney who drafted it).** This could result in a claim being brought against you.

>> **Paying pure lip service to data protection and not putting it at the heart of your business will be looked on unfavorably by any supervisory authority.** If, during an audit or in the course of investigating a complaint, a supervisory authority sees that you have merely copied a Privacy Notice from another business, it may take enforcement measures against you, such as by serving an enforcement notice or issuing a fine. See Chapter 21 for more on sanctions.

Enforcement notices are made public. Even though you may not be fined, this can still potentially have a negative impact on your reputation when your customers discover it — or when your competitors advertise it for you.

Communicating Your Privacy Notice

If you're collecting personal data directly from the data subject, the information included in the Privacy Notice must be provided at the point of collection of the data.

It's a common misconception that you need people to "agree" or "consent" to your Privacy Notice: That is not the case. Consent is just one of the lawful grounds of processing personal data (which I discuss in Chapter 3). Asking for consent to the whole Privacy Notice will not be "informed consent" (as discussed in Chapter 3) and therefore will be invalid. You merely need to advise people of what's in your Privacy Notice, not obtain their consent or their agreement to it.

You'll need a separate Privacy Notice for employees, which is typically provided directly to them rather than on your website. See Chapter 13 for more on this topic.

Communicating via email

If you haven't obtained the personal data directly from the data subject — maybe you obtained it from an online business directory, for example — you must link to your Privacy Notice in the first email that you send them.

You should check that you are legally allowed to email such data subjects without their consent. (See Chapter 19 for more on this.)

Even though you may have already provided your Privacy Notice to data subjects at the time that they provided you with their data, it is a good idea to include a link to your Privacy Notice in the footer of each email you send.

Communicating via your website

If you have a website, it's the obvious place for you to display your Privacy Notice. Typically, you do so with a link to the Privacy Notice in the footer of each page of your website, as shown in Figure 8-4. I recommend providing this link at all points where you collect personal data, such as a newsletter sign-up box or your contact form.

FIGURE 8-4:
Link to your
Privacy Notice in
the website's
footer.

Alumni   Contact Us   Cookie Policy   Corporate Responsibility   Legal Notices   Privacy Policy   Slavery And Human Trafficking Statement

Communicating over the phone

If you're collecting personal data over the phone, you should refer people to your Privacy Notice. Typically, this is done before the call is started, with a recorded message that's delivered during a holding period. You can provide brief details of the most important parts of the Privacy Notice, such as the right to opt out of marketing communications, and then refer callers to your website for the full Privacy Notice.

Communicating in person

If you collect personal data in person (for example, in your store or at an event), you should make the Privacy Notice available at this point. It's sufficient to have a sign with brief details of the Privacy Notice and a link that refers people to the Privacy Notice on your website. You could also keep a printed copy of the Privacy Notice behind the counter, in case people want to read it because they can't access the website.

TIP

If you collect business cards at a networking event, perhaps by way of a prize drawing to garner more cards, you must post a sign with brief details of the Privacy Notice and a link that refers people to the Privacy Notice on your website. Again, consider having the full Privacy Notice in hard copy so that people who can't access the version on your website can review it if they want.

You can, in theory, provide all of your Privacy Notice orally. To include all the information set out in the GDPR, however, you would be speaking for a long time. And, you would need to keep a record of having provided the requisite information (and of any relevant consents provided to you orally).

The Consequences of Not Having an Appropriate Privacy Notice

Putting a Privacy Notice in place is one of your main compliance obligations under the GDPR. Not doing it properly isn't worth the consequences you might face. If you fail to put in place a Privacy Notice that includes all matters set out by Article 13 (or Article 14, as the case may be), a fine is only one potential negative outcome. This list describes fines and a few other outcomes:

>> **Fine:** You can be fined up to 20 million euros or 4 percent of your global turnover for the preceding financial year, whichever is higher. This is not to say that you *will* be fined that amount, but you could be liable up to that amount. The fine is ultimately determined by all the relevant circumstances. (See Chapter 21 for more on what supervisory authorities consider when deciding an appropriate fine.)

>> **Enforcement notice:** In addition to paying a fine, you could be served an enforcement notice, requiring you to put a compliant Privacy Notice in place within a certain period.

>> **Damaged reputation:** You risk suffering a negative impact on your business's reputation or operations by not having a Privacy Notice:

- Typically, enforcement notices are made public and often reported on by the media, which can have an adverse impact on your reputation and the trust that customers and prospects have in you.

- Savvy customers will notice if you fail to have a Privacy Notice on your website or if it isn't updated for the GDPR, which can decrease the trust they have in you.

- Competitors may decide to report you to the relevant data protection authorities, in the hope of causing you wasted management time and expense from having to deal with a regulatory investigation.

TIP

Implementing a Privacy Notice doesn't have to be a difficult or costly exercise. Yes, you do have to carry out your data inventory first (see Chapter 7 for more on this topic), but when that task is complete, it will be easy to use that data inventory and a template to create your Privacy Notice. Of course, you could also ask your lawyer to draft a Privacy Notice for you, but using a template will keep costs down. Using one that includes guidance notes on this complex document will be the most useful to you. You can obtain a Privacy Notice template with guidance at www.suzannedibble.com/gdprpack, which makes putting a Privacy Notice in place as pain-free as possible.

Chapter **9**

Cookie Policy

I n this chapter, I help you explore why you need a Cookie Policy and what needs to be in it. Cookies are relevant under the GDPR because *cookies* — small text files delivered to and stored on a visitor's computer or smartphone via websites they're browsing — can be used to identify a unique device, and the data is used to form a profile of browsing habits that can be linked to a specific individual.

REMEMBER

Although I talk mainly about cookies in this chapter, the rules apply to any information collected from a device, including mobile advertising identifiers collected by mobile apps.

The main legislation that governs cookie use in the European Union is the Privacy and Electronic Communications Directive 2002/58/EC, otherwise known as the ePrivacy Directive. This Directive has been implemented into each EU member state's national law. At the time of this book being published, amendments to this Directive are being negotiated between the European Parliament, the European Commission, and the European Council.

The ePrivacy Directive (as implemented into individual EU member state law) only applies to organizations established in that EU member state. However, one change that will definitely take effect is that the new ePrivacy Directive will expand the territorial scope of "the cookie law" to have worldwide reach, in the same way that the GDPR does. In summary, if the GDPR applies to your business, even if you're established outside of the European Union, the new ePrivacy Directive will also apply to you. See Appendix A for more on this topic.

Defining Cookies

As I mention at the beginning of this chapter, a *cookie* is a small text file delivered via a website you're browsing, which is then stored on your computer by your browser. In simple terms, the purpose of the cookie is to identify you as a website user on your computer. The next time you visit that website, it can access that information and recognize you as a returning visitor to the website.

Not all cookies are created equal, as you can see from Table 9-1, which explains the different types. Some cookies enable organizations to track your behavior on your browser, for example, so that they can target you for more relevant online advertising. Others are used to remember your website preferences (such as your language choices) or login details, enabling you to use and log in to that site easier.

TABLE 9-1 **Cookie Types**

Type	Description	Example
Essential	Provides the information requested by the website user	A cookie for a website shopping cart so that the website remembers your order at the checkout page
Non-essential	Any cookie that is not an essential cookie	Includes cookies for analytics purposes, for behavioral tracking, and for making logins easier ***
Session	Typically deleted when you close your browser; also known as in-memory, transient, or nonpersistent	A shopping cart on an e-commerce site that remembers the products or services you add to the cart, which remain when you load a new page
Persistent	Remains on your computer but expires on a specific date or after a set period	Tracks your behavior online so that advertisers can send targeted ads; also used for keeping you logged in to accounts
Secure	Can be transmitted only by way of an encrypted connection (such as https), making the cookie less vulnerable to being hacked	Cookies that collect special category data, such as where the browsing of health websites is being tracked, should be especially concerned to ensure that the cookie is secure
Functional	Helps to personalize your browsing experience	Remembers your choice of playlists and favorite content to help you find new content

Type	Description	Example
First-party	When the cookie is issued by the website that a user views directly, such as where a cookie set by ico.org.uk is saved onto the hardware of a browser of the ICO website	On an e-commerce website, facilitates logins to that site or for the advertising purposes of that website
Third-party	When the cookie has a different domain from the site you're browsing, such as where an adtech company serves a cookie to you when you are browsing a golfing website	Used by advertisers to track you across multiple websites*
Authentication	Verifies you are who you say you are	When you're using an API (an *application programming interface* that allows one system to talk to another)
Tracking	A third-party, persistent cookie that tracks your browsing behavior over a certain period.	Used by advertisers to send you targeted advertising**

* Third-party cookies are typically served when the page you're browsing has banner advertisements for organizations other than the organization whose website you're browsing. Some modern browsers contain privacy settings that let website users block third-party cookies.

** If you've ever clicked a link for a product on your favorite news site, only to see an ad for an identical product when you move on to Facebook or another website, you've picked up a tracking cookie by clicking a product link on the news site.

*** The ICO guidance is that analytics cookies are non-essential and consent is required. However CNIL, the French supervisory authority, has released guidance to say that in certain circumstances the use of analytics cookies will not require consent — for more details see https://www.cnil.fr/en/cookies-and-other-tracking-devices-cnil-publishes-new-guidelines.

Understanding the Rationale for a Cookie Policy

Many online users aren't aware that cookies are often used to track their behavior across different websites: They're delivered to a user's computer often without the user knowing and can be used to record the user's online habits, also without the user's knowledge.

The ePrivacy Directive requires websites to inform users about the cookies they use and to obtaining the user's consent before serving non-essential cookies to them. The precise method of obtaining consent is not specified in the ePrivacy Directive, but consent must be obtained to a GDPR standard — meaning it must be freely given, specific, informed, and unambiguous.

In addition to the ePrivacy Directive, the GDPR can also apply to data collected through cookies. This is because the data in cookies may also identify individuals and therefore qualify as "personal data" within the scope of the GDPR. Recital 30 of the GDPR says:

"Natural persons may be associated with online identifiers such as Internet protocol addresses, cookie identifiers or other identifiers. This may leave traces which, in particular when combined with unique identifiers and other information received by the servers, may be used to create profiles of the natural persons and identify them."

When cookies can identify an individual via the person's laptop or mobile phone or another device, the cookie data constitutes personal data, and the use of such cookies (or other identifiers) is within the scope of the GDPR.

Not all cookies are used in ways that will identify individuals, but many are: especially cookies that are used for analytics and advertising purposes, and cookies used to remember user preferences (such as enabling an easier log in by autocompleting log-in fields).

Lawful grounds for processing personal data obtained from cookies

If you're using cookies in ways that can identify an individual, under the GDPR you must also have lawful grounds for processing them.

The most likely grounds for processing personal data obtained through the use of cookies are consent and legitimate interests.

If consent is required for the use of cookies because the ePrivacy Directive applies to you, you will also require consent to process the personal data obtained through cookies under the GDPR. However, if the ePrivacy Directive does not apply to you, you may be able to use legitimate interests as a lawful ground to process personal data identified through cookies for the near future. (See Chapter 3 for more about the lawful grounds of processing and Appendix A for upcoming changes to the ePrivacy Directive.)

When you need consent, whether under the ePrivacy Directive, the GDPR, or both, then it must be prior consent. This means it should be obtained before cookies are *fired* (distributed to a user's computer) by your website. However, a large proportion of websites fire cookies immediately after a user lands on a website — before obtaining consent is possible, in other words. This is not compliant.

The ICO guidance on the use of cookies states that it may be possible to rely on a different lawful ground of processing for subsequent processing beyond the setting of cookies, but not for the following activities, where consent will always be the appropriate ground of processing:

>> Analyzing or predicting preferences or behavior or attitudes of individuals where this information subsequently is used to make decisions or take measures related to such individuals.

>> Tracking and profiling for direct marketing and advertising.

If the cookie data is anonymous, the GDPR doesn't apply to such cookies, but the ePrivacy Directive applies to all cookies, even when the cookie data is anonymous. This means that you may still need consent under the ePrivacy Directive, even where the GDPR does not apply.

Creating and Communicating Your Cookie Policy

As you saw above, the function of your Cookie Policy is to provide clear and comprehensive information to your website users about the cookies you're using and what type of cookies they are (functional or session, for example).

Assessing your cookies

To create your Cookie Policy, you need to know what cookies you're using on your website and what their purpose is. A small-business owner may not know the answer, especially if a website developer set up the website.

If you don't know what cookies are on your website and what they're for, ask your web developer or use a cookie audit tool, such as cookiechecker www.cookie-checker.com/. Ghostery is another tool that can help with this — it is a free browser plug-in that also categorizes the cookies, such as advertising, analytics, and the like. For other options, search the Internet using the term "**tool to show cookies on websites**". Resources such as cookiepedia can also be helpful to find out more about what different types of cookies do.

In order to write your Cookie Policy, you need to know:

>> What types of cookies are being used

>> What the cookie is used for

>> How long the cookie lasts (for example, is it a session cookie that only lasts for the browsing session or a persistent cookie that lasts beyond the session and if so what is the expiry date)

>> Who serves the cookie — is it a first-party or third-party cookie and if it is a third party cookie, who serves it

>> How to refuse the cookie at a later date

In addition, when you have the list of cookies your website uses, assess how *intrusive* the cookies are — how they follow users about for their online browsing, in other words. First party cookies such as shopping cart cookies are less intrusive, for example, than third-party persistent tracking cookies, which monitor your website users' online behavior on a long-term basis. If you're using more intrusive cookies, obtaining informed consent for the use of those cookies is all the more important for you.

The ICO guidance on the use of cookies is that "you should take particular care to ensure clear and specific consent for more privacy-intrusive cookies, such as those collecting sensitive personal data such as health details, or used for behavioural tracking."

Digital agencies and website publishers should take particular care when using cookies for Real Time Bidding (RTB). RTB is a system used by ad exchanges to broadcast the personal data (often of a sensitive nature) of the individual browsing the website or using the app to thousands of organizations in order to solicit potential advertisers' bids to deliver their ads on the website or app.

The ICO's investigations into RTB have found that, in the vast majority of cases, cookies used for RTB do not comply with the ePrivacy Directive and the GDPR. The ICO highlighted the following deficiencies:

>> Insufficient information provided to the data subject about the processing

>> Data subject consent not obtained for the processing of non-special category data and instead relying on legitimate interests

>> Explicit consent from the data subject not obtained for special category data (such as tracking online browsing about religious or health content)

>> Failing to carry out a Data Protection Impact Assessment (DPIA) (See Chapter 15 for more on this topic.)

>> Sharing with large numbers of third parties the detailed profiles of individuals without their knowledge

The ICO is continuing to investigate the situation and may carry out sweeps of the adtech industry. It will issue a further report in 2020.

The French supervisory authority, CNIL, issued an enforcement notice in October 2018 to a French digital agency called Vectaury that had obtained personal data for hundreds of millions of people from the RTB system. The enforcement notice required Vectaury to cease processing geolocation data for advertising purposes without an appropriate lawful grounds for processing. CNIL stated that "it is clear that Vectaury is unable to demonstrate that the data currently collected through real time bid requests are subject to informed, free, specific, and unambiguous consent." Vectaury was non-compliant in:

>> Bundling together a number of separate processing purposes under a single opt in

>> Not checking that consent had actually been obtained from the individual and only relying on contractual clauses to this effect

>> Using misleading and vague language on the first consent screen

>> Using pre-ticked boxes for consent

It is worth noting that Vectaury believed it was following the IAB framework (see glossary), something that the IAB disputes by pointing out that Vectaury did not follow its policies correctly.

However, in practical terms, for the majority of data controllers, the most important assessment is whether the cookie is "strictly necessary" or not. If it is strictly necessary, the cookie is exempt from consent. If the cookie is not strictly necessary, consent from the web user is required.

TIP

You can also take this opportunity of auditing the cookies used on your website to tidy up your use of cookies and delete any you don't really need.

Writing your Cookie Policy

In Chapter 8, I discuss how the GDPR requires data controllers to provide certain information to data subjects — via the Privacy Notice — about how they process personal data. You can provide information about cookies in your Privacy Notice. However, data controllers commonly have a separate Cookie Policy that specifies which cookies they're using.

The requirement to provide certain information about the cookies you use on your site comes mainly from the current ePrivacy Directive. To comply with this Directive, you must explain what the cookies are being used for and obtain the user's consent to store a cookie on the device.

The obligation under the ePrivacy Directive to obtain consent is only in relation to non-essential cookies. However, you should provide information for all cookies used, both essential and non-essential.

Neither the GDPR nor the ePrivacy Directive specifies the information that needs to be contained in the Cookie Policy. However, you should include, as a minimum, the following information you learned from your cookie assessment:

>> What types of cookies are used (such as advertising or analytics)

>> Who sets the cookie

>> How a user can refuse the cookie

According to the ePrivacy Directive, the language in your policy must be clear and comprehensive. The UK's supervisory authority, the ICO, says this means the "text should be sufficiently full and intelligible to allow individuals to clearly understand the potential consequences of allowing the cookies should they wish to do so." In other words, make sure users understand what the cookies do and what that means for them — for example, their browsing and shopping habits will be tracked, and they'll see ads that reflect the tracking.

The ICO guidance also states that you must consider the general levels of understanding that website users hold about cookies. The understanding is still pretty low, so the Cookie Policy needs to be easy to understand — especially for people who have no technical background. Therefore, listing the types of cookies your website uses isn't enough; you need to fully explain what each type of cookie is used for and how that affects the user.

When using a banner or pop-up to link to provide the requisite information and to gain consent, consider the user experience. Many users find pop-ups annoying and even confusing, so you may want to use them sparingly, if at all, or as unobtrusively as possible. See the next section for more about ways to communicate your Cookie Policy to users.

Posting your Cookie Policy

You can choose to have a straightforward Cookie Policy on a web page on your website with a prominent link to it on each page of your website (through a banner or pop-up on your website, for example) or you can use a more sophisticated tool to show the Cookie Policy and obtain the necessary consent (see the section below for potential tools).

If the link to the Cookie Policy is in a banner that shows at the top or bottom of the web page, it must be easily viewable and above the *fold* (the section of the website page users can see without scrolling down).

Many websites merely have a link to a Cookie Policy that is just a plain link in the footer of each page of the website (without a banner or a pop-up). This isn't likely to be prominent enough to be compliant.

In addition to the Cookie Policy, you need a separate cookie consent statement — either in a separately displayed cookie banner or a cookie pop up — that links back to the cookie notice, with a call to action to provide consent, such as "Accept cookies" and "Reject cookies" buttons.

The ICO guidance on the use of cookies states that:

>> Rather than just have a link that states "Cookie Policy," you should make it clearer what the link is about by using words such as "Find out more about how our site works and how we put you in control."

>> You must **not** have boxes that emphasize 'agree' or 'allow' (or presumably 'accept') cookies, as opposed to 'block' or 'reject' cookies, as this influences website users to consent to the use of cookies. There must be an option of similarly prominent boxes of accept and reject.

>> The initial consent mechanism you use when people land on your landing page of your website must allow the user to make a choice about whether to accept the use of cookies or not; merely having a 'more information' section where controls are located would not suffice.

Figure 9-1 shows an example of how a banner might display a link to a Cookie Policy. The banner pops out at the left side of the web page and provides a link that users can click to read more about the website's cookies.

WARNING

Consent under the GDPR must *not* be *opt-out* consent, where you must take some action — click a button or select a check box — in order to block cookies. The GDPR insists on *opt-in* consent, where the user must take affirmative action in order to allow cookies. As such, cookie policies that state that by continuing to browse the website, the user consents to the use of cookies, will not be compliant.

FIGURE 9-1:
The ICO's
cookie banner.

Cookie walls

Equally, the GDPR prohibits you from making consent a requirement of the service, so in stating that, in order to continue browsing, the website user has to accept cookies (known as a *cookie wall*), this would also be in breach of the GDPR.

The Dutch supervisory authority issued guidance that cookie walls are not compliant with the GDPR. It stated that it had increased monitoring of organizations using cookie walls and was instructing them to make the necessary changes to ensure GDPR compliance.

The ICO guidance is a little more permissive when it comes to cookie walls. The ICO refers to Recital 25 of the ePrivacy Directive that states that "access to specific website content may be made conditional on the well-informed acceptance of a cookie or similar device, if it is used for a legitimate purpose." The ICO's guidance is therefore that cookie walls are not permitted for 'general access' to websites but that it is possible to restrict certain content if the user does not consent to the use of cookies. However, the ICO does go on to say that if the use of a cookie wall is "intended to require or influence users to agree to their personal data being used by [the data controller] or any third party as a condition of accessing your service, then it is unlikely that user consent is considered valid."

The ICO also notes, in a blog post published by it on the same day as their guidance on cookie walls, that "we recognize there are some differing opinions as well as practical considerations around the use of partial cookie walls and we will be seeking further submissions and opinions on this point from interested parties."

The Austrian supervisory authority, however, rejected a complaint that consent obtained through a cookie wall of an online newspaper was not freely given. The newspaper had provided a free online version of the newspaper and also a subscription version without advertising. It only allowed users of the free version to have access if they accepted cookies for advertising purposes.

The European Data Protection Board is advocating for a complete ban on the use of any cookie walls as part of the amendments to the ePrivacy Directive. So, we may only receive clarity on the matter of cookie walls when the new ePrivacy regulations come into force. See Appendix A for more on this.

To ensure full compliance, you need a tool (discussed in the next section) that shows — before the cookies are fired — the cookies used on your site and allows website users to make granular choices regarding which cookies they're happy to accept.

Using tools to communicate your Cookie Policy and obtain consent

Some existing tools can enable you to be compliant to lesser or greater degrees. One such tool, Cookiebot, enables you to show the different types of cookies you use on your website and provides the website user with the option to continue to browse the website while using only necessary cookies (for which consent isn't required). Cookiebot also appears to have the ability to prevent cookies from firing until consent is obtained, though you do have to add certain code to your other plug-ins. (Check out Cookiebot's website at www.cookiebot.com for more information.)

Figure 9-2 shows the Cookiebot banner, which you can place at the top or bottom of your website.

FIGURE 9-2:
Cookiebot gives users a simple choice.

Users can click the Show Details tab to see the additional information shown in Figure 9-3. Clicking the About Cookies tab shows more information about the different types of cookies — for example, cookies for statistics or marketing.

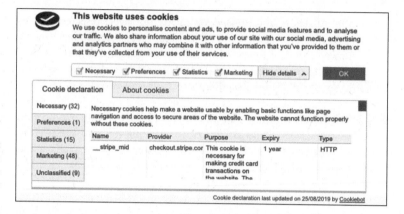

With Cookiebot, users cannot accept and refuse individual cookies; rather, the choice is simply between Preferences, Statistics, and Marketing. With other, more expensive GDPR solutions, such as One Trust (www.onetrust.com), you can allow your website users to make more granular choices about which cookies they're happy to consent to.

Another affordable WordPress plug-in that can be used to prevent cookies firing prior to consent being obtained (without having to add any code) can be found at https://wowq.io/gdpr-for-dummies. This plug-in also enables data subjects to access basic personal data about themselves (and update it), satisfying Recital 63 that states that best practice is for organizations to provide remote access to a secure self-service system where the data subject can have direct access to his or her personal data. In addition, the plug-in provides a Privacy Policy and Cookie Policy generator that automatically updates on your site for new guidance or amendments to regulations.

Looking into the Future of Cookies

The European Data Protection Board is determined to make amendments to the ePrivacy Directive that would end the under-the-radar surveillance that is carried on by tracking cookies. There has been fierce lobbying by affected industries who fear that any restriction on tracking cookies will have a significant effect on their profitability.

At the time of publishing this book, the amendments to the ePrivacy Directive are still being negotiated between the European Parliament, the European Council, and the European Commission and it will be very interesting to see where we end up on the issue of cookies.

For more on the proposed amendments, see Appendix A.

Sanctions for Not Having an Appropriate Cookie Policy

The current maximum fines for failing to comply with the cookie provisions established by the ePrivacy Directive are lower than for the GDPR (for example, the maximum fine is £500,000 in the UK), although this will increase to reflect GDPR fines when the ePrivacy regulations come into in force. (See Appendix A for more on this.)

If the cookie is processing personal data and the GDPR applies to that processing, then not providing the relevant information (within either the Privacy Notice or the Cookie Policy) is in breach of GDPR's Article 13 — namely, the obligation to provide the requisite information to data subjects.

Failing to obtain prior unambiguous consent to cookies that process personal data could also mean that you are processing data unlawfully, unless you are able to rely on an alternative lawful grounds for processing.

The maximum fine for such breaches is €20m or up to 4 percent of the total worldwide annual turnover of the preceding financial year, whichever is higher.

Google was fined €50m by the French supervisory authority for failing to obtain valid consent and not being sufficiently transparent about its processing of personal data. CNIL stated that "the processing operations are particularly massive and intrusive because of the number of services offered (about 20) and the nature of the data processed and combined."

In practice, the fine for not providing a Cookie Policy or not obtaining consent is likely to be significantly lower than the maximum fine. No fines had been issued at the time this book was published, although the Bavarian supervisory authority has been carrying out "cookie sweeps" and is currently considering fines.

Chapter **10**

Drafting Data Processing and Data Sharing Agreements

When transfers of personal data are made between organizations — from data controller to data processor, from joint controller to joint controller, or from data controller to data controller — certain safeguards need to be put in place to ensure that the recipient organization protects the personal data disclosed to it as required by the GDPR. This chapter looks at the arrangements that must be in place before making such transfers.

I cover the concept of *data processors* in Chapter 5. The GDPR requires that you, as a data controller, enter into a written agreement (a *Data Processing Agreement*) containing the mandatory provisions set out in Article 28 of the GDPR with each of your data processors. I discuss those requirements here.

Chapter 5 also covers the concept of *joint controllers*. The GDPR sets out certain matters that must be agreed on between the joint controllers and communicated to the data subjects. I also discuss those matters here.

Finally, when transfers of personal data are made from one data controller to other data controller(s) who are not joint controllers, the transferring data controller must consider a number of matters before the transfer and potentially specific codes of practice (as instigated in specific jurisdictions) to follow. Although it is not mandatory for an agreement to be in place between a data controller and another data controller to whom it has transferred data (whether in writing or not), it is considered good practice to do so and helps to demonstrate accountability.

REMEMBER

The need to put certain documentation in place applies whether the recipient to whom you have transferred the personal data is established within the EU or outside of the EU. Obviously, if the organization receiving the data is based outside the EU, additional safeguards for that international transfer must be in place, as explained in Chapter 6.

Understanding Data Processing Agreements

Prior to the GDPR coming into force, data controllers already had an obligation to put in place a written agreement with their data processors. This agreement, however, only needed to require the data processor to process personal data in accordance with the data controller's instructions and to ensure the security of the data that it processed.

The GDPR has significantly extended the terms that need to be included in Data Processing Agreements between data controllers and data processors.

What to include in the Data Processing Agreement

Article 28 of the GDPR sets out these required matters, which must be included in any Data Processing Agreement. These include:

>> **What processing will take place:** Storing databases of client details and sending marketing emails on behalf of the data controller, for example

>> **Who the data subjects are:** Customers or employees, for example

>> **The types of data that will be processed:** Client names, addresses, and phone numbers, for example

- **Whether the data includes any special categories of data:** Medical details, ethnicity, or political views, for example
- **How long the processing will continue:** For as long as the service agreement between the data controller and the data processor is in force or for a more specified period, for example

Article 28 also prescribes certain obligations on the data processor, which must be included in any Data Processing Agreement:

- To only act on the data controller's *documented* instructions (unless required by law to act outside of the data controller's instructions)
- To impose confidentiality obligations on anyone authorized to process the relevant data (for example, by ensuring staff have signed confidentiality agreements, or are otherwise under a statutory duty of confidence)
- To ensure the security of the personal data that it processes in accordance with Article 32 of the GDPR (as spelled out in Chapter 16)
- To obtain consent from the data controller for any subprocessor appointments and to flow down the same data protection terms to the subprocessor (see below and Chapter 5 for more on subprocessors)
- To implement technical and organizational measures to assist the data controller in complying with the rights of data subjects
- To notify any data breaches suffered to the data controller, and to support it in carrying out any necessary Data Protection Impact Assessments (DPIAs) or consultations with supervisory authorities (see Chapter 15 for more on DPIAs)
- To either return or destroy, at the data controller's election, the personal data at the end of the relationship between the data controller and the data processor (except as required by law)
- To provide the data controller with all information necessary to demonstrate compliance with the GDPR and to allow for and to contribute to audits by the data controller or its agents

The following rules apply to the appointment of subprocessors:

- The data processor must enter into, with each subprocessor, a written agreement that contains the same data protection obligations as specified in the contract between the data controller and the data processor.
- If the subprocessor fails to meet its data protection obligations, the data processor who appointed the subprocessor remains liable to the data controller for the actions of the subprocessor.

These are the mandatory terms for inclusion in a Data Processing Agreement. In reality, further terms — such as warranties, indemnities, and insurance provisions — are likely to be included, depending on the negotiating position of the parties. (More on that topic a little later in this chapter.)

Responsibility for the Data Processing Agreement

The GDPR doesn't clarify whether the responsibility for putting a Data Processing Agreement in place is on the data controller or the data processor.

However, under the GDPR, data controllers may use only data processors who provide sufficient guarantees that they meet the requirements of the GDPR. Such guarantees are usually provided, at least in part, by way of contract (that is, in the Data Processing Agreement) and, as such, if you, as the data controller, do not insist on your data processor's entering into a Data Processing Agreement, you will be in breach of this obligation — and at risk.

The data processor may also be liable for a failure to enter into a Data Processing Agreement. This is particularly likely to be the case where the data processor is a large organization and has refused to sign a Data Processing Agreement provided by the data controller.

A data controller has a difficult decision to make when its data processor doesn't agree to put a Data Processing Agreement in place. The data controller may decide that it's preferable to choose an alternative data processor than to take the risk of continuing to work with the non-compliant data processor. This equally applies to data processors when their data controller customers won't enter into Data Processing Agreements.

Negotiating a Data Processing Agreement

Aside from the Data Processing Agreement containing the mandatory terms required by Article 28 of the GDPR, a data controller also typically wants to include certain other clauses to its benefit. Whether those clauses end up in the Data Processing Agreement ultimately depends on the negotiating power of each party.

With the GDPR introducing significantly increased fines and the chance of civil claims being brought by a data subject, negotiating Data Processing Agreements (particularly in relation to warranties, indemnities, and liability) has become a lot more difficult.

Warranties, indemnities, and liability caps, though not the only matters that are the subject of negotiation in a Data Processing Agreement, are certainly the main areas of contention, and so I discuss them further here. Examples of other areas that are commonly negotiated include the extent of audit rights, the time within which the data processor must notify the data controller of a data breach, and whether the data processor may charge for assisting the data controller in replying to data subject rights.

Warranties and indemnities

A data controller is likely to want certain warranties and indemnities from the data processor and to have these included in the Data Processing Agreement:

>> **A *warranty* is a statement of truth made by a party.** If the statement is proved wrong, the other party can sue over it. Warranties might be about compliance with data protection legislation, for example, or about having certain insurances in place or a number of other matters.

>> **An *indemnity* is the obligation to financially reimburse the other party on a pound-for-pound basis for the loss suffered by the other party.** An indemnity is preferable to a warranty as the indemnified party can request payment on demand rather than having to bring a claim in court for damages for breach of warranty. In addition, often the indemnity will sit outside the liability cap that the warranties are subject to. An indemnity requested by a data controller in the Data Processing Agreement might be for the data processor to reimburse the controller for any loss suffered by the controller as a result of the data processor not complying with its obligations under the Data Processing Agreement or under the GDPR.

Obviously, if you're the data processor, you'll want to resist providing these warranties and indemnities in order to minimize your potential liability. Indemnities will be strongly resisted and tend to create significant negotiating friction, so unless your negotiating position is strong, it may be better to leave them out and rely on warranties.

REMEMBER

Under the GDPR, data controllers can be liable for the actions of their data processors. The appropriate supervisory authorities can also enforce directly against data processors. Whether they would, when considering the amount of a fine to levy against a data controller, consider the role played by the data processor and allocate the level of the fine accordingly is unclear. Only if the data controller is completely fault-free would it escape any liability for the actions of its data processor.

Liability caps

If the data processor agrees to take on certain liability by providing warranties and indemnities in the Data Processing Agreement, it will want to make sure this liability is capped in some way and not unlimited. This may be a difficult negotiation, with the data controller pushing for a liability cap that's as high as possible.

One way of approaching the negotiation is to look at the risks involved. Although, in theory, fines of €20 million or 4 percent of global turnover can be made, in reality, what are the chances of this happening? You, as a data controller, need to look at these factors:

>> **The sensitivity of the data:** The more sensitive, the higher the liability cap.

>> **The type and complexity of the processing:** In particular, whether the processing operations are commoditized (in which case your processor will seek a lower liability cap) or designed specifically for just you (in which case you may be able to argue for a higher cap).

>> **The number of data subjects involved:** The more data subjects involved, the higher the liability cap.

>> **The due diligence already carried out on the processor:** This includes whether any past incidents have occurred, such as data breaches and how advanced their security systems are.

>> **The reputation of the processor**

>> **The history between the data controller and the data processor**

>> **The level and type of insurance in place by the data processor and by the data controller**

>> **Any subprocessors involved, and their reputation and the due diligence carried out on them**

>> **The term of the contract:** The longer the contract, the higher the liability cap over the lifetime of the contract.

>> **The price being paid for the services:** The price may go up if you insist on a high liability cap.

>> **Whether you're prepared to offer a similar liability cap:** The reason is that there may be no good reason for imparity in liability caps.

In high-value, complex transactions, data controllers typically require a higher cap for liabilities for data protection than for the general indemnities under the service agreement (a "super cap" or an "enhanced liability" cap). Data controllers also typically require data loss as a specific *head of loss* (category of loss) under which the data controller can bring a claim against the data processor. Other specific heads of loss include fraud prevention costs and breach notification costs.

Pre-GDPR agreements

If you had Data Processing Agreements in place before the GDPR took effect and you, as a data controller, still have these same agreements in force post-GDPR without amendment, you may want to consider *repapering* these agreements — revisiting and revising them as necessary, in other words.

I recommend doing this at the next point possible for negotiation, which is likely when the contract term renews. Although no industry standard dictates the amount of the liability cap under the GDPR, what is standard is that data controllers are continually renegotiating liability caps in Data Processing Agreements.

Creating a Data Processing Agreement

A contract referred to as a Data Processing Agreement is typically a stand-alone document, but it's also possible for such an agreement to include the mandatory data processing clauses in a wider commercial agreement, such as a services agreement between the data controller and the data processor.

If your data processor is a large organization with very large numbers of customers, such as DropBox or Mailchimp, these organizations will typically prepare their own data processing addendums and incorporate them into the terms you have already agreed to. Addendums are not stand-alone contracts, but documents that are appended to a contract and which are subject to the clauses (such as liability caps) that already exist within the main contract. Typically, this type of addendum is nonnegotiable, and if you don't want to agree to it, you can terminate the service.

When preparing your own Data Processing Agreement, keep these points in mind:

>> **The agreement must be in writing but may be concluded electronically (Article 28 (9) of the GDPR).** Parties may also sign the agreement by hand and then scan and email the signature to the other party. In this case, the related email correspondence must be documented and retained.

>> **The agreement may be drafted in English but translations may be required.** If the data controller or data processor is established in an English-speaking country, or if either belongs to an international group of companies and English has been chosen as the group-wide language, then the Data Processing Agreement should be drafted in the English language. Supervisory authorities in jurisdictions where a data controller or data processor is based may require translations into the local language, if the agreement isn't already in the local language.

>> **Data processors based outside the EU must also have in place safeguards for international transfers.** (See Chapter 6.) One such safeguard involves standard contractual clauses, which look like they contain similar clauses to the mandatory processor terms. They aren't the same, however, and hence a separate Data Processing Agreement must still be entered into (or you can include the mandatory processor clauses under Article 28 in a wider commercial agreement).

>> **Having a lawyer or an attorney draft the agreement is always wise.** This ensures that all mandatory terms are included and that the agreement is to your best possible advantage.

If you don't want to hire someone to draft a customized agreement for you, consider purchasing a template and completing it for your business. My GDPR compliance pack includes a Data Processing Agreement (with guidance notes); see more at www.suzannedibble.com/gdprpack.

Understanding Data Sharing Agreements

If you're sharing data with a joint controller (see Chapter 5 for more on this topic), Article 26 of the GDPR states that there must be an "arrangement" in place between the data controllers.

TIP

Article 26 does not necessarily require a written agreement, but having a written agreement in place to evidence the arrangement is best practice and helps to demonstrate accountability.

Equally, if you, as a data controller, are sharing personal data with another independent data controller (not a joint controller, in other words), I recommend having an agreement in place (particularly where the data sharing is systematic, large-scale, or risky) even though the GDPR doesn't specifically require it. The agreement helps you justify the data sharing and demonstrate that compliance issues have been considered and sets out how the parties agree to solve them.

Article 26 of the GDPR states that the joint controllers shall "in a transparent manner" determine their respective responsibilities for compliance — in particular, in relation to the provision of information to data subjects and the exercise of data subject rights. The exception to this is where EU law or national law of any EU member state sets out the respective responsibilities.

Article 26 goes on to say that the essence of the arrangement shall be made available to data subjects (presumably, in Privacy Notices) and that a contact point may be designated for data subjects. Regardless of the nature of the arrangement and the division of responsibilities between the joint controllers, a data subject may exercise their rights against each of the joint controllers.

Creating a Data Sharing Agreement

A joint controller Data Sharing Agreement is different from a controller-to-controller Data Sharing Agreement.

As a reminder, joint controllers are two or more controllers who together determine the purposes and means of processing — and therefore share the responsibilities of — the data controller. See Chapter 5 for more on this.

What I refer to as an independent controller is a controller that is not a joint controller.

Accurately assessing whether you're transferring data to a processor, a joint controller, or another independent controller is vital because the type of agreement you must put in place will differ, depending on the nature of the other party. If in doubt, take legal advice.

For a joint controller Data Sharing Agreement, you need to include these two elements:

>> **Matters prescribed in Article 26 of the GDPR:** Namely, this is to specify each party's responsibilities for compliance with the GDPR (particularly with regard to information rights under Article 13 and 14 and the exercise of data subject rights).

>> **A designated contact point:** You may want to consider designating a contact point for data subjects, and to include the points specified for a controller-to-controller Data Sharing Agreement.

For both joint controller and controller-to-controller Data Sharing Agreements, although not legally required, it would be good practice to include these elements, too:

>> An obligation on each party to comply with data protection legislation (not just the GDPR but any applicable data protection legislation)

- A description of the data that's being shared and whether it's special category data

- An obligation on each party to provide assistance to the other in the event of a data subject exercising their rights

- Provisions for data retention

- Provisions about onward transfers of the data to a third party

- A description of the security that's in place to protect the data

- An obligation to inform the other party of any data breach

- Agreement on how to deal with any investigation by a supervisory authority

- A mutual indemnity for each party to reimburse the other for any loss suffered as a result of the other's actions or inactions

The ICO provides guidance on what to include in Data Sharing Agreements, at `https://ico.org.uk/media/for-organisations/documents/1068/data_sharing_code_of_practice.pdf`. At the time this book was published, this document had not been updated to reflect the GDPR. The ICO has, however, announced that it is preparing a new Code.

What to Do with Your Agreements

After you've drafted your agreements, negotiated them, agreed on the final text, and had them all signed, you'll want to keep them securely stored and accessible.

Data Processing Agreements

You don't need to file your Data Processing Agreement with any authority or perform any kind of registration with it. Be sure to keep it on file, however, so that you can easily refer to it when necessary, such as when

- Any data breach occurs

- You initiate the exercise of data subject rights that you need the processor's assistance with

- A new subprocessor is proposed by the processor

- You consider auditing the processor

>> Any associated agreement, such as the services contract, is terminated

>> An investigation by a data supervisory authority takes place

>> Any change occurs in the scope of the processing

>> You require the processor's assistance in carrying out a Data Privacy Impact Assessment, or DPIA (which is described in Chapter 15)

Data Sharing Agreements

You have no obligation to file or register your Data Sharing Agreement, or indeed even an obligation to have a written agreement for data sharing. You should, however, keep it on hand and revisit it when any of these circumstances requires it:

>> Exercise of a data breach

>> Investigation by a supervisory authority

>> Exercise of a data subject right

Examining the Consequences of Not Having the Appropriate Agreements in Place

Of course, you might face consequences — of varying degrees and which I discuss in this section — if you don't have GDPR-compliant Data Processing or Data Sharing Agreements in place.

Data Processing Agreements

In theory, you can be fined as much as €10 million or 2 percent of global turnover for the preceding financial year, whichever is higher, for the specific failure to have a Data Processing Agreement in place. In addition, you risk fines of up to €20 million or 4 percent of global turnover for the preceding financial year, whichever is higher for a breach of the security principle. (See Chapter 4 for more on the principles.)

In reality, fines for not having a Data Processing Agreement in place are likely to be much lower than this limit — if the first fine in relation to this particular offence is anything to go by: The data protection authorities in Hamburg fined a small shipping company €5,000 under the GDPR for not having a Data Processing Agreement in place.

At the other end of the scale, the UK's Information Commissioner's Office fined Yahoo's UK arm £250,000 before the GDPR took effect (when the maximum fine was £500,000). This was in relation to a number of breaches, however, and a large amount of data, and wasn't solely in relation to not having a Data Processing Agreement in place. Hence, this is unlikely to be indicative of the level of any future fines for not having a Data Processing Agreement in place.

Data Sharing Agreements

In theory, the maximum fine for not complying with Article 26 of the GDPR and not having a "transparent arrangement" between joint controllers could lead to a fine of up to €10 million or 2 percent of global turnover for the preceding financial year, whichever is higher.

In practice, fines are likely to be much lower, and no cases of fines for the breach of Article 26 existed at the time this book was published. See Chapter 21 for more about how fines and other sanctions are determined.

Because the GDPR doesn't have a requirement to have a controller-to-controller transfer in writing, in reality the relevant provisions of GDPR are likely to be one of the following:

>> Breaches of the general principles (described in Chapter 4)

>> Not having a lawful ground of processing (described in Chapter 3)

Chapter **11**

Writing Opt-In Wording

If you as a data controller need to rely on consent as your lawful grounds for processing personal data (see Chapter 3 for more about lawful grounds for processing), you may choose to use opt-in wording together with a tick box to obtain that consent.

Opt-in wording is a message to data subjects briefly explaining how their personal data — should they choose to give it — will be processed and used. The wording must be presented with an empty tick box, so the data subject must affirmatively tick that box to agree to the necessary processing.

Opt-in wording must be concise, specific, and easy to understand. Opt-in wording is often used in *just-in-time notices,* which are notices that appear on your website at the point where users provide personal data, such as a name and an email address. (For more on just-in-time notices, see Chapter 8.)

The opt-in wording should refer and link to your Privacy Notice (see Chapter 8) so that data subjects can be informed about how you will use their personal data.

Opt-in wording is complicated by the application of the ePrivacy Directive to certain marketing activities. The ePrivacy Directive requires consent in certain situations, as described below. The ePrivacy Directive was implemented into individual member state's law with certain variations. This chapter focuses on the

UK's implementation, but I have included a link in Chapter 22 to a summary of the differences in implementation in EU member states.

If you don't get the opt-in wording correct, your consent may not be valid. This chapter explains when you need to use opt-in wording and how to ensure that you get it right.

Understanding When to Use Opt-In Wording

If you are relying on the lawful grounds of consent to process personal data, you will generally need to use opt-in wording to obtain that consent. In some cases, you will need *explicit* consent opt-in wording (if you are processing special category data, for example).

If, however, you are instead relying on legitimate interests to process personal data (checking always that the ePrivacy Directive does not require consent), then you do not need opt-*in*, but you must offer an opt-*out*. I explore all of these situations in this section.

REMEMBER

Consent is just one of the six lawful grounds for processing (which I discuss in Chapter 3), so do ensure that consent is actually required or is the most appropriate grounds for processing before you obtain it. You will be unable to change the grounds for processing at a later date without a very good reason, and it is almost never possible to swap to a different ground if you initially relied upon consent.

Opt-in particulars

The GDPR standard of consent requires the data subject to perform an *affirmative act* to indicate their consent. This means that the data subject must choose to take a clear action, such as such as ticking a box, to indicate consent. You cannot obtain consent using pre-ticked opt-in boxes, opt-out boxes, or other default settings that are preset to opt-in.

Recital 32 of the GDPR states:

"Consent should be given by a clear affirmative act . . . such as by a written statement, including by electronic means, or an oral statement. This could include ticking a box when visiting an Internet website, choosing technical settings for information society services or another statement or conduct

which clearly indicates in this context the data subject's acceptance of the proposed processing of his or her personal data. Silence, pre-ticked boxes, or inactivity should not therefore constitute consent."

This means that tick boxes are not the only way to obtain consent — you could, for example, collect consent through an oral statement such as someone saying, "Yes, I agree." However, it may then be difficult for you to prove you had consent at a later date.

Similarly, you do not always need to use opt-in wording. If it is obvious that people are consenting, then opt-in wording is not necessary. For example, if a website provides a box for data subjects to enter their email address to receive newsletter updates, with a button underneath saying "Subscribe" or "Sign-up," then the act of entering an email address and clicking the button will suffice as the affirmative act. You do not also need to add opt-in wording saying "I consent to processing of my email address in order to send me newsletter updates" in this case.

In Figure 11-1, the user clearly knows that entering an email address and clicking Sign Up means consenting to being sent a daily email. You should also include a link to your Privacy Notice at the point that people enter their email address or other personal data.

FIGURE 11-1: Agreeing to receive a daily email.

A Sign Up box

If, however, you are proposing to use the personal data for more than one purpose, such as sending a free report and then sending further follow up marketing emails or sharing the personal data with other organizations, then you should use opt-in wording and a tick box to enable the granular consent that is required by the GDPR.

Opt-ins for lead magnets

I am often asked about what opt-ins are required for *lead magnets* and follow-up marketing emails. Lead magnets are typically free pieces of valuable content, such as a special report or a training series that online marketers will advertise in order to obtain the name and email address of people who are interested in the particular subject matter covered by the free content.

The online marketer emails the free lead magnet to the person who has signed up, but they also want to send such person follow-up marketing about a related product or service.

My view is that in order to send the lead magnet, you do not need opt-in wording or a tick box for consent if it is clear what the person is signing up for (in the same way that it is clear that a person is signing up for the daily email in the example of the *Guardian* newspaper above). So, if, for example, my ad says "sign up for my free GDPR Checklist" and there is a box to provide the email address, I would not need a further tick box for people to signify their consent for their personal data to be processed in order for me to send them the GDPR Checklist. I would, however, need to link to my Privacy Notice with words such as "to see how we use your personal data, click here to read our Privacy Notice."

If, however I wanted to send follow-up marketing emails to those people who had signed up for the GDPR Checklist, I would require consent to send such emails to individual subscribers (see below for the definition of individual subscribers) and would therefore need to add a tick box for people to provide their consent to receive the further marketing emails. (See Figure 11-2.)

The reason I would require consent to the follow-up marketing emails is because my organization is established in the EU and therefore the ePrivacy Directive applies to me — this law (which is separate to, but sits alongside, the GDPR) requires prior consent for sending marketing emails to individual subscribers. As a result of the ePrivacy Directive requiring consent, the GDPR also requires consent. Hence the tick box is required to obtain that consent.

If, however, your organization is established outside of the EU, the ePrivacy Directive does not apply and you may seek to rely on legitimate interests as a ground for processing the personal data for the follow up emails. You would need to carry out a Legitimate Interests Assessment form, keep it on file and provide the right to opt out. (See Chapter 12 for more.)

FIGURE 11-2:
Adding the
necessary
tick box.

Note that the ePrivacy Directive is soon to be amended to expand the territorial scope to match that of the GDPR, so that if the GDPR applies to you, the ePrivacy Directive will as well. See Appendix A for more on this.

Instead of advertising the free lead magnet, you may choose to advertise the follow-up marketing (such as the newsletter that includes details of special offers) and, as a thank you for signing up, provide people with the free content. It is possible to incentivize the opt-in, though not to the point where people are penalized for not opting in, such as by differential pricing or refusing to provide a service.

When to use opt-out wording

Opt-out wording is a message to data subjects explaining that they must take action — such as ticking a box — to object to their data from being used in a certain way, such as objecting to their email address being used to send marketing emails. You should use opt-out wording (rather than opt-in wording) if you're proposing to process personal data under the lawful grounds of legitimate interests, as opposed to consent.

As an example, if you are established outside of the EU and therefore the ePrivacy Directive does not currently apply to you, you can use the legitimate interests grounds for processing to send existing customers emails about similar products or services. In this case, you may use opt-out wording and ask people to tick the box if they want to opt-out of receiving future emails. You should advise the person signing up of their right to object to the processing at any time, so that if they don't want to opt out immediately, they can do so at any time in the future — for example, by adding the following words underneath your opt out wording: "you may unsubscribe at any time by clicking the link at the bottom of our emails."

If you are established in the EU, you need to consider the application of the ePrivacy Directive and the soft opt-in — see the next section in this chapter for more on that.

Figure 11-3 shows an example of opt-out wording for marketing communications that's used whenever a new customer is providing personal data for a holiday they have just purchased. If this organization is relying on legitimate interests as a lawful grounds for processing the personal data (and if established in the EU, the soft opt in applies), this opt-out wording is compliant.

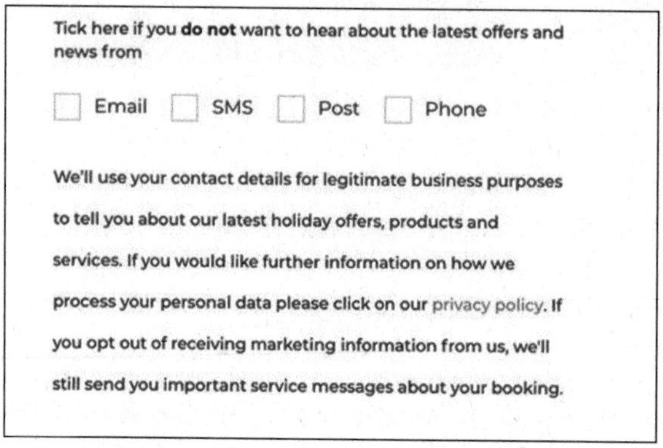

Tick here if you **do not** want to hear about the latest offers and news from

☐ Email ☐ SMS ☐ Post ☐ Phone

We'll use your contact details for legitimate business purposes to tell you about our latest holiday offers, products and services. If you would like further information on how we process your personal data please click on our privacy policy. If you opt out of receiving marketing information from us, we'll still send you important service messages about your booking.

FIGURE 11-3:
This opt-out wording clearly states that the user must tick the box to *not* receive emails.

The ePrivacy Directive and the soft opt-in

The ePrivacy Directive is a separate law to the GDPR and it has additional rules that apply on top of those set out in the GDPR. Specifically, it covers unsolicited electronic marketing, use of cookies, and confidentiality of electronic communications.

The ePrivacy Directive was implemented into each member state law with certain variations. In the UK, it was implemented as the Privacy and Electronic Communications Regulations (PECR). This law is the focus of this section. In Chapter 22, you find a link to a summary of how each EU member state has implemented the ePrivacy Directive.

The PECR requires consent for unsolicited marketing by email, fax, or text to individual subscribers. An *individual subscriber* is a natural person as opposed to a corporate subscriber which is a separate legal entity (such as a limited company, LLP, Scottish partnership, or a government body).

You may send unsolicited direct marketing emails and texts to corporate subscribers without consent. Note that corporate subscribers do not include businesses that trade as sole traders or partnerships.

Consent *is* required for unsolicited marketing by email, fax, or text to individual subscribers. If consent is required under PECR then, even if you think you have other potential grounds for processing under the GDPR, your lawful grounds under the GDPR should also be consent. In these cases, you will therefore need to use opt-in wording to obtain that consent, rather than relying on opt-out wording.

However, there is one instance when such consent is *not* required and this is known as the "soft opt-in" rule. In this case, you can instead rely on opt-*out*.

The soft opt-in rule applies where:

>> You have obtained the data subject's contact details in the course of the sale or negotiations for the sale of a product or service to that data subject.

>> The email marketing you send relates to similar products and services only.

>> The data subject is given the option to opt-out at the time that its contact details are collected, and in each subsequent communication.

As such, if you want to rely on the soft opt-in (a slightly confusing name, since it actually refers to opt-*out* based email marketing), you need to provide opt-out wording at the point of collecting that personal data.

Explicit-consent opt-in wording

If you are relying on explicit consent when processing special-category data (see Chapter 3 for more on this), you need to consider your opt-in wording even more carefully.

The main difference between *normal* consent and *explicit* consent is that explicit consent wording must contain an express statement of consent. Put another way, you should explicitly use the word "consent," rather than assume consent is obvious from the context (unlike the example of the "Subscribe" or "Sign-up" button above, these would not be sufficient for explicit consent). This means that, unlike normal consent, you cannot infer consent from a data subject's actions, even if those actions make it apparent that the data subject is consenting.

Explicit consent opt-in wording needs to state expressly those elements of the processing that require explicit consent, such as the fact that automated decision-making is being used or that special category data (such as health data) will be processed for clearly specified purposes.

REMEMBER

An electronic signature would be equally as compliant as a handwritten signature.

If, for example, you were running a health spa and collecting personal data about health matters in case a user needs urgent medical treatment or to check that they are not allergic to any of the health treatments they will take, you would require explicit consent and would need to state the element of processing that requires the explicit consent. Your opt-in wording would therefore need to look something like the example shown in Figure 11-4.

The explicit element of the opt-in wording should be separate from any other consent you're seeking, so in the example in Figure 11-4, you would not be able to have one signature to consent both to the processing of the health data and to direct marketing. The processing for sending direct marketing from related third parties would require further opt-in wording and tick boxes, as shown in Figure 11-5.

Please let us know any medical conditions you suffer from by ticking the appropriate boxes below. By signing the form below, you explicitly consent to us processing this personal data. We require your explicit consent for this processing because it constitutes health data. We will process your personal data in accordance with our Privacy Notice that is printed overleaf.

☐ Pregnancy

☐ Mobility problems

☐ Active/under active thyroid

☐ Verrucas/warts

☐ Heart problems

☐ Epilepsy

☐ Skin diseases/disorders

☐ Diabetes

☐ Metal pins/plates

☐ Claustrophobia

☐ Ear infections

☐ Cancer

☐ Surgery in the last 3 months

☐ Nuts or wheat allergies

☐ Seafood/shellfish allergies

Signed ....

Print name ....

Date...

FIGURE 11-4: This wording clearly states that explicit consent is required.

Please let us know any medical conditions you suffer from by ticking the appropriate boxes below. By signing the form below, you explicitly consent to us processing this personal data. We require your explicit consent for this processing because it constitutes health data. We will process your personal data in accordance with our privacy notice that is printed overleaf.

☐ Pregnancy

☐ Mobility problems

☐ Active/under active thyroid

☐ Verrucas/warts

☐ Heart problems

☐ Epilepsy

☐ Skin diseases/disorders

☐ Diabetes

☐ Metal pins/plates

☐ Claustrophobia

☐ Ear infections

☐ Cancer

☐ Surgery in the last 3 months

☐ Nuts or wheat allergies

☐ Seafood/shellfish allergies

Signed ....

Print name ....

Date..

Please tick below if you would like to receive emails from our partners with health-related offers:

☐ STU Spa

☐ ABC Supplements

☐ XYZ Weight Loss

FIGURE 11-5:
You must name third parties to receive consent on their behalf.

If you are proposing to share personal data with third parties and those third parties need consent for their processing (for example, they plan on sending direct marketing emails to the data subjects), those third parties should be specifically named in the consent, as they are in Figure 11-5.

WARNING

Consent isn't valid if you ask data subjects to agree to receive direct marketing from "carefully selected partners" or another, similar generic description. Nor is consent valid where data subjects are provided with a long list of general categories of organizations. See the nearby sidebar, "Information Commissioner's Office fines Everything DM Ltd £60,000," for an example of what not to do.

UK'S INFORMATION COMMISSIONER'S OFFICE (ICO) FINES EVERYTHING DM LTD £60,000

The ICO fined Everything DM Ltd £60,000 for sending 1.42 million emails without the correct consent. Everything DM, direct marketing specialists based in the UK, acquired lists of email addresses and sent emails on behalf of its clients for a fee.

When the ICO investigated, it found that while some data subjects had consented to receiving emails from unspecified "partners" and/or "third party companies," those consents weren't valid because neither Everything DM nor the third-party clients on whose behalf Everything DM was sending emails had been specifically named in those consents.

In addition, the emails gave the impression they were sent by the clients directly, but Everything DM actually sent the emails.

Steve Eckersley, ICO director of investigations, said, "Firms providing marketing services to other organizations need to double-check whether they have valid consent from people to send marketing emails to them. Generic third-party consent is not enough, and companies will be fined if they break the law."

Creating and Communicating Your Opt-In Wording

You should include opt-in wording wherever you are collecting personal data and relying on consent as your lawful grounds for processing, unless it is clearly obvious from the circumstances that, by providing personal data, the data subject will be consenting. You will typically see opt-in wording presented within just-in-time notices. (See Chapter 8 for more on this.)

The do's and don'ts of opt-in wording

The opt-in wording should be concise, easy to understand, and user-friendly. If the opt-in wording is difficult to understand or confusing — in particular, by the use of double negatives — the consent isn't valid. For example, the opt-in shown in Figure 11-6 isn't valid.

FIGURE 11-6:
This opt-in
wording is
too confusing
to be valid.

☐ Tick here if you would not like us to not send you emails about similar products and services.

The opt-in wording should be specific. If the consent is too vague and all-encompassing, it isn't valid. For example, the opt-in wording shown in Figure 11-7 isn't valid.

FIGURE 11-7:
This opt-in
wording is too
vague to be valid.

☐ Tick here if you are happy for us to keep your data on file and use it as we see fit from time to time

The opt-in wording should be clear about the purposes of the processing and the type of processing. Figure 11-8 shows an example of concise, easy-to-understand, user friendly opt-in wording from luxury travel magazine *Conde Naste Johansens*. It clearly states the purposes of the processing (to send certain types of information to the data subjects) and the type of processing activity (to send emails and brochures). It should ideally state why the date of birth is requested, as under the data minimization principle, only personal data necessary for the stated purpose should be collected.

The consent for data processing should be obvious, prominent, and not bundled with other terms and conditions. So, if you're collecting personal data at the same time you're selling a product or service or otherwise need to incorporate terms and conditions, you must have separate tick boxes for accepting terms and conditions for the sale and a separate tick box for giving consent to the data processing. Figure 11-9 is an example of opt-in wording where consent is not bundled with the terms and conditions.

You need to provide granular (more detailed) options for:

>> **Different purposes for the processing:** You might have one purpose to send direct marketing emails yourself and a second purpose to share the data with third parties for their marketing purposes.

>> **Different types of processing:** Examples are sending emails, sending postal marketing, and sending text marketing.

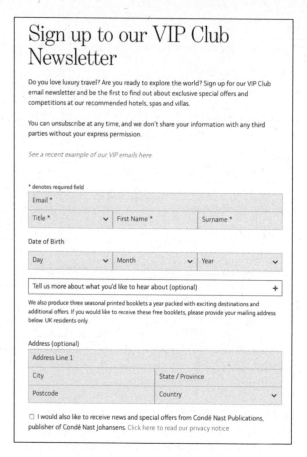

Sign up to our VIP Club Newsletter

Do you love luxury travel? Are you ready to explore the world? Sign up for our VIP Club email newsletter and be the first to find out about exclusive special offers and competitions at our recommended hotels, spas and villas.

You can unsubscribe at any time, and we don't share your information with any third parties without your express permission.

See a recent example of our VIP emails here.

* denotes required field

| Email * |
| Title * | First Name * | Surname * |

Date of Birth

| Day | Month | Year |

| Tell us more about what you'd like to hear about (optional) | + |

We also produce three seasonal printed booklets a year packed with exciting destinations and additional offers. If you would like to receive these free booklets, please provide your mailing address below. UK residents only.

Address (optional)

| Address Line 1 |
| City | State / Province |
| Postcode | Country |

☐ I would also like to receive news and special offers from Condé Nast Publications, publisher of Condé Nast Johansens. Click here to read our privacy notice

FIGURE 11-8:
Opt-in wording that is clear and specific is valid.

☐ Tick here to agree to our Terms and Conditions

☐ Tick here to consent to us sharing your personal data with XYZ Limited for them to send you details of similar products and services

FIGURE 11-9:
Keep consent separate from terms and conditions.

Figure 11-10 shows an example of opt-in wording that provides granular options for different types of processing.

You may see separate wording where certain types of processing, such as email and text, require *opt-in consent* and postal marketing asks for data subjects to *opt out*. This is because of the ePrivacy Directive, which provides that consent is required for email and text marketing. However, the ePrivacy Directive does not require consent for postal marketing, meaning you can generally rely on the lawful grounds of legitimate interests instead when it comes to processing of personal data for postal marketing (see Chapter 19 for more on this). In such a case, processing for postal marketing will require an opt-out (as data subjects have the right to object to processing where legitimate interests is the lawful ground of processing). If a data subject opts out of postal marketing, you must cease the processing immediately.

FIGURE 11-10:
Allowing the data
subject to make
choices.

Tick the following boxes to let us know how you would like to receive details of our special offers:
☐ email
☐ text
☐ telephone

For an example of opt-in wording together with opt-out wording, see Figure 11-11.

FIGURE 11-11:
You can provide
opt-in and
opt-out wording
together.

Tick the following boxes to let us know how you would like to receive details of our special offers:
☐ Tick here if you would like us to send you our special offers by email
☐ Tick here if you would like us to send you our special offers by text
☐ Tick here if you would not like us to send you our special offers by post

Avoiding consent fatigue

Recital 32 of the GDPR also states that the consent must not be unnecessarily disruptive to the data subject's experience. While you must adhere to the transparency principle (see Chapter 4 for more on this) and provide data subjects with sufficient information to make an informed choice, you must be wary of *consent fatigue*. This is when users provide consent without bothering to read the Privacy Notice or understanding the consequences of consenting, because they're overburdened with information, presented with too many consent requests, or the process of providing consent is simply too cumbersome.

To help data subjects avoid consent fatigue, be as specific and succinct as possible in the opt-in wording and use links within the opt-in wording to layered Privacy Notices. (For more on using links to aid reading comprehension, see Chapter 8.)

REMEMBER

You shouldn't try to obtain consent to (and therefore do not need opt-in wording for) the Privacy Notice itself. Consent is just one of your lawful grounds for processing. If you ask for consent to the Privacy Notice, you are effectively putting all of your processing on the grounds of consent. In any event, a Privacy Notice will be too long, and describe too many different processing activities, for anyone to be able to give valid consent to it in its entirety.

Keeping records of consent

Finally, as a data controller, you must keep records of consent, including

>> Who consented

>> When they consented

>> How they consented

>> What they were told about the processing

>> Whether they subsequently withdrew consent

As such, any tick boxes or other consent mechanisms used to capture consent online should ideally be integrated with appropriate record-keeping systems so that evidence of these consent records are retained.

Consequences of Not Having the Appropriate Opt-In Wording

If you do not obtain valid consent, either where you have chosen this as your lawful basis for processing or where consent is required by law, then you may be subject to fines of up to €20 million, or 4% of your total worldwide annual turnover in the previous financial year, whichever is higher.

REMEMBER

To help ensure that your consent is valid, and that you don't process personal data unlawfully — and therefore face a potential fine — make sure your opt-in wording meets the criteria in this list. You must ensure that

- » Consent is the most appropriate ground for processing.

- » The consent for the opt-in is separate from the consent for terms and conditions.

- » The wording is clear and not confusing.

- » The wording is specific about what you're going to do with the data, not vague and all-encompassing.

- » The wording is clear about the purposes of the processing and the type of processing.

- » You aren't using pre-ticked boxes, opt-outs, or default settings.

- » Where you require explicit consent, you specifically state the element of the processing that requires the explicit consent.

- » The method of obtaining consent isn't disruptive to the user experience.

Chapter **12**

Writing a Legitimate Interests Assessment Form

As I discuss in Chapter 3, one of the six lawful grounds for processing personal data is where the processing is necessary for the purposes of the legitimate interests pursued by the data controller or by a third party. However, to be lawful, these interests must not be overridden by the interests or fundamental data protection rights and freedoms of the data subject, in particular when the data subject is a child.

If you intend to rely upon legitimate interests as your lawful grounds for processing, it is a good idea to document a Legitimate Interests Assessment (LIA), a three-step test to determine whether you do, in fact, have a legitimate interest to conduct the processing, the necessity of the processing in order to achieve your legitimate interest, and whether data subjects' rights and freedoms outweigh your interest. In this chapter, I explain when to use an LIA form and what to consider when you do; I also discuss what to do with it when you have it complete.

TIP If you haven't yet read Chapter 3 on the matters to consider when you rely on the legitimate interests grounds for processing, I recommend doing so now to help put this chapter in context for you.

Knowing When to Use a Legitimate Interests Assessment Form

Each and every time you intend to rely on the legitimate interests grounds for processing personal data, it is a good idea to complete an LIA form and keep it on record. Retaining a record will help evidence compliance with your accountability obligations. The exercise of filling out the form will help you to decide whether or not the legitimate interests ground is likely to be appropriate or not.

There are some types of activity that the GDPR specifically mentions as potentially capable of being conducted in reliance on legitimate interests:

>> Fraud prevention

>> Network and information security

>> Detection or prevention of criminal acts or threats to public security

However, it would still be good practice to conduct an LIA in these cases, particularly if (for example) deploying security tools that might be intrusive (for example, monitoring Internet behavior).

Although the GDPR also specifically mentions the following legitimate interests, the UK's Information Commissioner's Office (ICO) advises that more consideration is needed when carrying out an LIA for these specific legitimate interests:

>> Intragroup administrative transfers (namely, transfers of personal data for administrative purposes between group companies, typically when group companies have shared services such as IT, HR, legal, finance, and so on)

>> Marketing

In reality, often organizations will not carry out LIAs for intra group administrative transfers and will only carry out LIAs for marketing where behavioral advertising is involved.

Completing a Legitimate Interests Assessment Form

The purpose of an LIA is to help you determine whether you can rely upon legitimate interests as the lawful basis for your processing under GDPR. An LIA form has three main parts, which I discuss in detail throughout the rest of this section: a Purpose test, a Necessity test, and a Balancing test.

TIP

The following sections provide you with some considerations to think about when you're actually doing the assessment. You could also take a look at the LIA template provided by the ICO at https://ico.org.uk/media/for-organisations/forms/2258435/gdpr-guidance-legitimate-interests-sample-lia-template.docx.

Purpose test

The first part of a Legitimate Interests Assessment should be a *Purpose test*, in which you determine whether you have a legitimate interest to conduct the processing. You should consider the following:

>> Why you want to process the data

>> What benefit you expect to receive from processing the data

>> Whether any third parties benefit from your processing of the data

>> Whether there are any wider public interests in your processing of the data

>> How important the benefits to you and/or the third party and/or the public are

>> What the impact would be if you didn't proceed with the processing

>> Whether the processing will comply with data protection and other applicable laws

>> Whether the processing will comply with applicable industry codes of practice or guidelines

>> Whether there are any ethical issues with the processing

Necessity test

The second part of the LIA form is the *Necessity test*, in which you determine whether the processing is actually *necessary* to achieve your legitimate interests — that is, whether you must conduct this processing to achieve the purposes that are your objective.

Necessary in this test doesn't mean that the processing itself has to be absolutely essential, but it must be targeted and proportionate. In other words, the method of processing must not exceed what is necessary to achieve your purposes.

You need to consider whether

>> The processing will help you achieve your purpose

>> The processing will help a third party achieve its purpose

>> The processing is reasonable and proportionate to achieve the purpose

>> You can achieve the purpose without the processing

>> You can achieve the purpose by processing less data or processing the data in a less intrusive way

TIP

Be honest when you answer these questions. Could you achieve the processing in less intrusive ways or in ways that involve less data? If that's the case yet you choose not to use the less intrusive methods, you need to justify your actions in the LIA and explain why the less intrusive methods are not reasonable alternatives.

Balancing test

The third and final part of the test is the *Balancing test,* in which you determine

>> The impact of the processing on the data subject's interests, rights, and freedoms

>> Whether the impact overrides your legitimate interests

The UK's ICO recommends that, before you carry out the Balancing test, you should use the DPIA screening checklist to assess whether you need to carry out a DPIA, which I discuss further in Chapter 15.

For the Balancing test, you need to consider the following, which I explain further throughout the rest of this section:

>> The nature of the personal data

>> The reasonable expectations of the data subject

>> The likely impact on the data subject

Nature of the data

The UK's ICO recommends that you consider the nature of the data — specifically, whether it's

>> Special-category data, such as medical data or data relating to religious beliefs (see Chapter 3 for more)

>> Criminal-offense data

>> Data that people consider to be private, such as financial information

>> Children's data

>> The data of vulnerable individuals such as the elderly or mentally challenged

>> Data about people in the context of their personal lives or private lives, for example, personal finance data

REMEMBER

The more sensitive or private the data and the more vulnerable the individual, the more likely the data subject's rights and freedoms will be at risk.

Reasonable expectations

Finally, you need to consider whether people will expect you to use their data in the way that you are proposing to. You should think about whether

>> You have an existing relationship with the data subject.

>> You used the data subject's data in the past.

>> You collected the data directly from the data subject.

>> You have explained the data processing and its purposes, — by providing a Privacy Notice to data subjects when you collected their data, for example.

>> You collected the data from a third party and, if so, what they told the individual about how the data would be used.

>> You have any direct feedback on the expectations of data subjects, such as from market research or consultation.

>> The data was collected recently or long ago.

>> Any changes in technology or otherwise would mean that you're processing the data in ways the data subject wouldn't expect.

>> The purpose for the processing and the method of processing are obvious and likely to be understood by your data subject.

>> Any particular circumstances would mean that the data subjects would or would not expect the processing.

>> Any imbalance exists in the relationship between you and the data subject so that you have power over the data subject.

You should also consider the nature of any relationship with the data subject (for example, existing customer, old customer, prospect, or someone who has never heard of you).

You don't have to prove that data subjects do in fact expect you to use their data the way you are. You just have to show that a reasonable person would expect the processing in those particular circumstances. A *reasonable person* is a hypothetical person who shows average care, skill, and judgment in his actions; the person serves as a comparative standard.

Impact on the data subject

In thinking about the likely impact the processing will have on the data subject, consider whether the processing may

>> Result in a high risk to the rights and freedoms of your data subjects — if so, you need to carry out a Data Protection Impact Assessment (DPIA). (See Chapter 15 for more on this topic.)

>> Result in any risk to the rights and freedoms of your data subjects

>> Result in any physical harm to the data subjects

>> Result in any financial loss, identity theft, or fraud

>> Result in any loss of control by the data subject over their personal data

>> Result in any significant economic or social disadvantage (such as reputational damage, discrimination, or loss of confidentiality)

>> Adversely impact data subjects exercising their individual rights (privacy rights or any other rights)

>> Adversely impact data subjects accessing services or opportunities

>> Add value to a product or service that the data subject uses

TIP

When considering these points, think about not just the likelihood of the risk but also the severity of any harm caused to the data subject. The higher the risks, the more your interests will need to be compelling.

If you identify risks to the rights and freedoms of data subjects but a DPIA isn't necessary, you still need to consider any safeguards you can put in place to reduce the impact on data subjects.

Safeguards might include:

>> **Switching to an alternative lawful basis:** Consent could be an option here.

>> **Enhancing transparency:** Make it absolutely clear to data subjects when they provide their data how you will be processing their personal data and for what purpose.

>> **Reducing data retention timescales:** By keeping the personal data for less time, you are reducing the potential impact on the data subject.

>> **Collecting less data:** In this case, you would collect only the data you absolutely need to achieve your purposes.

>> **Providing data subjects with the right to opt out:** I discuss opting out in Chapter 11.

>> **Not collecting data from children or vulnerable individuals:** This ensures that the data collected is from data subjects who can make informed choices about whether to object to the processing or not.

>> **Pseudonymize data:** This entails removing any parts of the data that could reasonably be used to identify a specific person.

>> **Security measures:** This could include adding more levels of encryption, instituting multifactor authentication, and restricting access within your organization. (See Chapter 16 for more.)

When you have considered all these safeguards, determine whether your interests should take priority over any risks to your data subjects. This is not an exact science. Subjectivity is unavoidable, but you should be able to show that you took into account all relevant considerations, took a balanced view, and are able to justify the decision you reached.

If you're unsure about whether your interests take priority, you may want to consider another lawful grounds for your processing.

What to Do with Your Legitimate Interests Assessment Form

After you have carried out your Legitimate Interests Assessment (LIA) form, here's what to do with it:

>> **Keep the form on file:** Again, keeping a record of this assessment helps evidence compliance with your GDPR accountability obligations.

>> **Review the form periodically:** If anything changes with your processing that may impact the matters considered as part of the LIA, revisit the form. Carry out the balancing exercise again, and consider whether additional safeguards are required or whether you need to stop the processing.

WARNING

If the outcome of your assessment is that the rights of the data subject override your legitimate interests, you cannot rely on legitimate interests as a grounds for processing. If you cannot find another appropriate lawful grounds for processing, you must not carry out the processing.

REMEMBER

If the LIA identifies high risks to the data subject, you likely need to carry out a DPIA. (See Chapter 15.)

Consequences of Not Carrying Out a Legitimate Interests Assessment

If you rely on the grounds of legitimate interests to process personal data when it was not appropriate for you to do so, you will be processing personal data unlawfully. An LIA can help you avoid this risk. If you process data unlawfully in reliance on legitimate interests you could face the following potential consequences:

>> **You could be subject to the maximum amount of fines.** The maximum is €20m or 4 percent of your total annual worldwide turnover in the preceding financial year, whichever is higher.

See Chapter 21 for more details on what's considered when regulatory authorities are considering sanctions.

>> **A data subject can bring a civil claim against you.** If groups of data subjects are affected, you could face a class action.

Chapter **13**

Writing Other Documents

The previous chapters in this part of the book explore various documents that you'll want to create (or that you must create) to stay compliant with the GDPR. As part of that compliance, you need to produce certain other documents, as set out in this chapter.

Data Protection Impact Assessments

A Data Protection Impact Assessment (DPIA) is required when you're carrying out processing that is likely to result in a high risk to data subjects. For more detail on what those risks might be, when a DPIA is required, and how to mitigate the identified risks, see Chapter 15.

A thorough DPIA helps you record evidence demonstrating that you have considered all potential risks that processing the data might cause and that you have met your accountability obligations. You should carry out a DPIA at the start of the project — before you commence the processing — and conduct it in tandem with planning for the project.

TIP

If you have a Data Protection Officer (also discussed further in Chapter 15), consult that person, as well as any concerned stakeholders, throughout the DPIA process.

This list, which isn't exhaustive, shows the types of information you need to review as part of the DPIA process:

>> Scope of the processing

>> Purposes of the processing

>> Intended benefits of the processing for data subjects

>> Intended benefits of the processing for you as the data controller

>> Intended benefits of the processing for any third parties

>> Types of data subjects that will be affected

>> Description of the processing

>> Types of personal data involved in the processing

>> Sources of the personal data

>> Length and frequency of the data processing

>> Volume of data to be processed

>> Considerations for data minimization

>> Lawful grounds for processing

>> Risks of the processing

>> Whether results will be disclosed to third parties

>> Security of processing

>> Assessment of data quality

>> Arrangements to address data subject rights

>> Data retention and disposal

>> Special arrangements for vulnerable individuals

>> Actions required

>> Your decision

If the DPIA indicates that the processing would result in a high risk — in the absence of measures taken by you to mitigate the risk — you need to consult with your supervisory authority before you carry out the data processing. See Chapter 21 for more about supervisory authorities.

Data Subject Access Requests and Response Records

As I discuss at some length in Chapter 14, a *data subject* is an individual whose personal data is collected, held, or processed. That chapter also details the eight rights of data subjects, one of which is the right to access their own personal data (which you as a data controller might have collected and processed). When data subjects access this right, they submit a Data Subject Access Request, which I discuss in this section.

Data Subject Access Requests (DSAR)

If you receive a Data Subject Access Request (DSAR) from a data subject, requiring you to disclose the information you hold about them, you need to complete a Data Subject Access Request record to show that you have complied with your obligations. (See Chapter 14 for more about Data Subject Access Requests.)

This list, which isn't exhaustive, shows the types of information you need to record in a Data Subject Access Request record:

» Date you received the DSAR

» Who the DSAR was received from

» Form of the DSAR

» Whether a form of identity was provided

» Whether the data subject was an employee, a client, or another type of data subject

» Whether the DSAR was made by a third party on behalf of the data subject

» Date of your response to the DSAR

» Nature of your response to the DSAR

» Whether any further action was taken by the data subject

Keep the DSAR record on file as evidence of your accountability obligations and to record your actions in case of an investigation.

Response to a DSAR

When a data subject submits a DSAR to you, you need to prepare the response letter enclosing the relevant information and documents.

Sending only the information and documentation you're legally obliged to disclose is extremely important because otherwise you could erroneously disclose sensitive business information that will adversely affect the business. See Chapter 14 for more on this.

You must respond to a DSAR without undue delay, the details of which are in Chapter 14. Your response should include the following information in relation to the personal data that's processed relating to the data subject who submitted the DSAR (note that this isn't an exhaustive list):

>> Types of personal data

>> Purposes of the processing

>> Recipients of the personal data

>> What safeguards are in place if the personal data is transferred outside the European Economic Area (EEA)

>> Sources that the personal data is collected from

>> Retention period for the personal data

>> Whether the personal data is used for automated decision-making or profiling

If you're unable to provide certain requested information because of one of the available exemptions (note that these vary throughout EU member states), you should explain which of the exemptions you're relying on. I discuss various exemptions in Chapter 14.

If you're unable to reply to the DSAR for any of the following reasons, in each case you must inform the data subject and advise them of their right to complain to the supervisory authority in the relevant EU member state:

>> You require further information to verify the identity of the data subject or the person making the DSAR on behalf of the data subject.

>> You requested further information because you were unable to verify the identity of the data subject making the DSAR (or the third party doing so on behalf of the data subject), and the requested information hasn't been forthcoming.

>> You have conducted a thorough search for the requested information and have determined that you have never processed personal data about the data subject or don't currently process personal data about the data subject and any personal data has been destroyed or erased in accordance with retention policies.

REMEMBER

Keep copies of the response and records of all disclosed data so that you know exactly what you have provided to the data subject in case the data subject requests further data or there is an investigation by a supervisory authority.

Data Breach Records

The GDPR, in Article 33(5), dictates that you must keep a record of any data breach that takes place relating to your organization. Another article — Article 35(5) — explains that this documentation will include any facts relating to the breach, its effects, and any subsequent remedial actions taken. By documenting this information, you will enable the supervisory authority to verify your compliance. (This is in addition to your data subject notification requirements. See Chapter 17 for more details.)

The following list, which isn't exhaustive, shows what a data breach record should, ideally, include:

>> Date of the data breach

>> Number of people affected by the breach

>> Nature of the breach

>> Description of the breach

>> Date you became aware of the breach

>> How you became aware of the breach

>> Description of the data involved in the breach

>> Likely consequences of the breach

>> Actual consequences of the breach

>> Whether all affected data subjects have been informed

>> Whether you have informed your data protection supervisory authority and, if so, on what date

>> What remedial action has been taken

Data Protection Policies

A Data Protection Policy isn't strictly required by the GDPR. Medium to large organizations often use this type of policy, however, to explain to data subjects how they process personal data and how they're complying with the GDPR.

Under legislation from certain EU member states — the UK, for example — an "appropriate policy document" needs to be in place if you process special-category data or criminal-convictions data. A Data Protection Policy is likely to suffice for the purposes of the "appropriate policy document."

In the UK, the appropriate policy document must include

>> The condition for the processing of special category data or criminal convictions data that you rely on in the Data Protection Act (DPA) of 2018, as set out in Parts 1–3 of Schedule 1; see Chapter 3 for more about conditions for such processing.

>> The lawful basis for the processing (as set out in Article 6(1) of the GDPR); see Chapter 3.

>> Whether the personal data is retained and erased in line with your retention policy, which I discuss later in this chapter; if not, you must explain the reasons why not.

The Data Protection Policy should include the following items (note that this isn't an exhaustive list):

>> Whether you have a Data Protection Officer (DPO) and, if so, their contact details; see Chapter 15 for more about DPOs.

>> A description of the data protection principles and how you adhere to them; Chapter 4 covers these principles.

>> The fact that you have put in place procedures to deal with any suspected personal data breach, which I cover in Chapter 17.

>> A description of data subject's rights and requests (the topic of Chapter 14).

>> What you have in place to ensure compliance with accountability obligations; see Part 3 of this book.

>> A description of your record keeping of your data processing activities.

>> What training you have in place for your staff in relation to data protection. (See Chapters 18 and 24 for a discussion of staff training.)

>> How you comply with the privacy by design and default obligations, which I discuss in Chapter 15.

>> Whether you carry out automated decision-making that has a legal or similarly significant effect on data subjects (see Chapter 14); if so, how you're complying with the GDPR in this regard.

>> A description of when you're able to share personal data with third parties.

Data Retention Policies

A Data Retention Policy can help you demonstrate compliance with the storage limitation principle of the GDPR, which I discuss further in Chapter 4. In short, according to the GDPR — in Article 5(1)(e) — personal data must be

>> Kept in a form that permits identification of data subjects for no longer than is necessary. You can keep the data only for as long as you need it to process it for whatever purposes you collected it.

>> Stored for longer periods only when the personal data will be processed for archiving purposes in the public interest, for scientific or historical research, or for statistical purposes.

TIP

The key information to remember under this principle is that you must not keep personal data for longer than you need it.

Your Data Retention Policy should, ideally, include the following (which isn't an exhaustive list):

>> The scope of the policy, such as all data stored in certain specified locations

>> Your data disposal policy

>> What you have taken into account when setting retention periods

>> Type of data

>> Purpose of the data

>> Review period

>> Retention period or criteria for each type of data

>> Roles and responsibilities of people within the organization who are involved with the storage, retention, or deletion of personal data

The policy should be flexible enough to allow for destruction or erasure in advance of the stated retention periods if you no longer need such data.

The UK's Information Commissioner's Office (ICO) advises that small organizations may not need a documented retention policy if they're engaging only in occasional, low-risk processing. Even if you don't have a retention policy, however, you're still obligated to review (regularly) any data you hold and then delete or anonymize accordingly.

REMEMBER

Reviewing your retention policy at regular intervals is a good practice. Doing so allows you to see whether any amendments are required, especially where you have lengthy retention periods or where data subjects are likely to be adversely affected.

Additional Privacy Notices

If you have employees, then in addition to your general Privacy Notice (see Chapter 8 for more), you should also have a Privacy Notice for your employees and potential employees:

>> **Employee Privacy Notice:** This Privacy Notice doesn't need to be posted on your website and should be provided to employees whenever they become employees (or as soon thereafter as is possible). This should include the same information as contained in your wider Privacy Notice but only what's relevant to your employees.

>> **Candidate Privacy Notice:** You should also provide job applicants with a Privacy Notice. It should not be the same as your employee Privacy Notice, because you won't be processing the data in the same way as set out in the employee Privacy Notice until they actually become employees. Again, the Privacy Notice should set out the same information as in your general Privacy Notice, but only what's relevant to candidates.

TIP

If you provide individuals with a candidate Privacy Notice before you hire them, you should still provide a copy of the employee Privacy Notice when they become employees.

4

Data Subject Rights, Protection, and Security

Introducing the eight data subject rights

Knowing how to handle Data Subject Access Requests (DSARs)

Conducting a Data Protection Impact Assessment (DPIA) to anticipate data security issues and mitigate risks

Hiring a Data Protection Officer (DPO) to ensure that you uphold data protection

Implementing data security practices so that you stay GDPR-compliant

Reviewing your reporting and recordkeeping requirements in the case of a data breach

Chapter **14**

Data Subject Rights

A *data subject* is an individual whose personal data is collected, held, or processed. When you, as an individual, provide your data (for example, your name, email address, and phone number) to an organization, you are the subject of the data — that is, the data subject. *Personal data* is defined in the GDPR as "any information relating to an identified or identifiable natural person," including information that may be referenced via particular identifiers such as a name, location data, or via factors relating to physical, genetic, or social identity of that natural person. Chapter 3 spells out what is and is not personal data. A *natural person* is an individual human being, as opposed to a legal person such as an organization.

A key part of the GDPR, you likely won't be surprised to know, is to provide for certain rights for data subjects. According to the Information Commissioner's Office (ICO), the UK saw a 100 percent increase in the exercise of data subject rights in *the first three months* after GDPR came into effect. (See the nearby sidebar, "GDPR awareness is on the rise.")

Going forward, I fully expect to see an increase in not only the frequency of data subjects exercising their rights but also the number of complaints to supervisory authorities (see Chapter 21) when such exercise of rights isn't correctly responded to. As a *data controller* (the entity who controls the data), you must know the rights that individuals have under the GDPR, what your obligations are to uphold those rights, and what consequences you face if you don't properly respond to these data subject rights. I discuss these issues throughout this chapter.

GDPR AWARENESS IS ON THE RISE

The UK's Information Commissioner's Office (ICO) ran two GDPR-awareness campaigns to inform the public of their data protection rights. Because data subjects are exercising their rights more frequently, the campaigns are considered successful. People's awareness varies regarding the data protection rights they have. Topping the list is the "right to access your personal data," with 58 percent of participants aware of such right. According to the survey, the least-known rights are the "right to move data from one provider to another" and the "right not to be subject to automated decision-making and profiling," with 27 percent and 30 percent aware, respectively. Find out more here:

```
https://ico.org.uk/media/about-the-ico/documents/2259732/annual-
    track-2018.pdf
```

Data processors also need to be aware of and be able to recognize the exercise of data subject rights, as data processors will need to pass the request to the appropriate data controller as soon as possible. The data processor must not reply directly to the data subject in relation to the exercise of data subject rights.

General Matters Relating to Data Subject Rights

The GDPR provides eight main rights for EU data subjects, strengthening the rights provided for in the previous data protection regulations. Before I describe those rights in detail, I explain in this section the general issues that apply to all data subject rights.

Territorial scope of data subject rights

A data subject is entitled to exercise data subject rights under the GDPR. A *data subject* is an identified or identifiable natural person. As I show in Chapter 1, GDPR applies to all data processed by entities established within the EU (including the data processing of US data subjects, for example). The GDPR applies to entities established outside of the EU to the extent that they process personal data of people within the EU to offer them goods or services or monitor their behavior.

If a data controller is established within the EU, all data subjects (wherever they are located in the world) are entitled to the data subject rights set out in the GDPR. If a data controller is established outside of the EU, only data subjects within the EU are entitled to exercise the data subject rights set out in the GDPR.

Form in which a right is exercised

The GDPR does not mandate the form of how a data subject exercises a right, such as a Data Subject Access Request (DSAR) or the right to rectification. The data subject can make the request verbally or in writing (including via social media) and to any person within an organization. A request isn't required to include a description of the right or to refer to the right by a formal, legal name. (For more on DSARs, see below.) Your staff must be trained to recognize the exercise of data protection rights, or else, if it's just you in your business, you must remain vigilant. The time limit for replying within one month starts upon receipt within the organization. Reception staff, mailroom staff, executives, secretaries, assistants, social media teams, and others all must know how to recognize the GDPR data subject rights and where to escalate that communication within the organization.

REMEMBER

Although the GDPR doesn't prescribe the form of how to exercise a data subject right, you may want to provide a standard form for data subjects to use. Note, however, that data subjects aren't required to use your online form and can submit the request to exercise a data subject right in any way they like.

Article 12 of the GDPR states that where the data subject makes the request by electronic means, the information shall be provided by electronic means where possible, unless otherwise requested by the data subject.

In relation to DSARs, Recital 59 of the GDPR recommends that wherever personal data is processed by electronic means, you provide a way for the data subject to file an DSAR electronically.

Deadline for replying to requests

You must act without undue delay whenever you receive a request to exercise a data subject right and in any event within one month of receipt of the request. What *undue delay* means depends on the particular circumstances, but the GDPR provides for a long stop for your reply of one month from your receipt of the request.

The time limit of one month begins to run on the day the request is received (or on the date that the further information is requested, whether or not that day falls on a weekend or another non-workday, until the same calendar date in the next month. Here are a couple of examples to further illustrate the time frame:

>> You receive a DSAR on Friday, February 11. You start the month time limit from Friday, February 11, so you must reply to the request by March 11 (even though February has only 28 or 29 days).

>> You receive a right to rectification request on Sunday, August 30. The time limit starts Sunday, August 30. You must reply to the request by September 30 (because September has 30 days).

Note: If the date for reply in the following month falls on a weekend or a public holiday, you have until the next working day to respond.

TIP

As shown in these examples, the number of days you have to respond varies depending on the number of days in the month and whether the day is a weekend or bank holiday. If you need to fix the time period for operational reasons, the safest strategy is to instigate a response period of 28 days.

In certain circumstances, you may be able to extend the time period to reply to a request. If the request is complex or you have received multiple requests from the data subject, you may be able to argue that you're entitled to extend the time limit by two months.

If you decide that you need this additional time to respond, you must reply to the data subject, within one month from the date you receive the request, in order to do the following:

>> Inform the data subject that you need additional time.

>> Explain the reasons for the delay.

Charging a fee

In most cases, you can't charge a fee to comply with data subject rights. Where the request is "manifestly unfounded or excessive in particular because of their repetitive character," you may charge a "reasonable fee" for your administrative costs of responding, or you can refuse to act on the request altogether (Article 12(5)).

The onus is on you as data controller to prove the request manifestly unfounded or excessive — that is, clearly unrealistic — should the data subject challenge you.

If the data subject requests further copies of the data, you may charge a reasonable fee based on your administrative costs for doing so. The GDPR provides no guidance regarding what a reasonable fee might be.

The UK's Data Protection Act 1998 allowed a fee of £10, which was quite a deterrent to data subjects making requests. If a data subject made a request in the heat of the moment, for example, the data controller's ability to request the £10 fee was often all it took to make the data subject reconsider the request.

Requesting identification

Article 12(6) of the GDPR states that if you have "reasonable doubts" about the identity of the person making the request, you may ask for additional information to confirm the data subject's identity.

What personal data you hold, the nature of that personal data, and what you're using it for can help you determine whether you may request additional information. These scenarios provide examples of when you can and cannot request additional information from a data subject:

>> You receive a DSAR from John Smith. The only personal data you hold about him is his name and email address, which you hold for marketing purposes. The request comes in via john.smith@hotmail.com, the same email address you hold on your system for this individual. Nothing in the email with the request or otherwise gives you any doubt regarding his identity. You are therefore unable to request additional information about his identity.

>> You receive a DSAR from Jane Smith in relation to sensitive medical data that you hold about her. The request came in via letter with the same address as the one you hold for Jane Smith on your records. The letter doesn't mention her health number, however, and her address is publicly available. Due to the sensitive nature of the data, you would be entitled to request further information to confirm Jane's identity. In this case, a passport or driver's license may be appropriate.

Refusing to comply

If you determine a request to be "manifestly unfounded or excessive," particularly taking into account whether it's a repeat request, you may either charge a reasonable fee (see the earlier section on this matter) or refuse to deal with the request (Article 12(5)).

If you refuse, you must let the data subject know within one month why you aren't taking action. You must also explain the data subject's right to complain to a supervisory authority (see Appendix B for a list of supervisory authorities) and/or to seek judicial redress in the courts.

Requests by or on behalf of others or from children

Another person can request to exercise a data subject right on behalf of the data subject, including

>> A lawyer

>> Someone who has power of attorney for the data subject

>> Someone who has a written request from the data subject

If you receive a request from a third party, you must verify that they are acting on behalf of the data subject. Accordingly, you may request additional information (such as the written request or power of attorney) to confirm that the third party isn't acting improperly. You will need to check written requests carefully and ensure any authority is authenticated and verified to prevent forgery and any unlawful disclosure to somebody who is not in fact authorized to receive such reply.

REMEMBER

Rights about data concerning children are likely to be exercised by parents, but if the child exercises a right directly, you must still respond. If an adult has written on behalf of the child, you may want to respond directly to the child if you think they will understand their rights. In deciding whether you think a child will understand their rights, you should take into account:

>> The child's age

>> The nature of the data

>> The inappropriateness of replying to the adult — for example, because of abuse allegations

If the child authorizes a reply to the parents or it's evidently in the best interests of the child, you can reply to the parents.

TIP

The presumed competence of a child will vary according to the European jurisdiction where the child resides. For example, in Scotland a 12-year-old person is considered "of sufficient age and maturity to be able to exercise their right of access, unless the contrary is shown." This presumption isn't shared by England, Wales, or Northern Island, so look into this issue as necessary.

Exemptions

Article 23 of the GDPR enables member states to introduce laws to provide for specific exemptions from data subject rights to safeguard such matters as:

- >> National security

- >> Defense

- >> Public security

- >> Prevention of crime

- >> Public interest

- >> Protection of data subject rights

- >> Enforcement of civil law claims

The UK's Data Protection Act of 2018 provides for certain exemptions, including:

REMEMBER

- >> If you process personal data for scientific or historical research or statistical purposes, you don't have to comply with the GDPR in relation to DSARs, the right to rectification, the right to restrict processing, or the right to object. Nor do you need to comply with the right to be informed (for indirectly collected data) or the right to be forgotten.

  This exemption doesn't apply to commercial research purposes, such as customer satisfaction surveys or market research.

- >> Similar exemptions apply if you're archiving in the public interest.

You can explore exemptions further at the ICO website (`www.ico.org.uk`).

The consequences of failing to respond correctly

You may face the potentially significant consequences of not replying properly to data subject rights. The GDPR gives regulators the power to fine data controllers up to €20 million or up to 4 percent of the total worldwide annual turnover of the preceding financial year, whichever is higher, for noncompliance with data subject rights.

However, because the fines are to be "effective, proportionate, and dissuasive," (Article 84(1)) not every failure to comply will result in a fine of €20 million. You may receive warnings or other orders to comply before you're issued a fine. See Chapter 21 for more about the powers of supervisory authorities (SAs) and what SAs must take into account when considering noncompliance with data subject rights.

Enforcement actions

At the time of this book's printing, no enforcement actions under the GDPR for failure to comply with data subject rights have taken place, because of the length of time for investigation.

SCL Elections was issued an enforcement notice and a fine for £15,000 under the previous data protection legislation (where the maximum fine was £500,000) for failure to respond to a DSAR from a US citizen, highlighting the point that the nationality of the data subject is irrelevant.

A Swedish digital marketing company Bisnode, which has an office in Poland, was fined €220,000 by the Polish supervisory authority for a failure to comply with the obligation to provide information to data subjects under Article 14.

Defining the Eight Data Subject Rights

This section describes the eight rights provided to data subjects by the GDPR. Later sections of this chapter delve deeper into the most commonly exercised right — namely, the right of access (see the section "Data Subject Access Rights [DSARs]") — and the most commonly misunderstood right — namely, the right of erasure (see the later section "The Right to Be Forgotten").

The right to be informed

A key transparency requirement under the GDPR is the data subject's right to be informed about what personal data is being collected and how that data is used.

To effectively honor this right, which enables you to build trust with your data subjects, you must provide concise and easily accessible information — written in plain language — about their right to be informed. The place to provide this information to the data subject is in your Privacy Notice. (See Chapter 8 for more on what needs to be included in your Privacy Notice.)

Getting it wrong on the right to be informed leaves you at risk of fines and of damaging your reputation. The maximum fine for a failure to provide the correct privacy information, as I've stated elsewhere, is 20 million euros or 4 percent of your global worldwide turnover for the preceding financial year, whichever is higher. Complying with this right is easy, and the fines are high, so if you don't have a GDPR-compliant Privacy Notice in place, I advise doing so after reading Chapter 8.

In relation to the right to be informed, the GDPR distinguishes between personal data that you collect directly from the data subject and personal data you obtain from a third party (that is, someone other than the data subject, such as a data broker or a credit reference agency or even scraped from publicly available sources). The next few sections spell out the differences.

Personal data obtained directly from the data subject

If you have obtained the personal data directly from the data subject (for example, when they signed up for a free gift on your website), you must provide data subjects, for free, with certain mandatory *privacy information* (typically found in your Privacy Notice) at the time you collect the data. The information must include

- » Why you're processing the personal data
- » How long you'll retain the personal data
- » Whom you'll share the data with
- » Other details, which you can read more about in Chapter 8

So, if you're collecting personal data (such as names and email addresses) from your website, you should include a link to your Privacy Notice at the point of collection (for example, the email sign-up box). If you intend to use that personal data for marketing, additional rules apply, as discussed in Chapter 19.

You aren't obliged to provide the privacy information where the data subject already has the information. Say, for example, you are holding a live, in-person event for people and they signed up for the event via your website. At the point of sign-up on your website, you included a link to your Privacy Notice which included details about the processing of further personal data that will be requested at the live event. You would not have to provide them with your Privacy Notice at the live event because they had already received it at the point of sign-up.

Personal data obtained from a third party

Whenever you collect personal data from a third party (such as a third-party data broker or a government authority), you're obligated to provide the data subject with the privacy information within one month of receiving the personal data or at the time of the first communication or at the time of disclosure to a third party (whichever is earlier).

You aren't obligated to provide data subjects with privacy information in these circumstances:

>> If the person already has the information

>> If it would involve a "disproportionate effort" (Article 14(5)(B)) or would be impossible to provide in particular, for processing for archiving purposes, scientific or historical research, or statistical purposes

>> If providing the information would make it impossible to achieve (or seriously impair the achievement of) the objectives of the processing

>> Where the law requires you to obtain or disclose personal data and also provides appropriate measures to protect the data subject's legitimate interest

>> Where a professional secrecy obligation applies to you — for example, if you are a lawyer or an accountant, regulations designed to counter money laundering or a lawyer's duty of confidentiality to their clients

The right of access

Known as *subject access*, data subjects have the right to access their own personal data and can make a DSAR verbally or in writing. I cover this right in more detail later in this chapter.

The right to rectification

At times, personal data is collected in an inaccurate or incomplete manner, or may become so over time (for example, if a data subject moves and their address records are not updated). The *right to rectification* allows for data subjects to correct or complete that data as needed.

If you receive a rectification request, you must take reasonable steps to ensure that the data you hold on that data subject is accurate. What is *reasonable* depends on the nature of the data and the purposes of the processing. In this context, *inaccurate* means that the data is incorrect, untrue, or misleading as to any fact. If there is a disputed opinion regarding the data that is a reasonably held opinion, and it's clear that it's an opinion and not fact, it's difficult for a data subject to argue that the data is inaccurate and should be rectified.

The following points can help you determine a course of action:

>> **If you previously verified the data's accuracy,** you can take this into account in deciding what reasonable steps you must take.

- » **While checking the accuracy, restricting the further processing of the data is a good practice,** even if the data subject hasn't specifically exercised this right.

- » **If the data held was once inaccurate but now is accurate,** you should be able to retain the inaccurate data and the notes on file showing that it was corrected.

- » If, after checking the data, you're satisfied it's accurate, explain your decision to the data subject and inform them of their right to complain to the supervisory authority (see Chapter 21 for further details) and their ability to seek a judicial remedy in the courts.

- » If the data is inaccurate and you provided it to third parties, you must contact those third parties and inform them of the inaccuracy unless doing so involves disproportionate effort or is impossible.

In some cases, you can refuse to comply, as explained in the earlier section "General Matters Relating to Data Subject Rights."

The right to erasure

This right enables data subjects to request that their personal data be erased. I cover it in much more detail later in this chapter, in "The Right to Be Forgotten."

The right to restrict processing

When data subjects request the *restriction* of their data, that means you can store the data but not process it. Data subjects can submit the request verbally or in writing and you have one month to respond from the date of receipt of the request. In the case of restriction, you don't have to delete the data; for that, data subjects would need to request erasure.

Data subjects have the right to request the restriction of their personal data in these circumstances:

- » **The personal data might be inaccurate.** Processing of the data is halted while you investigate the accuracy.

- » **The data has been unlawfully processed.** In lieu of requesting erasure, the data subject requests restriction. See Chapter 4 for more about the lawfulness requirement of the GDPR's first principle.

- » **The data subject needs you to retain the data.** Even if you, as a controller, no longer need it, you may need to retain it if the data subject needs it to establish, exercise, or defend a legal claim.

>> **The data subject has requested the right to object to your processing the data.** While you determine whether you have a legitimate interest to override that request, the data is restricted. I discuss the right to object a bit later in this chapter.

The right to data portability

This right, which applies only to information the data subject has given to a data controller, allows data subjects to obtain and reuse their personal data for their own purposes across different services:

>> **What they can do:** Move, copy, or transfer personal data in a useable format and in a secure manner from one environment to another, whether it's from your systems to the data subject or to a new data controller.

>> **Why:** This right ensures that data subjects aren't locked in by digital controllers as a result of not being able to move their personal data. If data subjects have invested a large amount of time in adding personal data to an application or to a software, they may feel that they cannot move away from that data controller due to the time or money involved in re-creating that personal data. The right to portability means that they can insist that the data controller transfers their data to a new data controller, allowing the data subject to shop around.

The following list highlights scenarios in which the right to portability doesn't apply:

>> In cases where personal data is inferred about the subject, such as in health assessment outcomes and credit scores

>> In cases where processing is necessary for the performance of a task carried out in the public interest or in the exercise of official authority vested in the controller

And this list highlights scenarios in which the right to portability does apply:

>> When the data subject provides the personal data

>> When personal data is observed (location, activity logs, website search history, and so on) about the data subject

The right to data portability can be exercised only under these circumstances:

>> When the grounds for lawful processing (an issue I further discuss in Chapter 3) is

- Consent

- Explicit consent (for example, for special category data)

- Contractual necessity

>> When the processing is carried out using automated means

>> When the exercising of the right cannot adversely affect the rights and freedoms of others

The right to object

At your first point of contact with data subjects, you're obligated to inform them about their *right to object:* that is, their right to request that you stop the processing of their personal data in certain circumstances. Under the GDPR, data subjects have an absolute right to stop their data from being used for direct marketing. In other cases, data subjects can object to the processing of their data, although you may be able to continue processing if there's a compelling reason.

Rights relating to automated decision-making and profiling

When no human is involved in decision-making, which is instead carried out via automation, that is *automated decision-making.* When personal data is processed automatically to evaluate certain matters about an individual, that is known as *profiling.* Automated decision-making can include profiling.

Article 4(4) of the GDPR says that profiling is: "Any form of automated processing of personal data consisting of the use of personal data to evaluate certain personal aspects relating to a natural person, in particular to analyse or predict aspects concerning that natural person's performance at work, economic situation, health, personal preferences, interests, reliability, behaviour, location or movements."

The GDPR applies to all automated individual decision-making and profiling. Article 22 of the GDPR contains further provisions in relation to automated decision-making that produces legal effects or similarly significant effects on the data subject (such as automated mortgage or credit decisions or recruitment tests).

You can carry out automated individual decision-making that produces a legal effect or has a similarly significant effect only in cases in which the decision satisfies one of these three requirements:

>> Necessary for entering into or performance of a contract between the data subject and the data controller

>> Authorized by EU or individual EU member state law applicable to the data controller (for example, for the purposes of countering fraud or tax evasion) and which also provides suitable measures to safeguard the data subject's rights and freedoms and legitimate interest

>> Based on the data subject's explicit consent

If any of your processing falls under Article 22, you must ensure that you

>> Provide data subjects with information about the processing in your Privacy Notice (including the logic involved in the decision-making process as well as the significance of, and the possible consequences for, the data subject). See Chapter 8.

>> Implement suitable measures to safeguard the data subject's rights and freedoms and legitimate interests (at least the right for them to obtain human intervention, to express their point of view, and to challenge the decision).

>> Undertake regular checks to ensure that your automated systems are working as planned.

If processing involves special category data (see Chapter 3), automated individual decision-making may be used only in any one of these scenarios:

>> The data subject has given explicit consent to the processing.

>> The processing is necessary for reasons of substantial public interest on the basis of EU or member state law.

>> Suitable measures to safeguard the data subject's rights and freedoms and legitimate interests are in place.

TIP

Automated individual decision-making is considered to be high risk, so the GDPR requires you to carry out a Data Protection Impact Assessment (DPIA) to demonstrate that you have identified and assessed the risks and determined how to address them. See Chapter 15 for more about DPIAs.

If your automated individual decision-making doesn't produce legal effects or similarly significant effects, you can continue such decision-making in accordance with general GDPR principles.

Data Subject Access Rights (DSARs)

A *Data Subject Access Request,* or DSAR, is a written request made by the data subject for information they're entitled to ask for under the GDPR.

REMEMBER

Don't confuse a DSAR with a request under the Freedom of Information Act (FOIA) or similar legislation in other jurisdictions where data can be requested from a public authority.

Key changes to DSARs under GDPR

EU data subjects were able to submit DSARs to data controllers under previous data protection legislation, but the GDPR introduces three notable differences to the DSAR process:

>> You aren't allowed to charge a fee except in limited circumstances (which I discuss earlier in this chapter).

>> You must respond to the DSAR within 30 days. (The pre-GDPR time limit in the UK was 40 days.)

>> You must provide the data in electronic form wherever possible.

Data subjects may request the following items from the data controller:

>> Confirmation that you're processing their personal data

>> Copies of their personal data but not of data relating to other people

>> Other mandatory information as specified at Article 15(1) of the GDPR, such as the purposes of the processing, the categories of personal data being processed, the recipients (or categories of recipients) to whom you disclose their personal data, and how long you will store their data

Regarding the "Other information" mentioned in the last bullet in the list, you may have already provided this information in your Privacy Notice, which I discuss in Chapter 8.

Amending the data

Data is often transient and is being updated continuously. So, what do you do if the data has changed from when you receive the request to when you're ready to send out your response to the request? Generally, the relevant time point from which to send data is the time the request was received. If the personal data is being amended or deleted while you're dealing with the request, however, you may send the data that you hold at the point you send the response.

What you absolutely must not do is delete data that you don't want to supply to the data subject. Under the UK's Data Protection Act of 2018 (and other, similar European legislation), it's an offense to amend requested data to prevent its disclosure, punishable by an unlimited fine.

Section 173(3) of the UK's Data Protection Act of 2018 states, "It is an offence to alter, deface, block, erase, destroy or conceal information with the intention of preventing disclosure of all or part of the information that the person making the request would have been entitled to receive."

However, section 173(5) goes on to say: "It is a defence for a person charged with an offence under subsection (3) to prove that (a) the alteration, defacing, blocking, erasure, destruction or concealment of the information would have occurred in the absence of a request made in exercise of a data subject access right, or (b) the person acted in the reasonable belief that the person making the request was not entitled to receive the information in response to the request."

Responding to a DSAR

In your response, you must provide the data in concise, clear language that the average adult person (or average child, if the request relates to a child) can understand. If the data is in some way encoded, you must provide a key to the code so that the data subject can interpret the data. However, if the data subject doesn't understand the language you respond in, you aren't obliged to provide a translation.

If a request for a DSAR is made electronically, you should make the requested data available in a commonly used electronic format, unless the data subject has requested otherwise.

Recital 63 of the GDPR recommends that you should, where possible, provide remote access to a secure, self-service system providing direct access to the relevant data, as long as this doesn't adversely affect the rights and freedoms of others, such as trade secrets or intellectual property.

The UK's Data Protection Act of 2018 has special provisions relating to data held by credit reference agencies. Unless otherwise specified, a DSAR to a credit reference agency applies only to information relating to the individual's financial standing. Credit reference agencies must also inform individuals of their rights under section159 of the UK's Consumer Credit Act 2006.

Disclosing data that includes information about other people

Under the UK's Data Protection Act of 2018, you don't have to comply with the DSAR if you would have to disclose information about another identifiable person, except if that other identifiable person has agreed to the disclosure or you can reasonably comply with the request without that person's agreement. Similar legislation applies in other EU jurisdictions.

Concerning whether it's reasonable, you need to think about these factors:

>> The type of data you would be disclosing

>> Any duty of confidentiality owed to the other person

>> Whether you have sought the agreement of the other person

>> Whether the other person is capable of giving agreement

>> Any express refusal of agreement by the other person

TIP

The crux here is to balance the rights of the data subject making the request with the rights of the other person — often, a difficult exercise. In these instances, I highly recommend that you carefully document your decision and your decision-making process and keep it on file.

REMEMBER

You cannot refuse to provide data merely because it was obtained from another person. Only when the data inextricably involves the data of another person can you refuse to disclose it on this ground.

Regarding processors and DSARs

A *data processor* is a third party who processes personal data for you under your instructions. If one of your data processors receives a DSAR relating to personal data for which you're the data controller, the data processor must pass that DSAR to you as soon as possible.

Your Data Processor Agreement should include provisions obliging the processor to pass the DSAR to you as soon as possible. See Chapter 5 for details about data processors, and Chapter 10 for more on Data Processor Agreements. I advise also having suitable contractual provisions between you and your processors obliging them to assist you with a DSAR (or any other data protection rights).

REMEMBER

You cannot fail to respond to, or request, a time extension due to data not being available because a data processor failed to act in a timely manner.

Exemptions to data being provided as part of a DSAR

Specific EU member state legislation provides for certain exemptions to the data you need to disclose in response to an DSAR. Schedule 2 of the UK's Data Protection Act of 2018 provides a number of exemptions, including

>> Legal professional privilege during legal proceedings or confidentiality between a legal advisor and a client.

>> Self-incrimination.

>> Corporate finance where compliance is likely to affect the price of corporate finance instruments or would adversely affect a person's decision in relation to corporate finance.

>> Management forecasting or management planning of an organization to the extent that disclosure would be prejudicial to such forecasting or planning.

>> Negotiations with the data subject if such disclosure would be likely to prejudice negotiations with the data subject. This relates only to the negotiations themselves and not to the underlying claims that are the subject of the negotiations. After the negotiations are complete, this exemption no longer applies.

>> References for education, training, or employment of the data subject, the placement of the data subject as a volunteer, the appointment of the data subject to any office, or the provision by the data subject of any service.

>> Copies of written exams/exam scripts and exam marks.

>> Journalistic, academic, artistic, and literary purposes.

For more on these exemptions, see Chapter 18.

REMEMBER

Other EU member states may have different exemptions. If you can't determine whether you need to comply with a DSAR (or any other request from a data subject), consider contacting your supervisory authority for guidance or even a GDPR lawyer or consultant. A list of supervisory authorities appears in Appendix B.

Responding to a Data Subject Access Request

Though a DSAR can be quite legitimate, many are used as fishing expeditions or to uncover confidential HR procedures regarding redundancy and discipline. You, therefore, must be able to respond to an DSAR in accordance with the law but also in a sensitive manner.

If you have employees within your organization, I recommend that you

>> **Identify one person within your organization who will be responsible for handling DSARs.** This is a job for the Data Protection Officer (see Chapter 15), if you have one; if you don't, choose another suitable employee.

>> **Put in place a DSAR handling policy for all staff, and train relevant staff how to respond to DSARs.** Remember to include the receptionist, the mail carrier, and the social media team.

>> **Train all staff on how to recognize an DSAR.** Emphasize the importance of forwarding the DSAR to the employee who has DSAR responsibility.

The flowchart shown in Figure 14-1 has steps for dealing with a DSAR.

SUBJECT ACCESS REQUEST

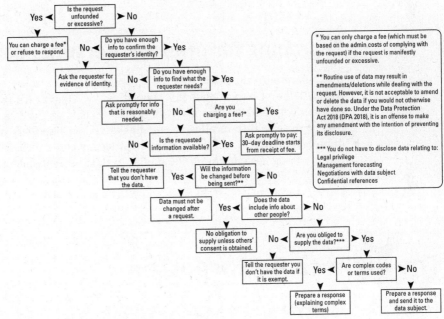

FIGURE 14-1:
Handling a DSAR.

FACEBOOK ARGUES THAT IT'S TOO TOUGH TO RESPOND TO DSAR

Michael Veale, of University College, London, submitted a DSAR to Facebook on May 25, 2018, the day GDPR came into force. Facebook replied (after the 30-day deadline) by saying it was too difficult to find all the relevant information.

Veale considered Facebook's response to be "unsatisfactory" on the basis that his data could be used to signify medical history, sexual orientation, or religion — essentially, highly personal and sensitive information. As a result, Veale lodged a formal complaint to the Irish Data Protection Commissioner (DPC). The DPC opened a statutory inquiry into the matter, anticipating that the matter will be referred to the European Data Protection Board because it involves cross-border processing.

As at the time of publishing this book, the statutory inquiry is still ongoing. Facebook is subject to another 10 investigations by the Irish DPC for matters ranging from questions over users' consent, to failure to notify supervisory authorities within 72 hours of a data breach.

Searching for relevant personal data

If you have not yet conducted a data mapping exercise (a key activity to comply with GDPR and inform your Privacy Notice; see Chapter 8), you must carefully consider where all the personal data is that you hold on the data subject. The data may be stored electronically, on a central server, on a memory stick, in the cloud, or on a hard drive. It might also be in hard-copy paper records. If paper records are in a filing system, the GDPR applies to them. Personal data may be included within emails, word processing systems, telephone records, payroll systems, or CCTV, for example. I discuss what constitutes personal data and where it's stored in Chapter 3.

The Right to Be Forgotten

Article 17 covers the right of erasure, or as it's commonly known, the right to be forgotten. A data subject can write to you and say, "I want to exercise my right to be forgotten." In this case, you have the obligation to forget that data subject and erase the vast majority of the personal data you hold about that person.

The right to be forgotten is different from an opt-out. If you have relied on consent as a ground for processing and a person opts out of marketing and receiving your emails, that isn't the same as a person requesting to be forgotten. In the case of an opt-out, you must have a record of the person opting out, which is typically kept on a suppression list. You need to keep at least that much information because the data subject's name might find its way into your database in the future, and you need to know that this data subject has said, "I don't want to receive those marketing emails."

The right to be forgotten is commonly misunderstood. Data controllers often mistakenly believe that it applies in all circumstances and that the obligation to delete data applies to all data. Neither assumption is the case, and the right is more restrictive than you might assume.

When the right to be forgotten applies

If a data subject chooses to exercise the right to be forgotten, you must erase personal data within the timescales discussed at the start of this chapter, when *one of* the following grounds applies (so it isn't an absolute obligation):

>> **The personal data is no longer necessary for the reason the data was collected or processed in the first place:** In this case, you should consider deleting the data because of the data minimization principle, which mandates that you should store and process information only for a specific purpose. See Chapter 4 for a discussion of the six data protection principles.

>> **The data subject withdrew consent on which the processing is based and there's no other legal ground for the processing:** So, on the flip side, you would *not* have to delete the personal data if a data subject withdraws consent to processing, but you have a legal obligation to keep records for a certain period.

For example, the limitation period for contractual claims in the UK is six years, so you might need to keep contracts for that time period. You can also keep email chains in which you've discussed elements of service or contractual terms, or anything that you would need to produce to defend a legal claim or to establish or exercise a legal claim.

>> **The personal data is processed on the ground of legitimate interests or public interests** *and* the data subject objects to the processing *and* there's no overriding legitimate interest for you to continue to process the data.

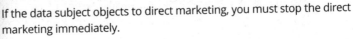

If the data subject objects to direct marketing, you must stop the direct marketing immediately.

>> **You're processing the data unlawfully.** If you are, you're in breach of the first data principle and liable for a fine of €20 million or a fine of up to 4% of annual worldwide turnover for the preceding financial year. See Chapter 4 for a discussion of the six data protection principles.

>> **The personal data has to be deleted for compliance with a legal obligation.** Such as to comply with a court order.

>> **The data was collected in relation to processing for the offer of online services to a child.** You should give particular attention to a request for erasure from a child (or from an adult who provided consent when they were a child) as they may not have realized the risks when they provided their personal data.

When the right to be forgotten doesn't apply

You don't have to delete all of a data subject's data if your basis for processing was not consent and you have an ongoing need and legal grounds for the processing, such as legitimate interests. It would be in your legitimate interest, for example, to maintain customer details on a suppression list to make sure you don't annoy customers by sending them information they've requested that you not send to them. To make sure that doesn't happen, you have to keep the data on file regarding their wishes. Does this infringe on their rights and freedom? No, because you're giving them what they've asked for.

Neither do you have to delete all of a data subject's data if you need to keep information for legal reasons. You're allowed to keep the information if the data processing is necessary for compliance with a legal obligation or for the establishment, exercise, or defense of legal claims.

The other, less common circumstances in which the right to be forgotten doesn't apply are listed here:

>> For exercising the right of freedom of expression and information

>> For compliance with a legal obligation or for the performance of a task carried out in the public interest or in the exercise of official authority

>> For reasons of public interest in public health

>> For archiving purposes in the public interest

Notifying third parties to whom you have transferred data

If you have transferred data to third parties and you're required to delete either all data or certain data to comply with the right to be forgotten, you must take additional steps to comply depending on whether the personal data has been shared privately with others or has been made public online:

>> **The data has been shared privately with others.** In this case, you must inform every recipient that the data subject has requested erasure. If asked, you must also inform the requesting data subject about these recipients.

>> **The data has been made public in a social network or web forum or elsewhere online.** You must take "reasonable steps," taking into account available technology and cost, to notify other data controllers so that they can take the necessary measures to delete the personal data in question, including links to and copies of it.

Erasing data from backup systems

In many cases, you might be able to delete the personal data from your live systems immediately. The personal data in backup systems, however, might remain for a designated retention period before being overwritten.

Keep these two key points in mind regarding information that a data subject has requested you erase. You must

>> **Stop using the data.** If the data will remain stored in a backup system, that backup must not be usable.

>> **Explain to the data subject what will happen to the data.** This includes live and backed-up instances.

If you have received a valid request to erase a data subject's data, you're required to erase the data from both live and backup systems. How you do so depends on

>> Your data retention schedule, including your backup retention policy

>> The technology available to you

The UK's ICO notes that if data cannot be immediately overwritten, backup data must be put "beyond use" and must not be used for any other purposes than holding it until it is deleted in line with the schedule for overwriting.

Children's data

The GDPR provides for the enhanced protection of children's personal data. If you based the processing of data on consent given by a child, you should prioritize the request to have that data erased, especially if that data exists in an online environment. You must comply even if the request is made when the data subject is no longer a child because, as a child, the person might not have understood associated risks when consenting to the processing.

Search engine results

The right to be forgotten emanated from a 2014 Spanish case (*Google Spain SL, Google Inc. v Agencia Espanola de Proteccion de Datos, Mario Costeja Gonzales*) in which a consultant, Mr. Gonzales, requested the removal of search engine links to Internet articles about his home repossession. He claimed this was damaging his business, because the first articles appearing in any online search pertained to his home repossession that had happened many years previously. The European Court of Justice (ECJ) ruled in his favor. The content is still online, but the search engines don't connect that content with searches for the consultant.

In a case that was heard by the ECJ in September 2018, the French supervisory authority, CNIL, sought a ruling that would enhance its powers to remove outdated or embarrassing content from Internet domains in any jurisdiction (not just on domains within the EU). Google fought the claim, arguing that this ruling would enable authoritarian regimes to limit free speech. Judgment was given by the ECJ in September 2019 and they ruled that there is no obligation for Google (or any other search engine operator) to remove data from Internet searches on domains outside of the EU. However, the court added that a search engine operator must put measures in place to discourage Internet users from going outside of the EU to find that information. Google currently uses a geoblocking feature that prevents EU users from being able to see delisted links.

In June 2018, Canada's supreme court ruled that Canadian courts do not have the power to force Google to remove links globally, so if the ECJ rules in favour of CNIL, it will be interesting to see whether other jurisdictions follow.

Chapter **15**

Data Protection by Design and by Default

The new obligations introduced by the GDPR include the requirement to implement data protection principles that safeguard individuals' rights. This is known as data protection *by design and by default*. What this essentially means is that you consider data protection and privacy upfront in order to integrate protection into your processing activities effectively— starting with the design stage and continuing throughout the whole life cycle. The idea is to take a preventative approach in which you proactively anticipate privacy issues and risks before they happen.

Previously known as *privacy by design,* this concept of data protection by design and by default is not a new one. Many organizations have implemented this approach as a matter of good practice, but the GDPR formalizes these requirements.

This chapter begins with a section fully describing data protection by design and by default, in case you aren't familiar with the concept. From there, I go on to discuss the Data Protection Impact Assessment (DPIA), a tool that can help you uphold data protection. Lastly, the chapter looks at the Data Protection Officer, a person dedicated to ensuring you uphold data protection.

Defining by Design and by Default

As I mention in the introduction, data protection by design and by default, though not new, is a concept that the GDPR formalizes. In this section, I further define this concept, taking the parts *by design* and *by default* separately.

REMEMBER

This obligation applies to data controllers and to all relevant individuals within a data controller's organization: from the director level to the IT team to the people using the processes and systems on a day-to-day basis.

TECHNICAL STUFF

Article 42 of the GDPR deals with certifications. Article 25(3) of the GDPR envisages certifications under Article 42 being used as a way to demonstrate compliance with these design/default requirements. The GDPR sets out the following in relation to certifications:

>> Certifications will be voluntary.

>> The process of obtaining certification will be transparent.

>> A certification does not reduce the responsibility of the data controller or the data processor when it comes to compliance with the GDPR.

>> Certifications will be granted subject to certain criteria.

>> Certification shall be issued for a maximum period of three years and may be renewed under the same conditions.

>> Certification will be withdrawn where the criteria are no longer met.

However, as at the time of print, no such certifications exist.

Data protection by design

Data protection by design — as specified in Article 25(1) of the GDPR — means you must consider data protection issues at the outset of the design of any system, service, product, or process and on a continuous basis.

As part of this, the GDPR requires you, as a data controller, to

>> Use appropriate technical and organizational measures to implement data protection principles.

>> Integrate safeguards into your processing to protect the data subject's rights and otherwise meet the requirements of the GDPR.

REGARDING OTHER ORGANIZATIONS

The GDPR (in Recital 78) makes it clear that data protection by design applies to other organizations involved in the supply chain even if these other organizations are not processing personal data, including any producers of applications, services, and products that are based on the processing of personal data or that process personal data to fulfill a task. These producers should consider users' right to data protection when developing and designing such products, services, and applications. Their intent should be to help data controllers and data processors fulfill their data protection obligations.

When you, as a data controller, choose suppliers of products and services related to your processing of personal data, consider whether the designers have incorporated data protection by design.

Equally, producers of products or services that relate to the processing of personal data should bear in mind that data controllers are likely to evaluate products and services based on whether they're developed or designed in accordance with data protection by design principles. The GDPR doesn't apply directly to developers, designers, and others who are not data controllers or data processors in this context, so they won't face sanctions if they fail. However, it's likely to their competitive advantage to do so.

For example, the following circumstances would require data protection by design:

>> Developing new IT systems, services, products, and processes that involve processing personal data

>> Developing organizational policies, processes, business practices, and/or strategies that have privacy implications

>> Planning the physical design of products

>> Embarking on data sharing initiatives

>> Using personal data for new purposes

The GDPR does not prescribe the technical steps that organizations can take to ensure compliance with the privacy-by-design obligations. In reality, data protection by design may involve you taking the following actions:

>> Minimizing the amount of personal data being collected and processed

>> Pseudonymizing personal data as soon as possible

>> Being transparent with regard to the functions and processing of personal data

>> Enabling the data subject to monitor the data processing

>> Enabling the data controller to create and improve security features

>> Ensuring that personal data is deleted when no longer necessary and otherwise in accordance with retention policies

Data protection by default

Data protection by default — as specified in Article 25(2) of the GDPR — means that you, as the data controller, must process only the personal data necessary to meet your specific purpose. This restriction is closely linked to the principles of data minimization, purpose limitation, and storage limitation (as discussed in more detail in Chapter 4).

Some people think that data protection by default means you must set all privacy settings to "Off" by default, but that isn't the case. What you need to do depends on the particular circumstances of the processing. If the processing involves risks to data subjects, it may be necessary for the strictest privacy settings to apply automatically — that is, "by default."

In any event, you should always consider the following in order to comply with the data protection-by-default obligations (which isn't an exhaustive list):

>> Providing data subjects with appropriate ways to exercise their rights

>> Ensuring that any choice given to data subjects is a "real" choice

>> Ensuring that personal data isn't made publicly available by default

>> Making privacy settings appropriate for the risks involved

>> Processing additional data only if the data subject consents to it

>> Processing the personal data that you actually require for only your specific purpose

>> Being transparent in relation to the processing of personal data

>> Enabling data subjects to understand the different stages of processing

>> Implementing appropriate security for the personal data

Conducting a Data Protection Impact Assessment

A *Data Protection Impact Assessment (DPIA)* is an evaluation you undertake as the data controller or the data processor. A DPIA is a process that enables you to identify and assess potential risks involved in the processing of personal data, look to mitigate those risks, and then decide whether the risks are still high. You must conduct this evaluation if you believe that processing certain personal data will involve a high risk to the rights and freedoms of the data subjects whose data you're processing.

In this section, I give an overview of the DPIA process, including how to ascertain risks and mitigations. Next, I look at when a DPIA is required and certain exemptions that might apply. Finally, I explain what to do if you determine that the identified risks are too high.

The DPIA process

The first thing to do in the DPIA process is to seek the advice of your Data Protection Officer (if you have one) and any other concerned stakeholders. (I talk more about seeking such advice later in this chapter.) You carry out the assessment, analyze the results, and then determine whether you can proceed with the data processing or need to consult your supervisory authority.

TIP

You may carry out a single DPIA for a set of similar processing operations that present similar high risks.

Chapter 13 has more details about which matters the DPIA will review, but the assessment should contain at least the items in this list:

>> Systematic description of the processing operations

>> Purposes of the processing, including, where applicable, the legitimate interest pursued by you — marketing or fraud prevention, for example.

>> Assessment of the necessity and proportionality of the processing operations in relation to the purposes

>> Assessment of the risks to the rights and freedoms of data subjects

>> Measures envisaged to address the risks, including safeguards, security measures, and mechanisms to ensure the protection of personal data

Where appropriate, you should seek the views of data subjects or their representatives on the intended processing. If you can demonstrate, however, that doing so would compromise the confidentiality of your business objectives or undermine security or simply be impractical, be sure to document the reasoning as part of your DPIA.

TIP

Conduct ongoing reviews of the processing to determine whether it's being carried out in accordance with the DPIA — particularly when the risks in relation to the processing operations may have changed.

Identifying risks and mitigations

If you believe that the processing of certain personal data will involve a high risk to the data subjects involved, consider the potential impact on those individuals. Your aim is to identify any harm or damage your processing may cause — physical, emotional, or material. In particular, look at whether the processing could contribute to any of these conditions:

>> Inability to exercise rights (including but not limited to privacy rights)

>> Inability to access services or opportunities

>> Loss of control over the use of personal data

>> Discrimination

>> Identity theft or fraud

>> Financial loss

>> Reputational damage

>> Physical harm

>> Loss of confidentiality

>> Reidentification of pseudonymized data

>> Any other significant economic or social disadvantage

When you have identified the risks, your next step is to first determine and record the source of each risk and then consider your options for reducing each risk. This list provides examples of actions you might take to mitigate potential risks:

>> Deciding not to collect certain types of data

>> Limiting the scope of the processing

>> Reducing the length of retention periods

>> Taking additional technological security measures

- >> Training staff to ensure that risks are anticipated and managed

- >> Anonymizing or pseudonymizing data where possible

- >> Creating internal processes to avoid risks

- >> Using a different technology

- >> Putting clear Data Sharing Agreements into place

- >> Making appropriate changes to Privacy Notices

- >> Offering individuals the chance to opt out where appropriate

- >> Implementing new systems to help individuals to exercise their rights

You should ask your DPO for advice. The preceding list isn't exhaustive, and you may be able to devise other ways to help reduce or avoid the risks.

Record whether the measure would reduce or eliminate the risk. You can take into account the costs and benefits of each measure when deciding whether they're appropriate.

When a DPIA is required

Data Protection Impact Assessments aren't new, but the GDPR (in Article 35) now requires controllers to carry out a DPIA prior to the processing where that type of processing is likely to result in a high risk to the rights and freedoms of natural persons. The GDPR specifies, in particular, processing that uses new technologies (such as Artificial Intelligence or Robotic Process Automation). And, of course, you must consider the nature, scope, context, and purposes of the processing.

Article 35 of the GDPR goes on to say that a DPIA shall in particular be required in any of these cases:

- >> Systematic and extensive evaluations of data subjects based on automated processing and on which decisions are based that produce legal effects or similarly significantly affect the natural person

- >> Processing on a large scale of special-category data or criminal-convictions data (see Chapter 3 for more about special category data)

- >> Systematic monitoring of a publicly accessible area on a large scale (such as CCTV or another type of video surveillance)

Recital 90 of the GDPR states that in addition to considering the nature, scope, context, and purposes of the processing, the sources of the risk should also be taken into account.

When a DPIA isn't required

You may be exempt in certain circumstances from carrying out a DPIA. For example, you won't be required to do a DPIA if you're processing personal data on the lawful grounds of either legal obligation necessity or public interests necessity, and the law regulates the specific processing operation (or set of operations) in question, and a DPIA has already been performed as part of a general assessment in the context of that legal basis.

REMEMBER

However, even if this set of circumstances applies to you, if EU member states require an assessment prior to data processing, you must still do the DPIA.

TIP

Even if a DPIA isn't strictly required by the GDPR or EU member state law, it is good practice to carry out a DPIA to consider and mitigate any risks of processing.

See Chapter 3 for more about the lawful grounds for processing personal data.

When to consult your supervisory authority

If you carry out a DPIA and it reveals that even after mitigating the risks as much as you can, the processing would still result in a high risk to the rights and freedoms of the data subject, the GDPR states (in Article 36) that you must consult your supervisory authority.

The supervisory authority must provide written advice to you, the data controller (and where applicable to the data processor), within eight weeks of receiving the consultation request. The supervisory authority can extend this period by up to a further six weeks if the processing is particularly complex. If any additional time is needed, it must write to you within one month of receiving the consultation request to explain the reasons for the delay. The 6- and 8-week periods may be put on hold while the supervisory authority is waiting for requested information from you.

The supervisory authority may take actions against you if you continue with the processing and they believe that it infringes the provisions of the GDPR.

You're likely to have to provide the following information:

>> Responsibilities of you as controller, any processor, joint controller, subprocessors, and so on

>> Purposes of the processing

>> Means of the processing

- >> Measures and safeguards to be put into place to protect the data subject

- >> Contact details of your Data Protection Officer (DPO), if you have one

- >> Copy of the DPIA

- >> Any other information required by the supervisory authority

Code of conduct

The supervisory authorities in each EU member state have been tasked with establishing and making public a list of the kind of processing operations that are subject to the requirement for a DPIA and those that don't require a DPIA. At the time this book was written, such lists had not been published.

Understanding the Data Protection Officer

A *Data Protection Officer (DPO)* is a person that you, as a data controller or a data processor, may be required to hire. Throughout this section, I discuss whom you might hire to fill this role and what responsibilities come with it. I also discuss when you're required to hire a DPO and their protections. I end the section with a quick look at choosing an external consultant to serve as your DPO.

What a DPO is

The DPO has a specific role and specific responsibilities, according to the GDPR, in relation to data protection and your processing of personal data. The DPO you appoint, who may be a staff member (either existing or new) or an external consultant, should have expert knowledge of data protection law.

Although the GDPR doesn't specify the exact credentials a DPO needs to have, it does say that the DPO's credentials should be in proportion to the type of processing carried out and the level of protection the personal data requires. Therefore, if you're a data controller or processor where the processing of personal data is complex or carries certain high risks, the DPO should have advanced knowledge and abilities. If your data processing is limited, however, you might not need such advanced expertise.

If you have a group of companies, you don't necessarily have to appoint a DPO for each group company. However, the DPO must be easily accessible to each group company or branch.

If the DPO of a group of companies doesn't speak the local language or isn't sufficiently familiar with the laws in a certain EU member state, you should consider having more than one DPO within the group.

The DPO's responsibilities

The DPO should be fully involved from the start in all issues that relate to data protection.

The GDPR defines (in Article 39) these tasks of the DPO:

>> Inform and advise you and your employees about your obligations to comply with the GDPR and other data protection laws.

>> Monitor compliance with the GDPR and other data protection laws with your data protection polices, including assignment of responsibilities, awareness-raising, and training of staff involved in processing personal data and conducting internal audits.

>> Provide advice on DPIAs and monitor their performance.

>> Cooperate with your supervisory authority.

>> Act as the contact point for your supervisory authority on issues related to data processing.

Your DPO is required to take account of the risk associated with your processing operations and therefore should take part in your DPIA. That person must consider the nature, scope, context, and purposes of the processing and provide risk based advice.

If, for some reason, you decide not to follow any advice provided by your DPO, you should keep records of your decisions and your reasons for those decisions, to help demonstrate accountability.

You may give your DPO other tasks and duties, as long as they don't lead to a conflict of interest with the DPO's primary tasks. Your DPO cannot determine the means or purposes of the processing of personal data. (As such, the head of marketing is unlikely to be able to act as the DPO.)

When a DPO is required

You must appoint a DPO in the following circumstances, all of which I explain further in this section:

- >> When you're a public authority

- >> When your core activities consist of regular and systematic monitoring of data subjects on a large scale

- >> When your core activities consist of processing special categories of personal data on a large scale

- >> When EU member state law requires it

Regarding public authorities

Public authorities is not a defined term within the GDPR. Organizations such as universities, publicly funded museums, and state schools are likely to be public authorities.

Regarding core activities

Core activities are your primary business activities. The data processing must be an "inextricable part of the data controller's or data processor's activity." If you need to process personal data to achieve your key objectives, this is a core activity. For example, if you process personal data for HR purposes, this processing won't be part of your core activities unless you're an HR service provider.

Regular and systematic monitoring of data subjects includes all types of web-based tracking and profiling and also offline processing and tracking — for example, for the purposes of behavioral advertising.

Regular has been defined to mean one or more of the following:

- >> Ongoing or occurring at particular intervals for a particular period

- >> Recurring or repeated at fixed times

- >> Constantly or periodically taking place

Systematic is defined this way:

- >> Occurring according to a system

- >> Prearranged, organized, or methodical

- >> Taking place as part of a general plan for data collection

- >> Carried out as part of a strategy

Large scale relates to the number of data subjects rather than to the size of the organization. The following are considerations regarding whether the processing is large scale:

>> Large number of data subjects impacted, as either a large number in total or a percentage of the relevant population (no guidance has been provided on what "large" means)

>> Volume of personal data

>> Range of different data being processed

>> Duration of the processing

>> Permanence of the processing

>> Geographical extent of the processing

Regarding EU member state law

In Germany, for example, companies that employ at least 9 people in the automated processing of personal data or at least 20 people who are employed in non-automated processing of personal data are required to appoint a DPO. Be sure to check your member state legislation to assess whether further requirements may oblige you to appoint a DPO even though you don't fit into the criteria set out here.

REMEMBER

Even though certain EU member states might not require you to appoint a DPO, you may enjoy certain advantages for doing so. For example, in France, if you appoint a DPO, you don't need to make prior declarations to the French supervisory authority, CNIL.

DPO protections

The DPO is put in place to perform an important job — to ensure that data protection measures are implemented and enforced — and, as such, must be able to perform the job unhindered. To that end, a DPO has certain protections:

>> The DPO should be independent:

  • You should not instruct the DPO on how to carry out any tasks.

  • You may not dismiss or penalize DPOs for performing their tasks.

>> The DPO must report to the highest management level. This doesn't necessarily mean that the DPO has a direct reporting line to the board of directors, but that the person must be able to access the highest level of senior management.

>> The DPO isn't personally liable for your data protection obligations or for any breaches of the GDPR or other data protection laws.

Additionally, you as the data controller or processor must do the following to help the DPO:

>> Provide your DPO with all resources necessary to carry out his or her tasks.

>> Provide the DPO with access to personal data and processing operations.

>> Enable the DPOs to maintain their expert knowledge.

DPO contractors

If you choose to use an external consultant to be your DPO, the consultant should have the same position, tasks, and duties as though you had an employee carrying out the role.

The DPO contractor isn't personally liable for your data protection obligations or for any breaches of the GDPR or other data protection laws.

You may decide to appoint a DPO internally and then use external consultants (and/or internal members of staff) to support the DPO. You should not, however, refer to external consultants or other internal team members (who are not actually the DPO) as a DPO, because this position brings certain requirements.

Chapter **16**

Data Security

O
ne of the key elements that underpins GDPR is how you, as a data controller or a data processor, secure and protect the personal data you collect, store, and process. Data security isn't just an IT issue — it affects every area of your operations, and it involves everyone at every level of your business.

Chapter 17 covers data breaches, specifically detailing what obligations you have under GDPR in the event that your organization experiences one. This chapter takes a more general look at data security practices that need to be embedded within your organization if they are to be effective.

Reviewing Data Security

Data security, often also known as *information security* — and, in the case of securing electronic data, *cybersecurity* — concerns the protection of data and information assets that are used to store and process data. These assets can be paper-based, such as filing cabinets and hard copy documents, or they can be electronic systems, such as computers, databases, and software.

The data we collect, store, and process is constantly increasing, as businesses capture more data about more people, topics, clients, or staff. At the same time, the threats to data security are constantly evolving, from cyberattacks, malware, theft, and competitors to environmental hazards such as fire or flood.

To remain relevant and effective, your data security practices need to be part of an ongoing process of continuous improvement, as shown in Figure 16-1. I discuss the relevant components of that process throughout this chapter.

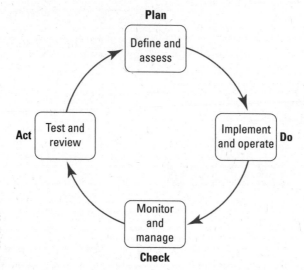

FIGURE 16-1:
The continuous
improvement
process.

REMEMBER

If you're reliant on third parties for data storage and/or processing functions, always check and verify their terms and conditions for the availability of their systems and services. This is particularly relevant when utilizing cloud- or Internet-based services that could impact your business operations.

Data security is often broken down into these three key areas, discussed next:

>> **Confidentiality:** Protecting data against unauthorized access, distribution, or publication

>> **Integrity:** Protecting data against unauthorized modification, corruption, or tampering

>> **Availability:** Protecting data against unplanned loss, destruction, or unavailability

Confidentiality

Confidentiality is about protecting data against unauthorized access, distribution, or publication. A key tenet of this concept is the *need-to-know* principle. Here's a basic question to ask whenever you provide any individual or entity with access to data or data processing systems: Does this person have a genuine need to know?

This question is particularly relevant when it comes to modern computing systems, where providing access to applications and databases to both internal and external parties must be carefully considered. One way to manage such access is through the use of appropriate access controls and user privileges that limit or restrict the level of access and visibility of data within your systems to only that are required to perform specific roles. Such access should be based around the concept of "least privilege," ensuring that users are not given more access than they need to perform their specific role or function. Users with enhanced privileges, such as system administrators, should not use their privileged accounts for normal, day-to-day work.

Where you do need to provide access to data, it's also worth asking whether the data needs to be provided complete and in its original form, whether you should cut it down by removing fields or elements or fields, or whether you need to consider *pseudonymization*, a technique that removes any part of the data that can directly identify specific individuals. (See the nearby sidebar, "Pseudonymization versus anonymization," for more information on that topic.)

PSEUDONYMIZATION VERSUS ANONYMIZATION

To pseudonymize a data record involves taking information that can directly identify a person, such as a name or date of birth, and removing it or replacing it with artificial identifiers. Doing so enables the data to be processed or transferred without enabling the data subjects to be re-identified. It's useful in cases where the identities of the data subjects are neither required nor relevant because the data can still support other types of data analysis.

Data that has been pseudonymized can be restored to its original state by adding back any identifying information that was removed. The anonymization of data on the other hand occurs whenever any information that can identify a particular person — directly or indirectly (for example, by singling out an individual using a cookie ID in order to track their browsing habits) — is stripped out by means of permanent deletion of identifiers or another process. For data to be truly anonymized, the process must be irreversible.

Confidentiality is also a key driver in the classification of data and data assets. Many businesses, organizations, and public sector bodies have specific guidelines on how they classify their data assets to ensure that need-to-know is enforced. It can also be used as a way of valuing data assets in terms of the impact to your business should the data be compromised or made public.

Integrity

Data *integrity* is concerned with protecting data against unauthorized modification, corruption, or tampering. Essentially, this means ensuring that the data you store and process is correct, accurate, and consistent over its entire life cycle. You need to be in a position in which you're confident that the data hasn't been tampered with or compromised in any way as it moves from one system or individual to another.

In many areas of business, data integrity is as important, if not more so, than confidentiality. Imagine for a moment you were buying something online. You need to have complete confidence that the value of pounds, euros, or dollars you paid is the same that arrives with the seller at the other end of the transaction for your purchase to be completed. This is data integrity at work.

Key approaches when considering data integrity include

>> **Validating data inputs and data outputs:** This involves ensuring software and applications only accept, produce, or respond to known good inputs and have strong error handling and validation routines.

>> **Protecting against system or hardware failure:** Calls for deploying systems on *high-availability* — resilient or cloud-based platforms that reduce single points of failure, in other words.

>> **Using encryption to protect data transfers:** This involves using appropriate technologies such as Virtual Private Networks (VPN) to safeguard the data being transferred, and/or Transport Layer Security (TLS) to encrypt the traffic end-to-end.

>> **Implementing safeguards that reduce the likelihood of human error:** Steps here could include having supervisors double check sensitive operations that staff are undertaking.

For high-value and high-impact data processing, actively ensuring nonrepudiation for specific events or transactions is essential. (*Non-repudiation* means being able to provide proof, potentially legal in nature, of the origin and integrity of the data involved in the transaction.)

Availability

Availability entails ensuring that data and data processing systems are available when they're needed. Imagine going to the bank to withdraw money. You reach the bank teller and are informed that, unfortunately, the bank systems are down and your request cannot be processed. That would be frustrating, wouldn't it? If you need to withdraw cash from the bank, you don't want to hear, "The systems are down and will be unavailable for the next 28 days. Sorry for the inconvenience." You need your money now, not in a month's time!

Ensuring that access to data and data processing systems is there when users need the data is essential for most businesses. Some key elements for consideration include

>> Backup and recovery solutions for data, files, systems, and applications

>> Disaster recovery (DR) and business continuity planning (BCP) that detail how your business will handle a major issue that impacts operations

>> High-availability and cloud-based solutions that show how you achieve resilience in data storage and processing systems

>> How you will manage the impact of environmental factors (such as fire and flood) or other security incidents

>> How resilient your systems are to disruption and whether they can continue to operate under adverse conditions, such as those caused by a security incident or technical fault

Article 32 Security Obligations

Article 32 of the GDPR states, "Taking into account the state of the art, the costs of implementation and the nature, scope, context and purposes of processing as well as the risk of varying likelihood and severity for the rights and freedoms of natural persons, the controller and the processor shall implement appropriate technical and organizational measures to ensure a level of security appropriate to the risk."

Essentially, this mouthful means that the security measures you implement to protect personal information must be proportionate to the risk that your processing poses, particularly the risk "from accidental or unlawful destruction, loss, alteration, unauthorized disclosure of, or access to personal data transmitted, stored, or otherwise processed."

REMEMBER

Article 32 does not govern only cybersecurity issues or cover only digital and electronic systems. It can also apply to the protection of data not stored or processed electronically, such as any data held in paper-based documents that are housed in physical file cabinets or records storage.

Article 32 doesn't outline a specific set of security controls you need to implement. Instead, it encourages data controllers (that's you) and data processors (which may be you or another entity) to implement "appropriate" controls based on the risk. Consider these controls:

>> Assessment of the value and nature of the data and processing activities

>> Implementation of suitable security policies, processes, and procedures

>> Maintenance of appropriate confidentiality, integrity, and availability (including resilience) of data and processing systems

>> The recovery or restoration of access to data and processing systems in a timely manner

>> Pseudonymization or encryption of personal data

>> Testing and evaluating the effectiveness of security controls

>> Implementation of and/or certification against established security frameworks, such as Cyber Essentials, ISO 27001, or NIST (National Institute of Science and Technology) Cybersecurity Framework, all of which are discussed later this in chapter, in the section "Introducing Security-Related Frameworks."

Implementing effective and proportionate security controls (the topic of the later section "Protecting Your Data") helps to protect individuals from the harm and distress caused by loss or abuse of personal information. When personal data is compromised, individuals may suffer from identity theft, financial loss, fraud, or physical harm as a result or otherwise find themselves the target of criminals. Even where such consequences are unlikely to happen, individuals are still entitled not to have their data used in unlawful or unauthorized ways.

Good data security practices are also important for legal and regulatory reasons and can be used to demonstrate compliance with broader aspects of GDPR.

Identifying Your Data Assets

The first step in effective data security involves the following activities:

>> Identifying your *data assets* — the data your business stores, processes, and manages, in either hard copy or electronic form

>> Valuing those assets in terms of their loss or impact to your business

TIP

If you have a lot of special category data, you may also want to look at classifying your data so that it becomes easier to enforce the need-to-know principle. Classifying information clarifies expectations on how it should be handled and who should have access to it. A typical business classification scheme could include:

>> **Public:** Information that is published by the organization or in the public domain (website content and brochures, for example).

>> **Internal:** Information that is not particularly sensitive but should only be handled by and shared with employees or trusted partners (intranet pages and internal emails, for example).

>> **Confidential:** Information that should be limited to specific personnel with a genuine need to know based on their role (personal information and legal guidance, for example)

>> **Protected:** Especially sensitive information that should be carefully protected and accessed only by a specific few individuals (sensitive personal information and security plans, for example).

Identifying and valuing your data assets is an essential step if you're going to implement suitable, proportionate controls to protect your data. All too often, organizations fail to take the first step in correctly identifying and valuing their assets and then either spend too much time and money protecting what they have or, worse still, don't do enough to safeguard their data. The latter issue all too often ends in a security breach (sometimes referred to as a *cyberattack*), as discussed in Chapter 17, with all the implications that carries.

When it comes to identifying your data assets, it's important to consider all types of data assets, separating them into their operational or functional uses and assigning each asset an *information asset owner* (IAO). The IAO is responsible for valuing the data asset and ensuring that it's managed appropriately and protected according to its value to the business.

A good way to assess the value of a given data asset is to assess the impact to your business from a breach of confidentiality, integrity, or availability — just one of these, or two, or all three. When valuing your data assets, you should consider factors such as these:

>> If the data became public, how would that impact your business?

>> If the data became inaccurate or inconsistent, how would that affect your business?

>> If you lost the data or it became inaccessible, what would that do to your business?

>> How long would it take to rebuild or re-create the data?

>> If the data was temporarily inaccessible, how long would it be before it impacted your business (hours, days, weeks)?

That last question is particularly relevant in terms of selecting and implementing suitable disaster recovery options to ensure that the impact to your organization is minimized but aligns with your operational requirements.

TIP

A great way to manage your data assets, in terms of identifying and valuing them, is with an *information asset register* (IAR). This can be anything from a simple spreadsheet to a comprehensive database (depending on the size and complexity of your business) as long as it's suitable for your organization. Asset registers are also useful evidence that you know and understand your data assets should you ever need to respond to a security breach or regulatory investigation.

Protecting Your Data

After you have identified your data assets and worked out their value to your business, you need to look at what you should be doing to actually protect them. These are known as *security controls* and are typically broken down into four areas: technical, procedural, personnel, and physical.

These four control types are often used together to layer your security defenses. The controls you actually deploy within your organization will vary based on the different types of data assets you have, the value those assets are assigned, existing threats that could target those assets, and the availability of the appropriate security controls that help to safeguard the assets.

Typically, the process used to define a set of security controls is based on what is known as a *risk assessment*, which is addressed in the later section "Conducting regular testing and assessments." In a risk assessment, you look at the value of the asset, the threats posed to the asset, the likelihood of an attack or failure being realized, and any existing mitigating security controls. You then use the results to assign a risk level to your data assets and to prioritize your efforts based on (and in order of) risk level. This way, you turn attention to the highest risks first, mitigating, avoiding, transferring, or accepting those before moving on to the next highest-risk areas.

REMEMBER

Taking steps to ensure that you have deployed security controls around sensitive and personal information helps you to protect those assets and your business operations. Doing so also goes a long way toward meeting your legal obligations for protecting personal information. When it comes to GDPR, being able to prove that you're actively managing the risks to data, taking steps to protect data, and deploying relevant security controls will count for a lot even if you experience a security breach.

Technical controls

Technical controls are composed of various technologies, systems, and software used to protect electronic data. They ensure that only valid users of a given system can access data on a *need-to-know* basis. Technical controls include

>> Firewalls and network perimeter defenses to protect your network and the devices and data that use it.

>> Antivirus solutions to spot and prevent computer malware attacks.

>> Roles-based access controls (RBAC) that ensure users have only the minimum privileges they need to perform their duties and can access only the systems and data they absolutely need.

>> Strong passwords or 2-factor authentication to improve user access security and prevent brute-force attacks.

REMEMBER

Two-factor authentication (2FA) is a security technique that requires the user attempting to access a system to be verified and authenticated with multiple factors. Rather than simply enter a username and password (one factor) and gain access, the user must also, for example, enter a code sent to a mobile device. (That second step is what is meant by the second factor.)

>> Device and network encryption to protect data at rest on computers, mobile devices, and tablets and to safeguard data as it travels around your network and externally (where relevant).

REMEMBER

Encryption is a technique that converts data into an unreadable format, protecting it from unauthorized systems or individuals. To access the data, the user must have the correct decryption key, which converts the data back to a readable format. In this way, data can be protected from unauthorized access and eavesdropping either at rest or in transit:

- **At rest:** On a computer storage device, hard drive, or mobile device

- **In transit:** Being sent or transferred over networks, such as over the Internet

» Data loss prevention (DLP) technology that notifies you whenever you're leaking data by way of user activity or network compromise. (*Data leaks* are one of the most common types of security breach and typically result from either a successful cyberattack, where malicious 3rd parties extract data from a victim's systems and networks, or by employees accidentally or deliberately emailing or uploading company data to external systems.)

Procedural controls

Procedural controls include the policies, processes, and procedures that all users must follow to protect data and may include

» Information security policies to help define your organization's approach to protecting data

» Social media policies outlining acceptable use of social media platforms to your staff, such as what they can and cannot do on social media, including whether they're allowed to discuss business topics online

» Email policies designed to provide guidance on how email should and should not be used within your organization

» Acceptable-use policies to give staff clear guidance on how to use company computer systems and other company-provided assets

» Data breach policies which outline how data breaches are handled, who is responsible for managing the breach, and when notifications need to occur

Personnel controls

It is an unfortunate fact of life that no matter how good your organization's technical security controls, employees doing the wrong thing, or not following the rules, are one of the main causes of security breaches. In this regard, personnel controls help you ensure that your employees can be trusted to have access to systems and data and are properly educated on how to handle it. Typical personnel controls include:

>> Pre-employment checks verify that potential employees or freelance staff are who they claim to be and have the skills and experience they claim.

>> Criminal record checks (where available — some EU member states do not allow such checks) and security vetting ensure that staff are safe to handle potentially sensitive information.

>> Security awareness training helps staff safeguard your systems and data.

>> Internal policy training helps staff understand how to comply with your internal policies and procedures.

Physical controls

Physical controls can provide real-world barriers between a would-be perpetrator and your organization's data. But they can also help protect data against environmental threats such as natural disasters, terrorist attacks, and accidental disruption. Physical controls that protect your offices can include such items as:

>> Lockable filing cabinets and information storage areas

>> Smoke detectors and fire alarms

>> Intruder alarms

>> Security doors

>> A no-tailgating policy preventing unauthorized personnel from entering sensitive areas

>> A *clear desk* (or *secure desk*) policy that helps ensure sensitive information isn't left lying around on employee desks

Handling Security Incidents

Under the GDPR, a personal data breach doesn't always mean that someone has stolen your data. A security incident leading to a personal data breach could be the result of any number of different accidental or malicious events, such as fire or flood destroying the data, a hard disk failure corrupting electronic data, or a work laptop containing personnel records being left on a train.

And despite all your best efforts to prevent anything bad from happening, you can still fall victim to *cyberattacks,* incidents in which intentional attempts are made — whether successful or not — to expose, alter, or disable data. Someone releasing *malware* (software designed to cause damage to a computer, server, or network) into your systems is just one example of a cyberattack.

When you experience a security incident in which data is compromised, you must be able to determine that the event took place as well as how to respond to and recover from it. Also, you must do the necessary assessments and testing to ensure that the security measures you have in place are working. These issues are covered throughout this section.

Detecting security incidents

Introducing measures to protect data is important but not necessarily enough on its own unless you have a way to identify whether a security-related event has actually occurred. Under GDPR, you're required, where feasible, to notify the appropriate supervisory body of a security breach within 72 hours of your becoming aware of the breach. (Chapter 17 covers details regarding notification and other issues related to data breaches.)

If you can't confirm that a breach has actually occurred, you're in a weak position and risk breaking the law or announcing that an event has taken place without being able to confirm it or understand the impact.

Detecting a security incident can mean different things depending on the type of incident and the complexity of the environment. A simple security incident could be something that's easy to spot and understand, such as a staff member informing their manager that an email has been sent to the wrong recipient.

Other security incidents can be more challenging to identify, especially in high-tech corporate environments with multiple internal and external systems interacting in real time. In these scenarios, you are likely to require the implementation of automated systems that log events and raise alerts with qualified incident responders based on rules designed to identify the actions of advanced, skilled computer hackers.

Detecting security incidents is as much about employee training and awareness, policies and procedures, and clearly defined roles and responsibilities as it is about technical capabilities. Staff need to understand how to report suspected security incidents, and whom to report them to, and appreciate how they will be handled. You also need to consider options for out-of-band reporting — also known as *whistle-blowing* — so that systemic activities or authority-based abuses can be reported without fear by the individuals concerned.

REMEMBER

The last thing you need as a business is to be informed by the press or a regulator that you've had a serious security breach that no one within your organization was aware of or had ignored!

Responding to security incidents

Even if you've deployed advanced technical solutions to detect and respond automatically to security incidents, your main method of responding will likely be key individuals working through manual processes.

Before you can respond to a suspected security incident, however, you must be prepared to do so by planning and documenting how you will identify and respond to different types of security incidents. Each type of incident requires a specific set of actions:

>> A flood that ends up destroying paper archives requires different actions by different personnel compared to a ransomware attack against your computer system.

>> An email containing special category data sent in error to the wrong recipient, for example, needs to be identified and dealt with quickly. This situation, however, isn't likely to need too many advanced technical skills.

>> A long and sustained cyberattack, resulting in huge quantities of data being exfiltrated from your business, is likely to involve a lot of specialist external skills for a thorough investigation.

All these scenarios have one important factor in common: They require you to follow documented processes and procedures so that you can

>> Confirm the nature of a security incident

>> Decide whether the event is a genuine incident or a false positive

>> Take action to contain the breach and limit the damage

>> Identify the cause

>> Determine whether security incident is reportable to regulators or to affected data subjects

TECHNICAL STUFF

Regarding data security, a *false positive* occurs when you think you have a vulnerability in your system or that your system has been compromised in some way. In reality, however, all is well. A software bug or unrecognized network traffic can cause a false positive. A *false negative*, which is the opposite, happens when you think everything is fine; in this case, unfortunately, some type of security breach has actually occurred.

Alongside any actions taken to identify and deal with the issue at hand, you have additional issues to consider:

>> What is the data involved or at risk? Is any of it personal information?

>> Was it the result of malicious or non-malicious activity (human error, for example)?

>> Is the incident a one-off or part of a larger issue?

>> What is the scope of the data involved, and which systems are impacted?

>> Should you disconnect impacted systems to preserve data or prevent further losses? This can be a way of preventing some types of cyberattack but can also impact the ability to conduct detailed forensic analyses of the attack.

>> Will you need to preserve evidence for future criminal or civil action?

>> How will you deal with any public or press reaction to the incident?

>> What is your plan for limiting the reputational impact to your business?

>> Do you need to notify any regulatory or supervisory bodies within a specific time frame?

>> Is there a potential need to notify data subjects and provide help and support? (See Chapter 17 for more on this topic.)

Obviously, more advanced technical systems can provide significant help when it comes to responding to security incidents. An advanced system must still be tailored to your specific business and operational needs, and even then, can typically only help you with purely technical issues.

Planning, documenting, and testing your data security response plans is a useful exercise. It helps to highlight critical gaps and can potentially save you from severe sanction if a genuine security breach occurs.

Recovering from security incidents

When it comes to recovering from a data security incident, effective planning and testing help to minimize the impact to your business. Here are some key areas to consider:

>> **Backup and recovery plans for key data and systems:** These provide you with a point-in-time recovery solution, should you lose important systems or data, and allow you to recover operationally from more minor incidents.

>> **Disaster recovery planning (DRP):** Essentially, this term specifies how you reduce the impact of technical and IT-related issues impacting your business operations. DRP tends to cover the key technology systems you need to maintain operational effectiveness while your main systems are offline or unavailable. DRP can cover anything from individual laptops to whole data centers.

>> **Business continuity planning (BCP):** This is a plan regarding how you manage and continue business operations in the event of a major issue impacting your business. Typically, this covers more than just IT, including premises and office facilities, logistics, supply chain, public relations, and staffing.

>> **Cyber-resilience:** Building and configuring systems that can continue to operate effectively despite adverse cyber-events is a relatively new area. It's gaining more and more recognition based on the idea that cyberattacks launched with enough resources and determination will always succeed to some extent.

Your plans for recovering from security incidents need to factor in timescales for recovery — in particular, how long it will take you to recover key systems and data following a breach — and any regulatory or supervisory obligations you have to ensure that systems and data are available.

A good way to start looking at your recovery plans is when you're identifying and valuing your data assets. When you're looking at each asset and its value to the business, consider the impact of the data not being available for a variety of timescales, such as 1 hour, 1 day, 2–3 days, 1 week, and 1 month. This is where you can start to consider the recovery plan for each data asset to ensure that it can be recovered in line with business requirements.

TIP

After you recover your systems and data following an incident, take time to

>> Glean lessons learned from the incident and feed them back into your planning and operations

>> Review your data assets and confirm or reevaluate their value to the business

>> Review your security controls

>> Assess the effectiveness of your ability to detect a security incident

>> Update your response and recovery plans

Conducting regular testing and assessments

Implementing security controls is essential for the data security of your key information assets. But how do you know whether the controls you have implemented actually work? How do you know whether you have significant weaknesses that a potential attacker can exploit to gain access to your special category data?

The only way to know whether your security controls are truly effective is to assess and ultimately test them. Security testing can be conducted in various ways, including

>> **Walk-throughs:** These simple paper-based exercises assess your controls and look for areas of potential weakness usually conducted by internal staff with knowledge of the systems and controls.

>> **Red Teaming:** A specialist external adversarial team is brought in to conduct a review and challenge the perceptions and implementation of your security controls, plans, and assumptions.

>> **Vulnerability assessments:** Your systems and infrastructure are scanned, either as a one-off exercise or continually as part of an ongoing security regime, using specialist tools that look for weaknesses in the setup and/or configuration.

>> **IT health checks:** Also known as *white hat testing,* this occurs when external security testing specialists are provided with detailed information about your systems, network, and applications with a view to conducting extensive internal testing. The aim is to look for and identify security vulnerabilities so that you can fix them.

>> **Penetration testing:** This type of testing is similar to IT health checks, but the testers conduct *gray hat* or *black hat testing,* which involves attempting to hack into your systems based on little to no understanding of your infrastructure. This means it can be potentially disruptive to your business operations should the testers adversely impact live systems. The aim of a penetration test is to simulate a lifelike, usually external, attack against your business so that you can assess the strength of your security controls and your resilience to a genuine cyberattack.

TIP

Any of these testing approaches should be employed at least annually, to verify your organization's security and reduce the risks posed by poor system configuration, software weaknesses, and application coding errors that can be introduced over time. Indeed, it's generally considered best practice to test your security controls following any major changes to your systems, infrastructure, or applications to ensure that the changes themselves haven't introduced security flaws that can be used to attack your business.

TIP

Testing your disaster-recovery and business-continuity plans and processes regularly is also a good practice. Changes over time to your supply chain or staffing or the general way your business operates can have a significant impact on your ability to survive a major business-affecting incident. Such factors need to be assessed in order to ensure that, should the worst happen, your organization can survive and recover.

Introducing Security-Related Frameworks

Security frameworks are collections of policies, processes, standards, guidelines, and controls that an organization has implemented to formally manage risks to its information and data. This section provides an overview of security frameworks that may be helpful to you as a small-business owner who needs to comply with data security obligations under the GDPR.

International frameworks include those provided by the International Standards Organization (ISO); national frameworks might be more suited to smaller businesses. Although the names, such as ISO 27001:2013, look very technical and may even be intimidating, these security frameworks provide the same benefit: They're here to help and support your data security efforts.

ISO 27001:2013

ISO 27001:2013, generally referred to as ISO27001 or ISO27k, is the recognized international standard for an information security management system (ISMS). An ISMS includes a set of policies, processes, standards, guidelines, and documented security controls an organization implements to formally manage its information risks.

The standard is designed to fit an organization of any size, from small businesses to large multinational corporations. Assessment of (and certification against) the standard is achieved for a given scope area. This can be an entire organization, an operational function such as a data center hosting function or a call center function, or several different functions that combine potentially different operational areas of a business.

To achieve ISO27001 certification, an organization must prove that it has an effective ISMS in place and that it's effectively managed and maintained under a process of constant review and improvement.

When looking to utilize external or third-party organizations as data processors, a data controller should ensure that the scope of the ISO27001 certification covers all areas of the processors' business involved in the processing. This should include

>> All data centers housing computing resources involved in the processing, including storage, processing, backup, and disaster recovery locations

>> All sites and personnel involved in the day-to-day support of those processing resources

>> All sites and personnel with access or potential access to the processing facilities or data, including data storage, backup, and disaster recovery facilities

>> Any subprocessors, subcontractors, and third-party suppliers with access to your data

It's also worth remembering that ISO certifications are international in nature, so it's important to verify that all locations within the scope of the certification that are likely to be involved in the processing or storage of your data are in countries that are suitable and acceptable for handling a processing your data.

Organizations that become ISO27001-certified generally have reasonably effective information security practices and are regularly assessed for renewal of their certification, so they're likely to be a good choice as processors, subject to the scope of the certification and their geographic locations.

ISO 27005:2018

When it comes to information security management, it's important to have a process for identifying and managing the risks posed to data and information. Known as an *information risk-management process*, it helps your organization identify its data assets, understand the impact of the loss or compromise of those assets, and manage the risks posed to the assets throughout their life cycle.

The recognized international standard for information risk management is ISO27005:2018 or ISO27005. ISO27005 can be used to support an effective ISO27001 regime, though it isn't necessary to achieve ISO27001 certification, as long as you use a suitable alternative information risk-management process.

ISO27005 does not document a specific risk management methodology, but instead advocates a process of continual risk management based on these factors:

- **Business context:** Here you define the criteria for how risks are identified and managed within your organization. This probably includes how information asset roles and responsibilities will be defined, how impact and likelihood will be assessed, what the organization-specific risk tolerance levels are, and how risks will be measured and prioritized. The latter is usually done based on either qualitative methodology (judgment and experience) or quantitative methodology (a mathematical formula to identify potential costs).

- **Risk assessment:** In this stage, you identify your data assets, identify the threats applicable to each asset, assess the impact and likelihood of a risk to those assets materializing, and then prioritize which assets need risks to be addressed most urgently.

- **Risk treatment:** Whenever risks are above your risk-tolerance level, making them unacceptable to your organization, you need to look at how you should manage them, typically by one of these methods:

  - *Mitigation:* Implement security controls to reduce the risk.

  - *Transfer:* Share the risk with another party, such as an insurer.

  - *Avoidance:* Look for ways to eliminate the risk completely.

- **Risk communication:** Here you ensure that the key stakeholders, data assets owners, and other individuals or groups involved in the information risk management cycle understand their roles and responsibilities, are clear on how information risk decisions should be managed, and know why certain actions need to be taken.

- **Constant risk review:** A key activity in information risk management is the constant monitoring and review of information risks. Systems, data, and the threats that exist around them are constantly changing. That's why it's important to have a process of constant review; ideally, built into change management processes to identify and manage risks that could be introduced over time, but also conducted regularly where systems and operations are more static.

Cyber Essentials (Plus)

Cyber Essentials and Cyber Essentials Plus are part of an initiative by the UK's National Cyber Security Centre (NCSC) to help businesses improve their cybersecurity and gain a form of certification that can be used to improve trust between organizations and their supply chain businesses.

The main difference between Cyber Essentials and Cyber Essentials Plus is that Cyber Essentials is a self-assessment option and Cyber Essentials Plus means that your security controls have been independently verified by a certification body.

Both certifications are designed to ensure that you have addressed the most common types of cyberattack, such as hacking, phishing, and brute force attacks, which aim to "guess" passwords. The certification looks at five key technical areas of your infrastructure:

>> **Firewalls:** How you're protecting your technical boundaries and Internet-facing systems and ensuring that only safe and essential services can be accessed from outside your boundary

>> **Secure configuration:** How you configure, lock down, and control systems and services, ensuring that systems are providing only the services required for their function and reducing inherent vulnerabilities

>> **User access controls:** How you control and manage user access to systems, applications, and data and ensure that access is the minimum required for users to perform their role

>> **Malware protection:** How you protect your systems and applications against malware, viruses, and worms and ensure that only valid software can be executed

>> **Patch management:** How you manage firmware, operating system, and software/application updates (often referred to as *patches*) in a timely manner to reduce vulnerabilities and therefore the potential for a cyberattack

In much the same way as ISO27001 certification, Cyber Essentials certification can cover all or part of your IT infrastructure, systems, and applications, but it's generally considered best practice to certify your whole IT infrastructure to ensure that you're properly protecting your data and systems.

REMEMBER

Cyber Essentials is entirely focused on digital systems and infrastructure that can be attacked from the Internet. It doesn't cover systems that are unable to be attacked from the Internet. Neither does it cover security controls protecting non-digital data, such as paper-based files and records.

NIST Cybersecurity Framework

The National Institute of Science and Technology (NIST) Cybersecurity Framework provides data security guidance to private sector companies and organizations. Primarily aimed at organizations based in the United States, the framework has been widely adopted outside of the US because of its quality and depth and the fact that it's well maintained.

Much of the content in this chapter is based on these functions of the NIST Cybersecurity Framework:

- » **Identify:** Develop an understanding of your organization's data assets, systems, functions, and risks.

- » **Protect:** Implement appropriate, proportionate, and suitable security controls to protect systems and data commensurate with the risk and value of the asset.

- » **Detect:** Implement appropriate solutions and processes to identify suspected cybersecurity events.

- » **Respond:** Implement suitable processes and procedures to protect your assets after a cybersecurity event is detected.

- » **Recover:** Develop and test plans and procedures to restore systems and services to an operational state in a timely manner, commensurate with their value to the business.

The NIST Cybersecurity Framework is a voluntary scheme against which organizations self-assess. When you start down the path of using the framework, a typical approach takes you from your as-is profile to a target profile:

- » **As-is:** You first assess your current state — your *as-is profile* — to verify your existing controls and identify your information security maturity level.

- » **Target:** After you understand where you are now, you should define a *target profile* for your business; the target is where you need to be. Then plan the activities to achieve the required level of security.

The NIST Cybersecurity Framework is an effective way of improving your organization's data security *posture* (or strength). It is, however, likely to require a serious commitment on your part in terms of money, time, and resources to implement effectively.

Data Controller and Data Processor Liabilities

Data controllers carry the largest burden under GDPR and must be able to demonstrate compliance with GDPR and relevant data protection legislation. Should you as a data controller be investigated by a supervisory authority, such as the UK's Information Commissioner's Office (ICO), you'll want to be able to prove that you've done your due diligence regarding your data protection obligations.

A data controller is responsible for compliance with the GDPR, regardless of any terms of business or contractual agreement between the controller and a data processor. They are also potentially liable for any damage and related claims for compensation if processing conducted on their behalf infringes the GDPR — unless they can prove they aren't in any way responsible for the event giving rise to the breach. (See Chapter 5 for more about the controller's and processor's individual responsibilities.)

REMEMBER

Data processors involved in an infringement of the GDPR may be liable to the data controller under the terms of their contract for services. They may also be included in any action taken by an individual or an investigation conducted by a supervisory authority (such as the ICO) and may be subject to penalties or required to make corrective actions.

A data processor can also be subject to a claim by an individual who decides to take the processor to court for damages caused by their processing. In such cases, a processor is liable for damages only if they have failed to comply with the processor requirements of GDPR or have acted against or without the data controller's lawful instructions.

The role of subprocessors

When a processor performs data processing services on behalf of another processor, it is called a *subprocessor*. Subprocessors are typically used when a processor needs to outsource some or all of the processing function performed on behalf of a data controller. For example, if company A engages service provider B to process data on its behalf, and service provider B then outsources some of that processing to service provider C, then A is the data controller, B is the processor, and C is the subprocessor.

Here's another real life example of when a subprocessor may be involved in data processing:

1. You (the data controller) employ an event management company (the data processor) to organize a function.

2. You provided the event management company (the data processor) with a list of potential attendees (the data subjects).

3. The event management company then hired a printing company (the subprocessor) to print and deliver the invitations to those attendees.

Like any other processor, a subprocessor can be held liable for damages if they have failed to comply with the processor requirements of GDPR or if they have acted against or without the data controller's lawful instructions relayed to it by the processor.

The processor remains liable to the controller for any subprocessor infringement of the processor's data protection obligations. Essentially, this means that if a subprocessor is at fault for a breach of GDPR, the processor — and not the subprocessor — is liable for compensating the controller. Any liability between the subprocessor and processor is based on the terms of their contractual obligations.

Doing your due diligence

When engaging a data processor, it's the data controller's responsibility to make sure the data processor is competent to provide the processing services in line with the data controller's GDPR and data protection obligations.

Article 28(1) states that data controllers are required to use data processors that can provide sufficient guarantees that they have the relevant data security controls and organizational safeguards in place to protect the data commensurate with the risk posed.

Such guarantees could be in the form of certification against industry standards, like ISO27001 or Cyber Essentials, or it could be obtained by assessing their technical expertise, reviewing their policies and procedures, and, where relevant, auditing compliance with your requirements on an ongoing basis.

In addition to satisfying itself that the processor is suitable and capable, the data controller must also ensure that there's a legal or contractual agreement with the processor that covers the requirements of Article 28(3) as well as providing the processor with clearly documented instructions on the processing activities.

Breaches caused by data processors

While data controllers retain the primary responsibility for compliance with the GDPR, both controllers and processors need to understand the nature and implications of data security breaches that can be caused purely by processors failing in their specific responsibilities. Chapter 17 covers a handful of data security breaches that have been seen or reported in the real world. They are designed to highlight a common set of issues that can and are experienced when processing personal data.

Sanctions for data breaches caused by data processors

If a data breach happens that is purely the fault of the data processor, the supervisory authority (such as the ICO) can choose to take a number of actions against the processor themselves, without recourse to the data controller. These include

>> Issuing warnings or reprimands for processing operations that infringe the regulations

>> Ordering the processor to comply with subject access requests where the controller is unable or unwilling to do so itself

>> Ordering the processor to improve their operations to bring them into compliance with their obligations, which can include the manner of the improvements and a time limit on their implementation

>> Imposing a temporary or permanent limitation or ban on the processor's activities

>> Ordering the processor to rectify or erase personal information and/or restrict processing activities

>> Withdrawing (or ordering the withdrawal of) any regulation-related certificate

>> Ordering the processor to cease or suspend the transfer of data with third countries or international organizations

>> Issuing an administrative fine in addition to, or instead of, any of these sanctions

Chapter 17 has more information about potential consequences for data controller-caused data breaches.

Chapter **17**

Data Breaches and Reporting Obligations

As a data controller or a data processor, your obligation is to secure personal data that you process. If your organization suffers a personal data breach, you have to carry out certain reporting and recordkeeping requirements. Although the only data breaches you tend to hear about are those of large companies, small businesses can suffer data breaches, too. Data breaches more often than not happen accidentally and thus aren't always a result of malicious intentions.

In this chapter, I describe the types of breaches, provide insight on assessing how significant a breach is, and give guidance on determining whether a breach has actually occurred. An important aspect of breaches, under the GDPR, is sending notifications related to the breach — to either the supervisory authority or the affected data subjects (or, if you are a data processor, to the relevant data controller) — and documenting breaches and how you handle them. Lastly, I cover the consequences of breaches.

Understanding What Constitutes a Breach

According to the GDPR, a *personal data breach* is a "breach of security leading to the accidental or unlawful destruction, loss, alteration, unauthorized disclosure of, or access to, personal data transmitted, stored or otherwise processed." This definition is a lot to take in, so in this list I break it down and explain it in segments:

>> **Accidental:** As I mention in the introduction to this chapter, not all data breaches are intentional. Some can happen as a result of carelessness or by other accidental means.

>> **Unlawful:** This term refers to any act or omission that violates the GDPR or any other laws or regulations, such as altering personal data in order to not have to disclose it as part of a Data Subject Access Request.

>> **Destruction:** When personal data is destroyed, that means it no longer exists or no longer exists in a form that is of any use to the data controller.

>> **Loss:** This term means that the data controller no longer has control of, or access to, the personal data or no longer has the personal data in its possession.

>> **Alteration:** This term means that the data has been changed in character or in composition and can include corrupted or inaccurate data.

>> **Unauthorized disclosure:** This term refers to disclosure of personal data (or access) by recipients who are not authorized to receive (or access) the data.

REMEMBER

Personal data breaches aren't caused solely by hackers breaking into your online systems and stealing personal data. Personal data breaches can also happen as a result of these (and other, similar) scenarios:

>> Staff members leave hard copy files of personal data on airplanes or public transportation.

>> Email with personal data is sent to the wrong recipient.

>> Staff members lose mobile devices, laptops, or memory sticks that contain personal data.

>> Personal data is altered without authorization.

>> Personal data becomes unavailable due to a server malfunction so that the data is no longer accessible.

>> Personal data undergoes unauthorized destruction.

>> Personal data is lost in the postal mail.

>> Hackers make personal data unavailable by using ransomware.

>> Hackers obtaining personal data through social engineering techniques such as phishing and spear phishing.

TECHNICAL
STUFF

Phishing is where hackers pretend to be a trusted entity (a law firm, for example, or the tax authority) in an attempt to persuade you to click on a link within the message. After the link is clicked, a program installs malware or ransomware on your computer. The malware can then detect confidential data that you input onto other web pages, such as passwords for online banking. The ransomware encrypts your files so that you can't access them until you pay the ransom. Spear phishing is where hackers disguise themselves as a trustworthy friend or entity to acquire personal data, typically through emails or online messaging. Spear phishing attacks target a specific victim, whereas phishing attacks are not personalized to victims.

Categorizing breaches

Breaches can be characterized in three main ways — note that a data breach could involve one or two or all three of these types:

>> **Confidentiality:** An unauthorized or accidental disclosure of, or access to, personal data that happens when someone who should not have the data acquires it or gains access to it.

>> **Integrity:** An unauthorized or accidental alteration of personal data that occurs when data is rendered unusable or has been changed or made incomplete.

>> **Availability:** An accidental or unauthorized loss of access to, or destruction of, personal data. The loss of access refers to the scenario when the people who should have access to the data are denied that access. Examples of availability breaches are described in this list:

- *Data has been deleted either accidentally or by an unauthorized person.*

- *In the case of securely encrypted data, the decryption key has been lost.*

- *The normal service of an organization has been significantly disrupted; for example, experiencing a power failure or denial-of-service attack, rendering personal data unavailable.*

Note that, in each type of availability data breach case, if you (the data controller or data processor) cannot restore access to the personal data — for example, from a backup — this is regarded as a *permanent loss of availability* and is therefore a personal data breach.

A *temporary loss of availability* could also be a data breach where the lack of access would result in an adverse impact on the rights and freedoms of data subjects. If a temporary loss of availability is caused by planned system maintenance, however, that is not a data breach.

The European Data Protection Board (EDPB) provides guidance on data breaches following a loss of availability, as follows:

>> If critical medical data about patients is unavailable at a hospital, even temporarily, this may present a risk to individuals' rights and freedoms, such as operations being canceled and lives put at risk. This would be a data breach that requires notification. (I talk more about the format for such notifications in the "Sending Notifications" section, later in this chapter.)

>> If a media company's systems are unavailable for several hours because of a power outage and the company is prevented from sending newsletters to its subscribers, this is unlikely to have an impact on the data subjects' rights and freedoms and would not be a data breach that requires notification.

>> A company might suffer infection by ransomware that leads to a temporary loss of availability (temporary, presuming that the data can be restored from backup). In this case, a network intrusion has occurred, so notification could be required if the incident comprises a confidentiality breach (personal data is accessed by the hacker) that presents a risk to the rights and freedoms of data subjects.

REMEMBER

Ransomware is malicious software that encrypts data, making it unusable. Victims receive the decryption key after paying ransom money to the perpetrator.

Assessing Data Breaches

The GDPR makes it clear (in Recital 87) that when a security incident occurs with regard to personal data, you need to act quickly to determine whether a personal data breach has in fact occurred. If so, you must quickly consider what impact the risk of this data breach will have on the rights and freedoms of individuals. In this section, I discuss the potential consequences set out by the GDPR and the risk factors you need to consider.

When you consider the risk that a data breach will have on the rights and freedoms of individuals, keep in mind these two factors: the likelihood of the risk and the severity of the risk. These factors will help you to decide (if you are a data controller) whether you need to send notifications to your supervisory authority and to the affected data subjects. This must be an objective assessment. When in doubt, err on the side of caution, and notify. If you are a data processor, you need to notify the relevant data controller of any data breach regardless of risk.

You must if possible notify your supervisory authority about a breach within 72 hours of knowing that a personal data breach occurred — issues I cover in more detail later in this chapter, in the section "Sending Notifications." However, the clock doesn't start ticking toward that 72 hours until you have determined that the incident is actually a breach. You're allowed an investigation period during which the 72 hours is not counting down. I cover these topics in the "Sending Notifications" section as well.

The GDPR refers to the impact on "natural persons" and not on "data subjects affected by the breach." This term means that you must consider a wider impact than for only the data subjects, though they are your first (immediate) concern.

A *natural person* is an individual human being, as opposed to a *legal person* which may be a private business entity or non-governmental organization or a public organization, such as a governmental organization.

Addressing potential consequences

When you're considering the risk to the rights and freedoms of individuals, focus on the potential negative consequences on individuals, as described in the GDPR (in Recital 85):

>> Loss of control over their personal data

>> Limitation of their rights

>> Discrimination

>> Identity theft or fraud

>> Financial loss

>> Unauthorized reversal of pseudonymization

>> Damage to reputation

>> Loss of confidentiality of personal data protected by professional secrecy

>> Emotional distress of the individual

>> Any other significant economic or social disadvantage to the natural person concerned

The GDPR cautions that a personal data breach, if not addressed in an appropriate and timely manner, may have any combination of these negative impacts on individuals.

REMEMBER

If the data breach involves special-category data (see Chapter 3 for more on this topic), you can assume that the rights and freedoms of individuals are impacted and that a notification is necessary. The same data breach may affect individuals in different ways; for example, vulnerable individuals (such as children) may be more affected than others. As such, you should consider the risks case-by-case and look at all relevant factors.

Weighing risk factors

The European Data Protection Board (EDPB) recommends that you consider the following criteria when assessing whether breach-related risks will impact the rights and freedoms of natural persons:

>> **The type of breach:** A confidentiality breach where medical information has been disclosed to unauthorized parties, for example, may have consequences different from circumstances when medical information has been lost and is no longer available. A further consideration would be the identity and motive of the third party breaching the data; for example, if the breach is a disclosure in error to a small number of people, all of whom have agreed to delete the data, this will be a lower risk breach than one where hackers have obtained data with a view to profit from it.

>> **The nature, sensitivity, and volume of personal data that has been compromised:** The more sensitive the data, the higher risk of harm to the individuals affected. Breaches concerning health data, identity documents, or financial data such as credit card details can all cause harm on their own. If used together, they could be used for identity theft. A list of customer-deliveries data may seem fairly innocuous, but if it specifies when deliveries are paused (for example, because customers are away on holiday), it has the potential to cause harm to individuals: Burglars could use this information to steal goods from homes while the data subjects are away from home.

The breached data doesn't have to constitute a large volume for there to be a risk to the individual. A breach concerning data about just one person (such as lost medical records or disclosing a vulnerable individual's address) could involve a high risk to that data subject, triggering the obligation to notify the supervisory authority and the individual.

If the effects of the data breach are long term or permanent, the impact is greater.

>> **Ease of identification of individuals:** Consider how easy it would be for a party who has access to compromised personal data to identify specific individuals, not just with the compromised data but also with other data they may hold. If data is encrypted and the third party doesn't have the key or the data is otherwise pseudonymized, it won't be easy for the third party to identify individuals.

>> **Severity of consequences for individuals:** Consider whether the potential harm to individuals could include severe consequences, such as identity theft or fraud, physical harm, psychological distress, humiliation, or damage to reputation. The severity of consequences will likely be greater to individuals where special categories of data have been compromised.

>> **Special characteristics of the individuals concerned:** Consider whether the consequences could be even more severe when dealing with vulnerable individuals (such as children or vulnerable adults); typically, they are.

>> **Special characteristics of the data controller:** If you're, for example, a data controller holding medical data, the risk of a breach impacting individuals is greater than if you're a media company whose mailing list has been breached.

>> **The number of affected individuals:** Generally, the higher the number of affected data subjects, the greater the impact of the breach. A data breach relating to a single individual could have a high impact, however, if the data is special-category data and/or the individual is a vulnerable individual.

Although not listed in the EDPB guidance, you may also want to consider the identity and motive of the third party breaching the data. Consider who has access to the compromised data and what their motives are. Has an innocent individual received personal data via an email sent to the wrong email address? Or is a criminal enterprise selling financial details on the dark web?

Becoming aware of the breach

You may become aware of the data breach soon after it happens or not until weeks or even months later. The GDPR allows for this situation, and the countdown for sending notifications about the breach starts only after you actually become aware of it.

The EDPB guidance indicates that a data controller should be regarded as having become aware when the data controller has a reasonable degree of certainty that a security incident has occurred that has led to compromised personal data.

This is not to say that you can merrily go about your business without caring whether data breaches have taken place. The security obligations under GDPR require you to implement all appropriate technical protection and organizational measures that help you to monitor and establish immediately whether a breach has taken place.

This list describes examples (based on EDPB guidance) regarding when the data controller would become aware in various scenarios:

>> **Losing data on an electronic device:** If you lose a USB key with unencrypted personal data on it, you may not be able to say for certain whether unauthorized third parties have gained access to that personal data. However, the loss is a data breach that must be notified because there's a reasonable degree of certainty that an availability breach has occurred.

  You, as the controller, become aware of the breach when you realize that the USB key has been lost.

>> **Unauthorized disclosure:** If you're told by a third party that they have received personal data accidentally, this unauthorized disclosure is clear evidence of a confidentiality breach.

  You become aware of the breach when you're notified by the third party.

>> **Network intrusion:** When you detect a possible intrusion into your network, you investigate to establish whether personal data has been compromised and you realize that is the case.

  You become aware of the breach when you realize that personal data has been compromised.

>> **Hacking or other types of cybercrime:** If a cybercriminal contacts you after having hacked into your system and demanding a payoff to release the files they've stolen, you would check your system to confirm that you have suffered an attack.

  You become aware of the data breach after the confirmation.

Investigating the breach

When you discover a security incident or you're informed of a potential data breach by a third party, you're allowed a short period of investigation to confirm whether a personal data breach has occurred. During the period of investigation, you, as the data controller, aren't regarded as being aware of the breach. As such, the notification timescales don't start yet. You must, however, start your investigation as soon as possible after becoming aware of the security incident or potential breach.

After you have carried out your initial investigation, you will probably need to conduct a more detailed and thorough investigation. The 72-hour notification timer, however, starts after your initial investigation shows, with a reasonable degree of certainty, that a personal data breach has occurred.

Responding to a breach

When you decide a personal data breach has occurred, your next step is to decide whether the risks arising from the personal data breach will affect the rights and freedoms of data subjects and then take appropriate action. That action may include making notifications, which I discuss in the following sections. Other appropriate actions to consider (such as making and following PR plans and remediation plans) are outside this book's scope. Here's an example of a data breach response:

1. A third party notifies you that the third party has received an email impersonating you, which contains accurate personal data relating to the third party.

2. This notification informs you that your system has been breached.

3. You carry out an urgent investigation to determine whether your system has been breached and then follow your internal processes to detect the breach.

4. You confirm the breach and are now aware of the personal data breach. You identify that multiple individuals whose personal data you hold have been affected.

5. You consider whether the breach is likely to have an impact on the rights and freedoms of individuals and whether you need to notify your supervisory authority and the affected individuals. This seems highly likely given the malicious nature of the incident and the volume of individuals affected.

6. You take appropriate remedial action to address the breach.

If your organization is larger, your breach response plan should include these items:

>> Procedures for analyzing and containing a potential security breach

>> Reporting mechanisms

>> Operational responsibility for managing a breach and contact information for the person/team responsible

- >> Instructions for whether and how to escalate an incident

- >> Processor management plans

- >> A communications plan, including steps for notifying affected individuals

- >> A remediation plan

- >> Details of external resources, such as lawyers, insurers, and IT, PR, and HR personnel

- >> A documentation plan

TIP

Whether a data breach happens accidentally or via malicious means, it is important to have a PR response plan in place to help you communicate quickly and effectively with data subjects. Doing so can help allay fears and minimize damage to your professional reputation. I can highly recommend Alan Stevens for reputation management (www.mediacoach.co.uk/crisis-media-management).

Sending Notifications

If you have assessed that the data breach involves some risk to the rights and freedoms of data subjects, you must notify your supervisory authority (or SA, also known as a data protection authority).

In the case of a personal data breach, the GDPR, in Article 33(1), requires that you, as the data controller, notify the supervisory authority without undue delay. When possible, notify the supervisory authority no later than 72 hours after having become aware of the breach. And, if there's a delay in notifying — that is, within 72 hours — be sure to provide the reasons for the delay.

The GDPR has an exception from making the notifications to your supervisory authority where the personal data breach is unlikely to result in a risk to the rights and freedoms of natural persons.

REMEMBER

When in doubt, err on the side of caution and notify. You suffer no penalty for notifying in circumstances that later turn out not to comprise a personal data breach.

TIP

Work out which supervisory authority is your lead authority. For example, if you're established in the UK and all affected data subjects are in the UK, the supervisory authority will be the ICO. If you are not established in the EU, EDPB guidance is to make the notification to the supervisory authority of the country in which your Representative (see Chapter 6 for more on Representatives) is established. See Chapter 21 for more about determining your lead authority.

TIP

If you decide not to notify, you should still keep a written record of your decision and reasoning for not notifying the breach — and you should do this on a data breach record form (as you should with breaches that you notify). See Chapter 13 for more on this topic. If your supervisory authority decides that you should have notified, you may be subject to sanctions (which I discuss at the end of this chapter).

Notifying the supervisory authority

Article 33(3) of the GDPR states that the notification to the supervisory authority should, at minimum,

>> Describe the nature of the personal data breach, including (where possible):

- *The categories and approximate number of data subjects concerned*

- *The categories and approximate number of personal data records concerned*

>> Communicate the name and contact details of the data protection officer or other contact point where more information can be obtained

>> Describe the likely consequences of the personal data breach

>> Describe the measures taken or proposed to be taken by the controller to address the personal data breach, including, where appropriate, measures to mitigate its possible adverse effects

The GDPR doesn't define *categories of data subjects* or *personal data records*. The EDPB suggests the following explanations:

>> **Categories of data subjects:** The various types of individuals whose personal data has been affected by the breach. This could include children and other vulnerable groups, people with disabilities, employees, customers, or suppliers.

>> **Categories of personal data records:** The different types of records that a data controller may process, such as health data, educational records, social care information, financial details, bank account numbers, and passport numbers.

Even if you don't yet know precise information such as the number of data subjects affected, do not delay in notifying. The GDPR allows you to provide approximate numbers. Additionally, you can provide information in phases, which may be useful when a complex breach has taken place. For example, you can provide an initial notification to a supervisory authority within the 72-hour time period and then follow that up later once you have gathered more information with a supplemental notification.

You must provide reasons for any delay in providing relevant information to the supervisory authority.

Although Article 33(3) of the GDPR lists the minimum amount of information you must provide, you can of course provide more information than required. Do this wherever it may be helpful, such as naming the data processor if the processor caused the breach and if they suffered an incident that may affect other data controllers.

The supervisory authority may of course request further information as part of its investigation.

As a data controller, you may want to seek advice from the supervisory authority about whether you need to notify affected individuals. However, in some instances, such as potential identity theft, you obviously need to notify affected individuals and you must do so without delay. (See the later section "Notifying data subjects" for more on this topic.)

You could suffer a number of data breaches over a short period of time relating to the same or similar types of personal data about large numbers of data subjects. This might be the case where, while investigating one breach, you identify other, similar breaches. Rather than having to notify each of these breaches individually, you may submit a bundled notification that covers all the breaches. If, however, the breaches involve different types of personal data, breached in different ways, you should submit individual notification for each breach.

Here's an example that the UK's supervisory authority, the ICO, provides:

1. You detect an intrusion into your network and become aware that files containing personal data have been accessed, but you don't know how the attacker gained entry, to what extent the data was accessed, or whether the attacker also copied the data from your system.

2. You notify the ICO within 72 hours of becoming aware of the breach, explaining that you don't yet have all relevant details but that you expect to have the results of your investigation within a few days. After your investigation uncovers details about the incident, you give the ICO more information about the breach without delay.

Notifying data subjects

Article 34(1) of the GDPR states: "When the personal data breach is likely to result in a high risk to the rights and freedoms of natural persons, the controller shall communicate the personal data breach to the data subject without undue delay."

The criteria for notifying the supervisory authority of the breach is that there's a risk to the rights and freedoms of natural persons. The criteria for notifying the affected individuals is that there's *a high risk* and therefore this is a higher threshold.

If you initially decide that there's *not* a high risk to the rights and freedoms of individuals, keep careful records of this decision and the reasons for it. The supervisory authority may require you to notify data subjects even if you have decided not to; the authority may even impose sanctions on you if you haven't notified data subjects when you should have done so.

TIP

The risk to data subjects may change over time, so keep this point under review: A notification may not be necessary initially. As further matters come to light or the risk changes — for example, because data is released into the public domain or accessed in a further breach — that would change the risk to *high*. A high risk requires notification to data subjects.

Some data breaches might require law enforcement investigations. Although you must notify individuals as soon as possible, the GDPR understands that early disclosure of a breach could, as stated in Recital 88, "unnecessarily hamper the investigation of the circumstances of a personal data breach." On the advice of law enforcement authorities, you may delay notifying data subjects of the breach while those investigations are ongoing.

What to include in a notification to data subjects

Article 34(2) of the GDPR instructs you to use clear and plain language in the notification to data subjects. Regarding what to include, you must provide similar information that you provided to the supervisory authority — namely:

>> Description of the nature of the breach

>> Name and contact details of the data protection officer or other contact point

>> Description of the likely consequences of the breach

>> Description of the measures taken or proposed to be taken by the controller to address the breach, including, where appropriate, measures to mitigate its possible adverse effects

Additionally, you should provide, where appropriate, advice to data subjects on any steps they can take to mitigate risks, such as resetting passwords.

How to communicate to individual data subjects

Recital 86 states that you, as a data controller, should cooperate with supervisory authorities in deciding how to communicate with affected data subjects. However, as the controller, you probably have in mind the most effective ways to communicate with your data subjects. If urgency requires it, though, you should notify data subjects immediately, without waiting for the supervisory authority's input.

Merely posting the notice on your website or in a blog isn't sufficient notification. This list highlights ways to communicate the breach to data subjects:

>> Notify the individual directly, unless doing so would involve disproportionate effort (for example, because their contact details are not known or were lost due to the breach). If it would involve disproportionate effort, you should make a public communication, such as a notice in a national newspaper.

>> Several different types of channel might be appropriate to communicate the notice directly to individuals — direct email, SMS or other direct message, for example. Other transparent communication methods include prominent website notice, letter by post, and prominent advertisements in print media.

>> Make the data breach the sole focus of the communication. Don't combine the notice with other communications — including it in an email about other matters, for example.

>> If data subjects are affected from a number of different countries and speak different languages, you may need to communicate the notification in the local language to ensure that data subjects can understand the notification.

>> However, if your communications with the data subjects concerned are always in English, then English would generally suffice for the notification to those data subjects, even if they reside in non-English speaking countries. If you communicate with the data subjects in a different language, the notification would also need to be in this language.

>> If a particular channel has been compromised, clearly you should be careful of using this channel to communicate the breach notification, as this channel could also be used by attackers impersonating you.

At the point you're able to do so, you must notify the data subject directly, even if you have previously made a public communication. You may be unable to communicate directly with a data subject because, for example, you lack sufficient information to do so. If you later receive information that allows direct communication with the data subject — such as when the data subject provides you with that information — you must then notify the data subject directly about the data breach.

EXAMPLES OF WHEN TO NOTIFY DATA SUBJECTS IN CASE OF A PERSONAL DATA BREACH

In the "Categorizing breaches" section, earlier in this chapter, I set out three examples of when you may be required to send notifications in the case a of a personal data breach.

Now I provide further examples of data breaches where you would need to notify not just the supervisory authority but also the data subject:

- Hackers steal bank details of customers.
- An employee loses a file containing patients' health data.
- An attacker publishes usernames, passwords, and purchase histories online.
- Medical records become unavailable for 24 hours.
- The personal data of a large number of data subjects is mistakenly sent to the wrong mailing list.
- A direct marketing email is sent to a large number of recipients in the To: or Cc: fields so that each recipient can see the email address of other recipients.

These next two examples of data breaches would *not* require you to notify the supervisory authority and the data subject:

- A brief power outage lasts several minutes and customers are unable to access their records.
- A USB key with a securely encrypted backup of personal data on it being stolen during a break-in without the thieves having access to the encryption key.

When notifications to individuals aren't necessary

Article 34(3) of the GDPR sets out the circumstances in which notifications to individuals are not required:

>> You have applied appropriate technical and organizational measures to protect personal data prior to the breach — in particular, those measures (such as encryption) that render the personal data affected by the breach unintelligible to any person who isn't authorized to access it.

- » Immediately following a breach, you have taken subsequent measures to ensure that the high risk posed to individuals' rights and freedoms is no longer likely to materialize — for example, you have identified an individual who accessed personal data and taken action against them before they could do anything with it.

- » Contacting individuals would involve disproportionate effort — for example, because you do not hold their contact details, or their contact details were lost in the breach. In this case, a public communication or similar measure must be made to inform the data subjects in an equally effective manner.

Keeping Internal Records

Whether you notify or not, you should keep a record of the data breach on your data breach form. (For more on this topic, see Chapter 13.) Article 33(5) of the GDPR requires you to keep a record of these items:

- » Facts relating to the breach
- » The effects of the breach
- » The remedial action you have taken

You should also keep records of

- » Your investigation
- » Any steps to be taken to prevent a recurrence of the breach
- » Info on whether training is necessary

Although it isn't required by the GDPR, you should also consider whether any other steps are advisable, such as notifying banks, credit card companies, police organizations, insurers, professional bodies, or anyone else who can help to minimize the risk of harm to the affected individuals.

Data Processors and Data Breaches

This section is written from the perspective of the data controller, but if you are a data processor, obviously you will need to consider this in light of you being a data processor.

If you use a data processor (see Chapter 5 for more on this) and your data processor suffers a data breach in relation to the personal data of your data subjects, the data processor must inform you "without undue delay" of the breach as soon as it becomes aware of the breach.

REMEMBER

Data processors are obliged to notify the data controller of ANY data breach, regardless of the risk to the rights and freedoms of individuals.

The processor is not required to notify the supervisory authority or the data subjects directly about a breach unless it's personal data related to their role as data controller, such as personal data relating to their clients.

The data processor's requirements on breach reporting should be included in your Data Processing Agreement. (See Chapter 10 for more on this agreement.)

Sanctions for Data Breaches

If you suffer a personal data breach caused by your failure to comply with the principles of the GDPR, such as maintaining the security of personal data, you could be fined up to 20 million euros or 4 percent of your global turnover for the previous financial year, whichever is higher.

If you fail to notify the supervisory authority and/or data subject when you should have done so, you could be fined up to 10 million euros or 2 percent of your global turnover for the past financial year, whichever is the higher.

In the year after the GDPR came into force, EU organizations reported almost 60,000 data breaches. So far, fewer than 100 fines have been issued by regulators, as investigations continue. These range from fines for minor breaches, such as emails mistakenly being sent to the wrong recipient, to major hacks affecting millions of individuals and making front page headlines.

In July 2019, British Airways was fined £183m (representing 1.5% of its turnover) and Marriott was fined £99m (representing 3% of its turnover) for the data breaches they suffered as a result of hackers breaching their security systems. As at the time of publishing of this book, British Airways is having to fight a group action for compensation from affected data subjects.

OTHER LAWS THAT MAY APPLY TO DATA BREACHES

In addition to the GDPR, more specific laws may apply to data breaches, such as these:

- The Privacy and Electronic Communications Regulations in the UK require communications service providers to notify the UK's supervisory authority, the ICO, of any personal data breach.

- The Electronic Identification and Trust Services (eIDAS) Regulation requires UK trust service providers to notify the ICO of a security breach.

- The EU Network and Information Security (NIS) Directive requires operators of essential services and digital service providers to report security incidents to network and information systems that have a "significant" or "substantial" impact to the competent national authority.

Most US data protection state laws specify:

- Fines for organizations that fail to notify data breaches

- Notifications to data subjects affected by the breach

- Notifications to regulatory boards

For example, in Texas, organizations can be fined up to $250,000 for a single data breach under the Identity Theft Enforcement and Protection Act and under the California Consumer Privacy Act 2018, affected data subjects are entitled to up to $750 each for a data breach affecting their personal data. Under HIPAA (Health Insurance Portability and Accountability Act of 1996, a law that provides for data protection in relation to medical data), organizations can be fined up to $1.5 million for each non-compliance with such law.

Although I cannot comment on the accuracy of this Digital Guardian report, "The definitive guide to US data breach laws" may be a useful reference point:

https://info.digitalguardian.com/rs/768-OQW-145/images/the-definitive-guide-to-us-state-data-breach-laws.pdf

5

The Workplace, Marketing, and Beyond

Chapter **18**

GDPR and the Workplace

I f you have people working for you in your organization — whether they're full-time or part-time employees, agency workers, volunteers, apprentices, interns, or hired on contract, such as freelancers or associates — you'll hold lots of personal data about them, for various purposes. These purposes include — but aren't limited to — paying salaries, paying taxes, providing benefits, offering training, monitoring performance, and storing sickness and disability records.

A lot of the personal data you'll process for employees is *special-category* data, previously known as sensitive data, which requires additional protection because it relates to matters where people have been negatively targeted, for example, or discriminated against (as discussed in Chapter 3).

In addition to the GDPR, you should consider local laws in processing employee data, not just general employment law — such as the obligation in many European countries to consult with works councils when proposing or making changes to employment arrangements — but also EU member-state–specific employee data regulations or laws about certain elements of data processing, such as surveillance.

When I refer to 'employees' or 'employment' in this chapter, I am referring to anyone who works for you, whether they be full-time or part-time employees, agency workers, volunteers, apprentices, interns, or hired on contract, such as freelancers or associates.

Choosing Appropriate Lawful Grounds of Processing for Employee Data

As with the processing of any personal data, you must have lawful grounds for processing employee data. In this section, I explore which lawful grounds are appropriate for processing employee data, as well as which ones you can rely on for processing the personal data of job candidates and former employees.

Lawful grounds of processing for employee data

Typically, your lawful grounds for processing employee data will be one of these:

>> **Consent:** The employee has provided consent to the processing.

>> **Contractual necessity:** Processing is necessary to fulfil the employment contract.

>> **Legal necessity:** Processing is necessary for compliance with legal obligations.

>> **Legitimate interests:** Processing is necessary for your legitimate interests.

Before the GDPR went into effect, many organizations sought to rely on the consent of the employee to process their data. However, post-GDPR, relying on consent for processing employee data isn't a good idea, because the GDPR makes it clear that consent is valid only where consent is freely given. This is problematic, for two reasons:

>> **Pressure to provide consent:** In the context of an employment relationship, an imbalance of power often exists between the employer and employee. In that situation, the employee may feel pressure to provide consent — so *it isn't freely given.* Recital 42 of the GDPR specifically states:

"In order to ensure that consent is freely given, consent should not provide a valid legal ground for the processing of personal data in a specific case where there is a clear imbalance between the data subject and the controller."

In addition, the European Data Protection Board said in an opinion on data processing at work that:

"Employees are seldom in a position to freely give, refuse or revoke consent, given the dependency that results from the employer/employee relationship. Unless in

exceptional situations, employers will have to rely on another legal ground than consent — such as the necessity to process the data for their legitimate interest."

>> **An employee might withdraw consent at any time.** If you didn't have other grounds on which to process the data, you would need to delete that data, which may be a problem for you.

REMEMBER

Consent may be appropriate for employees in exceptional circumstances where they have a genuine choice to consent, such as an employee survey. If the employee doesn't have a genuine choice, however, you should not rely on consent as a grounds for processing that data.

WARNING

Some EU member states require consent for employee data processing, leading to lengthy consent documents for employees to sign, so check local laws on this.

Table 18-1 describes examples of typical employee data processing and the grounds for processing that may be appropriate.

TABLE 18-1   **Legal Grounds of Processing for Employee Data**

To Do This . . .	Employer Needs to . . .	Legal Grounds
Pay employee salaries	Collect and process employee names and bank details	Processing is necessary to fulfil an employment contract.
Pay employee taxes	Collect and pass employee data to the tax authorities	Processing is necessary to comply with a legal obligation.
Train employees or monitor performance	Collect and pass certain employee data to third-party training or software providers	Processing is necessary for the legitimate interests of the employer.

REMEMBER

You need to carry out the Balancing test and complete a Legitimate Interests Assessment (LIA), which I discuss in Chapter 12, to rely on legitimate interests as a lawful ground for processing.

REMEMBER

If you're processing special-category data such as health data or personal data revealing ethnic origin (see Chapter 3 for more about special-category data), your processing of such special-category data needs to fall within an exemption to the general prohibition of processing special-category data. One such exemption is where the processing is necessary for the purposes of carrying out the obligations and exercising specific rights of the data controller or of the data subject in the field of employment and social security and social protection law.

Lawful grounds of processing for candidate data

If you're hiring new employees and you have candidates apply directly to you or by way of an agency, your lawful grounds for processing their personal data on a CV, cover letter, or application form is typically that the processing is necessary for your legitimate interests.

You need to decide on a retention period for this personal data, particularly where the candidate doesn't become an employee. (See Chapter 13 for more about data retention policies.)

WARNING

If you want to keep the personal data of the candidate on file in case another employment opportunity arises that is suitable for that candidate, you will need to obtain the candidate's consent for this processing and keep a record of the consent.

TIP

You may want to retain personal data related to unsuccessful candidates in case they bring a claim against you arising from the recruitment process. If so, you should keep the data until the limitation period for bringing a claim expires. Limitation periods vary across the EU.

Lawful grounds of processing for data about former employees

You may need to continue to process an employee's data even when that employee is no longer employed by you. You'll likely want to continue to process the personal data of former employees in these two cases:

>> **Pension-related matters:** If you're processing for pensions-related matters, your lawful grounds for processing are that the processing is necessary to fulfil a legal obligation.

>> **Legal claims:** If you're processing for legal-claims–related matters, your grounds for processing are for your legitimate interests.

REMEMBER

The definition of processing is very broad and includes storing personal data, so even if you are only retaining the data in case of future legal claims (whether or not any legal claims arise), you are still processing the data.

In the case of retaining employee records for potential legal claims where the personal data comprises special-category data, Article 9(2)(f) permits the processing of special-category data where the processing is necessary for the establishment, exercise, or defense of legal claims.

TIP

Guidance from the UK's supervisory authority, the ICO, in relation to retaining personal data for potential legal claims is that:

>> You should delete information that could not possibly be relevant to a potential legal claim.

>> Unless there is some other reason to retain the personal data, the data should be deleted when such a legal claim could no longer arise (for example, because a statutory limitation period has expired).

You should also consider any legal or regulatory requirements to retain records, such as information required for tax and audit purposes or information about health and safety.

Writing and Communicating an Employee Privacy Notice

You'll create a Privacy Notice (covered in Chapter 8) for your customers and website users and upload it to your website. Separately, you need to have a Privacy Notice for your employees that explains how you process employee data.

What to include

An employee Privacy Notice is fairly similar to your main Privacy Notice in content. In the employee Privacy Notice, however, you're referring only to personal data that's processed relating to employment. You need to include these areas:

>> Data protection principles.

>> Description of the personal data you process.

>> How you collect the personal data.

>> How you use the personal data.

>> Purposes for which you process the employee data.

>> How you use special-category data.

>> How you process criminal-convictions data.

>> Whether you use automated decision-making and, if so, what it's for and what the processes are and how employees can require human involvement.

>> Transfers to third parties.

>> Transfers outside of the EEA and the measures in place for safeguarding the data.

>> Measures in place to ensure data security.

>> Your data retention policy.

>> Rights of access, correction, erasure, and restriction for the employees.

>> The right of the employee to withdraw consent.

>> Details of your Data Protection Officer, if you have one. (See Chapter 15 for more on whether you need one.)

What to do with it

Provide the employee Privacy Notice to a potential employee at the time they become an employee. If you haven't already provided existing employees with an employee Privacy Notice, do so as soon as possible. Ask employees to read the notice carefully and to sign where indicated to confirm that they have read (and understood) the policy.

WARNING

Don't ask employees to *agree* to the contents of the notice. Doing so is requesting consent for all your employee data processing. You don't want to do that, for reasons mentioned earlier, in the "Lawful grounds of processing for employee data" section, earlier in the chapter

Managing subject access requests from employees

Data subjects may submit Data Subject Access Requests (DSARs) to a data controller to request information about personal data that the data controller is holding about them. An employee is a data subject, so that person has the right to send you a DSAR. (The procedure for replying to a DSAR is set out in Chapter 14.) Complying fully with that procedure is extremely important and will help you avoid providing an employee with ammunition to use against you.

Often, an employee will submit a DSAR only when you're already having problems with that employee. Employees may try to use a DSAR to extract information from you in the middle of a redundancy exercise, for example, or a disciplinary procedure.

That an employee will typically only submit an DSAR during an existing problematic situation puts more of the onus on you to correctly manage DSARs from employees, as opposed to any other type of data subject. Although time periods are particularly important, the most important area in which to "get it right" in replying to an employee DSAR is the actual disclosures and understanding what you're legally obliged to disclose and what you don't need to disclose.

In the next several sections, I explain the exemptions that govern what you don't have to disclose (and under what circumstances) before getting into the details of how to actually respond to an employee's DSAR.

Understanding exemptions

Article 23 of the GDPR allows EU member states to introduce exemptions to various provisions in GDPR, including DSARs, by way of national legislation.

In Germany, data controllers do not have to provide data subjects with access to personal data processed about such data subject where:

>> Doing so would reveal confidential data, such as data about third parties and data that is protected by German law such as trade secrets.

>> The personal data comprises archived data (data that is retained only due to legal or statutory retention provisions because the data cannot be deleted).

>> The personal data is backup data (data that is stored exclusively to secure or safeguard data).

>> The personal data is retained exclusively for data protection audits.

In order to benefit from the last three exemptions, German organizations must implement appropriate measures to ensure that the data cannot be processed for other purposes. In addition, they must document their decision to deny access to the personal data.

The UK has a number of exemptions from the requirement to provide all requested data; I discuss throughout this section the ones most relevant to employees.

Regarding information relating to other individuals

First, you aren't obliged to disclose information if that would involve disclosing information relating to another individual who can be identified from the information — *except* in either of these two scenarios:

>> The other person has consented to the disclosure.

>> It's reasonable to disclose the information to the data subject without consent.

   To determine whether it's reasonable to disclose information without consent, you need to consider all relevant circumstances, including

   - The type of information

   - Any duty of confidentiality owed to the other individual

   - Any steps taken to seek the consent of the other individual

   - Whether the other individual is capable of giving consent

   - Any express refusal of consent by the other individual

An individual can be identified from information to be provided to a data subject by a data controller if the individual can be identified from either of these:

>> That information

>> That information and any other information that the controller reasonably believes the data subject is likely to possess or obtain

In the employment context, if, for example, a DSAR was submitted by an employee in the middle of a disciplinary procedure, a statement by another colleague about that employee may not be required to be disclosed, even if the name of the colleague is redacted, because it might be obvious who the colleague is.

Regarding legal advice privilege

Legal advice privilege is relevant when personal data is contained in confidential communications between you and your lawyers, where those communications are for the purpose of giving or receiving legal advice. If you're in the middle of a grievance procedure and your lawyers have written to you with advice about how to handle the procedure and how much to offer in settlement for the employee to go quietly, you wouldn't need to disclose such correspondence to an employee who has submitted a DSAR.

This is relevant only to lawyers and doesn't extend to advice provided by human resources (HR) advisors. However, there's a further exemption for intentions in relation to negotiations with the data subject to the extent that they would be likely to prejudice those negotiations. If your HR advisor had written to you about negotiations with the data subject, this correspondence may be exempt and, therefore, you aren't required to disclose it.

Alongside legal advice privilege is *legal professional privilege,* which applies to confidential communications between lawyers and clients where that communication is created for the dominant purpose of ongoing or reasonably contemplated civil or criminal litigation. Again, note that this exemption relates only to advice from lawyers and not from HR advisors.

TIP

Simply copying a lawyer on an email doesn't constitute legal privilege; the lawyer must be providing legal advice, or litigation must be reasonably contemplated.

WARNING

Be careful when forwarding emails, because legal privilege can be lost when you do so.

Regarding management forecasts

Another relevant exemption is *management forecasts* (in which management may be planning to make personnel changes within the organization) to the extent that it would be likely to prejudice the conduct of the business or activity concerned. The UK's supervisory authority, the ICO, provides the following example:

"The senior management of an organisation is planning a reorganization. This is likely to involve making certain employees redundant, and this possibility is included in management plans. Before the plans are revealed to the workforce, an employee makes a subject access request. In responding to that request, the organisation does not have to reveal its plans to make him redundant if doing so would be likely to prejudice the conduct of the business (perhaps by causing staff unrest before the management's plans are announced)."

Regarding references

One more relevant exemption is that of references given (or to be given) in confidence for these purposes:

>> The education, training, or employment (or prospective education, training, or employment) of the data subject

>> The placement (or prospective placement) of the data subject as a volunteer

- » The appointment (or prospective appointment) of the data subject to any office

- » The provision (or prospective provision) by the data subject of any service

If in doubt about what to disclose, consult a lawyer or a data protection consultant.

Responding to an employee DSAR

After you have verified the identity of the employee, you have 30 days to reply. The 30-day countdown begins as soon as you have made that identification. See Chapter 14 for more about the exact timescales required for your reply. You should reply in writing and include the following details:

- » **The types of personal data you process about the employee:** Examples are bank details, national insurance number, medical records, home address, and date of birth.

- » **The purposes for which you process the data:** The purpose might be to pay the employee, for example, or to pay tax, to judge fitness for work, or to send employee communications.

- » **To whom you disclose the personal data — either the recipients of the data or categories of recipients of the data:** This might be your payroll provider, for example, or your pensions provider and the tax authorities.

- » **Any transfers outside of the EEA and the appropriate safeguards that are in place:** You might transfer employee data to your payroll provider who is outside of the EEA or to a group company outside of the EEA for centralized HR purposes, for example. For the relevant safeguards for such transfers, see Chapter 6.

- » **Any sources of data when data isn't collected directly from the data subject:** This is either the names of the sources or categories of the sources.

- » **Your retention periods and a summary of your retention policy:** See Chapter 13 for more about retention periods and for what details your retention policy should include.

- » **Any use of automated decision-making:** If you use automated decision-making, you need to explain the details of this, including any logic involved in the decision-making and any envisaged significant consequences for the data subject.

Monitoring Employees

An employee has a right to privacy in the workplace. However, the employee's right to privacy needs to be balanced with the employer's legitimate interests in protecting its systems and confidential information.

As an employer, you may monitor your employees to protect your business, but you must conduct the monitoring in accordance with certain principles.

In this section, I describe the ways in which you might monitor employees and the principles you must follow. I also explain what are — and what are not — legitimate cases of monitoring. (Using CCTV is a particularly intrusive type of monitoring, so I spend more time discussing matters related to it.)

Types of employee monitoring

Employees might incorrectly use email, the Internet, and the telephone in ways that can lead to problems for the employer, such as damage to reputation, employee performance issues, potential loss of business, and certain liabilities for the employer, such as those relating to defamation, harassment, discrimination, copyright infringement, hacking, transmitting viruses, and disclosure of confidential information and trade secrets. To help prevent these issues, you, as an employer, may want to monitor employees' actions in these areas:

>> **Email:** Computer programs can search across all emails for keywords or email addresses that may pose a threat.

>> **Internet use:** Programs can block the use of certain websites, and you can view the employee's browsing history.

>> **Telephone use:** You may monitor phone calls for quality control, volume, and cost and to review employee performance or ensure compliance.

>> **CCTV:** This system can be used in the workplace and surrounding areas, generally for security and safety; I further explain aspects of CCTV with regard to a code of conduct, among other factors, in the "CCTV" section, later in this chapter.

>> **Vehicle tracking:** You may want to monitor your employees' journeys, whether in company cars or on trucks or vans, for example, to ensure compliance with law and productivity.

>> **Fitness tracking:** Your health insurance provider may issue Fitbit devices or other fitness tracking devices to employees to monitor movement and process health data.

>> **Social media:** You may monitor employees' social media accounts to ensure that they aren't bringing the organization into disrepute.

>> **Background checks on candidates:** You may want to carry out background checks on candidates before offering them a job, which is also a form of monitoring.

You must ensure that any monitoring is compliant with local employment laws, data protection laws, human rights laws, and other specific laws, such as in relation to the interception of communications and Germany's Secrecy of Telecommunications Act, which makes it a criminal offense for employers to monitor employees' personal emails.

If you're established outside the EU, you are subject to the GDPR wherever you monitor employees in the EU (even if the monitoring is done, for example, from the US).

Principles for employee monitoring

If you want to carry out workplace monitoring, you should ensure compliance with these principles:

>> **Necessity:** You must be able to show that the monitoring of your employees is truly necessary.

>> **Legitimacy:** You must have lawful grounds for collecting and processing the personal data.

>> **Proportionality:** Your monitoring must be proportionate to the issue you're dealing with.

>> **Transparency:** You must clearly notify employees of the monitoring you will conduct.

Throughout this section, I look at each of these principles in more detail.

Necessity

Before you carry out any form of workplace monitoring, you must be confident that the monitoring is truly necessary. As part of your deliberations, you should consider whether less intrusive methods would also achieve your purpose.

Suppose that you want to eliminate harassment in the workplace by preventing employees from accessing or displaying offensive materials in an open plan office. To achieve this, you decide to monitor Internet and email use. In this case, you need to show that you could not resolve the issue by sending staff to harassment training and dealing effectively with any reported cases of harassment or by other, less intrusive methods.

You have a few options for how to conduct less intrusive methods of monitoring. You could limit monitoring to any of these factors:

>> **Location:** Not monitoring changing rooms, toilets, break areas, or places of worship

>> **Time:** Using spot checks rather than continuous monitoring

>> **Data:** Not monitoring employee's personal messages, for example

>> **Recipient:** Allowing only the HR manager to have access to the data

>> **Data subject:** Monitoring only high-risk employees rather than every employee

Article 35 of the GDPR requires you to carry out a DPIA if the workplace monitoring involves any of these factors:

>> New programs, systems, or processes that make changes to existing ones and the processing is likely to result in a high risk to the rights and freedoms of individuals

>> Automated processing (including profiling) that produces legal or other significant effects for employees

>> Large-scale processing of special categories of personal data or criminal-convictions data

>> Large-scale, systematic monitoring of a publicly accessible area

TIP

Employee monitoring is likely to involve a high risk to the rights and freedoms of the monitored employees. This means that a DPIA is necessary in all cases of employee monitoring. Chapter 13 provides a list of what the DPIA includes; Chapter 15 provides details about the DPIA process.

Legitimacy

To carry out workplace monitoring, you must have a lawful basis for the monitoring. EU member state employment law regarding the legality of employee monitoring varies, so you should consult a specialist in the relevant member state to advise on this topic.

In addition, certain member states have works councils that may need to approve the extent of any workplace monitoring, before it may legally be put into place.

If workplace monitoring is permitted by member state law, for data protection purposes you need to determine your lawful grounds for processing. Consent is rarely an appropriate lawful grounds of processing for workplace monitoring because of the imbalance in the employment relationship. For this reason, you need to rely on other grounds — more likely than not, the legitimate interests grounds.

REMEMBER

You, as an employer, have a legitimate interest in protecting your organization from threats, but this must be balanced with each employee's right to privacy. To help ensure that you maintain this parity, conduct a Balancing test, which is part of the Legitimate Interests Assessment (LIA), covered in Chapter 12.

Proportionality

Your workplace monitoring must be proportionate to the concern you're trying to address. For example, continuously monitoring all employees' emails to ensure that nobody is disclosing confidential information isn't considered proportionate.

Transparency

You must be transparent with employees about what type and amount of workplace monitoring is taking place. If employees haven't been notified that they're being monitored, they will have a greater expectation of privacy.

In many court cases involving workplace monitoring, the fact that no notification of workplace monitoring was provided had a strong negative bearing on the outcome of the case for the employer.

Merely notifying employees about workplace monitoring isn't the same as receiving consent to the monitoring. As I mention earlier, consent rarely, if ever, is an appropriate lawful ground of processing for workplace monitoring.

TIP

To be transparent with employees, you should provide them with the following information in an IT policy:

>> The standards and rules for using company software and equipment, such as email, Internet, and telephones.

>> Notification to employees that their use of such software and equipment may be monitored.

>> Explanations of how usage will be monitored, for what purposes, and to whom it will be disclosed.

>> Details on how much private use is allowed (such as adding personal appointments to the online work calendar).

You cannot actually specify that employees may not use your equipment for private use, because courts have ruled that employees have a right to such private use. You may specify that employees use work email accounts only for work-related matters, but that they can log on to the Internet to use personal email accounts, such as Gmail or Hotmail, for private matters.

>> Descriptions of any disciplinary action that will be taken if employees breach policies.

TIP

In some EU member states, it may be a requirement for works councils to approve any such policy, so, again, be sure to double-check.

REMEMBER

In some instances, it may be possible to not notify an employee of monitoring, such as where the employee is under investigation for theft. In some EU member states, monitoring without notification isn't permitted in any circumstances; in others, a narrow scope is permitted. Be sure to double-check.

TIP

The European Data Protection Board suggests that the IT policy should be reviewed annually to see whether any changes need to be made to it, such as whether less intrusive means of achieving the aim are available.

Identifying legitimate monitoring

If you comply with the data protection principles — particularly those of necessity, legitimacy, proportionality, and transparency — you can legally carry out workplace monitoring.

The European Data Protection Board guidance gives examples of legitimate monitoring, including the following:

>> "An employer monitors the LinkedIn profiles of former employees that are involved during the duration of non-compete clauses. The purpose of this monitoring is to monitor compliance with such clauses. The monitoring is limited to these former employees. As long as the employer can prove that such monitoring is necessary to protect his legitimate interests, that there are no other, less invasive means available, and that the former employees have been adequately informed about the extent of the regular observation of their public communications, the employer may be able to rely on legitimate interests as lawful grounds for processing."

> » "Processing location data can be justified where it is done as part of monitoring the transport of people or goods or improving the distribution of resources for services in scattered locations (e.g., planning operations in real time), or where a security objective is being pursued in relation to the employee himself or to the goods or vehicles in his charge. Conversely, data processing is considered to be excessive where employees are free to organise their travel arrangements as they wish or where it is done for the sole purpose of monitoring an employee's work where this can be monitored by other means."

Recognizing monitoring that isn't legitimate

Several types of employee monitoring may not be legitimate. In this section, I look more closely at various types and the factors affecting them.

Regarding special-category data

Justifying workplace monitoring that involves the monitoring of special-category data can be difficult. (See Chapter 3 for more on this topic.) Where monitoring is particularly intrusive, this is unlikely to be legitimate.

Regarding covert surveillance

In certain EU member states, covert surveillance is unlawful unless

» You have obtained express permission from your supervisory authority

» An exemption applies

Check the member state's data protection laws and employment laws in this regard. You also may need to consider works councils, trade unions, and any collective agreements.

Regarding background checks

If you carry out background checks on potential employees (such as social media reviews, educational and professional qualifications, or criminal records), you must be careful not to blacklist people (that is, make a list of people you won't employ), because it is considered to be a disproportionate intrusion into an individual's privacy and is generally illegal. You must consider such checks on a case by case basis and delete the data once you have made a decision about the employment for that particular role.

Article 10 of the GDPR states that you can only process criminal convictions data under the control of official authority or when the processing is authorized by EU or member state law providing for appropriate safeguards. Article 10 goes on to say that you cannot keep a comprehensive register of criminal convictions unless it is kept under the control of official authority. This is an absolute prohibition against data controllers keeping a list of criminal convictions, for example, to screen against for future employees.

In the UK, in addition to having a lawful grounds of processing to process criminal convictions data, you must meet a specific condition in Schedule 1 of the Data Protection Act of 2018. The most likely condition for employee checks is that processing is necessary for the purposes of performing or exercising obligations or rights which are imposed or conferred by law on the controller or the data subject in connection with employment, social security, or social protection. However, the condition is limited to where there is a legal obligation to carry out a background check or where rights to carry out background checks are conferred by law (such as where employees work with children and vulnerable adults), so this will not apply automatically to all processing of criminal convictions data for background checks. A further condition is that the potential employee has provided consent. However, it must be made clear that the potential employee does not have to consent in order to be considered for the role, in order to ensure that the consent is freely given and therefore valid.

The UK's ICO advises that you should only carry out criminal records checks for potential employees that you intend to appoint, rather than for all short-listed candidates.

REMEMBER

If you are processing criminal convictions data in the UK, you need to have a "relevant policy document" which explains procedures for complying with the GDPR principles and its erasure and retention policies — see Chapter 13 for more on this.

In Poland, the use of background screening for potential employees is not only questionable under the GDPR but also the Polish Labor Code. To minimize the risks of noncompliance, you should obtain the candidate's explicit, prior consent to the background checks and make it clear that their consent is not conditional upon them obtaining employment (so that a free choice is given).

Certain EU member states, such as Finland, have specific laws against blacklisting. Be sure to check local employment laws and data protection laws when carrying out background checks.

Other monitoring that may not be legitimate

The European Data Protection Board Guidance provides several examples of what *isn't* legitimate monitoring:

>> **Social media accounts:** Don't assume, just because somebody's social media profile is public, that you can use this information for your own purposes. You still must have lawful grounds for processing, such as legitimate interests. It's more likely to be legitimate to inspect social media accounts if they're related to business purposes (such as LinkedIn) rather than to private purposes (such as Facebook).

>> **Job applicant information:** You may process personal data of job applicants only to the extent that the processing is necessary and relevant to the performance of the job they're applying for. There are no legal grounds for you to require job applicants or employees to "friend" you or otherwise share with you their private social media accounts.

>> **Monitoring software:** You're unlikely to have legal grounds under legitimate interests to deploy wide-reaching software packages that do any of the following, because the processing involved in such technologies is disproportionate:

- *Log keystrokes and mouse movements*

- *Take screen captures (either randomly or at set intervals)*

- *Log applications used (and how long they were used)*

- *Collect video from webcams*

>> **Employee devices:** Your employees might use their own equipment under, for example, a Bring Your Own Device (BYOD) policy, which allows them to use their own equipment (phones, laptops, and tablets, for example) to conduct company business and access company data. It is unlikely to be legitimate for you to monitor the location and traffic of those devices if that monitoring also collects data relating to the employee's private and family life.

TIP

If you want to monitor for business purposes, you must put systems and processes in place that prevent the collection of data in relation to the employee's private life.

>> **Fitness monitoring devices:** If you provide your employees with fitness monitoring devices, the resulting health data should be accessible only to your employee and not to you. When you're choosing a fitness monitoring device or service, carefully review the Privacy Notice of the manufacturer or service provider of the service or device, to ensure that it doesn't result in unlawful processing of health data of your employees.

- **Facial expressions:** It is unlikely to be lawful for you to monitor your employee's facial expressions by automated means — for example, to identify deviations from predefined movement patterns in a factory. The European Data Protection Board guidance states that employers should refrain from the use of facial recognition technologies.

- **Private use of company vehicle:** If employees are permitted to use company vehicles for private use, they should be able to temporarily disable location tracking when circumstances justify it, such as a visit to a doctor. If this isn't possible, general tracking of the company vehicle in these circumstances is unlikely to be legitimate.

- **Vehicle webcam:** If you decide to continuously monitor vehicles with a video camera inside the cabin that records sound and video, the purpose of which is to improve the driving skills of your employees, this is unlikely to be legitimate.

- **Emails to customers:** Suppose that you want to send an email to a customer with a link to the name and location of the employee tasked with delivering a package. You want to include a passport photo of the delivery person so that the customer can confirm the person's identity. This is legitimate monitoring.

CCTV

The *closed-circuit television (CCTV)* system uses cameras to capture images displayed on monitors, often in a secure room. Organizations place the cameras in various areas for surveillance or security purposes, but access to the video feeds are limited (closed-circuit) and not publicly distributed. If you capture an image of an individual via CCTV, whether the person is standing still or moving, this data is *biometric data,* which is based on a person's physical characteristics and can be used to identify that person. A person's iris, fingerprints, voice, and gait — and even the way they use a mouse — are all examples of biometric data.

Biometric data is special-category data. You therefore need to not only have lawful grounds for processing (such as legitimate interests), but also fall within an exemption for processing special-category data. See Chapter 3 for the exemptions for processing special-category data.

Certain EU member states may make consultation with the supervisory authority a prerequisite of using CCTV, so be sure to check.

REMEMBER

Though CCTV is a more intrusive form of monitoring, the same data protection principles apply to it as to less intrusive processing of personal data, such as the data minimization principle, the transparency principle, and the legitimacy principle. (I discuss all six data protection principles in Chapter 4.)

TIP

Rather than use CCTV, consider whether you can use less intrusive methods of achieving your purpose — such as improving lighting, installing alarms, installing access cards for entry doors, or implementing other security measures.

You should also consider these actions:

>> Use a fixed camera rather than a mobile camera.

>> Position cameras so that you narrow the extent of the monitored area to the area of concern in order to minimize processing that is not necessary for the purpose.

>> Avoid private areas such as toilets and individual workspaces.

>> Avoid zooming in.

>> Allow for the blurring or deletion of images or parts of the recording.

>> Freeze images.

>> Use voice messages over the CCTV (for example, to send warnings to individuals who may be acting inadvertently (such as trespassing without noticing), and shut down cameras in specific areas.

>> Be mindful of the period of retention of the CCTV footage — it should be retained only as long as necessary for the purpose for which the CCTV was being used (where footage may be required for legal proceedings, for example).

>> Conduct staff training on the misuse of CCTV footage and the potential consequences of doing so.

>> Put into place a CCTV policy and regularly review this policy.

Regarding transparency

In terms of transparency and notifying data subjects of the use of CCTV, the notice needs to be visible and placed within a reasonable distance of the area being monitored. You may use a sign with the CCTV camera symbol to make people aware that CCTV is being used. The sign must also state the purposes of the monitoring, name the data controller, and provide contact details for the data controller.

You must follow up with a Privacy Notice if a data subject contacts you. (See Chapter 8 for more about Privacy Notices.)

Regarding a DSAR and CCTV footage

If a data subject submits a Data Subject Access Request (DSAR), relevant CCTV footage must be included in your response to that DSAR. If the footage shows images of other people, you should preserve their privacy by blurring their images before including that footage in your response. See Chapter 14 for more about DSARs in general; I discuss DSARs, as related to employees, earlier in this chapter.

Regarding Data Protection Impact Assessments

A Data Protection Impact Assessment (DPIA; covered in Chapter 15) should be carried out before installing CCTV if any of these conditions applies:

>> The video surveillance is considered to be high risk to the rights and freedoms of the affected individuals.

>> The video surveillance involves systematic monitoring of a publicly accessible area on a large scale.

>> Video surveillance has been included on any lists published in member states of the processing where a DPIA is required.

Codes of conduct

Certain countries may have codes of conduct relating to the usage of CCTV in the workplace. The UK's ICO Employment Practices Code — which isn't legally binding — states that

>> You should carry out an impact assessment to consider whether the benefits of using CCTV outweigh any adverse impact — in particular:

   • "Where possible, monitoring should be targeted at areas of particular risk and confined to areas where expectations of privacy are low."

   • "Continuous monitoring of particular individuals is only likely to be justifiable in rare circumstances."

- >> Unless covert monitoring is necessary, you should provide your employees with a clear notification that video monitoring is being carried out and where and why it is being carried out.

- >> You should display obvious notices (such as on the walls near the CCTV) to notify people that monitoring is taking place and why.

If you're considering undertaking covert monitoring and not notifying employees, the Employment Practices Code suggests that:

REMEMBER

- >> Your senior management authorize the monitoring after having considered the issue carefully and being satisfied that there are grounds to suspect criminal activity or similar and that if individuals were to be notified about the monitoring, this would jeopardize the prevention or detection of such crime.

  Covert monitoring will rarely be justified, and it should be used only in exceptional circumstances and where the number of people involved in the investigation is limited.

- >> You don't let covert monitoring be ongoing — end it as soon as the investigation is complete. Set clear rules limiting the disclosure and access to data that's obtained as part of the monitoring.

- >> You don't use covert monitoring in areas where workers would expect to have privacy (such as in toilets, changing rooms, or private offices). If you suspect a serious crime and you consider such covert monitoring necessary, you should involve the police.

- >> Any information you obtain through covert monitoring should be used only to prevent or detect a crime or other malfeasance. You should delete any other information collected, unless it reveals information that no reasonable employer could be expected to ignore.

The ICO has also produced a code of practice on the use of surveillance systems, which is expected to be updated for the GDPR:

- >> Use of a surveillance camera system must always be for a specified purpose that is in pursuit of a legitimate aim and necessary to meet an identified pressing need.

- >> The use of a surveillance camera system must take into account its effect on individuals and their privacy, with regular reviews to ensure that its use remains justified.

- There must be as much transparency in the use of a surveillance camera system as possible, including a published contact point for access to information and complaints.

- There must be clear responsibility and accountability for all surveillance camera system activities, including images and information collected, held, and used.

- Clear rules, policies, and procedures must be in place before a surveillance camera system is used, and these must be communicated to all who need to comply with them.

- No more images and information should be stored than that which is strictly required for the stated purpose of a surveillance camera system, and such images and information should be deleted after their purposes have been discharged.

- Access to retained images and information should be restricted, and there must be clearly defined rules on who can gain access and for what purpose such access is granted; the disclosure of images and information should take place only when it is necessary for such a purpose or for law enforcement purposes.

- Surveillance camera system operators should consider any approved operational, technical, and competency standards relevant to a system and its purpose and work to meet and maintain those standards.

- Surveillance camera system images and information should be subject to appropriate security measures to safeguard against unauthorized access and use.

- Effective review and audit mechanisms should be in place to ensure that legal requirements, policies, and standards are complied with in practice, and regular reports should be published.

- When the use of a surveillance camera system is in pursuit of a legitimate aim and there's a pressing need for its use, it should then be used in the most effective way to support public safety and law enforcement with the aim of processing images and information of evidential value.

- Any information used to support a surveillance camera system that compares against a reference database for matching purposes should be accurate and kept up-to-date.

VICARIOUS LIABILITY FOR EMPLOYERS OF DATA BREACHES BY EMPLOYEES

As an employer, you are vicariously liable for the actions of your employees — they act on your behalf and if they incur a liability in doing so, generally speaking it is your liability as the employer. This is why you need to ensure appropriate training, not just for GDPR compliance, but for all applicable laws and regulations.

The Morrisons case has highlighted the potential liability for employers with regard to employees and data breaches. The facts of this case are that Andrew Skelton, a disgruntled senior IT auditor at Morrisons (a UK nationwide supermarket) who was going through disciplinary proceedings, copied the payroll data of almost 100,000 Morrisons staff onto a USB drive and posted it onto a public file sharing site.

Mr. Skelton was convicted under the UK's Computer Misuse Act 1990 and the Data Protection Act 1998 (the data protection legislation in force before the GDPR) and was sentenced to 8 years in prison. The UK's supervisory authority, the ICO, investigated the matter and decided that Morrisons had not breached the Data Protection Act 1998 and that no enforcement action against Morrisons was necessary.

However, that was not the end of the matter. More than 5,000 Morrisons employees brought proceedings against Morrisons in a class action for breach of the Data Protection Act, breach of confidence, and misuse of private information. The employees alleged that Morrisons was vicariously liable for the actions of Mr. Skelton.

The High Court decided that although Morrisons was not primarily liable for the data breach because Morrisons had taken appropriate technical and organizational measures to prevent the unlawful use of payroll data (other than not being able to delete the data from Mr. Skelton's computer, which in itself would not have prevented the data breach).

However, worryingly for employers, the High Court also decided that Morrisons was vicariously liable for the actions of Mr. Skelton. Morrisons appealed to the Court of Appeal on this point and the Court of Appeal agreed with the High Court. The Supreme Court of the United Kingdom will consider the issue on November 7, 2019.

If the Supreme Court agrees with the Court of Appeal, employers may find themselves in a position where they have taken all necessary steps to protect data, yet are still liable for the actions of rogue employees, leading to employers suffering significant adverse financial consequences. Morrisons is looking at a potential liability of more than £100 million.

The Court of Appeal stated that the solution to such vicarious liability would be to put insurance in place. Employers should therefore consider whether insurances are in place to adequately protect them against vicarious liability for data breaches.

Chapter **19**

Keeping Your Marketing GDPR-Compliant

Applying data protection rules to marketing activities is one of the areas of data protection that is most confusing to organizations. This is because for certain forms of marketing, a number of other regulations apply in addition to the GDPR, such as EU member state laws derived from the EU's ePrivacy Directive and other local laws that are specific to certain sectors.

In addition, marketing often involves a large number of third parties, such as third-party platforms that send your email messages on your behalf and third parties such as publishers, advertisers, and tech companies who place ads for you and provide consent management tools.

To explain how the GDPR applies to marketing activities, I first tackle what constitutes marketing and then explore issues that are relevant no matter what type of marketing you engage in — from choosing a lawful grounds for processing to what happens when you don't comply. Finally, I look at online and offline marketing separately, further breaking each of those large topics into their smaller components to look at the ins and outs of Facebook marketing, email and affiliate marketing, events, exhibitions, and more.

Marketing, Defined

When considering marketing, you need to think about direct versus indirect marketing. I've created Table 19-1 to help you see the differences.

TABLE 19-1   **Direct versus Indirect Marketing**

Type of Marketing	Processes Personal Data?	GDPR Applies?
Direct	Likely	Yes
Indirect	Unlikely	No

The European Data Protection Board (EDPB) Guidance specifies that *direct marketing* is "any form of sales promotion targeted toward particular individuals." This broad definition includes messages sent by charities and other not-for-profit organizations for fundraising purposes. The following list further breaks down and examines the scope of this definition:

>> **Sales promotion:** The promotion doesn't even need to offer anything for sale — it might simply consist of a message that furthers the aims of the organization or communicates a free offer. The communication may be mainly about something that isn't a sales promotion but if even a small part of the communication is a sales promotion, however, it falls within the definition of direct marketing.

>> If, for example, you send an email to your email database to inform them that your store is closing all day on Sunday and you have a post script notifying the data subjects of a forthcoming sale, that still constitutes a direct marketing email.

- >> **Offering free services:** Even if you're sharing information about free, value-added services such as training, a podcast, or even a blog, if such content is related to your organization's purposes, this communication, if it's made directly to the individual — for example, by email, text, or postal mail addressed to the data subject — constitutes direct marketing.

- >> **Website banner or magazine insert ads:** Because the marketing effort needs to be directed toward particular individuals for it to be considered direct marketing, marketing communications such as untargeted website banner ads and magazine inserts don't constitute direct marketing for the purposes of GDPR.

WARNING

The ePrivacy Directive may potentially soon expand to cover any advertisements that are "presented to" an individual, including banner ads where personal data is processed, meaning that consent would be required for such ads, so keep an eye on this legal development if you believe that you'll be affected by it. This point is being negotiated between EU institutions and as at the time of publishing, it is not known quite where the negotiations will end up.

- >> **Administrative messages:** Communications that are merely transactional or administrative don't fall into the scope of direct marketing. Sending an email to confirm an order or state that the office is closed isn't a direct marketing communication.

- >> **Market research:** Market research isn't considered direct marketing as long as it's genuine market research. If it's direct marketing disguised as a survey for market research or including an element of promotion or collecting data to use in future marketing, the direct marketing rules apply — whether or not you call it market research.

REMEMBER

If you're processing personal data to carry out market research or for statistical purposes and are using the lawful ground of legitimate interests for the processing, your Privacy Notice should inform data subjects of their right to object to the processing. (See Chapter 8 for more about what else needs to be contained in your Privacy Notice.)

- >> **Via electronic means:** If the direct marketing message is electronic and sent by email, text, automated call or fax, the ePrivacy Directive also applies. (See more on this topic in the section "The inter-relationship with the ePrivacy Directive," later in this chapter.)

General Matters Regarding the GDPR and Marketing

When you process personal data for marketing purposes, you must comply with all the data protection principles set out in the GDPR. (See Chapter 4 for more about these principles.) The principles that are especially relevant to marketing are described in this list:

>> **Processing data lawfully and fairly:** You must explain to the data subject, in your Privacy Notice (covered in Chapter 8), who you are and specify that you plan to use the personal data for marketing purposes. You also need to notify the data subject if you plan to disclose the data to third parties, especially if you share or sell the data for the third party to market to the data subject. (You'll likely need the consent of the data subject in order to do so.)

>> **Limiting the purpose:** You won't use the personal data for any purposes other than the ones for which you have notified the data subject. So, if you have collected the data for purposes other than marketing, you cannot decide to start marketing to the data subject, because that's a different purpose.

>> **Accuracy:** You must ensure that personal data is accurate and kept up to date. If your marketing list is outdated and doesn't accurately reflect a data subject's preferences for marketing, it's in breach of the GDPR.

Throughout the rest of this section, I cover various considerations you must keep in mind as you conduct marketing activities for your organization. These include choosing an appropriate lawful grounds for processing, using the proper opt-in etiquette, understanding the impact of the ePrivacy Directive, and discovering what to expect when you don't comply.

The lawful grounds for processing

The two main lawful grounds for processing when sending marketing communications are consent and legitimate interests. (See Chapter 3 for more about these two, and all other, lawful grounds for processing.)

Deciding on a lawful grounds for processing personal data for marketing purposes is an area that many organizations confuse. They think that marketing is all about consent and then try to obtain consent when it isn't necessary or appropriate. Or they rely too heavily on legitimate interests while failing to carry out the necessary Balancing tests or to consider the impact of the ePrivacy Directive that, in the main, requires consent for direct marketing by email, text, automated call, or fax. (For more on the Balancing test as part of the Legitimate Interests Assessment [LIA], see Chapter 12.)

Consent

The GDPR doesn't specify that consent must be obtained for all direct marketing communications. In fact, Recital 47 states that "the processing of personal data for direct marketing purposes may be regarded as carried out for a legitimate interest."

However, if consent is required under the ePrivacy Directive for certain processing, it's also required under the GDPR. Therefore, if you send unsolicited direct marketing by email, text, fax, or automated call, you need to obtain consent of the data subject. (One exception is when the soft opt-in applies; see the later section "Email and text marketing" for more on this topic.)

WARNING

You cannot send a direct message to somebody to ask for their consent to marketing, because this message in itself constitutes direct marketing. You need to obtain consent by other marketing methods, such as a general sign-up process on your website, banner ads that aren't targeted specifically at the individual, general postal mailings, or inserts in magazines, for example.

Chapter 3 covers the criteria for valid consent and managing consent and for the right of the data subject to withdraw consent at any time. This list includes a reminder of the most important information you need to know about consent and marketing:

>> **Consenting to marketing is known as *opt-in:*** Your wording for the opt-in must be effective — a task that organizations often fail to achieve. Chapter 11 shows you how to structure the opt-in, and I discuss the soft opt-in later in this chapter.

>> **Sharing data with third parties:** If you're sharing personal data with third parties who seek to rely on that consent (for their own marketing purposes, for example), you must explicitly name these third parties when you're obtaining the consent to be able to share the data. Even naming precisely defined categories of third parties is unacceptable.

For example, a statement such as this one won't lead to valid consent being provided: "We will share your data with carefully selected third parties so that they can contact you about retail opportunities" or "We will share your data with banks, insurance companies, and lawyers so that they can provide you with special offers related to this product." The statement must instead be as specific as this one, with separate tick boxes for each third party: "Tick here to receive offers from Widget Limited, ABC Limited, XYZ Bank Plc."

WARNING

If a data subject has provided consent to their data being passed to a third party, that third party cannot then pass that data to another third party.

>> **Buying a marketing list:** If you're buying a marketing list, you must ensure that the appropriate consents have been obtained. If the data was obtained by the seller of the marketing list before the date on which the seller initially contacted you, the consent is unlikely to be valid.

WARNING

Even if a seller of a marketing list assures you that the appropriate consents have been obtained, you must carry out solid due diligence on the seller and on the consents obtained. If you don't and the consents prove not to have been obtained in reality, you will not have the appropriate consents and will therefore be processing personal data unlawfully. This carries the maximum fine of €20m or 4 % of global turnover for the preceding financial year, whichever is the higher.

Legitimate interests

As I mentioned previously, Recital 47 states that "the processing of personal data for direct marketing purposes may be regarded as carried out for a legitimate interest." If you're relying on legitimate interests, you must still carry out a Legitimate Interests Assessment (LIA) and keep it on file. (See Chapter 12 for more on the LIA.) A lot depends on whether a relationship is preexisting between the data subject and the data controller and whether the data subject would reasonably expect to receive that marketing communication.

If you're relying on legitimate interests to send the direct marketing communications, you must advise the data subject of the right to object to the processing (effectively, to opt out of the marketing) at any time. Article 21(3) states that "where the data subject objects to processing for direct marketing purposes, the personal data shall no longer be processed for such purposes."

You must also provide the details of the processing, a statement that you're relying on legitimate interests for the processing, a description of what those legitimate interests are, as well as a notification of the right to object to the processing in your Privacy Notice (which I cover in Chapter 8).

B2B marketing and B2C marketing

Many people believe that the GDPR doesn't apply to business-to-business (B2B) marketing, but this isn't the case. If an individual can be identified from the processing, the GDPR applies equally to B2B marketing and to business-to-consumer (B2C) marketing.

The distinction between B2B marketing and B2C marketing is made in the ePrivacy Directive, which I discuss further in the section "The inter-relationship with the ePrivacy Directive," later in this chapter.

A few examples illustrate the point:

>> If you're sending a marketing email to john.smith@widgets.com (unless several people named John Smith are working at Widgets.com — and even if you're sending marketing messages relating to products or services for the widgets business rather than to John Smith personally), this still constitutes the processing of personal data. The GDPR applies.

>> If you're sending an email to admin@widgets.com, this in itself isn't personal data, because an individual cannot be identified from this data. The GDPR doesn't apply.

>> Even if you're sending *solicited* marketing — marketing messages that have been requested, in other words — you still must comply with the GDPR principles because you're processing personal data. (See Chapter 3 to find out what constitutes personal data.)

REMEMBER

As I discuss in the earlier section "Marketing, Defined," the GDPR covers all direct marketing communications where you are processing personal data, including direct marketing sent by post, phone, fax, email, text, or otherwise. The GDPR also covers online ads that are targeted at individuals — via their browsing history, for example.

Opt-outs and suppression lists

The GDPR provides in Article 13 that you, as a data controller, must notify data subjects about their right to withdraw consent (where consent is the lawful grounds for processing) and to object to the processing (where legitimate interest is the lawful grounds for processing). This notification is typically included within the Privacy Notice.

In addition, Recital 70 states:

> "Where personal data are processed for the purposes of direct marketing, the data subject should have the right to object to such processing, including profiling to the extent that it's related to such direct marketing, whether with regard to initial or further processing, at any time and free of charge. That right should be explicitly brought to the attention of the data subject and presented clearly and separately from any other information."

This means that the right to object (or, as it's more commonly referred to, the right to *opt out*) should be set out at the point where you obtain the data subject's details. You cannot merely include it within your Privacy Notice or your terms and conditions, where it would be easier to miss. In practice, you could do something similar to what you see in Figure 19-1.

1. Create your Economist.com account

First name

Last name

E-mail address

Create password (Must be 8 characters long)

Select your country

Your registration will be provided in accordance with our terms and conditions. You accept these terms when you submit your order

2. Let us know if we can contact you

The Economist Group will like to keep you informed about exclusive offers, events and new product developments in line with our privacy policy. If you would prefer not to be contacted please tick the box

☐ No, please do not contact me

Sign up

FIGURE 19-1:
Allow data subjects to opt out at the point where you collect their information.

TIP

Here are a few other points to keep in mind regarding opt-outs:

» **You must allow the data subject to opt out from all marketing activities.** This includes postal marketing, email marketing, text marketing, and any other marketing you send.

» **You must comply with the request to opt out as soon as possible and without charge to the data subject.** You cannot, for example, insist on a data subject calling a premium-rate phone number to opt out. Incidental costs, such as the cost of an Internet provider to send an email, aren't considered as charging for the opt-out.

» **If a data subject chooses to opt out, you should add the data subject to a data suppression list.** Do this rather than delete all of the data subject's details, in order to ensure that if the data subject ends up on your marketing list again, you know not to email them. This suppression list is typically provided and facilitated by your email marketing software.

TECHNICAL STUFF

A *suppression list* is a list of personal data about data subjects who have opted out of marketing where, rather than deleting the data subject's personal data entirely, you retain just enough information to ensure that their preferences are adhered to in the future.

>> **If a data subject opts out from receiving direct marketing messages, you must not email them any direct marketing messages or ask them by email to opt in.** Numerous large fines have been levied on data controllers who have sent direct marketing emails to data subjects who have previously opted out. (One example, among many, is EE Limited, a UK telecommunications provider that was fined £100,000 [approximately $122,000] for sending promotional email messages to customers who had previously opted out of marketing communications.)

>> **If a data subject has opted out in a national list of preferences for direct marketing (held by some EU member states), don't send direct marketing messages to that data subject.** Screen these lists and cleanse your own lists of the data subjects who have opted out, before sending direct marketing communications.

If you have a specific opt-in from a data subject, it takes priority over their having opted out on a national list of preferences.

The inter-relationship with the ePrivacy Directive

The EU's *ePrivacy Directive* governs direct marketing sent by electronic communications in the form of email, text, fax, or automated call.

The ePrivacy Directive requires consent to be obtained for using nonessential cookies and regulates the use of certain electronic communications (email, text, fax, and automated call) for sending direct marketing messages.

At the time of writing this book, the ePrivacy Directive applies only as implemented by individual EU member states and relates only to organizations established within those member states. However, the European Parliament, the European Commission, and the European Council are now negotiating amendments to the ePrivacy Directive that would extend the territorial scope to match that for the GDPR. See Appendix A for more on this.

In addition, the proposed amendments to the ePrivacy Directive extend the scope of the direct marketing communications from email, text, fax, or automated calls to any direct message, including WhatsApp messages, Facebook messages, Snapchat messages, or any other over-the-top (OTT) service. It has also been proposed that the text be changed to messages that are "presented to" rather than "sent to" — this would include marketing messages that aren't sent directly to the data subject, such as banner ads and other display ads.

EU member states implemented the ePrivacy Directive into national law in slightly different ways. The UK, Sweden, Slovenia, Portugal, Luxembourg, Latvia, Hungary, France, Finland, and Estonia, for example, distinguish between sending unsolicited direct marketing messages to individuals and to corporate entities:

>> Opt-in consent is required in order to send unsolicited direct marketing messages to individuals, which includes someone trading as a sole trader and a partnership.

>> Opt-out consent is permitted in order to send unsolicited direct marketing messages to corporate entities.

All other EU member states make no such distinction and require opt-in consent for unsolicited direct marketing messages to individuals and to corporate entities.

The soft opt-in rule is described in the section below on Email Marketing.

The UK implemented the ePrivacy Directive via the Privacy and Electronic Communications Regulations, which is often referred to as PECR.

The consequences of getting it wrong

If you don't comply with the GDPR in your marketing efforts, you run the risk of losing the trust of your customers and prospects. You also risk having customers and prospects complain about your noncompliance to the relevant supervisory authority.

On receiving a complaint, the supervisory authority typically investigates. If you aren't in compliance, the supervisory authority issues one of the following:

>> **An enforcement notice:** This requires you to make changes to your practice or to stop the data processing.

>> **A fine:** A fine can be as much as €20 million (approximately $22 million) or 4 percent of your global turnover for the preceding financial year (whichever is higher). See Chapter 21 for more about fines for noncompliance with specific obligations.

Online Marketing

Online marketing has many names. You may have heard it called online advertising, digital marketing, or web advertising, among others. In short, it's a form of marketing that uses the Internet to spread a message about an organization's brand, services, and products. Methods include email, social media, display advertising, and more.

Facebook marketing

If you advertise on Facebook, as long as you aren't uploading personal data to Facebook, Facebook is the data controller. Users of Facebook are served ads in accordance with their privacy settings on Facebook.

If, however, you upload personal data to Facebook — for custom audiences you create on Facebook from a list of your existing contacts, for example — you're the data controller and you need to consider your lawful grounds for processing the personal data that you are uploading for the purposes of serving them Facebook ads.

WARNING

Some people argue that a data controller is able to upload personal data to Facebook to create custom audiences on the basis of legitimate interests and that consent isn't necessary. However, a decision in late 2018, of the Higher Administrative Court of the Federal State of Bavaria (in Germany) cast some doubt on this when the Court upheld the decision of the Bavarian Data Protection Authority that banned advertisers from uploading personal data in such a way without explicit consent, for the following reasons:

>> Facebook obtains additional information about data subjects from matching email addresses, even if a data subject hasn't registered with Facebook.

>> It also shows Facebook that a data subject is a customer of a particular company or online store. This can involve special category data being shared with Facebook, such as when people subscribe to a political party or purchase a certain type of medication.

>> Facebook doesn't notify data subjects that the data has been shared and doesn't give them a chance to object.

The Bavarian Data Protection Authority dismissed claims that *hashing* (a security measure that transforms a set of data into another of the same length via mathematical means) would solve the problem. The Authority further commented that this decision also has implications for Facebook's *lookalike audiences* (an audience chosen by Facebook who are comprised of individuals who are similar to your existing contacts but who have likely never interacted with your organization) and the Facebook *pixel* (the code you put on your website that tracks users' behavior when they browse your website and enables Facebook to serve them targeted ads on the Facebook platform).

The case was decided before the GDPR came into force, but the Bavarian Data Protection Authority asserts that the relevant principles still hold under the GDPR and that other supervisory authorities are likely to follow its stance.

The decision does not go as far as to say that explicit consent is mandatory in every case where a data controller wants to upload personal data for the purposes of using custom audiences. The Court considered legitimate interests and found that the Balancing test would not go in favor of the website owner in this case. The Court also commented that it would be possible for the website owner to obtain consent because the email addresses were collected during the process of placing an online order.

It also remains to be seen whether there is any distinction in uploading personal data where there is no chance of special-category data being involved and where a privacy notice has advised the data subject of this use and provided the opportunity to opt out.

TIP

If you do decide to upload your email list using Facebook's Custom Audiences feature, ensure that this list is up-to-date and that data subjects who have unsubscribed from your email list aren't included in the list that's uploaded to Facebook.

Facebook Fan Pages

Due to a decision by the European Court of Justice in June 2018, the administrator of a Fan Page on Facebook is jointly responsible with Facebook for the processing of the personal data of visitors to the page. I provide the details of *the Court of Justice of the European Union (CJEU) V. Wirtschaftsakademie Schleswig-Holstein* in Chapter 5, where I discuss joint controllers.

This case was decided under the Data Protection Directive, pre-GDPR and with no mention in that legislation of joint controllers. However, the reference to *joint responsibility* is equivalent to that of joint controllers under the GDPR.

The practical implications of this case for organizations that use Facebook Fan Pages are that you need to:

» Provide your Privacy Notice to visitors of your Fan Page (or ensure that Facebook has done so)

» Enter into a joint controller arrangement with Facebook

» Supply prior consent to use Facebook pixels, which I discuss later in this chapter

Facebook has provided a Joint Controller Addendum that you can view at

`www.facebook.com/legal/terms/page_controller_addendum`

The Facebook Like button

In a non-binding opinion linked to the *Wirtschaftsakademie* case about Facebook Fan Pages, Michal Bobek, Advocate General of the European Court of Justice, has opined that when you place a Facebook Like button on your website, you're jointly responsible with Facebook for the collection and transmission of the data subject's personal data (and therefore a joint controller, which I discuss further in Chapter 5).

This opinion was requested by the Higher Regional Court of Düsseldorf in Germany after consumer advocates in Germany applied for an order requiring Fashion ID, an online fashion store, to remove the Like plug-in, arguing that merely by embedding the Facebook Like button on its website, Fashion ID was causing Facebook to gather personal data about its website users — even if they didn't click the Like button and even if the user had no Facebook account.

It remains to be seen whether this opinion will be followed by the court, but it seems likely.

Cookies and pixels

In light of recent guidance from the Information Commissioner's Office (ICO) in the UK and the Commission Nationale de l'Informatique et des Libertés (CNIL) in France, cookies must not be deployed until affirmative consent to the use of such cookies is obtained. This consent necessitates more than the user continuing to browse a website, even if a cookie policy on the website has specified that cookies are being used.

This may cause problems for website owners wanting to use Facebook pixels on their sites in order to carry out retargeting on Facebook. (*Retargeting* is where Facebook takes hashed personal data about your website users and uses this data to show such website users your ads about the relevant content they were browsing on your website.)

TIP

If you're using Facebook pixels on your website, IAB Europe, the European-level association for the digital marketing and advertising ecosystem, recommends that you include the following wording in your cookie policy:

> *"We use technologies, such as cookies, to customize content and advertising, to provide social media features and to analyze traffic to the site. We also share information about your use of our site with our trusted social media, advertising and analytics partners. [See details — link to your Privacy Policy.]"*

Facebook has also made some changes so that Facebook pixels can be set as first-party cookies in addition to third-party cookies. This is because many website browsers now block third-party cookies. Facebook allows you to change your advertising settings within Facebook to set either first- and third-party cookies or just third-party cookies. You can also set the pixel to analytics only or to advertising and analytics.

See Chapter 9 for more about cookies and your Cookie Policy.

Facebook Messenger

If you're using Facebook Messenger marketing to send advertising to users while the personal data is on Facebook's platform, you aren't the data controller.

TIP

Facebook has its own rules about using Facebook Messenger, to protect the Messenger platform from spam. You can view more at

```
https://developers.facebook.com/docs/messenger-platform/policy/
policy-overview
```

REMEMBER

As soon as you extract personal data from Facebook (perhaps you have asked for email addresses to enter a free prize draw), you are the data controller in relation to that personal data and you need to ensure that you have lawful grounds for processing and to provide the data subject with a copy of your Privacy Notice.

Facebook Groups

If you run a Facebook group, you're allowed to ask people applying to join the group up to three questions in order to ensure that they intend to be responsible members of the group. If you're using these three questions to obtain an email address (to send a free report related to the topic of the Facebook group, for example), then, as I explained above, when you take those emails from the Facebook platform, you become the data controller and you need to consider your lawful grounds of processing for using that personal data. If you cannot rely on legitimate interests, you will need to obtain consent for the use of that personal data.

If you intend to send follow up marketing emails to Facebook group members in addition to sending them the free report, you will also need to consider your lawful round of processing for this follow up marketing. Consent needs to be granular and provide the data subject with a true choice as to whether they consent or not (see Chapter 3 for more) so you cannot request the two consents in the same question. Facebook does not allow the functionality for tick boxes in the Facebook group questions, so you would need to use two of the three questions in order to obtain the two consents.

Your Facebook questions might look like this:

> Q1 "Enter your email address in the box below if you want to receive our free report on XYZ. We use your personal data in accordance with our privacy policy that you can see at [INSERT URL]."

> Q2 "If you would also like to receive our newsletter that provides updates, news, discount vouchers and details of special promotions, please type YES below."

You may be able to combine the consents into one question if you express the free report to be a thank you gift for subscribing for your newsletter. Your question might say:

> "Enter your email address if you want to receive our newsletter. To thank you, we will send you our free report on XYZ. We use your personal data in accordance with our privacy policy that you can see at [INSERT URL]."

By expressing the free report to be a thank-you gift, this arguably falls within the ICO's guidance that it's permissible to incentivize an opt-in. If you're marketing in EU member states other than the UK, check the relevant regulator's approach to this topic.

TIP

A tool designed to help you capture email addresses from your Facebook questions and import these addresses into your customer relationship management (CRM) system is Group Funnels. You can find out more about it at `https://bit.ly/2sU0m0a`. This is an affiliate link — a link that tracks any sales made through this link and for which you receive a small amount of commission. I've personally used this software and experienced great results with it.

Display advertising

Display advertising is the use of banner ads in graphical or text form that appear in specifically designated areas of a website or social media platform.

If you're using cookies with banner ads to carry out retargeting, you need to consider the updated cookie guidance from the ICO and CNIL, which requires affirmative consent before the cookie is deployed. See Chapter 9 for more about cookies.

Behavioral advertising

If you're carrying out online behavioral advertising (where you or an agency on your behalf are presenting targeted ads to web users by collecting information about their website browsing behavior), then if personal data is being processed as part of that advertising, the GDPR will apply. Due to the GDPR's wide definition of 'identifiers', such processing will almost always comprise the processing of personal data.

In addition to GDPR compliance, you must consider the ePrivacy Directive when using online behavioral advertising, because cookies or similar devices are sure to be used in this form of advertising. The ePrivacy Directive requires consent for the use of non essential cookies. This standard of consent is the same as for consent under the GDPR. See Chapter 3 for more about consent.

In order to obtain consent to cookies, you may want to consider the IAB Europe framework. It helps website operators and publishers, consent management providers, and vendors such as supply-side platforms (SSPs), exchanges, demand-side platforms (DSPs), ad servers, and data management platforms comply with the GDPR. You can find out more about how the IAB Europe framework can help with consent issues at https://advertisingconsent.eu.

WARNING

If your advertising network uses real-time bidding (or you're an advertising network that uses real-time bidding), note that such auctions are being challenged as not compliant with the GDPR. (In *real-time* bidding, you can bid for ad space based on current data, such as market conditions and performance data; if you're using Facebook ads, Google ads, LinkedIn ads, or other social media ads, you're likely using real-time bidding.)

The reason that real-time bidding is being challenged is that the advertiser or advertising agency often uses the data from the bid to create a profile of the individual — their interests, for example — and integrates this with other data sources to build an even more detailed profile of the individual. Mostly, this is carried out without the individual's knowledge.

Usually, the data contained in the bid request doesn't identify an individual by data (name or address, for example) but rather by a randomized persistent identifier or user ID. Because the GDPR defines personal data very widely, such identifiers would be considered personal data and hence all provisions of the GDPR apply. This means you need to have lawful grounds for processing (consent) and to be transparent about the processing and the purposes of the processing.

If you're using online behavioral advertising (OBA), you need to be compliant with the GDPR's provisions about profiling (covered in Chapter 14).

The GDPR defines *profiling* as "any form of automated processing of personal data consisting of the use of personal data to evaluate certain aspects relating to a natural person, in particular to evaluate certain personal aspects concerning that natural person's performance at work, economic situation, health, personal preferences, interests, reliability, behavior, location, or movements."

In October 2018, the French supervisory authority, CNIL, put Vectaury, a French advertising network, on notice to cease the processing of personal data because it had not gained valid consent to the processing and had not been transparent about using real-time bidding as part of its profiling strategy. Vectaury claimed it had implemented the IAB Consent Framework (as I referred to earlier), but CNIL said that the consent was not informed, not specific, and not given by affirmative action.

Keep in mind these important concepts from the *Vectaury* case:

>> **Make the mobile app consent process effective.** The standard process doesn't provide information on the processing of location data and doesn't make available an easily accessible list of third-party recipients with whom the personal data would be shared.

>> **Provide sufficient processing information.** You need to provide sufficient information about the processing before a data subject is asked to consent. (See Chapter 8 for more details about the information that needs to be provided in a Privacy Notice.)

>> **Provide a list of third parties with whom the data is being shared.** You must provide the list to the data subject in a clear and easily accessible way before the data subject is asked to decide whether to consent.

>> **Allow different purposes of processing be consented to individually, as with parties with whom data will be shared.** The default should always be no consent.

>> **Use options with equal weighting for consent.** An example is Accept All, Reject All, and Choose Cookies.

>> **Obtain and retain all records of consent.** As with any consent for the processing of personal data, you need to keep careful records of the consent provided. See Chapter 3 for more on this.

Keep these guidelines in mind when it comes to OBA:

>> Ad networks like Google's Adsense or Facebook's Audience Networks ads are likely to be data controllers because they have control over the way the data is processed and the purposes of the processing. This means that they have to comply with the GDPR as a data controller.

>> A website publisher may also be a joint controller with the ad network. The way the responsibilities fall within that joint controller relationship depends on the nature of the relationship. (See Chapter 5 for more about joint controllers.)

>> The ePrivacy Directive applies to online behavioral advertising because it relies on the use of cookies or other, similar devices. (See Chapter 9 for more on the use of cookies.) Note that online behavioral advertising typically involves the use of third-party cookies.

Email and text marketing

When it comes to email and text marketing, you need to consider not only compliance with the GDPR but also the ePrivacy Directive.

The implementation of the ePrivacy Directive varies across EU member states, with some states requiring opt-in consent for unsolicited direct marketing messages for both corporate subscribers and individual (non-corporate) subscribers. See the earlier section "The inter-relationship with the ePrivacy Directive) to read more about which EU member states require opt in consent for unsolicited direct marketing messages for both corporate subscribers and individual subscribers.

In the UK, under the Privacy and Electronic Communications Regulations (PECR), you can send unsolicited direct marketing messages to corporate subscribers (namely, limited companies, LLPs, Scottish partnerships, and government bodies). Note that this doesn't include businesses that trade as sole traders or partnerships. You must, however, identify yourself in the email or text. If the email address includes personal data such as `james.smith@abc.com`, the individual has the right to require you to stop sending marketing to their email address.

There is a prohibition against sending unsolicited direct marketing messages to individual subscribers, unless they have provided their prior consent or the soft opt-in applies.

The soft opt-in, as I describe in Chapter 11, applies in the UK if the following conditions are met:

>> You have obtained the contact details of the recipient of that email in the course of the sale or negotiations for the sale of a product or service to that recipient.

>> The email is in respect of your similar products and services only; and

>> The recipient has been given a simple means of refusing the use of his contact details for the purposes of such direct marketing at the time that the details were initially collected, and, where he did not initially refuse the use of the details, at the time of each subsequent communication. (Such a refusal must be free of charge, except for the costs of the transmission of the refusal.)

Other EU member states interpret the soft opt-in slightly differently:

>> In Austria and Denmark, you're allowed to rely only on the soft opt-in where the contact details have been obtained in the course of a sale and not in negotiations leading to the sale.

>> In certain EU member states — the UK and the Netherlands for example — the data subject doesn't need to have bought anything for the soft opt-in to apply. *Negotiations* means that a prospect has actively expressed an interest in buying your products or services — for example, by requesting a quote or asking for further details.

   Arguably, people who have added goods to an online shopping cart but haven't checked out yet could be said to have actively expressed an interest, thereby allowing use of the soft opt-in to enable follow-up emails to encourage them to continue with their purchase.

WARNING

If you're a not-for-profit organization or charity, take care when seeking to rely on the soft opt-in — the soft opt-in refers to "obtaining contact details in the course of a sale or negotiations for the sale of a product or service." Hence, it doesn't include any contact details you have obtained as a result of campaigning or fundraising.

To rely on the soft opt-in, you must have obtained the contact details of the data subject directly from that data subject. If you received the details from a third party (for example, from the purchase of a marketing list), you wouldn't be able to rely on the soft opt-in.

REMEMBER

If you rely on the soft opt-in, you may only send texts or emails about similar products or services. To ascertain whether they're similar, ask yourself whether the customer would reasonably expect to receive the email from you. If you were sending a follow-up email about an upgrade to an existing product, the customer would reasonably expect to hear about it. If, however, you sold the customer a motorboat and then sent an email advertising double glazing, this item wouldn't be one that the customer would reasonably expect to hear about.

As a data controller, when sending direct marketing emails or texts, you must

>> Inform the recipient of your identity

>> Ensure that the message is identifiable as a commercial communication

>> Ensure that promotional offers are clearly identified and that the conditions to qualify for them are clear

Affiliate marketing

In *affiliate marketing*, you market other organizations' products or services in return for a percentage of the price paid by the customer. You aren't sharing your customer's or prospect's data with the third-party organization, but rather are emailing your customers and prospects about the products and services of a third party and including a link to their website or landing page for the particular promotional offer.

If you want to send offers from third parties to your customers and/or prospects, the ICO guidance is to ensure that you have the appropriate consent from such individuals to receive sales promotions from third parties. It is unlikely that such third parties would need to be specifically named and consented to individually.

TIP

If you are carrying out affiliate marketing, also ensure that you are disclosing the fact that you are acting as an affiliate and may earn commission on any sales made through your link.

Automated calling

An *automated calling system* automatically calls a telephone number and then plays a prerecorded message when the call is answered. This doesn't include the automated calling of telephone numbers to facilitate a live call once the individual answers the telephone.

You must always obtain opt-in consent before using automated calling systems with your data subjects, regardless of whether it's a B2B call or a B2C call.

Certain EU member states (including the UK and Poland) require the caller to disclose their identity and contact details in the prerecorded message.

Offline Marketing

Offline marketing, sometimes referred to as traditional marketing, is any marketing that doesn't occur on the Internet. Types include face-to-face networking, events, snail mail, and others, which I discuss further in the following sections.

Prospecting and networking

Prospecting occurs when you identify an individual with whom you want to do business, regardless of whether they're within a corporation.

Individuals within organizations often identify individuals in other organizations via social media or at networking events and then follow up with them to see whether they're interested in doing business. Perhaps someone has given you their business card at a networking event or you have obtained their email details from searching the Internet.

Can you then email this individual without their prior consent?

Under the GDPR, you need to think about your lawful grounds for processing the personal data of the individual (name and email for example). If you're hoping to rely on legitimate interests, you need to carry out a legitimate interests assessment. (See Chapter 12 for more on the LIA.) You should provide the individual with your Privacy Notice (or a link in your email) and give them the right to opt out. You might say something like this:

> "I hope you don't mind my following up after our conversation at XYZ. If you're not interested, just let me know and I won't contact you again."

However, it isn't so much the GDPR that determines whether you can email someone, but rather the ePrivacy Directive. Under this Directive, in some EU member states you cannot send unsolicited direct marketing emails to anyone. In certain EU member states, such as the UK, you can send unsolicited direct marketing emails to corporate subscribers. (See the earlier section "Email and text marketing" for more.) If your prospect is working for a corporation and you're emailing them in their capacity as an employee of that corporation (rather than as an individual), you can follow up by email without consent (and relying on legitimate interests as your lawful grounds of processing for GDPR purposes).

This point takes me back to the definition of direct marketing, which I discuss at the beginning of this chapter. That definition is "any form of sales promotion directed toward particular individuals." So, if you send this email:

> "It was good to meet you at X. How do you fancy meeting up for a coffee some time?"

arguably, it wouldn't be a direct marketing email and would instead be outside the scope of the ePrivacy Directive.

TIP

Another way to safely follow up is to ask the person at the networking meeting or on social media, "Is it okay for me to send you an email to follow up?" This is effectively obtaining their consent to the email. You would however need to keep a record of that consent.

Of course, if you just gather up business cards at networking meetings and send unsolicited sales emails to individuals without having spoken to them, this won't be GDPR-compliant. It isn't particularly effective marketing, either.

Events

If you collect individuals' personal data at events you attend, speak at, or exhibit in — by asking them to drop their business card in the box to enter a prize drawing to win your book, for example — this doesn't mean you can then automatically send them direct marketing emails about your promotions. You would need to consider the application of the GDPR and the ePrivacy Directive to sending direct marketing emails, as set out earlier in this chapter.

You could arguably invite event attendees to drop their business cards in a box to receive your newsletter and, as a thank-you, enter the person's name into a prize drawing. The ICO in the UK has made clear that incentivizing opt-ins is acceptable, though other EU member states may not share this view.

Otherwise, you could ask people to mark their business cards to signify their consent to receive promotional materials, or you could have a hard copy sign-up form on which people can tick a box to receive promotional materials.

You should also have a copy of your Privacy Notice available at the point where people are providing their data and draw their attention to it.

Exhibitions

Often, exhibition organizers believe that they can share attendees' details with exhibitors or with other attendees without gaining consent from the attendees. This belief is incorrect. If they are passing personal data to third-party exhibitors who would require consent to process such data in the way they intend (for example, to send marketing emails), those exhibitors should be individually named and consent be obtained separately for each individual exhibitor.

Blanket consent to share attendees' details with every exhibitor isn't sufficiently granular, and the attendees should be given the opportunity to identify which of the exhibitors they *want* to hear from. Often, attendees receive QR codes on their name badges, and then exhibitors ask attendees who have expressed an interest whether they can scan the QR codes to obtain their details and send them follow-up emails.

Referrals

If you run a refer-a-friend scheme, where a customer or prospect is asked to provide their friends' details so that you can contact them, you're obtaining the personal data of a third party without their consent. You need to consider the legal grounds for processing the personal data and, because the friend wouldn't generally expect to hear from you, this is unlikely to fall under legitimate interests.

TIP

One solution would be to implement a system whereby an email is created for the referrer to send to the friend with a code or a unique link, so that you know who has referred the friend. Then you aren't processing the personal data of the third party until they sign up for the offer.

Postal marketing

The ePrivacy Directive has no bearing on postal marketing. If you use personal data in your postal marketing, you need to comply with the GDPR. If you send direct marketing messages by post addressed to "the owner" or "the resident," or if it's mail that isn't even addressed, such as junk mail, personal data isn't being processed and you don't need to comply with the GDPR. Having said that, other laws in individual EU member states may apply to the delivery of unsolicited mail or the content of such junk mail.

If you process personal data as part of sending direct mail by post, you need to consider your lawful grounds for processing. Chances are good that you're already processing data by storing the data before sending mail, so you should already have a lawful basis for such processing.

If an individual hasn't consented to receive direct marketing messages by post, the other possible lawful grounds for processing is legitimate interests. You need to carry out the Legitimate Interests Assessment (LIA) as well as the Balancing test (as I discuss in Chapter 12). This list describes a few examples of people who would expect to hear from you:

>> Someone who has just bought something from you would likely expect to hear from you.

>> Someone who has indicated interest in your products and services in some way (by liking your Facebook page or signing up for your email list, for example) might reasonably expect to hear from you.

>> Someone who has a driveway in need of repair at their house receives an offer from you for a new driveway. Would this homeowner reasonably expect to hear from you? This scenario isn't cut-and-dried, so make sure you carry out your LIA and are prepared to justify your decision to process personal data on this basis.

If the data subject opts out of direct marketing by mail, you must stop sending them postal marketing.

Non-automated calls

A *non-automated* phone call is one that a person makes by manually dialing a number and then speaking with whoever answers (whether or not they're using a script as a guide).

Some EU member states permit business-to-business non-automated marketing calls, and others don't. Germany requires opt-in consent for marketing calls to individuals and opt-out consent for marketing calls to businesses. The UK allows opt-out consent for marketing calls to both individuals and businesses.

Search the following sites before using any number for marketing calls:

>> **Telephone Preferences Service (TPS):** Individuals can use this free service to register as opting out of unsolicited sales and marketing calls:

```
www.tpsonline.org.uk/tps/index.html
```

>> **Corporate Telephone Preference Service (CTPS):** This area of TPS allows corporate subscribers to opt out of receiving unsolicited sales and marketing calls:

```
www.tpsonline.org.uk/tps/whatiscorporatetps.html
```

Chapter **20**

Children, Charities, and Associations

s I've discussed elsewhere in this book, as a data controller you have extra considerations when it comes to the processing of children's personal data. In this chapter, I take a more in-depth look into getting consent from children, what lawful grounds for processing are appropriate, and the additional rights children have under the GDPR.

I also cover charities and associations in this chapter. Associations (churches and professional clubs, for example) have no rules specific to them to follow, but they must comply with the GDPR the same as any organization is required to do. Charities, on the other hand, have specific points relating to fundraising activities to consider under the GDPR.

Children

A *child* is anyone under the age of 18. A person with *parental responsibility* has the legal rights and responsibilities for a child (younger than 18) that are normally afforded to parents. Often, this is a child's natural parents, but sometimes it is not.

According to Recital 38 of the GDPR, children may be less aware of risks and consequences associated with the processing of personal data. And children may also not understand their rights concerning the processing of personal data. As such, children require "specific protection," and Recital 38 goes on to state, "Such specific protection should, in particular, apply to the use of personal data of children for the purposes of marketing or creating personality or user profiles and the collection of personal data with regard to children when using services offered directly to a child."

According to this Recital, however, the specific protection doesn't extend to "preventive or counselling services offered directly to a child." In these cases, consent from the person holding parental responsibility for the child isn't necessary.

WARNING

Essentially, you have the responsibility to protect the rights and freedoms of the child, and you'll need to prove that you provide this protection should you be investigated by a supervisory authority. To adequately protect a child, you must design your processing from the outset, taking children and their ages into account. As a general rule, younger children need more protection than older children.

TIP

You may want to carry out a Data Protection Impact Assessment (DPIA) before you process any child's personal data to assess the impact of the processing on the rights and freedoms of the child. If you are marketing to children, this will generally be considered by supervisory authorities to result in a high risk to the rights and freedoms of the child and therefore you must carry out a DPIA before doing so. (See Chapter 15 for more about DPIAs.)

So, as you can see, children are provided with certain additional protections over and above those that adults enjoy under the GDPR — protections I discuss further throughout the rest of this section.

Differences for children under the GDPR

The GDPR makes it clear that children's personal data deserves specific protection. It also brings in new requirements for the processing of a child's personal data where you offer an online service directly to a child.

If you offer an online service directly to a child (and not by way of an intermediary, such as a school) and you're relying on consent as your lawful basis for the processing, only children over a certain age are able to provide their own consent. The age of consent varies, from 13 to 16, among EU member states. (See Chapter 3 for more on the age of consent.)

TIP

Even if the payment or funding for the service doesn't come directly from the child (for example, where an app is free but funded by advertising), this will still constitute offering online services directly to a child.

Keep a few things in mind regarding the consent of children:

>> **Obtain parental consent:** for children under the age of consent, unless the online service is an online preventive or counseling service, you must obtain the consent of the person who has parental responsibility for the child.

>> **Verify child's age:** you need to be able to verify that a child providing their own consent is old enough to do so. You don't need to verify their exact age, but you must verify that they're at the requisite age or older.

The GDPR provides no guidance regarding what you must do to verify the child's age, but consider what's technologically available in light of the risks in the processing. For more high-risk processing, for example, you need to take more steps to verify that the child is old enough to provide consent.

>> **Verify parental responsibility:** you also need to verify that the person providing consent for the child is actually the person with parental responsibility.

WARNING

Even if you do not specifically target children with your marketing for online services, you should take a cautious approach and still require verification of age or parental consent (and verification of parental responsibility).

The UK's Information Commissioner's Office (ICO) has given these examples:

>> **Low risk processing:** If you're processing a child's personal data to send them a band's newsletter, for example, a simple tick box lets the child confirm that they're at the requisite age to provide their own consent. A tick box may suffice to let the person consenting for the child confirm that they have parental responsibility.

> » **High risk processing:** If the child is signing up for a chat room, deeper investigation regarding the child's age is likely to be required. You could use a third-party age verification service or double-check the relationship between the person claiming parental responsibility and the child, such as providing copies of passports.
>
> If you ask for and use a passport for verification of age, you need to erase it as soon as you have verified the age of the child or the relationship.

The GDPR also introduces special rules about marketing to children or profiling them, which I discuss further in the "Marketing to children" section, later in this chapter. In addition, the GDPR requires that Privacy Notices for children are age-appropriate, a topic I discuss more in the later section "Privacy Notices geared to children."

Consent of parents and children

To process the personal data of children, you need to have lawful grounds for processing such data for that particular purpose, in the same way you do for adults. (See Chapter 3 for more on this topic.)

If you're processing the data of children based on consent, you need to consider the information in the following sections.

Competence

Regardless of whether you offer an online service to a child, you must ensure that anyone providing consent is *competent* — that is, the individual truly understands what it is they're consenting to. Without competency, the consent isn't informed (a requirement of consent under the GDPR) and therefore isn't valid.

Rules differ across the EU regarding whether a child is competent. For example, in the UK (apart from Scotland), no set age denotes when a child is considered competent. In Scotland, children 12 or older are presumed to be competent.

If you're unable to make individual assessments of the children, consider both of these factors:

> » The age range of the children whose personal data you're processing

> » The complexity of the request for consent

If a child isn't competent, you need to obtain the consent of the person with parental responsibility, unless it's apparent that doing so would be against the best interests of the child.

TIP

Your Privacy Notice must explain how an individual can withdraw consent where a person with parental responsibility provided the consent when the individual was a child, and the child has now become competent.

Contractual obligation as lawful grounds for processing

If you want to rely on the contractual grounds of processing for children's personal data, note that the legal age of capacity to enter into contracts varies across EU member states. The UK (with the exception of Scotland, where the legal age of capacity is generally 16) doesn't have a set age at which a child is considered to have the necessary legal capacity to enter into a contract.

TIP

If you want to rely on the contractual grounds of processing for children's personal data, you would be wise to take legal advice in this complex legal area.

Legitimate interests as lawful grounds for processing

If you want to rely on legitimate interests to process a child's personal data, you should note that Article 6(1)(f) of the GDPR (which has to do with the lawfulness of processing) explains when the data controller's legitimate interests can be overridden. In effect, any claim of legitimate interest is trumped by the "interests or fundamental rights and freedoms of the data subject which require protection of personal data, *in particular where the data subject is a child.*" (The emphasis is mine.)

Additional rights of children

Children enjoy all the same data protection rights that adults have (Chapter 14 covers data subject rights) as well as some additional rights, as explained in the next few sections.

Marketing to children

Recital 38 mandates that children must have specific protection when their personal data is used in marketing, because children are likely to be less aware of the risks, consequences, and safeguards.

If you want to market to children using their personal data, you need to consider the risks involved and how you can reduce those risks. You also must consider any specific legislation about marketing to children, which varies from EU member state to member state.

Profiling and automated decision-making

If you want to carry out profiling on children or use automated decision-making with them, you must carry out a Data Protection Impact Assessment, or DPIA. (See Chapter 15 for more on this topic.) The Recitals suggest that automated decision-making and profiling not be used when it comes to children, but this isn't backed up in the text of the GDPR itself. In any event, automated decision-making and profiling of children should not be the norm.

Privacy Notices geared to children

Children also have rights when it comes to the information provided to them — the same way that adults do. However, you must ensure that the information is provided in an age-appropriate way. If your target audience includes a wide range of ages, for example, you may need to have more than one Privacy Notice. If you have only one Privacy Notice, ensure that it's easily understandable by the youngest children in your target audience.

Even if you're obtaining the consent of a person with parental responsibility for the child, you still need to inform the child of their rights in relation to their data. If your target audience is pre-literate, you may need to produce an age-appropriate video (for example, a cartoon using simple language) to provide the necessary information.

Children exercising data protection rights

Children may exercise their data protection rights themselves if they are competent to do so. (See the earlier section "Consent of parents and children" for more on competency.) If you decide that a child is competent to provide consent, it's assumed that they're competent to exercise their data subject rights.

REMEMBER

Any person (child or adult) may authorize someone else to act on their behalf to exercise their rights. (For more on this topic, see Chapter 14.)

The data subject rights are those of the child and not of the person with parental responsibility. You should allow that person to exercise the child's data subject rights only when the child has authorized such person to do so, when the child lacks sufficient understanding to exercise the rights themselves, or when it's evident that this would be in the best interests of the child.

If a child isn't competent and a person with parental responsibility tries to exercise the child's data subject rights, it's usually appropriate to permit the adult to exercise the rights. An exception occurs when you have evidence that doing so would not be in the best interests of the child.

If you believe that the child can understand their rights, you should reply directly to the child. You may respond to the person with parental responsibility where the child has authorized it or where you believe that it would be in the best interests of the child.

The right to be forgotten

An individual may want to exercise the right to erasure (that is, the right to be forgotten) regarding data collected when the individual was a child. Recital 65 addresses this concern, stating that the right of erasure "is relevant in particular where the data subject has given his or her consent as a child and isn't fully aware of the risks involved by the processing, and later wants to remove such personal data, especially on the Internet." At this point, the fact that the individual is no longer a child is irrelevant.

If the data subject is no longer a child or has become competent to exercise their rights on their own behalf, you should — even if consent was provided by a person holding parental responsibility — accept the (now adult) data subject's request for erasure.

REMEMBER

If the child is competent to provide their own consent and to exercise their own data protection rights, always consider the wishes of the child before accepting a request to erase personal data that comes from a person with parental responsibility.

If a dispute about erasure arises between a child and the person with parental responsibility for the child — or where the child wants to have their personal data erased without the knowledge of the person with parental responsibility — you need to think about the level of understanding of the child. You must also consider what's in the child's best interests. If more than one person holds parental responsibility and they disagree about whether the child's personal data should be erased, consider the child's views. The best interests of the child should always be the most important factor in deciding whether to erase the data.

GDPR CASES INVOLVING CHILDREN

In August 2019, the Swedish supervisory authority fined a school in Sweden €18,630 for its trial of facial recognition technology to monitor the attendance of students. The trial only monitored 22 students over a period of 3 weeks. The data was stored on the hard drive of a computer at the school which was locked in a cabinet. Consent was obtained from the guardians of the children participating in the trial, but it was not possible to refuse to participate in the trial. The school did not carry out a risk assessment. The supervisory authority considered that the use of facial recognition technology and the processing of biometric data (a type of special-category data) in order to monitor attendance brought a disproportionate risk to the rights and freedoms of the children and that there were less invasive ways to monitor attendance. Hence the processing was in breach of Article 5 — the purpose limitation principle. The supervisory authority held that the school had failed to carry out a Data Protection Impact Assessment (as it should have done for processing that is likely to result in a high risk to the rights and freedoms of the children) and that it should have consulted with the supervisory authority in accordance with Article 36. (See Chapter 15 for more on this.) In addition, the supervisory authority said that any consent to the use of facial recognition software was not valid as the children and their guardians could not freely decide if they or their children wanted to be part of the trial. Finally, the school could not demonstrate an exemption for the general prohibition against processing special category data and did not have a sufficient legal basis for the data processing. The supervisory authority commented that the fine would have been higher had the trial been longer. In addition, the maximum fine for public authorities in Sweden is SEK10 million (approximately €1.35m or $1.5m).

In March 2019, the Norwegian supervisory authority fined the Bergen municipality €170,000 for its failure to secure the user accounts of children in the municipality's primary schools (and employees of the schools). Files containing personal data were unprotected and openly available. The fact that the data related to children was considered to be an aggravating factor when setting the fine.

Charities

The GDPR applies to all charities, not-for-profit organizations, and political organizations of all types, no matter their size and no matter their structure. In this section we look at GDPR considerations that are particular to charities.

Fundraising and marketing

Due to the wide definition of marketing, anything that promotes the aims and objectives of the organization is considered marketing. If you use personal data to do any of the following, it's considered marketing and you must comply with the GDPR rules on marketing:

>> Send newsletters

>> Inform people about a fundraising appeal

>> Share campaign materials

You may process personal data (see Chapter 3 for more on what constitutes personal data) in a number of areas of your daily operations, such as:

>> Promoting your charity and seeking funding

>> Identifying individuals who may support your charity's objectives

>> Getting feedback on new fundraising methods and activities

>> Holding records of supporters, donors, volunteers, beneficiaries, and other useful contacts

>> Supporting fundraising initiatives by individuals

All six data protection principles in the GDPR apply equally (see Chapter 4 for more on the six principles), and you must ensure that you have lawful grounds for processing. (See Chapter 3 for more on that topic.). For more on GDPR and marketing, see Chapter 19.

The ePrivacy Directive also equally applies. (Chapter 19 has more on this topic.) Note that the soft opt-in doesn't apply to non-commercial marketing, so you can't rely on the soft opt-in exemption for emails or texts about fundraising.

The ICO provides the following example to demonstrate how charities cannot reply on the soft opt-in: An individual sees a charity appeal in a newspaper and decides to donate a small amount of money by text message. However, the fact that the individual has decided to donate on this occasion (and provided their number to the charity as a result) doesn't mean that the charity has their consent to use their details to contact them about future campaigns. The charity cannot therefore use the individual's details for marketing purposes.

Certain EU member states may have fundraising preference services where individuals have opted out from charities contacting them. You must check such preference services before contacting individuals. In the UK, this service is called the Fundraising Preference Service and individuals can opt out from receiving communications from specific charities. Failing to check such a preference service may amount to a breach of the GDPR.

The ICO oversaw investigations of 59 charities who had failed to check the Fundraising Preference Service and as a result issued a warning to charities. The ICO said: "Charities that ignore the fundraising preference service run the real risk of causing distress and offence to people who just don't want to receive their marketing communications. The ICO has written to them to remind them they must act lawfully and responsibly in protecting people's personal data and in how they communicate with them. Our advice for charities is clear: They must not contact people registered on the FPS and, where we see this happening, we will investigate and take enforcement action where necessary."

Wealth screening and data matching

Wealth screening is an aspect of researching prospects to determine an individual's ability to donate. When a charity uses wealth screening, it's looking at indicators of wealth, such as property ownership, business affiliations, shareholdings, and more.

Often, where individuals have opted not to provide certain information about themselves, charities will engage external companies to obtain that information. Those external companies might use *data matching* (comparing a sets of computer records held by separate entities or by using publicly available data) to identify what data is missing; they then compile existing data or telephone numbers to fill the gaps in order to contact individuals to ask for donations.

If you carry out wealth screening or data matching, you need to work out your lawful grounds for processing. Consent will not always be necessary, but if you choose to rely on legitimate interests, ensure that you carry out a Legitimate Interests Assessment and keep it on file. (See Chapter 12 for more on this.)

You need to let people know that you are wealth screening or data matching. The typical place to provide this information is in your Privacy Notice. (See Chapter 8 for more on this.) You also need to inform the individuals of their right to opt out of such processing. Various charities in the UK that used wealth screening and data matching and shared the data with other charities without notifying the data subjects that they were doing so incurred fines for this activity.

REMEMBER

Just because personal data is publicly available doesn't mean that the GDPR doesn't apply to it. You still need to follow the principles (see Chapter 4) and have a lawful grounds for processing the data (see Chapter 3).

TIP

Check whether there are any additional laws or codes about fund-raising practice that prevents the sale or sharing of personal data by charities. In the UK, the Code of Fundraising Practice prevents the sharing of personal data by charities (whether for payment or not) unless the explicit consent of the individual has been obtained.

When sharing data, you must comply with the general rules for sharing personal data. (See Chapter 19 for more on this topic.)

Religious charities and door-to-door preaching

The GDPR applies to religious groups and churches. If prior to the GDPR coming into force, special data protection rules applied to religious groups or churches, these rules need to be brought into line with the GDPR.

With regard to the application of the GDPR to religious groups, the European Court of Justice gave a preliminary ruling in July 2018 clearly stating that religious communities are not exempt from GDPR compliance or other applicable data protection laws.

In the case of *Tietosuojavaltuutettu v Jehovan todistajat – uskonnollinen yhdyskunta*, the Finish supervisory authority brought the case against a group of Jehovah's Witnesses in Finland who had been carrying out door-to-door preaching. The preachers had been making notes about the names, ages, family circumstances, and religious beliefs of the individuals they spoke to in order to assist their memory when they made a further visit. This was done without the knowledge of the individuals concerned. The Jehovah's Witnesses argued that this processing was exempt from the GDPR in that it was a purely household or personal activity. The Court rejected this argument and said that the processing was within the scope of the GDPR.

In addition, the Court held that the Jehovah's Witnesses group was a joint controller, with its members who were carrying out the door-to-door preaching acting as the data controller, even if the community did not have access to the data. This was because the purpose of the door-to-door preaching was to achieve the aims of the religious community and the preaching was coordinated and encouraged by the community.

Although this case was based on the old Data Protection Directive (the European law that pre-dated the GDPR), this still proves significant for future application of data protection rules.

Volunteers

Volunteers are treated in exactly the same way as employees when it comes to GDPR compliance and charities are responsible for the actions of volunteers. You should therefore ensure your volunteers have received GDPR training. See Chapter 24 for more about employee training.

Security

Just because you are a charity does not mean that you can pay any less attention to the security of the personal data you process. In 2018, the British and Foreign Bible Society, a registered charity in the UK, was fined £100,000 by the ICO for failing to have adequate security measures in place, resulting in hackers being able to access the personal data of 417,000 individuals. The charity had failed to put a suitably strong password in place for remote access rights to the network.

Data protection fee

If you are a charity (or other not-for-profit organization) in the UK, you do not have to pay the data protection fee if the following criteria apply:

>> You only process information necessary to establish or maintain membership or support *or* to provide or administer activities for people who are members of the organisation or have regular contact with it

>> You only hold information about individuals whose data you need to process for this exempt purpose

>> The personal data you process is restricted to personal information that is necessary for this exempt purpose

ICO risk review report for charities

The ICO has shared a risk review report for charities, alerting charities to common areas of noncompliance with the GDPR by charities. You can view it at https://ico.org.uk/media/action-weve-taken/audits-and-advisory-visits/2259675/charities-audit-201808.pdf.

The key risks for charities are described in this list:

>> **Sending direct marketing communications without consent.** See Chapter 3 for more about relying on consent as your lawful grounds for processing.

>> **Not notifying individuals of wealth screening and data matching.** See the section on wealth screening and data matching earlier in this chapter.

>> **Processing special-category data without due care and protection.** See Chapter 3 for more about what constitutes special-category data.

>> **Not securing personal data and being susceptible to data breaches.** Chapter 16 covers data security, and Chapter 17 has information about your obligations for reporting breaches when they occur.

» **Accidental disclosure of data because staff training is lacking.** Chapter 16 covers the importance of training staff on security issues.

» **Not ensuring that volunteer access to data is limited and secure.** Chapter 16 provides more detail on security measures.

CASE STUDIES OF ENFORCEMENT: CHARITIES

Several UK charities were fined in recent years for misusing personal data and more specifically for engaging in these activities:

- Secretly screening millions of donors so that they could be targeted for additional funds
- Carrying out data matching by tracing and targeting new or previous donors to complete gaps in information from other sources
- Trading personal details with other charities, thus creating a large pool of donor data for sale

And here's a list of fines:

- **Royal Society for the Prevention of Cruelty to Animals:** £25,000
- **British Heart Foundation:** £18,000
- **International Fund for Animal Welfare:** £18,000
- **Cancer Support UK (formerly Cancer Recovery Foundation UK):** £16,000
- **Cancer Research UK:** £16,000
- **Guide Dogs for the Blind Association:** £15,000
- **Macmillan Cancer Support:** £14,000
- **Royal British Legion:** £12,000
- **National Society for the Prevention of Cruelty to Children:** £12,000
- **Great Ormond Street Hospital Children's Charity:** £11,000
- **WWF-UK:** £9,000
- **Battersea Dogs' and Cats' Home:** £9,000
- **Oxfam:** £6,000

(continued)

(continued)

As mentioned above, the ICO also fined the British and Foreign Bible Society £100,000 after cyberhackers gained access to more than 400,000 supporters' personal data. The ICO investigated the security breach and found that the organization had failed to take appropriate technical and organizational measures to secure the data.

In Italy, a number of websites affiliated with an Italian political party suffered a data breach, and the Italian supervisory authority required certain security improvements. The party's data processor didn't complete the improvements and had to pay a fine of €50,000.

Associations

An *association* is a group of people organized for a joint purpose. Common associations include churches, sports clubs, professional clubs, and recreational leagues that require membership (for knitting, gaming, bicycling, or any other activity or hobby, for example).

The GDPR applies to all associations that process personal data, regardless of the size of the association.

The GDPR assigns no special rules for associations; they must comply with the GDPR in the same way that other organizations do. However, if you're processing personal data merely to keep in touch with members and to advise them of future events, your compliance should be relatively simple.

If you're storing individuals' names and other contact details such as email addresses, you're processing personal data. You must do so in accordance with the data protection principles set out in Chapter 4.

TIP

Your lawful grounds for processing personal data to keep in touch with members are likely to be consent or legitimate interests. For existing members, the most appropriate grounds for processing are legitimate interests because the members are expecting to hear from you. For past members, consent may be necessary; see Chapter 3 for more on this topic.

You should also provide data subjects with all information required by Articles 13 and 14. For more about these articles and the Privacy Notice, see Chapter 8.

CASE STUDIES OF ENFORCEMENT: ASSOCIATIONS

The European Court of Justice ruled that a Swedish woman, Mrs. Lindqvist, who identified and included personal data of fellow church volunteers on her website without their consent, was in breach of data protection legislation. The creation of the website wasn't a personal activity and therefore she wasn't exempt from data protection legislation.

Mrs. Lindqvist was fined SEK4000 (approximately £300) for, among other problems, processing special category data without consent and transferring data outside the EEA.

Although this case was decided pre-GDPR, it's still relevant to show that associations cannot cite the exemption in Article 2(2)(c) (by a natural person in the course of a purely personal or household activity) to argue that the GDPR doesn't apply to them.

A Polish sports association was fined €12,950 for publishing in error the personal data relating to judges who were granted judicial licenses online, including addresses and identification numbers. On discovering the error, the association notified the Polish supervisory authority of the breach and tried but failed to rectify the breach. The fine reflected this failure and the large number of judges involved.

Chapter **21**

Supervisory Authorities, Remedies, Liabilities, and Penalties

Data protection authorities (DPAs) are independent public entities that provide advice on data protection issues and investigate complaints of violations. In particular, *supervisory authorities* (SAs) are DPAs helping to uphold the GDPR and relevant EU member state laws. One key change with the GDPR is that supervisory authorities — compared to DPAs of past data protection regulation — have greatly enhanced powers to impose large fines and other sanctions on organizations that aren't complying with the GDPR.

Each EU member state has its own supervisory authority, and some EU member states have more than one. Germany, for example, has one authority for each of its 16 states as well as an overarching Federal Commissioner for Data Protection and Freedom of Information.

The early sections of this chapter further explore what supervisory authorities are and the powers they hold, in addition to helping you determine who is your supervisory authority. The chapter ends with a look at what happens when data subjects lodge complaints — as they have a right to do — to a supervisory authority, with details on the resulting remedies, compensation, and fines.

Introducing Supervisory Authorities

As I state in this chapter's introduction, supervisory authorities (SAs) uphold the GDPR and relevant EU member state data protection laws. As such, SAs are meant to be completely independent from the member state's governments (and anyone else) — the GDPR mandates this in Article 52. Article 51 of the GDPR states that the supervisory authority is to "protect the fundamental rights and freedoms of natural persons in relation to processing and to facilitate the free flow of personal data within the Union."

To provide that protection, each supervisory authority has a number of tasks (set out in Article 57) to fulfil, including these:

>> Monitoring and enforcing the GDPR

>> Promoting public awareness of the GDPR

>> Promoting awareness of the GDPR with data controllers and processors

>> Handling complaints lodged by data subjects, bodies, or organizations

>> Cooperating with other supervisory authorities to ensure consistency of application of the GDPR across EU member states

Furthermore, Recital 122 makes clear that each supervisory authority is able to exercise its powers in relation to

>> Data controllers or processors that are established in the supervisory authority's member state

>> Data processing affecting data subjects on its territory

>> Data processing carried out by a data controller or processor not established in the European Union (EU) when targeting data subjects residing in its territory

Finding Your Supervisory Authority and Lead Authority

A supervisory authority can regulate data controllers and data processors who are established in their EU member state or whose processing affects or targets data subjects residing in its territory. For example, the French data protection authority CNIL can regulate controllers and processors who are established in France or where the processing affects or targets data subjects residing in France.

However, what happens when a data controller or data processor is established in multiple EU member states, or whose processing affects or targets data subjects residing in multiple EU member states? In these cases, a lead *authority* becomes necessary when data controllers or data processors carry out processing of personal data that impacts data subjects in more than one EU member state. In that scenario, a lead authority is chosen so that the parties involved have a single authority. I explain how to identify a lead authority below.

Supervisory authority

You need to know who your supervisory authority is, for the following reasons:

>> To know whom to contact to discuss a breach of the GDPR or other data protection legislation

>> To ask for advice or assistance

>> To know, most importantly, to whom to make notifications of data breaches

This list explains how to determine who is your supervisory authority:

>> **If you are established in one EU member state and that member state has more than one supervisory authority:** Germany is a prime example here. Your relevant supervisory authority is the one that has jurisdiction over the region where your organization has its headquarters. If you are headquartered in Berlin, for example, then the Berlin supervisory authority will be your supervisory authority.

>> **If you are established in one EU member state and that member state only has one supervisory authority:** As you might expect, your relevant supervisory authority is the supervisory authority of the member state in which you are established.

>> **If you have establishments in more than one EU member state or your processing is likely to substantially affect data subjects in more than one EU member state:** You will have a lead supervisory authority, which I discuss in the next section.

>> **If you are a non-EU established data controller or data processor subject to the GDPR:** You could be subject to the jurisdiction of multiple supervisory authorities.

REMEMBER

When the UK leaves the European Union, the UK's supervisory authority, the ICO, will not be an EU supervisory authority for the purposes of the GDPR. The ICO will, however, continue to be the independent supervisory body regarding the UK's data protection legislation.

Lead authority

The GDPR contains provisions to help data controllers and data processors which are established in more than one EU member state or which carry out processing that substantially affects (or is likely to substantially affect) data subjects in more than one EU member state, so that they need to deal with only a single supervisory authority, known as the *lead authority*, rather than supervisory authorities in multiple member states. This mechanism is often referred to as the *one-stop shop*.

The GDPR doesn't define the term *substantially affects*. The European Data Protection Board guidance is that supervisory authorities will interpret what it means on a case-by-case basis. They will consider the context of the processing, the type of data, the purpose of the processing, and factors such as whether the processing:

>> Causes, or is likely to cause, damage, loss, or distress to individuals

>> Has, or is likely to have, an actual effect in terms of limiting rights or denying an opportunity

>> Affects, or is likely to affect, individuals' health, well-being, or peace of mind

>> Affects, or is likely to affect, individuals' financial or economic status or circumstances

>> Leaves individuals open to discrimination or unfair treatment

>> Involves the analysis of the special categories of personal or other intrusive data — particularly, the personal data of children

>> Causes, or is likely to cause, individuals to change their behavior in a significant way

- >> Has unlikely, unanticipated, or unwanted consequences for individuals
- >> Creates embarrassment or other negative outcomes, including reputational damage
- >> Involves the processing of a wide range of personal data

The European Data Protection Board guidance states, "[T]he fact that a data processing operation may involve the processing of a number — even a large number — of individuals' personal data, in a number of member states, doesn't necessarily mean that the processing has, or is likely to have, a substantial effect."

Certain exceptions apply to the one-stop-shop mechanism. The lead authority may agree that another supervisory authority can take its own enforcement action if complaints come only from data subjects who reside within the territory of the other supervisory authority.

Your lead authority is the supervisory authority of the EU member state in which your "main establishment" is located. Usually, that's at your place of central administration, but if another of your establishments has the power to implement decisions about how personal data is processed, it is the main establishment.

If more than one entity makes decisions about how personal data is processed, it may be that there is more than one lead authority.

If you have an EU establishment but that is not the place of central administration, the European Data Protection Board guidance is that you should consider the following questions to determine which supervisory authority is your lead authority (although it notes that these are not an exhaustive list of questions and all of the circumstances should be considered):

- >> Where are decisions about the purposes and means of the processing given final sign off?
- >> Where are decisions about business activities that involve data processing made?
- >> Where does the power to have decisions implemented effectively lie?
- >> Where is the Director (or Directors) with overall management responsibility for the cross-border processing located?
- >> Where is the controller or processor registered as a company, if in a single territory?

What if it is difficult to identify the main establishment and difficult to determine where decisions are made about data processing (or perhaps decisions about the data processing are all taken outside of the EU)? The GDPR does not provide an answer in these circumstances. The EDPB guidance is that "the pragmatic way to deal with this would be for the company to designate the establishment that will act as its main establishment. This establishment must have the authority to:

>> Implement decisions about the processing activity; and

>> Take liability for the processing, including having sufficient assets

If the company does not designate an establishment in this way, it will not be possible to designate a lead authority."

Here's a more detailed example of how to work out which supervisory authority is the lead authority:

1. **A food retailer is headquartered in Paris, has a distributor in Germany, and sells only in France and Germany.**

   Its lead authority is the CNIL in France because its head office is in Paris.

2. **If a data breach occurs relating to French and German customers, the CNIL would investigate.**

   If necessary, CNIL would take enforcement action, such as levying a fine.

3. **The CNIL would consult with the relevant German supervisory authorities during its investigation.**

   The German supervisory authorities, however, would generally not be able to undertake their own investigation or take their own enforcement action (unless, for example, the breach related only to German data subjects).

4. **If a German data subject wants to make a complaint against the food retailer, the German citizen data subject may make such complaint to the relevant German supervisory authority.**

5. **The German supervisory authority would contact the CNIL.** The CNIL may either decide to investigate the complaint itself or agree that the German supervisory authority should investigate the complaint.

Organizations outside the EU

If you're an organization that doesn't have an establishment in an EU member state, you won't benefit from the one-stop-shop mechanism and therefore won't be able to determine a lead authority. Merely having a Representative (as discussed in Chapter 6), in an EU member state doesn't mean that you can benefit from the one-stop-shop mechanism.

In such circumstances, you must deal (via your Representative) with the supervisory authority in each EU member state where you're processing personal data of its citizens. To see more about appointing Representatives, see Chapter 6.

Forum shopping

You may prefer to deal with one supervisory authority over others, perhaps because you have a stronger relationship with them or because they're more lenient in enforcement matters. However, the GDPR doesn't allow *forum shopping*. This means you cannot choose a particular supervisory authority to be your lead authority.

You might attempt to work around this rule and choose your supervisory authority by claiming to have your main establishment in one EU member state. If, in reality, no effective exercise of management activity or decision-making over personal data processing occurs at the establishment, the relevant supervisory authorities will decide which supervisory authority (if any) is your lead authority. The relevant SA will use objective criteria and look at all evidence to make the decision.

This challenge to the lead authority was evidenced when the French supervisory authority, CNIL, disputed that the Irish supervisory authority was in actual fact the lead authority for Google, even though Google's EU headquarters is in Ireland. CNIL asserted that the Google entity in Ireland "did not have a decision-making power" in relation to the purposes and means of the relevant cross-border data processing activities. The CNIL therefore decided that the Irish supervisory authority was not the lead authority and that the CNIL could levy a fine, which it did of 50m euros.

You could, of course, actually restructure your group so that decision-making about data processing operations is moved to one of your establishments in a different EU member state. However, such a restructuring would not be a simple matter. Plus, you face the potential risk that the desired supervisory authority won't agree that it is the lead authority or that there is a challenge from another supervisory authority in the jurisdiction of affected data subjects.

REMEMBER

If you have more than one establishment within the EU that makes decisions about data processing operations, you could well have more than one lead authority.

UK establishments after Brexit

WARNING

After Brexit, the UK is no longer an EU member state and the UK's data protection authority, the ICO, will no longer be a supervisory authority for the purposes of the GDPR. Organizations established within the UK need to consider the following:

>> **If you process personal data in the UK and otherwise only in a single EU member state (and the processing substantially affects — or is likely to substantially affect — data subjects only within the UK and that other single EU member state),** then post-Brexit, the one-stop shop will not apply and your data processing will be subject to oversight from both the UK's supervisory authority (under UK data protection law) and the supervisory authority of the relevant member state in which you are processing data (under the GDPR).

>> **If you are established in the UK and in one other EU member state but your processing also substantially affects (or is likely to substantially affect) data subjects in EU member states other than where you are established,** your data processing in the context of your UK establishment will be subject to oversight by the UK's supervisory authority. However, your data processing in the context of your EU establishments (and any other processing substantially affecting data subjects in EU member states) will continue to be cross-border processing and you will need to work out the lead authority in respect of that cross-border processing.

   You will therefore have to deal with both the ICO and the lead authority.

>> **If you are established in the UK and two or more EU member states, then regardless of whether the processing substantially affects data subjects in other EU member states,** your data processing in the context of your UK establishment will be subject to oversight by the UK's supervisory authority. However, your data processing in the context of your EU establishments will continue to be cross-border processing and you will need to work out the lead authority in respect of that cross-border processing.

   You will therefore have to deal with both the ICO and the lead authority.

>> **If you're only established in the UK but your processing is likely to substantially affect individuals in any other EU member state,** you will, post-Brexit, have to deal with the ICO and each supervisory authority in each EU member state where individuals are located whose personal data you process in connection with those activities. In theory, you could be fined by the ICO and by the supervisory authority in every EU member state where data subjects are affected.

Reporting Data Breaches to Your Supervisory Authority

You should report data breaches to your supervisory authority or, where cross-border processing is involved, to your lead authority. See Chapter 17 for details about data breaches — specifically, regarding the obligations you have under GDPR.

Appendix B lists the supervisory authorities and their contact details.

Powers of Supervisory Authorities

Supervisory authorities have investigatory, corrective, as well as authorization and advisory powers. In this section, I list the details of each of these powers.

Investigatory powers

Article 58(1) of the GDPR sets out the investigatory powers of supervisory authorities. As such, authorities are given the power to

» Order the data controller and the data processor to provide any information it requires

» Conduct investigations into data controllers and data processors by carrying out data protection audits

» Carry out a review on certifications that may be issued by the supervisory authorities that certify organizations as being GDPR compliant (note that as at the time of publishing this book, no certifications are in place)

» Notify the data controller or the data processor of alleged infringements of the GDPR

» Obtain from the data controller and the data processor access to all personal data and all information necessary for the performance of the supervisory authority's tasks

» Obtain access to any premises of the data controller and the data processor, including any data processing equipment

Corrective powers

Article 58(2) of the GDPR sets out the corrective powers of supervisory authorities. They can:

>> Issue warnings to a data controller or data processor whose intended processing operations are likely to infringe the GPPR

>> Issue reprimands to a data controller or data processor where processing operations have infringed provisions of the GDPR

>> Order the data controller or data processor to comply with a data subject's request to exercise their rights in relation to their personal data

>> Order the data controller or data processor to bring its processing operations into compliance with the GDPR, in a specified manner and within a specified period

>> Order the data controller to notify individuals of a data breach

>> Impose a temporary or definitive limitation, including a ban on processing of personal data

>> Order the rectification or erasure of personal data or restriction of processing, and notify such actions to recipients to whom the personal data have been disclosed

>> Withdraw a certificate or order the certification body to withdraw a certificate or order the certification body not to issue certification if the requirements of the certification are not met, or are no longer met

>> Impose an administrative fine

>> Order the suspension of data flows to a recipient in a third country or to an international organization

Authorization and advisory powers

Article 58(3) of the GDPR sets out the authorization and advisory powers of supervisory authorities. They can:

>> Advise the data controller in accordance with the prior consultation procedure

>> Issue, on its own initiative or on request, opinions to the national parliament or the member state government or to other institutions and bodies as well as to the public on any issue related to the protection of personal data

- » Authorize certain processing, if the law of the member state requires such prior authorization
- » Issue an opinion and approve draft codes of conduct
- » Accredit certification bodies
- » Issue certifications and approve criteria of certification
- » Adopt standard data protection clauses for data processor appointments and for international data transfers
- » Authorize contractual clauses for international data transfers
- » Authorize administrative arrangements between public authorities for international data transfers referred to in Article 46 of the GDPR
- » Approve binding corporate rules for international data transfers

Remedies, Liabilities, and Penalties

Throughout this book, I emphasize the responsibility that you, as a data controller or as a data processor, have in regard to upholding the GDPR. Where applicable, in other chapters, I discuss what consequences you, as a data controller, face in a situation where you fail, for various reasons, to uphold the GDPR. I explore these consequences more fully here, but before I do that, I take a quick look at the data subject's right to lodge complaints.

Data subject complaints

Every data subject has the right to lodge a complaint with a supervisory authority of the EU member state of their habitual residence, place of work, or place of the alleged infringement if the data subject considers that the processing of personal data relating to them infringes the GDPR.

After the data subject has lodged the complaint with a supervisory authority, the SA is responsible for informing the data subject on the progress and the outcome of the complaint (including the possibility of a judicial remedy) within a reasonable period. If the complaint requires further investigation or coordination with another supervisory authority, intermediate information should be given to the data subject.

A data subject also has the right to require a not-for-profit body active in the field of the protection of personal data to lodge a complaint on their behalf with a supervisory authority.

Judicial remedies

A *judicial remedy* is action that a court of law takes in order to enforce a right or impose a penalty. Under the GDPR, data subjects have certain rights relating to judicial remedies, which I discuss in this section.

Judicial remedies against decisions of supervisory authorities

Data subjects and other affected parties have the right to an effective judicial remedy in relation to certain decisions of supervisory authorities — namely:

>> Any data subject or organization has the right to an effective judicial remedy against legally binding decisions concerning them taken by a supervisory authority.

>> Data subjects have the right to an effective judicial remedy where a supervisory authority doesn't handle a complaint or doesn't inform them within three months of the progress or outcome of the complaint.

Recital 143 explains that decisions of supervisory authorities that you may challenge in the courts include:

>> The exercise of investigative, corrective, and authorization powers by the supervisory authority

>> The dismissal or rejection of complaints

You may not challenge decisions that aren't legally binding, such as opinions issued or advice provided by supervisory authorities.

REMEMBER

Court proceedings against a supervisory authority are required to be brought before the courts of the member state where the supervisory authority is established.

Judicial remedies against data controllers or data processors

Data subjects whose rights have been infringed have the right to an effective judicial remedy against the infringing data controllers or data processors.

Data subjects need to bring court proceedings against an infringing data controller or data processor before the courts of the member state where either of these is true:

>> The infringing data controller or data processor is established.

>> The data subject has their habitual residence.

The data controller's and data processor's liability to provide compensation

Article 82 of the GDPR provides that, "Any person who has suffered material or non-material damage as a result of an infringement of this regulation shall have the right to receive compensation from the controller or processor for the damage suffered."

This list explains when the data controller and/or data processor is liable to provide the compensation:

>> A data controller is liable for the damage caused by the processing of data that infringes the GDPR (whether that processing has been conducted by the data controller itself or by a data processor on its behalf).

>> A data processor is liable only for the damage caused by its processing where either of these is true:

  • *It has not complied with obligations of the GDPR specifically relating to data processors.*

  • *It has acted outside of or contrary to lawful instructions of the data controller.*

>> A data controller or data processor isn't liable for damage if it can prove that it is in no way responsible for the event giving rise to the damage.

>> If more than one data controller or data processor, or both a data controller and a data processor, are involved in the same processing and are both responsible for damage caused by the processing, each data controller and each data processor is liable for the entire damage in order to ensure full compensation to the data subject.

>> If a data controller or data processor pays full compensation for the damage suffered to a data subject, that data controller or data processor is entitled to claim back from the other data controllers or data processors (involved in the same processing) that part of the compensation corresponding to their responsibility for the damage.

When it comes to determining which court will have jurisdiction, keep in mind that data subjects have two choices for bringing court proceedings against an infringing controller or processor. They can choose the courts of the member state where:

>> The infringing data controller or data processor is established

>> The data subject has their habitual residence

A 2-tiered system of fines

The GDPR has a 2-tier system for levying fines, depending on the nature of the infringement:

>> Up to 10m euros or up to 2 percent of the total worldwide annual turnover of the preceding financial year, whichever is higher

>> Up to 20m euros or up to 4 percent of the total worldwide annual turnover of the preceding financial year, whichever is higher

The lower tier of up to 10m euros or up to 2 percent relates to the following infringements of the GDPR:

>> Failure to obtain consent to the processing of data relating to children (Article 8) (data controllers); see Chapter 20

>> Failure to implement technical and organizational measures to ensure data protection by design and default (Article 25) (data controllers); see Chapter 15

>> Failure to agree with respective compliance obligations for joint controllers (Article 26); see Chapter 5

>> Failure to designate Representatives when not established in the EU (Article 27) (data controllers and data processors); see Chapter 6

>> Failure to appoint data processors correctly (Article 28) (data controllers); see Chapters 5 and 10

- ›› Subcontracting without the prior consent of the controller (Articles 28 and 29) (processors); see Chapters 5 and 10

- ›› Failure to process data only in accordance with the specific instructions of the data controller (Article 29) (data processors); see Chapters 5 and 10

- ›› Failure to maintain written records (Article 30) (data controllers and data processors); see Chapter 5

- ›› Failure to cooperate with supervisory authorities (Article 31) (data controllers and data processors)

- ›› Failure to implement technical and organizational measures to secure the data (Article 32) (data controllers and data processors); see Chapter 15

- ›› Failure to report breaches to the appropriate supervisory authority or to data subjects within the required timescales (Articles 33 and 34) (data controllers); see Chapter 17

- ›› Failure to notify the data controller without undue delay on becoming aware of a personal data breach (Article 33) (data processors); see Chapter 17

- ›› Failure to comply with the recommendations of a Data Privacy Impact Assessment (Articles 35–36) (data controllers); see Chapter 15

- ›› Failure to comply with the provisions in relation to the appointment of Data Protection Officers (Articles 37–39) (data controllers and data processors); see Chapter 15

The higher tier of up to 20m euros or up to 4 percent relates to the following infringements of the GDPR:

- ›› Failure to comply with the basic principles for processing personal data, including conditions of consent (Articles 5, 6, 7, and 9) (data controllers); see Chapter 3

- ›› Failure to comply with data subjects' rights (Articles 12–22) (data controllers); see Chapter 14

- ›› Failure to comply with provisions relating to international transfers (Articles 44–49) (data controllers); see Chapter 6

- ›› Failure to comply with obligations under EU member state laws in relation to specific processing situations, such as processing in the context of employment and processing for archiving purposes (data controllers and data processors); see Chapter 18

- ›› Noncompliance with an order imposed by a supervisory authority or a failure to comply with a supervisory authority's investigation (Article 58) (data controllers and data processors)

When considering the amount of the penalty, the supervisory authority considers the following issues, as stated in Article 83 of the GDPR:

>> The nature, gravity, and duration of the infringement, taking into account the nature, scope, or purpose of the processing concerned as well as the number of data subjects affected and the level of damage suffered by them

>> The intentional or negligent character of the infringement

>> Any action taken by the data controller or data processor to mitigate the damage suffered by data subjects

>> The degree of responsibility on the part of the data controller or data processor, taking into account technical and organizational measures implemented by them

>> Any relevant previous infringements by the data controller or data processor

>> The degree of cooperation with the supervisory authority when it came to remedying the infringement and mitigating the possible adverse effects of the infringement

>> The categories of personal data affected by the infringement

>> The manner in which the infringement became known to the supervisory authority — in particular, whether, and if so to what extent, the controller or processor notified the authority of the infringement

>> The level of compliance with measures previously ordered against the data controller or data processor concerned with regard to the same subject matter

>> The adherence to approved codes of conduct or approved certification mechanisms established by the supervisory authorities

>> Any other aggravating or mitigating factor applicable to the circumstances of the case, such as financial benefits gained (or losses avoided) directly or indirectly, from the infringement

Note: At the time this book was printed, no codes of conduct or certification mechanisms had been approved.

Other penalties

Individual EU member states may also lay down rules on other penalties applicable to infringements of the GDPR, provided that such penalties are effective, proportionate, and dissuasive. These penalties will apply in addition to those set out in the GDPR itself.

CAMBRIDGE ANALYTICA ILLEGALLY OBTAINED PERSONAL DATA

Professor David Carroll, a US academic, discovered that Cambridge Analytica had processed US voter information in the UK and that this gave him rights to request access to that information.

He submitted a Data Subject Access Request (DSAR) to Cambridge Analytica on January 10, 2017, and Cambridge Analytica's parent company, SCL Group, emailed him, requiring him to pay a small fee and to send proof of identity. He received a reply from an email address at SCL Group informing him to submit the fee and proof of identity to SCL Elections Ltd, Cambridge Analytica's agent.

Carroll duly sent in the fee and the proof of identity and on March 27, 2017, SCL Group, on behalf of Cambridge Analytica, sent Professor Carroll a spreadsheet that purported to contain all the personal data he was legally entitled to receive.

Carroll did not believe that the spreadsheet contained all the relevant data about him, nor was there a sufficient explanation of where the data had been obtained or how it would be used. He therefore complained to the ICO and in September 2017, the ICO wrote to Cambridge Analytica to share the professor's concerns.

Cambridge Analytica refused to reply to the ICO's questions and claimed that Carroll wasn't entitled to exercise a DSAR because he was not a UK citizen or based in the UK. SCL Group told the ICO that Professor Carroll was *"no more entitled to make a so-called 'subject access request' under the UK Data Protection Act than a member of the Taliban sitting in a cave in the remotest corner of Afghanistan."*

The ICO replied in October 2017 that this was not legally the case and reiterated that SCL would need to comply with the DSAR because wherever a data subject lives in the world, if their personal data is being processed by a UK company, the UK's data protection laws apply.

SCL replied to the ICO a month later, asserting that the ICO had no jurisdiction in the matter, stating that SCL Group did "not expect to be further harassed with this sort of correspondence."

The ICO then served a legal notice on SCL, ordering it to provide to Carroll all the data it held on him within 30 days or risk an unlimited fine.

(continued)

(continued)

SCL subsequently announced it had gone into liquidation. The ICO warned it that its decision to "close down and re-emerge under another name" would not shield it from liability. See more at:

www.theguardian.com/uk-news/2018/may/05/cambridge-analytica-uk-regulator-release-data-us-voter-david-carroll

6

The Part of Tens

Chapter **22**

Ten GDPR Resources

I've written this book to act as your number-one resource regarding the GDPR and what you're responsible for doing in order to remain GDPR compliant. This book can help lay a solid foundation for your understanding of the GDPR. With that foundation laid, you can enhance your GDPR knowledge with the resources listed here.

Suzanne Dibble's resources

Facebook group

```
www.facebook.com/groups/GDPRforonlineentrepreneurs
```

Yes, my top GDPR resource for you is my Facebook group, GDPR for Online Entrepreneurs — it's bursting with free resources (mainly in video format, for those who don't want to plow through lengthy guidance notes). It has an engaged community — 35,000 strong — of online business owners from around the world who are kept updated with the latest goings-on and who ask questions (and get answers) about the way the GDPR works in practice.

TIP

Ensure that you answer the questions to be accepted into the group.

GDPR Compliance Pack

www.suzannedibble.com/gdprpack

If you don't want to pay a fortune to a lawyer to draft your GDPR documentation — such as Privacy Notices, Cookie Policies, and Data Processing Agreements — take a look at my GDPR compliance pack, which contains over 20 documents and six instructive video guides about how to become GDPR compliant. The pack is affordably priced at £197 (about $240), which comes with 12 months of free updates.

GDPR updates email

Ongoing compliance with the GDPR is essential. To ensure that you are up to date with new guidance, new laws and regulations, case law and opinions, sign up for my GDPR updates emails that I send every two weeks.

To sign up, go to http://www.suzannedibble.com/gdprupdates.

Supervisory Authorities and EDPB Websites

It never hurts to go straight to the source when you want information.

The Information Commissioners Office

www.ico.org.uk

The Information Commissioner's Office (ICO), which is the UK's supervisory authority, has some useful guidance notes on the vast majority of areas of the GDPR. They provide practical examples, and the information is comprehensive. The only problem is that, due to the complexity of the GDPR, these guidance notes are often quite lengthy. They do, however, have some free checklists that are handy to use after you have a grasp on the subject area.

For a comprehensive guide to the GDPR, go to

```
https://ico.org.uk/for-organisations/guide-to-data-protection/
    guide-to-the-general-data-protection-regulation-gdpr
```

Supervisory authorities

A list of all of the supervisory authorities and their websites are included in Appendix B.

EDPB

The European Data Protection Board website is also very helpful and lists most of the EU-wide GDPR guidance at `https://edpb.europa.eu/`.

The EU Commission

```
https://ec.europa.eu/commission/priorities/justice-and-fundamental-
    rights/data-protection/2018-reform-eu-data-protection-rules_en
```

The EU Commission has a good website (which isn't particular to any individual EU member state) that includes a number of good guidance notes to help you become familiar with the provisions of the GDPR.

It also provides links to the EU model clauses:

```
https://ec.europa.eu/info/law/law-topic/data-protection/international-
dimension-data-protection/standard-contractual-clauses-scc_en
```

and to a list of the EU member states:

```
https://europa.eu/european-union/about-eu/countries_en
```

International Association of Privacy Professionals (IAPP)

```
https://iapp.org
```

The IAPP, which is the world's largest association of privacy professionals, has a wealth of information on its website. The association also hosts regular training events and conferences.

Note: This site provides content for privacy professionals, so if you're looking for relatively basic guidance on the GDPR, this site may not be for you.

TIP

If you intend to become certified as a privacy professional, IAPP also offers training and exams, leading to the CIPP, CIPM, and CIPT certifications.

Privacy Shield Searchable Database

```
www.privacyshield.gov/welcome
```

If you transfer to the United States any personal data from an organization that is established within the EU, it's an international transfer and needs special protection. If the organization to which you're transferring the personal data is part of the EU-US Privacy Shield Framework, this is sufficient additional protection. For more on international transfers, see Chapter 6.

If the organization is not part of the Privacy Shield, you need to look at additional protection, such as putting standard contractual clauses in place or obtaining consent. See Chapter 6 for more on this topic.

Go to `www.privacyshield.gov/list` to see whether a US entity is Privacy Shield-certified.

Easily Readable Online Text of the GDPR

```
https://gdpr-info.eu
```

If you have any desire to read the entire text of the GDPR — including the articles and recitals that I reference throughout this book — or, more likely, to refer to certain sections of it, this link is helpful.

Cookie Consent Tools

In Chapter 9, I list potential tools to use in order to obtain consent for the use of cookies and to provide the requisite information to the data subject.

GDPR Compliance Platforms

The three resources described in this main section are organizations that provide consulting services regarding many facets of privacy and security. They exist to help their clients mitigate risk. Let me give you an overview of their GDPR-related services.

OneTrust

`www.onetrust.com/products/gdpr-compliance`

The OneTrust platform includes a variety of tools to help medium-to-large-size organizations become, and remain, GDPR-compliant, including tools in these areas:

>> Self-assessment

>> Data mapping (designed to help organizations understand how data flows through the organization and to third parties)

>> Cookie compliance

>> Mobile app compliance

>> Consent management

>> Risk management

>> Breach response

This comprehensive and user-friendly platform has prices starting from £80 (about $98) per month for small organizations.

TrustArc

`www.trustarc.com`

TrustArc is similar to OneTrust in that it's a comprehensive platform that helps organizations monitor risk and identifies gaps in compliance.

TrustArc, which can also manage cookie consent preferences, has a number of marketing tools, such as consent management.

TrustArc has flexible pricing tailored to fit the needs of its clients; see the website for more information.

GDPR Mentor

```
http://gdprmentor.com
```

GDPR Mentor is a GDPR–compliance platform designed more for smaller businesses with prices starting at £25 (about $30) per month per user. Available tools include

>> Self-assessment

>> Data mapping

>> Data management

>> Third-party transferee management

GDPR Enforcement Tracker

```
www.enforcementtracker.com
```

CMS Law, a well-respected international law firm based in London and Frankfurt, has put together a handy spreadsheet of every fine that has been levied in relation to the GDPR.

If you're interested in seeing what types of noncompliance are drawing fines and the level of fines that are being levied, check out this helpful searchable database.

REMEMBER

You have no guarantee that similar acts of noncompliance will be treated in exactly the same way. The reason is that a supervisory authority normally considers a number of circumstances when deciding on the level of a fine, and each case is decided on its own facts.

Book Contributors' Resources

My thanks again to our technical editor Phil Lee of Fieldfisher. Phil is not only an excellent privacy lawyer; he (and his colleagues) also write a very informative and easy to read privacy blog at https://privacylawblog.fieldfisher.com/.

My thanks also to Lee Hezzlewood, cyber-security consultant and owner of Secure Thinking, a UK-based company providing specialist data protection and cyber-security services. Lee contributed Chapter 16 on data security and has a refreshingly straightforward way of explaining technical security matters. If you are in need of cyber-security services, I can't think of anyone better to help you out. You can contact Lee at:

Web: https://LeeHezzlewood.com

Email: support@LeeHezzlewood.com

Phone: +44 01282 902772

Chapter **23**

Ten Must-Have Skills for the DPO

I f you're looking to hire a Data Protection Officer (see Chapter 15 to find out whether you need to) or you're considering a new career in data protection as a DPO, this chapter's list of ten must-have skills for DPOs may prove helpful.

Many company executives believe that they can hire a fairly junior IT specialist or assign the office manager (or another existing generalist staff) to fulfil the role of DPO. This is not the case. The DPO needs to be appropriately qualified, or else you could be in breach of the GDPR.

REMEMBER

The DPO doesn't necessarily need to be a salaried employee; the position can, in fact, be outsourced. A group of companies might appoint a single DPO, provided that the person is easily accessible from each establishment.

The DPO's tasks, as defined in Article 39 of the GDPR, are listed here:

» Inform and advise you and your employees about your obligations to comply with the GDPR and other data protection laws.

>> Monitor compliance with the GDPR and other data protection laws, as well as with your data protection policies, including assigning responsibilities, raising awareness, training staff involved in processing personal data, and conducting (or being consulted on) internal audits.

>> Provide advice on DPIAs and monitor performance of the project to which the DPIA relates.

>> Cooperate with your supervisory authority.

>> Act as the contact point for your supervisory authority on issues related to data processing.

In this chapter, I explore the top ten skills required of a DPO.

Experience in Privacy and Security Risk Assessment

Article 39.2 of the GDPR requires DPOs to "have due regard to the risk associated with processing operations." This reflects other risk-based provisions of the GDPR, such as the requirement under Article 24 to implement "appropriate technical and organizational measures" in order to demonstrate compliance and to maintain security of processing. In both cases, the GDPR says the "appropriate" measures should "take into account the nature, scope, context, and purposes of processing as well as the risks" to data subjects.

This obligation is likely to require DPOs to provide guidance on risk assessments, Data Protection Impact Assessments (DPIAs), and best practices to mitigate risks.

For these reasons, it's helpful if your DPO has a strong background in privacy and security risk assessment. A background in IT programming, IT infrastructure, and Information System audits would also be useful in order for the DPO to provide meaningful and useful guidance in risk mitigation.

Knowledge of Data Protection Law and Practices

Article 37.5 requires the DPO to be a person with "expert knowledge of data protection law and practices." A DPO should certainly be very familiar with the GDPR and its application in practice, as well as other relevant data protection law and practice. This includes overseas data protection laws in any country where the organization has any presence.

Recital 97 provides some guidance around how to determine the necessary level of expert knowledge according to:

>> The data processing operations that are carried out

>> The protection required for the personal data processed by the data controller or the data processor

So, for example, if your organization processes health data, your DPO would need to have knowledge of processing health data and any specific laws or regulations relating to that type of processing.

REMEMBER

The GDPR doesn't require the DPO to be a qualified lawyer or have any formal legal qualifications.

Ability to Work Independently

Recital 97 states that DPOs should not have any conflicts of interest and be able to perform their duties and tasks in an independent manner — DPOs should be able to carry out their duties as they see fit, with no influence from the board of directors or other people within the organization. This necessitates a level of seniority, independence, and the ability to assert themselves.

The DPO is allowed to perform other functions within the organization, but cannot perform roles that conflict with the DPO role — such as when determining the purposes and means of data processing. An example of this would be where an Information Systems manager may want to scan everyone's email for data loss prevention purposes, but the DPO may consider that this is not appropriate from a GDPR perspective. If you combined the Information Systems manager and the DPO into a single role, there would be an obvious conflict. The DPO must be able to be completely independent within the role.

The DPO is also bound by secrecy and/or confidentiality considerations concerning the performance of their task, in accordance with applicable law.

Ability to Work Autonomously

Article 38.3 of the GDPR requires the data controller and data processor to "ensure that the DPO does not receive any instructions regarding the exercise of those tasks" and goes on to say, "[T]he DPO shall directly report to the highest management level of the controller or the processor."

The GDPR provides no guidance in defining "the highest management level," but presumably the DPO should report to the board of directors, and directly to a board member.

The European Data Protection Board guidance on DPOs states that:

"If the controller or processor makes decisions that are incompatible with the GDPR and the DPO's advice, the DPO should be given the possibility to make his or her dissenting opinion clear to the highest management level and to those making the decisions. In this respect, Article 38(3) provides that the DPO 'shall directly report to the highest management level of the controller or the processor.' Such direct reporting ensures that senior management (e.g., board of directors) is aware of the DPO's advice and recommendations as part of the DPO's mission to inform and advise the controller or the processor. Another example of direct reporting is the drafting of an annual report of the DPO's activities provided to the highest management level."

Because DPOs cannot receive instructions regarding the exercise of their tasks, the person must operate entirely autonomously, which, again, requires seniority and a high level of expertise.

Ability to Communicate Effectively

Article 39.1 requires the DPO to cooperate with the supervisory authority and act as the contact point for the supervisory authority on issues relating to processing. The DPO must therefore be able to communicate effectively with regulatory authorities.

A DPO of a group of companies or otherwise covering multiple jurisdictions may not be able to speak the language of each supervisory authority it needs to deal with. In this case, having a DPO who speaks the language of the main market(s) is at least recommended.

In addition, the DPO can, ideally, speak the language of the data subjects in order to handle requests and complaints from data subjects.

Because Article 39 requires the DPO to train staff within their organization, the person also must have good communication skills in this regard.

Ability to Negotiate Adeptly

The DPO may be in charge of negotiating Data Processor Agreements with suppliers and — because you want the person to achieve the best outcome for you without souring the relationship with the supplier — must therefore be a skilled negotiator.

Maintain Cultural Awareness and Sensitivity

Because the DPO is likely to deal with data controllers, data processors, and, potentially, data subjects from different countries around the world, the person needs to have cultural awareness and sensitivity in these dealings.

Demonstrate Leadership

Because the DPO is likely to be in a senior position within the organization, and because the position necessitates leading (or influencing) a diverse set of stakeholders, the DPO is likely to need solid leadership skills.

Ability to Embrace Change

Because risks are always changing and technology is ever evolving, a good DPO should be aware of the changing environment. Additionally, the DPO should be prepared to take quick action in embracing the changes that are necessary to respond to those risks.

Display Business and Interpersonal Acumen

DPOs should have broad business experience and a good understanding of the industry of the data controller and processors so that they can understand how data protection can be integrated into the organization's business functions as smoothly as possible.

In addition, the DPO will likely benefit from having these personal skills:

>> Integrity

>> Initiative

>> Organization

>> Perseverance

>> Discretion

>> Assertiveness in difficult circumstances

>> Able to resolve conflicts

>> Able to build working relationships

learning styles

» **Presenting training face-to-face and in small workshops**

» **Teaching data basics, job-based details, and your internal systems**

» **Providing refresher courses, multiple sessions, and reminders**

» **Making it safe for staff to report breaches and other privacy-related incidents**

» **Instituting a culture of privacy — from the top down**

Chapter **24**

Ten Ways to Train Employees to Be Good Stewards of Data

Human error causes the vast majority of data breaches. This makes it absolutely essential that you, as a data controller or processor, provide all relevant staff with suitable training on data protection matters.

In fact, Article 39 of the GDPR provides that the DPO shall provide staff involved in processing operations with training in data protection matters. And, the Information Commissioner's Office (ICO), the UK's supervisory authority, makes it clear that you must train your staff and continually refresh the training.

The UK's supervisory authority, the ICO, states: "The GDPR requires you to ensure that anyone acting under your authority with access to personal data does not process that data unless you have instructed them to do so. It is therefore vital that your staff understand the importance of protecting personal data, are familiar with your security policy, and put its procedures into practice. You should provide appropriate initial and refresher training."

You should train *all* staff who have *any* connection with personal data, such as in these jobs or areas:

>> Receptionist

>> Mail clerk

>> IT engineer

>> Marketer or social media consultant

>> Customer service representative

>> Product developer

>> Assistant or anyone else who sends external emails to more than one person

>> Member of board of directors

Not all staff need to have detailed knowledge of the GDPR, but they should have knowledge relevant to their function within the organization. Staff who open the mail, make social media posts, or answer the phones, for example, need proper training to recognize a Data Subject Access Request (DSAR).

This chapter describes my top ten tips for training your staff and helping them be good stewards of personal data.

Understand That One Size Doesn't Fit All

Every organization is different, and standardized online courses are unlikely to offer the scope of training that an organization requires. What makes more sense is to have training customized for your organization and then further customized for individual staff functions within the organization.

TIP

If customized training is out of budget for you, then you may want to start with standardized training and then supplement with bespoke training relevant to particular functions within your organization (such as marketing or IT).

Assess Individuals' Learning Styles

Assess the learning styles of each area of your workforce and decide the most appropriate medium for learning. Millennials might prefer customized digital training, for example. The board of directors, however, may benefit from face-to-face training as part of a *board away day* (annual sessions with training and team building exercises tailored for a company's board members).

Develop Engaging Training

Workshop style training in small groups is likely to engage staff much more than lecturing to them. In workshops, you can group different staff functions (such as HR, IT, customer services, and marketing, for example) so that they can discuss the issues relevant to their function. This enables each group to process deeper questions and concerns before sharing with the wider workshop any issues that are relevant to the whole organization.

Some elements of face-to-face training are useful to gain the buy-in of individual staff. You want to help them appreciate the importance of data protection within the organization. What you don't want is staff who view the training as a tick-box exercise without an understanding of the consequences of noncompliance with the GDPR and the role that they can play in that noncompliance.

Staff generally have differing levels of knowledge and experience in relation to data protection matters. The ability for them to be able to ask questions and have them answered individually is invaluable.

REMEMBER

If the budget in your small organization doesn't permit customization of training or face-to-face training, more affordable standardized online courses are, of course, better than nothing.

Teach the Basics to All Staff

All staff need to know the basics when it comes to the GDPR and data protection. This basic level of training should include an overview of these types of information:

>> The necessity of the GDPR in protecting personal data

>> The consequences, such as fines and reputational damage, that can result if staff don't comply with data protection laws

- >> The ways in which the principles of the GDPR apply to your particular organization

- >> Your organization's data protection policies and the location of hard copy or online documents

The basic training should also include:

- >> Practical tips on securing personal information (such as creating strong passwords, locking computers, and safely opening emails from unknown senders), sharing personal data, and recognizing and respecting data subject rights

- >> Information on where to obtain additional information and answers to questions

Provide Detailed Training per Function

After staff understand the basics of data protection, you should offer more detailed training for different staff functions. For example, you may want to consider training in these areas:

- >> **Customer services:** These employees need to recognize DSARs and know who to pass them to within the organization for the DSAR to be responded to appropriately.

- >> **Marketing:** Employees in this department need to understand the rules around direct marketing, lawful grounds for processing (such as consent and legitimate interests), and profiling/automated decision-making.

- >> **Product/service development:** Everyone in this area must understand the principle of privacy by design and the need for Data Protection Impact Assessments (DPIAs).

- >> **Senior leadership:** Everyone "up the ladder" must understand the importance of embedding a culture of privacy in the organization and the risks of not being compliant.

- >> **Procurement personnel:** Employees who are responsible for engaging data processors must understand the GDPR's due diligence requirements and the need for a Data Processing Agreement with data processors.

- >> **HR:** The HR staff need to understand the lawful grounds for processing for employee data, be able to recognize and deal with DSARs, and know the privacy rules about job applicants.

Train on Internal Systems and Procedures

If employees know what the GDPR says but don't know how to deal with it in practice, the organization is open to risk. To mitigate this risk, you must train employees on your internal systems and procedures for complying with the GDPR.

Here are a couple of examples to illustrate this point:

>> A staff member who opens the mail and receives a DSAR must know whom to pass it to in order to ensure that it's dealt with properly.

>> If a data breach occurs, the staff member who discovered the data breach should know exactly whom to contact within the organization to ensure (among other issues) that employees who are appropriately trained are:

- Containing the breach

- Dealing with the affected data subjects

- Making any necessary notifications

Reinforce Training with Reminders around the Workplace

In addition to holding regular refresher training, anything you can do to regularly reinforce the message of GDPR compliance with employees is a good thing. Here are a few examples:

>> **Provide reminders about past training.** Pin a poster in the staff's break room, for example. You can find a good example at

    https://media.kingseducation.com/assets/media/ke-downloads/
    policies/GDPR_Posters.pdf

>> **Appoint data protection champions within different staff functions.** *Champions* are responsible for answering questions from other staff and demonstrating best practices within that function.

>> **Offer rewards.** Give refresher quizzes (both online and in person) and awards for individual or team compliance.

Spread Out Training across Multiple Sessions

The GDPR is a large and complex area for employees to comprehend. Rather than try to cram all the information into one session, hold a series of shorter sessions. Studies have shown that people learn, retain, and act on information in a more effective way when they receive it in smaller chunks.

Having more than one training session also allows staff to attempt, between sessions, to implement what they have learned in their working environments. And, they have time to formulate meaningful follow-up questions.

REMEMBER

You also need to build GDPR training into new-employee onboarding courses.

Encourage a Culture of Openness

Employees must feel comfortable, and without fear of retribution, about reporting data breaches and any other circumstances that aren't GDPR-compliant. When employees are tempted to hide data breaches, it leads to larger repercussions for the organization, such as fines for failing to notify within the prescribed time limit.

Or, if an employee is tempted to hide a DSAR after not dealing with it as quickly as required, the organization may also face larger repercussions: The data subject who sent the DSAR may complain to the supervisory authority. If the organization is investigated, it could be fined.

Adopt a Culture of Privacy

Why train your staff to consider data protection matters if a culture of privacy doesn't exist throughout the entire organization? If you tell your staff to do one thing but senior managers dismiss the need for data protection or the board of directors shows noncompliance (for example, by failing to appoint a Data Protection Officer [DPO] when required or to let the DPO operate independently), your staff won't adopt data protection in practice.

As Elizabeth Denham, the UK Information Commissioner, said:

Arguably the biggest change is around accountability.

The new legislation creates an onus on companies to understand the risks that they create for others, and to mitigate those risks. It's about moving away from seeing the law as a box-ticking exercise, and instead to work on a framework that can be used to build a culture of privacy that pervades an entire organisation.

It means a change to the culture of an organisation. That isn't an easy thing to do, and it's certainly true that accountability cannot be bolted on: It needs to be a part of the company's overall systems approach to how it manages and processes personal data.

But this shift in approach is what is needed. It is what consumers expect. The benefit for organisations is not just compliance but also providing an opportunity to develop the trust of its consumers in a sustained way."

7

Appendixes

Appendix A

Upcoming Changes to Data Protection Laws

The GDPR introduces some key changes in European data protection law that I discuss in Chapter 2. In this appendix, I explore other data protection law changes inspired by our increasingly digitally reliant world and by the global impact the GDPR is sure to have going forward.

The ePrivacy Regulations

Now being negotiated between the European Parliament, the European Council, and the European Commission are amendments to the ePrivacy Directive that came into effect in 2002. Individual EU member states implemented this Directive as part of their national law, though there are differences in interpretation of the Directive and therefore differing national laws (as discussed in Chapter 19). The amendments to the ePrivacy Directive will take effect with the introduction of new ePrivacy Regulations.

REMEMBER

A Directive is a legislative act of the EU that requires all EU member states to implement a new law, yet allows some flexibility on how the laws' goals are to be met. A Regulation, however, is a binding legislative act that is applied in its entirety across all EU member states and is immediately applicable and enforceable.

The extent and scope of digital advertising has drastically changed since 2002. By updating the ePrivacy Directive to meet these changes, the aim of the amendments is twofold:

>> To ensure confidentiality of online communications

>> To end under-the-radar commercial surveillance

Every time you go online via a laptop, computer, or smartphone, you're under *commercial surveillance*: the monitoring and collection of your digital data (including the content of your emails, the websites you browse, and any purchases you make) and metadata (data that's descriptive of other data, such as titles and headings on a web page or the date and location of when you took photos). That digital data is then sold and used to target you with commercial advertising or political messaging. The majority of people don't realize the extent of this surveillance.

The amendments are being fiercely lobbied by the digital advertising industry, which fears that the revisions will have a significant adverse effect on their business. Media outlets in the digital advertising sector have predicted calamity and hail the amendments as "the biggest possible evil" and "the end of the digital economy."

The main reason the digital advertising industry fears the amendments is that it is proposed by the European Parliament that the consent needed for setting cookies should be given at the browser setting level and should be switched by default to no consent.

Surveys have shown that only 6 percent of people would bother to make a choice about cookie settings at the browser level. Online advertisers fear that this situation will be the end of online targeting. A study funded by the European Interactive Digital Advertising Alliance (EDAA) and IAB Europe found that "device-level" consent could wipe out up to half of the market (€526bn) and threaten up to 6 million jobs.

However, certain innovative businesses in the digital marketing sector have taken a different approach and changed their business model to reflect the increasing concern from web users about their online privacy:

>> **The French web search engine Qwant doesn't employ user tracking and doesn't personalize search results.** It states, 'The advertising business can never excuse practices where companies disrespect users' privacy and free choice, and Qwant is living proof that we can make advertising revenue without collecting and sharing personal data."

>> **PageFair also uses an alternative business model — contextual advertising instead of behavioral advertising.** PageFair describes contextual targeting as "ad placement done smartly" — which means, rather than rely on broad demographics, location, and simple browsing history, contextually targeted ads connect the right message to the right person at the right time. Contextual ad campaigns show users content similar to what's on the page they're browsing. According to PageFair, 615 million people block ads.

Aside from attempting to introduce consent for cookies at browser levels, the ePrivacy Directive amendments also propose these actions:

>> **Expanding the territorial scope of the ePrivacy Directive so that it matches that of the GDPR:** At the time of publishing this book, the ePrivacy Directive applies only to organizations established in the EU. After the amendments come into force, the new Regulations will have the same territorial scope as the GDPR, meaning that organizations outside the EU that are already subject to the GDPR will also need to be compliant with the new ePrivacy Regulations.

>> **Increasing fines to the same levels as the GDPR:** At the time of publishing this book, the fines for noncompliance with the ePrivacy Directive are limited to £500,000 in the UK and similar amounts in other EU member states. The proposed amendments to the ePrivacy Directive would see these fines be increased significantly so that they're the same maximum amounts as for the GDPR.

>> **Insisting that consent will be needed for all targeted online marketing communications:** Under the proposed amendments to the ePrivacy Directive, consent is king:

- Under the GDPR, consent is just one of the lawful grounds for processing. But under the new ePrivacy Regulations, in order to send marketing communications by email, text, over-the-top services (for example, Facebook Messenger, Snapchat, WhatsApp, or Skype messaging), or any other kind of online marketing message sent from you directly to an individual, you will be required to obtain the prior consent of that individual.

- The standard of consent will be higher to align with the GDPR standard of consent — namely, consent freely given by way of affirmative action (that is, not implied); using language that's clear, specific, granular, and distinguishable from other information, and that informs individuals what they're consenting to and that they can opt out in the future.

>> **Placing restrictions on the use of metadata:** At the moment, there are no restrictions on processing metadata. If I go for a run with my Strava app, there is nothing to say that Strava can't sell my data to third parties, which is of course their business model. It's this under-the-radar surveillance that the new ePrivacy Regulations seek to end. Under the proposed amendments, you can no longer process metadata unless the processing falls within one of the exemptions, such as processing for billing purposes or network management.

Not everyone agrees that consent under the proposed ePrivacy Regulations should match the GDPR standard. CIPL (a global privacy and security think tank based in Washington, DC, Brussels, and London) works with industry leaders, regulatory authorities, and policymakers to develop global solutions and best practices for privacy and the responsible use of data to enable the modern information age. CIPL is concerned that an over-reliance on consent will hinder the user's experience. They argue that consent should be required only for intrusive or harmful processing.

Here's what you need to do to prepare for the updated ePrivacy Directive:

>> Review your current marketing efforts, and assess your current consents.

>> Ensure that you're aware of, and are compliant, with existing laws, such as the GDPR.

>> Keep up-to-date with the progress of new data protection laws.

>> Recognize whether any of these possibilities in new data protection legislation could prevent your business from continuing in its current form.

>> Make a member of your team responsible *right now* for keeping up to date with the progression of the new ePrivacy Regulations and ensuring compliance with the new Regulations. If you have a Data Protection Officer, this would naturally be the appropriate person to take such responsibility.

US Data Protection Laws

The United States has no comprehensive data protection law covering all business sectors and all 50 states. Privacy legislation has been adopted on an ad hoc, piecemeal basis with sector-specific legislation being introduced when the circumstances have required it, such as the Video Privacy Protection Act 1988, the Driver's Privacy Protection Act 1994, and the Children's Online Privacy Protection Act.

The Federal Trade Commission (FTC) can bring enforcement actions against unfair or deceptive practices and enforce privacy and data protection regulations. The FTC has taken the view that deceptive practices also include the failure to keep personal data secure and the failure to comply with privacy notices.

The California Consumer Privacy Act

Some US states are more active than others in the area of data protection legislation. California, for example, has passed the California Consumer Privacy Act (CCPA), which will take effect on January 1, 2020.

The CCPA will affect any business (wherever in the world it's located) collecting or storing data about California residents, so most US businesses that operate on a national basis will likely adopt the higher standard of the CCPA for all of their data subjects, even if not all of their data subjects reside in California.

If you're already compliant with the GDPR, you will in part be compliant with the CCPA. However, the CCPA has some unique requirements and defines personal data more broadly than the GDPR.

The CCPA applies to any entity that aims to make a profit and that

>> Carries on business in California

>> Collects the personal data of California residents

>> Determines on its own or jointly with others the purposes and means of the processing

>> Meets one or more of the following criteria:

- *Has annual gross revenues in excess of $25 million*

- *Annually buys, receives for a commercial purpose, sells, or shares the personal data of 50,000 or more consumers, households, or devices*

- *Derives 50 percent or more of its annual revenue from selling personal data*

The CCPA does *not* apply to the processing of the personal data of individuals outside of California. It applies to every individual who is in California for other than a temporary or transitory purpose and every individual who is domiciled in California but is outside California for a temporary or transitory purpose.

The provisions of the CCPA include

>> Privacy notice requirements

>> Training programs for staff to understand the CCPA obligations

>> The right of consumers to access their personal information

>> The right to request deletion of personal information obtained from the consumer

>> The right to request disclosure of personal information collected and shared

>> The right to disclosure of categories of personal information sold

>> The right to opt out of the sale of personal information

>> The right to non-discrimination in relation to exercising data subject rights

The downside to the lack of a comprehensive US data protection law

That the lack of comprehensive privacy legislation in the United States might be a disadvantage economically is of real concern. The majority of other large non-EU economies (such as Brazil, Japan, New Zealand, Singapore, and South Africa) are putting into place comprehensive data protection laws. This, together with the misuse of personal data and high-profile security breaches, is putting pressure on US lawmakers to implement a comprehensive statewide data protection law.

Other economies (such as Canada, Israel, and Japan) are aligning their new data protection laws with the GDPR rather than with the frameworks proposed by the United States. This might cause US lawmakers to feel increased pressure to implement a comprehensive US privacy law that reflects the GDPR as well.

Global Data Protection

Countries have varying degrees of regulation and enforcement, a topic I explore a bit further in Chapter 1, but here's a quick overview of recent or upcoming data protection legislation worldwide:

>> **Brazil has passed the General Data Protection Law, which takes effect in February 2020.** This law applies to any processing of the personal data of Brazilian individuals, wherever in the world the processor is located. It is, in the main, aligned with the GDPR.

>> **A number of other countries are anticipated to pass data protection laws aligning with the GDPR.** These include Bosnia and Herzegovina, Montenegro, Ukraine, North Macedonia, Monaco, Switzerland, and potentially Malaysia, in addition to those who have already done so, such as Serbia and Jersey.

» **Hong Kong has published a New Ethical Accountability Framework.** This framework aims to persuade Hong Kong businesses to carry out privacy impact assessments similar to those required under the GDPR.

» **Certain other countries are also considering their first comprehensive data protection laws.** This list includes Honduras, the British Virgin Islands, Kenya, Indonesia, and Zimbabwe.

» **India has prepared a draft bill — the Personal Data Protection Bill — that's modeled on the GDPR.** The bill has significant differences, such as no right to be forgotten. However, a year after the draft bill was submitted, it is yet to be tabled in India's Parliament.

Appendix B

List of Supervisory Authorities

Austria
Österreichische Datenschutzbehörde
Barichgasse 40-42
1030 Wien
Tel. +43 1 52152 2550
email: dsb@dsb.gv.at
Website: http://www.dsb.gv.at/

Dr. Andrea Jelinek, Director

Belgium
Autorité de la protection des données -
Gegevensbeschermingsautoriteit
(APD-GBA)
Rue de la Presse 35 – Drukpersstraat 35
1000 Bruxelles - Brussel
Tel. +32 2 274 48 00
Fax +32 2 274 48 35
email: contact@apd-gba.be
Website: https://www.autorite
protectiondonnees.be/ -
https://www.gegevensbescherming
sautoriteit.be/

Mr. David Stevens, President

Bulgaria
Commission for Personal Data Protection
2, Prof. Tsvetan Lazarov blvd.
Sofia 1592
Tel. + 359 2 915 3580
Fax +359 2 915 3525
email: kzld@cpdp.bg
Website: https://www.cpdp.bg/

Mr. Ventsislav Karadjov, Chairman
of the Commission for Personal Data
Protection

Croatia
Croatian Personal Data Protection Agency
Martićeva 14
10000 Zagreb
Tel. +385 1 4609 000
Fax +385 1 4609 099
email: azop@azop.hr
Website: http://www.azop.hr/

Mr. Anto Rajkovača, Director

Cyprus
Commissioner for Personal Data
Protection
1 Iasonos Street,
1082 Nicosia
P.O. Box 23378, CY-1682 Nicosia
Tel. +357 22 818 456
Fax +357 22 304 565
email: commissioner@dataprotection.
gov.cy
Website: http://www.dataprotection.
gov.cy/

Ms. Irene Loizidou Nikolaidou,
Commissioner for Personal Data
Protection

Czech Republic
Office for Personal Data Protection
Pplk. Sochora 27
170 00 Prague 7
Tel. +420 234 665 111
Fax +420 234 665 444
email: posta@uoou.cz
Website: http://www.uoou.cz/

Ms. Ivana Janů, President

Denmark
Datatilsynet
Borgergade 28, 5
Tel. +45 33 1932 00
Fax +45 33 19 32 18
email: dt@datatilsynet.dk
Website: http://www.datatilsynet.dk/

Ms. Cristina Angela Gulisano, Director

Estonia
Estonian Data Protection Inspectorate
(Andmekaitse Inspektsioon)
Tatari 39
10134 Tallinn
Tel. +372 6828 712
email: info@aki.ee
Website: http://www.aki.ee/

Ms. Pille Lehis, Director General

Finland
Office of the Data Protection Ombudsman
P.O. Box 800
FIN-00521 Helsinki
Tel. +358 29 56 66700
Fax +358 29 56 66735
email: tietosuoja@om.fi
Website: http://www.tietosuoja.
fi/en/

Mr. Reijo Aarnio, Ombudsman

France
Commission Nationale de l'Informatique
et des Libertés - CNIL
3 Place de Fontenoy
TSA 80715 – 75334 Paris, Cedex 07
Tel. +33 1 53 73 22 22
Fax +33 1 53 73 22 00
email: NA
Website: http://www.cnil.fr/

Ms. Marie-Laure Denis, President of CNIL

Germany
Die Bundesbeauftragte für den
Datenschutz und die Informationsfreiheit
Husarenstraße 30
53117 Bonn
Tel. +49 228 997799 0; +49 228 81995 0
Fax +49 228 997799 550; +49 228 81995 550

email: poststelle@bfdi.bund.de
Website: http://www.bfdi.bund.de/

Mr. Ulrich Kelber, Federal Commissioner
for Data Protection and Freedom of
Information

NOTE: In Germany, the competence in the
field of data protection is split among
different data protection supervisory
authorities in Germany. Competent
authorities can be identified according to
the list provided under: https://www.
bfdi.bund.de/bfdi_wiki/index.php/
Aufsichtsbeh%C3%B6rden_und_
Landesdatenschutzbeauftragte.

Greece
Hellenic Data Protection Authority
Kifisias Av. 1-3, PC 11523
Ampelokipi Athens
Tel. +30 210 6475 600
Fax +30 210 6475 628
email: contact@dpa.gr
Website: http://www.dpa.gr/

Mr. Konstantinos Menoudakos, President
of the Hellenic Data Protection Authority

Hungary
Hungarian National Authority for Data
Protection and Freedom of Information
Szilágyi Erzsébet fasor 22/C
H-1125 Budapest
Tel. +36 1 3911 400
email: peterfalvi.attila@naih.hu
Website: http://www.naih.hu/

Dr. Attila Péterfalvi, President of the
National Authority for Data Protection
and Freedom of Information

Iceland
Persónuvernd
Rauðarárstígur 10
105 Reykjavík
Tel: +354 510 9600
email: postur@dpa.is
Website: https://www.personuvernd.
is or https://www.dpa.is

Ms. Helga Þórisdóttir, Commissioner

Ireland
Data Protection Commission
21 Fitzwilliam Square
Dublin 2
D02 RD28
Ireland
Tel. +353 76 110 4800
email: info@dataprotection.ie
Website: http://www.
dataprotection.ie/

Ms. Helen Dixon, Data Protection
Commissioner

Italy
Garante per la protezione dei dati
personali
Piazza di Monte Citorio, 121
00186 Roma
Tel. +39 06 69677 1
Fax +39 06 69677 3785
email: garante@garanteprivacy.it
Website: http://www.
garanteprivacy.it/

Mr. Antonello Soro, President of Garante
per la protezione dei dati personali

Latvia
Data State Inspectorate
Blaumana str. 11/13-15
1011 Riga
Tel. +371 6722 3131
Fax +371 6722 3556
email: info@dvi.gov.lv
Website: http://www.dvi.gov.lv/

Ms. Daiga Avdejanova, Director of Data
State Inspectorate

Liechtenstein
Data Protection Office, Principality of
Liechtenstein
Städtle 38
9490 Vaduz
Principality of Liechtenstein
Tel. +423 236 6090
email: info.dss@llv.li
Website: https://www.
datenschutzstelle.li

Dr. Marie-Louise Gächter, Commissioner

Lithuania
State Data Protection Inspectorate
A. Juozapaviciaus str. 6
LT-09310 Vilnius
Tel. + 370 5 279 14 45
Fax +370 5 261 94 94
email: ada@ada.lt
Website: http://www.ada.lt/

Mr. Raimondas Andrijauskas, Director of
the State Data Protection Inspectorate

Luxembourg
Commission Nationale pour la Protection
des Données
1, avenue du Rock'n'Roll
L-4361 Esch-sur-Alzette
Tel. +352 2610 60 1
Fax +352 2610 60 29
email: info@cnpd.lu
Website: http://www.cnpd.lu/

Ms. Tine A. Larsen, President of the
Commission Nationale pour la Protection
des Données

Malta
Office of the Information and Data
Protection Commissioner
Second Floor, Airways House
High Street, Sliema SLM 1549
Tel. +356 2328 7100
Fax +356 2328 7198
email: idpc.info@idpc.org.mt
Website: http://www.idpc.org.mt/

Mr. Saviour Cachia, Information and Data
Protection Commissioner

Netherlands
Autoriteit Persoonsgegevens
Bezuidenhoutseweg 30
P.O. Box 93374
2509 AJ Den Haag/The Hague
Tel. +31 70 888 8500
Fax +31 70 888 8501
Website: https://autoriteitper
soonsgegevens.nl/nl

Mr. Aleid Wolfsen, Chairman of the
Autoriteit Persoonsgegevens

Norway
Datatilsynet
Tollbugata 3
0152 Oslo
Tel +47 22 39 69 00
email: postkasse@datatilsynet.no
Website: www.datatilsynet.no

Mr. Bjørn Erik Thon, Director

Poland
Urząd Ochrony Danych Osobowych
(Personal Data Protection Office)
ul. Stawki 2
00-193 Warsaw
Tel. +48 22 531 03 00
Fax +48 22 531 03 01
email: kancelaria@uodo.gov.pl;
zwme@uodo.gov.pl
Website: https://uodo.gov.pl/

Mr. Jan Nowak, President of the Personal
Data Protection Office

Portugal
Comissão Nacional de Protecção
de Dados - CNPD
Av. D. Carlos I, 134, 1°
1200-651 Lisboa
Tel. +351 21 392 84 00
Fax +351 21 397 68 32
email: geral@cnpd.pt
Website: http://www.cnpd.pt/

Ms. Filipa Calvão, President, Comissão
Nacional de Protecção de Dados

Romania
The National Supervisory Authority
for Personal Data Processing
B-dul Magheru 28-30
Sector 1, BUCUREȘTI
Tel. +40 31 805 9211
Fax +40 31 805 9602
email: anspdcp@dataprotection.ro
Website: http://www.dataprotection.ro/

Ms. Ancuţa Gianina Opre, President of the
National Supervisory Authority for
Personal Data Processing

Slovakia
Office for Personal Data Protection
of the Slovak Republic
Hraničná 12
820 07 Bratislava 27
Tel.: + 421 2 32 31 32 14
Fax: + 421 2 32 31 32 34
email: statny.dozor@pdp.gov.sk
Website: http://www.dataprotection.gov.sk/

Ms. Soňa Pőtheová, President of the
Office for Personal Data Protection
of the Slovak Republic

Slovenia
Information Commissioner of the
Republic of Slovenia
Ms Mojca Prelesnik
Dunajska 22
1000 Ljubljana
Tel. +386 1 230 9730
Fax +386 1 230 9778
email: gp.ip@ip-rs.si
Website: https://www.ip-rs.si/

Ms. Mojca Prelesnik, Information
Commissioner of the Republic
of Slovenia

Spain
Agencia Española de Protección de Datos
(AEPD)
C/Jorge Juan, 6
28001 Madrid
Tel. +34 91 266 3517
Fax +34 91 455 5699
email: internacional@aepd.es
Website: https://www.aepd.es/

Ms. María del Mar España Martí,
Director of the Spanish Data
Protection Agency

Sweden
Datainspektionen
Drottninggatan 29
5th Floor
Box 8114
104 20 Stockholm
Tel. +46 8 657 6100
Fax +46 8 652 8652
email: datainspektionen@
datainspektionen.se
Website: http://www.
datainspektionen.se/

Ms. Lena Lindgren Schelin, Director
General of the Data Inspection Board

United Kingdom
The Information Commissioner's Office
Water Lane, Wycliffe House
Wilmslow - Cheshire SK9 5AF
Tel. +44 1625 545 700
email: casework@ico.org.uk
Website: https://ico.org.uk

Ms. Elizabeth Denham, Information
Commissioner

Credit: The European Data Protection Board

Appendix C

GDPR Checklist

The chapters in this book break down the data principles, documentation, and obligations you need to be aware of (and carry out) to be compliant with the GDPR. This appendix provides a handy list that shows altogether the activities you must complete to maintain that compliance.

To purchase the GDPR Compliance Pack, which provides all the legal document templates you need to become GDPR compliant, go to www.suzannedibble.com/gdprpack.

Does GDPR apply to me territorially?

If you're established in the EU — whether you're a data controller or a data processor— GDPR applies to all your processing of personal data. If you're established outside of the EU and your processing activities are related to either of the following, GDPR applies to that processing:

>> Offering of goods or services (whether or not a payment is made) to data subjects within the EU

>> Monitoring behavior of data subjects within the EU

See Chapter 2 for more on the topic of the territorial scope of the GDPR.

Does GDPR actually apply to the data I process?

If you process data that identifies, or is capable of identifying, an individual (including cookies and IP addresses) wholly or partly through automated means or manually as part of a filing system, then GDPR applies except where you are an individual processing the data in the course of a purely personal or household activity.

See Chapter 3 for more on what constitutes personal data.

What data do I process and for what purpose?

If you don't have transparency on from where you collect personal data, what processing of personal data you carry out, for what purposes you carry out the processing and to whom you transfer or share the personal data, you should prepare a data inventory of the personal data you process. This inventory must be a dynamic inventory that is consistently updated for recordkeeping purposes, unless exemptions apply.

See Chapter 3 for examples of data you may process. For guidance on how to prepare a data inventory, see Chapter 7.

Do I process special-category data?

If you process data comprising racial or ethnic origin data, political opinions, religious or philosophical beliefs, trade union memberships, genetic data, biometric data, data concerning health, or data concerning a person's sex life or sexual orientation, you are processing special-category data. Processing special-category data is prohibited unless your processing is exempted.

See Chapter 3 for more information on special-category data and the exemptions for processing it.

What are the lawful grounds of processing for each processing activity I've identified?

If you process personal data, you must have lawful grounds for processing such data. As I detail in Chapter 3, you can choose from one of the six lawful grounds for processing data for your specified purpose:

» The data subject has given consent to the processing of their personal data for one or more specific purposes.

» Processing is necessary for the performance of a contract to which the data subject is party or in order to take steps at the request of the data subject before entering into a contract.

» Processing is necessary for compliance with a legal obligation to which the data controller is subject.

» Processing is necessary in order to protect the vital interests of the data subject or of another natural person.

>> Processing is necessary for the performance of a task carried out in the public interest or in the exercise of official authority vested in the data controller.

>> Processing is necessary for the purposes of the legitimate interests pursued by the data controller or by a third party, except where such interests are overridden by the interests or fundamental rights and freedoms of the data subject, which require protection of personal data — in particular, where the data subject is a child.

REMEMBER

If one of your grounds has to do with legitimate interests, be sure to carry out the Legitimate Interests Assessment (LIA). See Chapter 12 for more on this topic.

Do I transfer personal data to third parties, and do I know what country each third party is in?

If you transfer your personal data outside of the EU, you must follow strict rules on transfers to third parties outside of the EEA. Determine whether the country in which the recipient of the data is established has an adequacy finding (where the EU has decided that no further safeguards are necessary for the transfer because the country has adequate data protection laws) or, if it's in the United States, whether it's certified under the Privacy Shield framework. You'll also need this information to add to your Privacy Notice.

See Chapter 6 for more about data transfers outside of the EU and Chapter 8 for more about Privacy Notices.

Do I have a GDPR-compliant Privacy Notice?

If you haven't updated your Privacy Policy for the GDPR coming into force, the chances are good that even if you have a Privacy Policy from pre-GDPR days, it isn't GDPR-compliant, because GDPR prescribes numerous details that need to be included in your Privacy Notice.

See Chapter 8 for what to include in your Privacy Notice.

Have I added my GDPR-compliant Privacy Notice to my website?

If you don't already have a link to your Privacy Notice on the footer of your website, add one so that it appears on every page of your website. If you do already have a link to your policy, make sure that you replace your old Privacy Policy with your new Privacy Notice.

See Chapter 8 for more on what to do with your Privacy Notice.

Have I sent my GDPR-compliant Privacy Notice to my subscribers and other data subjects?

If you change the wording of your Privacy Notice, the GDPR requires you to send your updated Privacy Notice to your subscribers and other data subjects to confirm, among other things:

>> How you collect and process their personal data

>> For what purposes you use their data

>> The legal grounds for processing such data

>> How you keep their data secure

>> Their rights in relation to such data

See Chapter 8 for what to include in your Privacy Notice and what to do with it.

Have I added opt-in wording to my sign-up boxes?

If you have a sign-up box on your website that collects email addresses (and perhaps other information) in return for your newsletter or other free content, you must have GDPR-compliant opt-in wording at the point of collection (underneath the sign-up box, for example), together with a link to your Privacy Notice.

See Chapter 11 for more about what your opt-in wording should say.

Have I obtained GDPR-compliant consent for electronic marketing communications?

If you don't have GDPR-compliant consent for your direct marketing communications where personal data is used, you need to obtain fresh consent. This is a complex area, so make sure you read Chapters 3 (about consent) and 19 (about marketing) before attempting to obtain consents.

Have I obtained GDPR-compliant consent for processing special category data?

If you are processing special-category data and your exemption to the general prohibition against processing special-category data is that you have the data subject's explicit consent, you must ensure that this consent meets the GDPR standard of explicit consent, perhaps by having the data subject sign the form where data has been collected or by using double verification.

See Chapter 3 for more about processing special-category data.

If I process special-category data or criminal-convictions data, have I implemented an "appropriate policy"? (UK ONLY)

If you are processing special-category data or criminal-convictions data and you are established in the UK, you need to put in place an appropriate policy document. You can read more about this in Chapter 13.

Do I have a procedure for recording consents, including explicit consent for special-category data?

If you are relying on consent to process personal data, the GDPR requires procedure for recording details of consents. Does your email marketing system track consent to opt-ins? Do you keep a filing system of hard copy consent forms?

See Chapter 3 for more about managing consent.

Have I put in place a system for managing opt-outs or a withdrawal of consent?

If you are processing personal data on the lawful grounds of consent, the GDPR requires you to keep records of opt-outs. Does your email marketing system manage this for you?

See Chapter 19 for more on this topic.

Have I put in place GDPR-compliant processor agreements with the third parties who process personal data on my instruction?

If you use data processors (organizations which process your personal data under your instruction, such as an email marketing service provider or cloud-based data services), under the GDPR, you must have a written agreement with your data processor. The GDPR prescribes what must be included in that agreement.

See Chapter 10 to see what must be included in these agreements.

Have I put in place a system for handling data subject rights?

If you don't have in place a system for handling data subject rights, you should do so as soon as possible. As a general rule, you can no longer charge for data subject requests and you must respond within 30 days.

See Chapter 14 for more on this topic.

Do I need to appoint a Data Protection Officer (DPO)?

If you don't know whether you need to appoint a Data Protection Officer, you should check this as soon as possible. The GDPR spells out who this might be along with their duties.

See Chapter 15 for more on DPOs.

Do I need to carry out a Data Protection Impact Assessment (DPIA)?

If your processing of personal data is likely to result in a high risk to the rights and freedoms of individuals, you must carry out a Data Protection Impact Assessment before starting the processing.

See Chapter 15 for more on DPIAs.

Do I have a system for data breach notifications?

If you don't have a system in place for data breach notifications, you should implement such a system as soon as possible. A *notifiable* data breach occurs when there is a loss, an alteration, unauthorized disclosure of, or access to personal data *and* when there is a risk to the rights and freedoms of individuals. If you suffer a notifiable data breach, you must notify the supervisory authority within 72 hours of the breach. If there is a high risk to rights and freedoms, you must also notify the affected individuals.

See Chapter 17 for more on data breach notifications.

Is your insurance adequate?

If you process personal data, you should consider your liability in light of increased GDPR fines and determine whether existing insurances are adequate. Contact your insurance broker to ensure that your insurance coverage is sufficient.

See Chapter 21 for more on fines and other consequences of GDPR non-compliance.

Do I have a Data Retention Policy in place?

If you do not yet have a Data Retention Policy in place, see Chapter 13 to find out what needs to be included in such policy.

Have I taken the necessary steps to keep my data secure?

If you are processing personal data, you need to implement appropriate data security to keep it secure. Data security is an issue that reaches far beyond your IT department to every area of your business and to all your employees. From implementing the right security controls to assessing and managing risks to properly training your staff, data security is a key element of GDPR because you, as a data controller, are responsible for securing and protecting the data you process.

See Chapter 16 for more about data security.

Do I need to pay the data protection fee? (UK ONLY)

In the UK, you may need to pay the data protection fee to the Information Commissioner's Office (ICO). This ranges from £40 for small businesses to £2,900 for larger businesses. See https://ico.org.uk/media/for-organisations/documents/2258205/dp-fee-guide-for-controllers-20180221.pdf for more information and to see whether you're exempt from paying the fee.

See Chapter 5 for more on the data protection fee.

If I have employees, have I worked out lawful grounds for processing their data and obtained signed copies of the employee Privacy Notice?

If you have employees (or other workers), you need to consider your lawful grounds of processing for each processing activity because it may no longer be possible to rely on consent. Relying on grounds other than consent is best because consent is unlikely to be valid due to the imbalance in the employment relationship. Where consent is necessary, this should be in a separate document to the employment agreement. You should ensure that an updated Privacy Notice is provided to employees.

See Chapter 18 for more on lawful grounds for processing for data related to employees and Chapter 13 for details of what the employee Privacy Notice should include.

If I have employees, have I arranged for data protection training for them?

If you have employees (and any other workers), they need to be aware of how to properly process data, how to record consents, how long to store data, when to report data breaches, and how to respond to data subject requests. If you require training for your employees, please email us at support@suzannedibble.com.

Please see Chapter 24 for more about employee training.

If I have employees, have I put systems in place for employee Data Subject Access Requests?

If you have employees (and any other workers), you should put in place systems for responding to Data Subject Access Requests. Data Subject Access Requests are most commonly submitted from employees in the context of a dispute.

See Chapter 18 for more about employee Data Subject Access Requests.

Appendix D

Glossary

anonymization: A process that strips out any information that can identify a particular person, by means of encryption or another method. For data to be truly anonymized, the process must be irreversible. *See also* pseudonymization.

article: Part of the General Data Protection Regulation (GDPR) that outlines the legal requirements organizations must follow to achieve and maintain compliance.

Article 29 Working Party: A guiding entity regarding data protection issues. The party ceased to formally exist when the GDPR came into effect, but its guidance is still relevant. It has been replaced by the European Data Protection Board. For simplicity, any guidance produced by the Article 29 Working Party is referred to in this book as being issued by the European Data Protection Board.

automated decision making: The process of making a decision by automated means without any human involvement.

binding corporate rules: Internal rules approved on an individual basis by supervisory authorities for data transfers within multinational organizations that allow such organizations to transfer personal data within the same group of companies to countries that do not provide an adequate level of protection without any further safeguards.

biometric data: Personal data resulting from specific technical processing relating to the physical, physiological, or behavioral characteristics of a natural person which allow or confirm the unique identification of that natural person, such as facial images or fingerprint data.

consent: Any freely given, specific, informed, and unambiguous indication of the data subject's wishes by which the person, by way of a statement or clear affirmative action, signifies agreement to the processing of their personal data.

controller (or data controller): The natural or legal person, public authority, agency, or other body that, alone or jointly with others, determines the purposes of the processing of personal data.

cookie: A small text file generated by the website on which the user is browsing, which is then stored on the user's computer by the website browser, with the aim of identifying the user.

Cookie Policy: A policy setting out how you use cookies within your organization.

corporate subscriber: A corporate body with separate legal status, such as companies, limited liability partnerships, Scottish partnerships, and some government bodies, that subscribes to a service for electronic communications services, such as email. This definition is relevant to the UK's PECR.

criminal-convictions data: Data about criminal allegations, proceedings, or convictions and personal data linked to related security measures.

cross-border processing: 1) The processing of personal data which takes place in the context of the activities of establishments in more than one EU member state of a controller or processor in the EU where the controller or processor is established in more than one member state; 2) the processing of personal data which takes place in the context of the activities of a single establishment of a controller or processor in the EU but which substantially affects or is likely to substantially affect, data subjects in more than one EU member state.

Data Processing Agreement: A legally binding agreement in writing between the data controller and data processor that contains the mandatory terms for the processing set out in the GDPR. Often referred to as a DPA.

data protection by design and by default: The concept requiring data controllers to put in place appropriate technical and organizational measures to implement data protection principles and safeguard data subjects' rights.

data subject: An individual whose personal data is collected, held, and/or processed by a data controller for varying purposes and who can be identified, directly or indirectly, by reference to such personal data.

directive: A legal act of the EU which requires EU member states to achieve a particular result, though the means to achieve such ends are not dictated. EU member states pass their own legislation to implement the directive, with a certain amount of flexibility. *See also* regulation.

direct marketing: The communication (by whatever means) of advertising or marketing material which is directed to particular individuals.

EEA: *See* European Economic Area.

EDPB: *See* European Data Protection Board.

enterprise: A natural or legal person engaged in an economic activity, irrespective of its legal form, including partnerships or associations regularly engaged in an economic activity.

ePrivacy Directive (ePD): The Privacy and Electronic Communications Directive 2002/58/EC, an EU directive on data protection and privacy in the digital age (as amended by Directive 2009/136).

European Data Protection Board (EDPB): An independent EU body that contributes to the consistent application of the GDPR and other data protection rules throughout the EU and promotes cooperation between supervisory authorities.

European Economic Area (EEA): An area uniting the EU member states and Iceland, Liechtenstein, and Norway — three countries that have adopted a national law implementing the GDPR.

European Union (EU): A political and economic union of 28 member states located primarily in Europe. Once the UK leaves the EU, there will be 27 member states. As at the time of publishing this book, the EU member states comprised Austria, Belgium, Bulgaria, Croatia, Cyprus, Czech Republic, Denmark, Estonia, Finland, France, Germany, Greece, Hungary, Ireland, Italy, Latvia, Lithuania, Luxembourg, Malta, Netherlands, Poland, Portugal, Romania, Slovakia, Slovenia, Spain, Sweden, and the UK.

EU member state: A country that is a member of the EU.

filing system: Any structured set of personal data which is accessible according to specific criteria, whether centralized, decentralized, or dispersed on a functional or geographical basis.

genetic data: Personal data relating to the inherited or acquired genetic characteristics of a natural person which give unique information about the physiology or health of that natural person and which result, in particular, from an analysis of a biological sample from the natural person in question.

group of undertakings: A controlling undertaking and its controlled undertakings. A controlling undertaking is a legal entity such as a company that can exercise a dominant influence over another legal entity (the "controlled undertaking") by such ways as ownership of another company's share capital, controlling a majority of votes in another company, or the ability to appoint more than 50% of the company's directors.

head of loss: A category of loss that can be claimed, such as fraud prevention costs and breach notification costs.

IAB: The Interactive Advertising Bureau, an advertising business organization that develops industry standards, conducts research, and provides legal support for the online advertising industry.

IAB Framework: A framework put together by the IAB to enable websites, advertisers, and their ad technology partners to obtain, record, and update consumer consent for their personal data to be processed in line with the GDPR.

individual subscriber: A living individual, including an unincorporated body of individuals, that subscribes to a service for electronic communications services, such as email. This definition is relevant to the UK's PECR.

identifiable natural person: A person who can be identified, directly or indirectly, in particular by reference to an identifier such as a name, an identification number, location data, or an online identifier or to one or more factors specific to the physical, physiological, genetic, mental, economic, cultural, or social identity of that natural person. *See also* data subject, personal data, sensitive data.

information society service: A service as defined in point (b) of Article 1(1) of Directive (EU) 2015/1535 of the European Parliament and of the Council — any service provided for renumeration, at a distance, by electronic means and at the individual request of a recipient of services.

Information Commissioner's Office (ICO): The UK's supervisory authority. When the UK leaves the EU, the ICO won't be a supervisory authority for the purposes of the GDPR. The ICO will, however, continue to be the independent supervisory body regarding the UK's data protection legislation.

international organization: An organization and its subordinate bodies governed by public international law, or any other body which is set up by, or on the basis of, an agreement between two or more countries.

international transfer: When personal data that is being processed (or will be processed) is sent to a third country or an international organization. *See also* third country, international organization.

joint controller: A data controller that acts together with at least one other data controller to determine the purposes and manner of the processing of certain personal data.

Just-in-time notices: A notice that can consist of text, video messages, or other forms of communication that appears at the point that data subjects input their personal data (for example, on an organization's website), providing a brief message explaining how their information will be used and typically linking to a Privacy Notice.

lead authority: The supervisory authority that has primary responsibility for matters arising out of cross border processing.

legal person: An entity that has a separate legal status to an individual, such as a company, a Limited Liability Partnership, or a government organization.

main establishment: 1) As regards a controller with establishments in more than one EU member state, the place of its central administration in the EU, unless the decisions on the purposes and of the processing of personal data are taken in another establishment of the controller in the EU and the latter establishment has the power to have such decisions implemented, in which case the establishment having taken such decisions is to be considered to be the main establishment. 2) As regards a processor with establishments in more than one EU member state, the place of its central administration in the EU, or, if the processor has no central administration in the EU, the establishment of the processor in the EU where the main processing activities in the context of the activities of an establishment of the processor take place to the extent that the processor is subject to specific obligations under this regulation.

natural person: A living human being.

PECR: The Privacy and Electronic Communications (EC Directive) Regulations 2003 as amended in 2004, 2011, 2015, 2016, and 2018, a UK law implementing the ePrivacy Directive.

personal data: Any information relating to an identified or identifiable natural person, including a name, an identification number, location data, an online identifier or to one or more factors specific to the physical, physiological, genetic, mental, economic, cultural, or social identity of that natural person. *See also* data subject, identifiable natural person, special-category data.

personal data breach: A breach of security leading to the accidental or unlawful destruction, loss, alteration, unauthorized disclosure of, or access to personal data transmitted, stored, or otherwise processed.

Privacy Notice: A notice providing certain information to data subjects about the use of their personal data, as required by the GDPR.

processing: Any operation or set of operations which is performed on personal data or on sets of personal data, such as collection, recording, organization, structuring, storage, adaptation or alteration, retrieval, consultation, use, disclosure by transmission, dissemination, or otherwise making available, alignment or combination, restriction, erasure, or destruction.

processor (or data processor): A natural or legal person, public authority, agency, or other body that processes personal data on behalf of and under the instructions of the controller.

profiling: Any form of automated processing of personal data consisting of the use of personal data to evaluate certain personal aspects relating to a natural person — in particular, to analyze or predict aspects concerning that natural person's performance at work, economic situation, health, personal preferences, interests, reliability, behavior, location, or movements.

pseudonymization: The processing of personal data in such a manner that the personal data can no longer be attributed to a specific data subject without the use of additional information, provided that such additional information is kept separately and is subject to technical and organizational measures to ensure that the personal data aren't attributed to an identified or identifiable natural person. *See also* anonymization.

recipient: A natural or legal person, public authority, agency, or another body to which the personal data are disclosed, whether a third party or not. However, public authorities that may receive personal data in the framework of a particular inquiry in accordance with EU or member state law shall not be regarded as recipients; the processing of those data by those public authorities shall be in compliance with the applicable data protection rules according to the purposes of the processing.

recital: Content that provides context regarding the GDPR articles and thereby provide guiding support regarding how to act in accordance with the articles.

regulation: A legal act of the EU that becomes immediately enforceable as law in all EU member states. *See also* directive.

representative: A natural or legal person established in the EU who, designated by the controller or processor in writing, represents the controller or processor with regard to their respective obligations under the GDPR.

restriction of processing: The marking of stored personal data with the aim of limiting their processing in the future.

special-category data: Personal data which includes racial or ethnic origin; political opinions; religious or philosophical beliefs; trade union membership; the processing of genetic data; biometric data for the purpose of uniquely identifying a natural person; or data concerning a natural person's sex life or sexual orientation.

supervisory authority: An independent public entity in each EU member state responsible for monitoring the application of the GDPR and contributing to the consistent application of the GDPR throughout the EU, bestowed with certain tasks and powers under the GDPR such as providing advice on data protection issues, investigating complaints of violations, and levying fines and other sanctions for noncompliance with the GDPR. Also known as a "data protection authority."

supervisory authority concerned: A supervisory authority that is concerned by the processing of personal data for one of these reasons:

>> The controller or processor is established on the territory of the member state of that supervisory authority.

>> Data subjects residing in the member state of that supervisory authority are substantially affected or likely to be substantially affected by the processing.

>> A complaint has been lodged with that supervisory authority.

third country: Any country outside the European Economic Area (EEA) — any country other than the EU member states, Iceland, Norway, and Liechtenstein, in other words. (The latter three countries have adopted a national law that implements the GDPR.)

third party: A natural or legal person, public authority, agency, or body other than the data subject, controller, processor, and persons who, under the direct authority of the controller or processor, are authorized to process personal data.

UK: The United Kingdom.

United Kingdom: The United Kingdom of Great Britain and Northern Ireland, including the countries of England, Scotland, Wales, and Northern Ireland (not including the Isle of Man, Guernsey, or Jersey, which are Crown dependencies).

Working Party: *See* Article 29 Working Party.

Index

A

above the fold, 153
access, right of, 214
accidental data breaches, 268
account handle, 48
accountability
  about, 35–36
  data protection and, 80–81
accuracy, data protection and, 85–86
adequacy finding, 103–104
adverse impact, 85
advertising
  behavioral, 325–328
  display, 325
advertising ID, 47
advisory power, 360–361
affiliate marketing, 330
affirmative act, 172
affirmative action, 31
alteration data breaches, 268
ambiguity, 62
amending data, 219–220
anonymization
  defined, 419
  of personal data, 49–50
  pseudonymization *vs.*, 245
appointing Data Protection Officer (DPO), 414
apps, for tracking location data, 47
archiving, processing special category data and, 76
article, defined, 419
Article 29 Working Party, 26, 93, 419
as-is profile, 263
assessing
  cookies, 149–151
  data breaches, 270–276
  learning styles, 387
assessments, conducting regular, 258–259
associations
  about, 335, 348
  case studies of enforcement for, 349

Austria, 403
authentication cookies, 147
authorization power, 360–361
automated calling system, 330
automated decision-making
  about, 340
  defined, 419
  rights related to, 217–218
automated processing, children and, 34
autonomous work, 382
availability
  data breaches and, 269
  data security and, 244, 247
  permanent loss of, 270
  temporary loss of, 270
avoidance, 261
awareness, of data breaches, 273–274
Axciom, 18–19

B

B2B (business-to-business) marketing, 316–317
B2C (business-to-consumer) marketing, 316–317
background checks
  on candidates, 298
  employee monitoring and, 302–303
backup plans, for key data and systems, 256
Balancing test, 72–73, 190–193
banner ads, 313
Battersea Dogs' and Cats' Home, 347
Bavarian Data Protection Authority, 321–322
BCP (business continuity planning), 257
BCRs (Binding Corporate Rules), 108–109, 419
behavior, monitoring, 28
behavioral advertising, 325–328
Belgium, 403
Binding Corporate Rules (BCRs), 108–109, 419
biometric data, 305, 419
black hat testing, 258
board away day, 387
Bobek, Michal (Advocate General), 323

Bosnia, 400

brand damage, 18–19

Brazil, 400

Brexit, 104, 108, 358

Breyer v. Bundesrepublik Deutschland, 48

British Airways, 19, 283

British and Foreign Bible Society, 346, 348

British Heart Foundation, 347

British Virgin Islands, 401

browser fingerprint, 48

Bulgaria, 403

business acumen, displaying, 384

business context, 261

business continuity planning (BCP), 257

business-to-business (B2B) marketing, 316–317

business-to-consumer (B2C) marketing, 316–317

by design and by default

    about, 229–230

    conducting Data Protection Impact Assessment (DPIA), 233–237

    data protection by default, 232

    data protection by design, 230–232

C

California Consumer Privacy Act (CCPA)(2018), 40, 284, 399–400

Cambridge Analytica, 367–368

Cancer Research UK, 347

Cancer Support UK, 347

candidate data, processing, 290–291

candidate Privacy Notice, 202

Carroll, David (professor), 367–368

case studies

    of enforcement for associations, 349

    of enforcement for charities, 347–348

categories

    of data subjects, 277

    of personal data records, 277

categorizing data breaches, 269–270

CCPA (California Consumer Privacy Act) (2018), 40, 284, 399–400

CCTV (closed-circuit television), 297, 305–309

champions, 389

change, embracing, 383

charging fees, 208–209

charities

    about, 335, 342

    case studies of enforcement for, 347–348

    data matching, 344–345

    data protection fee, 346

    door to door preaching, 345

    fundraising, 342–344

    ICO risk review report for, 346–347

    marketing, 342–344

    religious, 345

    security, 346

    volunteers, 345

    wealth screening, 344–345

Cheat Sheet (website), 9

children

    about, 335–336

    consent for online services, 66–67

    consent of, 338–339

    data for, 228

    data protection for, 34–35, 340–341

    DSARs on behalf of, 210

    under GDPR, 336–338

    marketing to, 339

    Privacy Notice and, 340

    profiling, 340

    rights of, 339–341

    verifying age of, 337

Children's Online Privacy Protection Act, 398

CIPL, 398

civil claims

    ability to bring, 36

    about, 17

CJEU (Court of Justice of the European Union), 25, 105

classifying information, 249

clear, affirmative act, 62

clear GIFs, 48

closed-circuit television (CCTV), 297, 305–309

CMS Law, 376

CNIL (Commission Nationale de l'Informatique et des Libertés), 151, 323, 327

code of conduct

    about, 237

    CCTV use and, 307–309

Code of Fundraising Practice (UK), 344

commercial surveillance, 395

Commission Nationale de l'Informatique et des Libertés (France-CNIL), 151, 323, 327

common law, 68

communicating

  Cookie Policy, 149–156

  to data subjects, 280

  effectively, 382–383

  employee Privacy Notices, 291–292

  opt-in wording, 180–184

  over phone, 143

  in person, 143

  Privacy Notices, 142–143

  via email, 142

  via websites, 143

CompariTech, 19

compatibility of purposes, 54, 55

competence, children and, 338–339

complaints, data subject, 361–362

completing

  data inventory, 120–129

  Legitimate Interests Assessment (LIA) form, 189–193

compliance

  about, 2–3, 8–9

  investments in, 3

  platforms for, 375–376

conducting

  Data Protection Impact Assessment (DPIA), 233–237

  regular testing and assessments, 258–259

confidential information, 249

confidentiality

  data breaches and, 269

  data security and, 244, 245–246

consent

  about, 31–32, 56–57

  of children, 34, 338–339

  for children for online services, 66–67

  defined, 419

  documenting, 65–66

  for electronic marketing communications, 413

  explicit, 75, 76–77, 110–111, 177–179, 413

  freely given, 57–59

  GDPR-compliant, 413

  as grounds for processing employee data, 288

  implied, 62

  incentivizing, 57

  informed, 59–61

  keeping records of, 184

  marketing and, 315–316

  obtaining fresh, 62–63

  opt-in, 153, 320

  opt-out, 153, 320, 414

  parental, 337, 338–339

  pressure to provide, 288–289

  specific, 59

  third-party, 61, 67

  tools for obtaining, 155–156

  withdrawal of, 31–32, 289, 414

  written, 98

consent fatigue, 183–184

consequences

  of data breaches, 271–272

  of non-compliance, 320

constant risk review, 261

consulting supervisory authority, 236–237

Consumer Credit Act (UK-2006), 220

content, 41

content element, 42

contractors, DPO, 241

contractual clauses, standard, 106–108

contractual necessity

  about, 67–68, 111–112

  as grounds for processing employee data, 288

contractual obligation, as lawful grounds for processing, 339

controller, defined, 419

controller-to-controller SCCs, 107

controller-to-processor SCCs, 107–108

controls, for data protection, 250–253

Cookie Policy

  about, 145–146

  communicating, 149–156

  creating, 149–156

  defined, 419

  posting, 152–154

  rationale for, 147–149

  sanctions for not having, 157

  writing, 151–152

cookie sweeps, 157

cookie walls, 154–155

Cookiebot, 155–156

cookiechecker (website), 149

cookiepedia, 149

T

About the Author

Suzanne Dibble has been a lawyer for over 20 years, qualifying as a corporate lawyer in one of the world's largest law firms, DLA Piper. There she led teams of professionals on multi-million-pound private equity deals as well as mergers and acquisitions, whilst also advising the boards of international blue-chip companies on all areas of company law.

Whilst at DLA Piper, Suzanne was seconded to Virgin's head office where she worked alongside Richard Branson. Amongst other key projects, she led a group-wide data protection project with great success. As a result of this success, she was nominated by Virgin and DLA Piper for the national Solicitor of the Year award and subsequently voted runner-up.

Suzanne was asked to move to ITV Plc, the UK's largest commercial broadcaster, where amongst other key strategic projects, she led the billion-pound project for digital switchover when the broadcaster moved from an analog signal to a digital signal.

Suzanne was then headhunted to be Legal Director of Hamptons International, then a UK subsidiary of the largest property development company in the world. Suzanne was soon promoted to Director of Operations and was responsible for the operations of over 1,000 staff and over 100 branches. As a result of Suzanne's role at Hamptons, she was listed in the *Who's Who of Young Business Leaders 2009* and the *Who's Who of Britain's Business Elite* in 2010.

Whilst pregnant with her first child, Suzanne set up her own legal practice in 2010, focusing exclusively on helping small businesses. When she became over-subscribed in her one-to-one consultancy business and in order to help even more small businesses, she established her online legal platform — the Small Business Legal Academy — in 2012, which provides templates, video guides, checklists, case studies, action plans, and an online community to help small businesses protect and grow their business affordably. Suzanne won a Law Society award for this pioneering work and 100% of Academy members surveyed said that they would recommend the Academy to other small-business owners.

In 2018, whilst consulting with one of the best-known global data companies on their GDPR compliance, Suzanne realized that she needed to provide more support to small businesses to help them come to grips with the complexities of the GDPR. She committed to post in her Facebook Group (GDPR for Online Entrepreneurs) one video a day for 90 days from the end of February 2018 until the introduction of the GDPR on May 25, 2018 in order to help break down this complex area into manageable chunks for small-business owners. The Facebook community exploded and grew to 40,000 people from around the world within just two months.

In response to requests from the Facebook community, Suzanne created her GDPR compliance pack that provides all the templates small businesses need to comply with the GDPR, together with video guides and checklists. The compliance pack received great acclaim with over 5,000 packs having been sold.

Suzanne is regularly asked to appear on TV and radio to provide comment on GDPR-related matters and has appeared on prime time national TV programs such as *Newsnight* and *Watchdog*, news channels such as the BBC News and Sky News, and many national radio stations such as Radio 4, Radio 5 Live, and Radio 2. Suzanne has also been featured in many national newspapers, magazines, and online articles.

In addition, Suzanne regularly speaks at international conferences on the topic of the GDPR, the ePrivacy Directive, and other legal matters, including the huge Digital Marketer's international conference in San Diego and the Data Protection World Forum. See www.suzannedibble.com/speaking for more about how to hire Suzanne as a speaker for your event.

As well as continuing to help small businesses with the GDPR, Suzanne's next project is Legal Buddy (www.legalbuddy.biz), which aims to make creating legal contracts so quick and easy that every business, no matter how small, looks forward to putting watertight contracts in place.

Dedication

To my mum and dad for always believing in me — it sounds a cliché, but without your faith in me, I know I wouldn't have achieved half of what I have done. I love you both always and thank you for all that you have done for me.

To my husband, Gordon, thank you for being the calm and centering influence in my life. Thank you for putting up with my wild flights of fancy and bringing practicality and stability. Your unwavering good humor has made writing this book a lot less painful than it otherwise would have been. Thanks for keeping the girls amused during all those "writing weekends" and for keeping me topped up with my herbal teas during late-night writing slogathons. I love you and am so pleased to be by your side in this magical journey of life.

To my girls, thank you for being my inspiration to keep challenging myself and succeeding in new ways. I hope that by doing so, I am helping you to see that you can achieve anything you set your minds to and that even if the achievement involves lots of hard work, discipline, and missing out on a few nice things, it is all worth it, especially of course, when you are helping people.

Author's Acknowledgments

Writing this book has probably been the hardest thing I have ever done (and I have faced plenty of difficult challenges during my career). Having to find time to write alongside the day job, bringing up two young children, running the household, and managing with shoulder pain whilst typing have been exceptionally difficult, and I thank my editors for their patience. What has kept me going is the thought that this book will (hopefully) help so many small-business owners come to grips with a complex and important area of the law in an easy and accessible way.

Huge thanks to my technical editors, particularly to Phil Lee of Fieldfisher — no better privacy lawyer will you find. Despite his already heavy workload, Phil agreed to be the technical editor because he shares my desire to make complex legal topics accessible to all — no matter what the size of the legal fees budget. Thanks, Phil, you're a total star.

To my fabulous assistant Roberta, thank you so much for being so trustworthy and reliable that I could leave you to get on with the very important job of keeping my clients and customers happy, while I focused on writing this book. You truly are a gem.

To my own Mary Poppins, Laura, thank you for coming along at just the right time in our lives and being such a capable nanny and so good with the girls (and of course, the third child Bertie . . .) — you allowed me to completely focus on writing the book and made life so much less stressful. I am forever in your debt.

To my coach, Sue Revell (the best coach any business owner could hire!), thanks for helping me with what was a difficult decision for me to write this book. Now the book is all written, I am so happy that I made the decision to write it, as I can see that it will help many thousands of small businesses and that makes me very happy.

To my community of female entrepreneurs, High Performing Women, thank you for your encouragement to keep going with the book, when times were hard. On my tenth wedding anniversary on holiday, when all I wanted to do was go to the beach with my family, you spurred me on so that I could meet my deadline. Keep being amazing and supporting each other!

Finally, to everyone in my GDPR Facebook group, thank you for being the inspiration for this book. Early on, after the start of the group, a member told us about his elderly mother who ran a small business that brought her great joy, who was in tears because she thought she would have to close it down due to the risks of being fined €20m for noncompliance with the GDPR. On hearing this, I determined to bring a sensible, practical, non-scaremongering approach to GDPR compliance to as many small businesses as I could — this book is a further way of getting that approach out there. Particular thanks to all of the GDPR experts in my Facebook group who take time to help others with their questions, for no reward other than the satisfaction that comes from helping people.

Publisher's Acknowledgments

Acquisitions Editor: Tracy Boggier

Senior Project Editor: Paul Levesque

Copy Editor: Becky Whitney

Editorial Assistant: Matthew Lowe

Sr. Editorial Assistant: Cherie Case

Proofreader: Debbye Butler

Production Editor: Magesh Elangovan

Cover Image: © bestfoto77/Shutterstock